i

i i
i i

'twas all so pretty
a sail it seemed
as if it could not be

and some folks thought
'twas a dream they'd dreamed
of sailing that beautiful sea

n

i i   i

n

n i

i

i

conse

nsu

s

n o

i ni ni

me

n i

clatu

r

e

a

n i n

co

su

f i

c s

su

s

n f i

n i n

m

summa

ma t

t

l at

i

i

o

n

but e

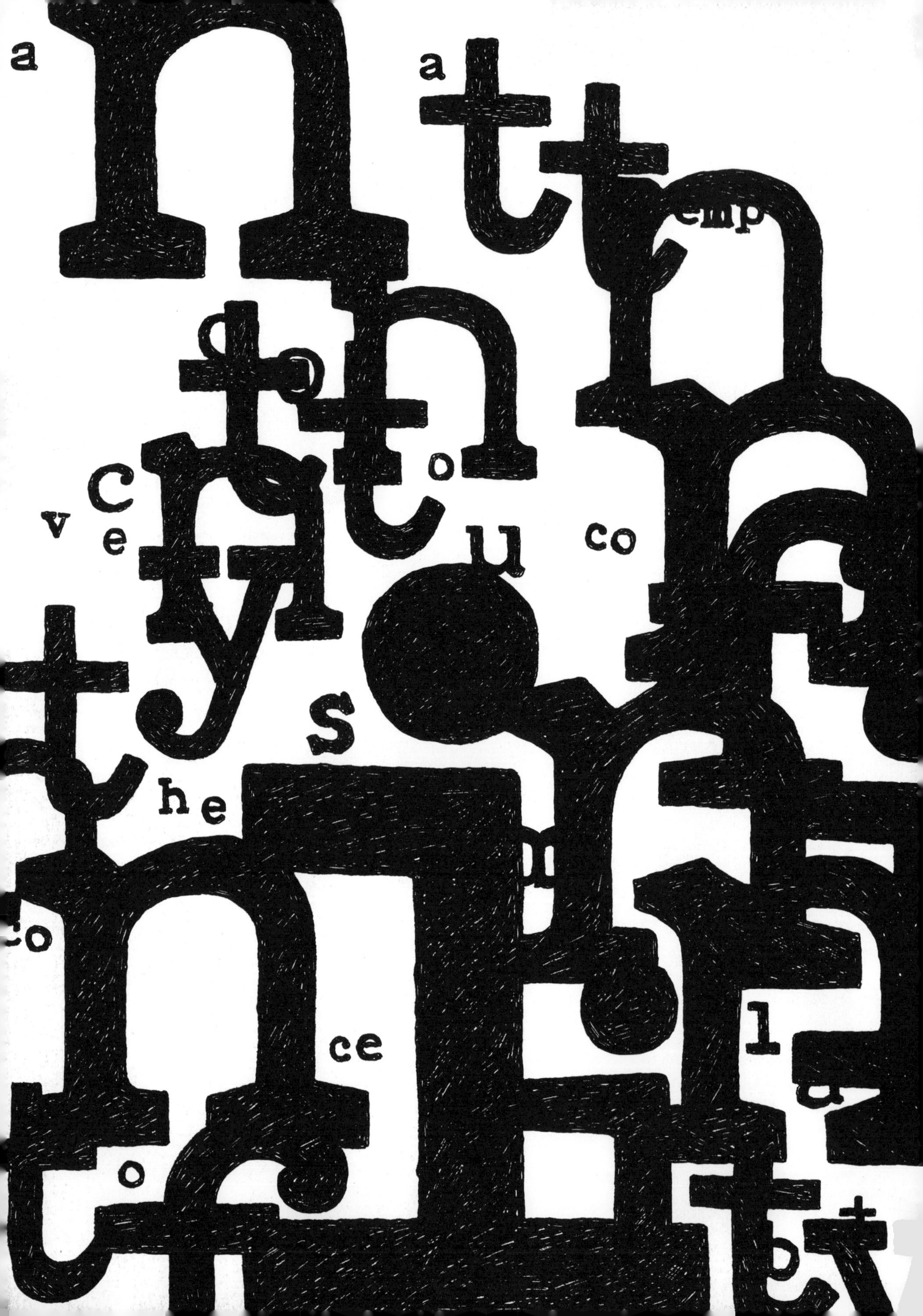

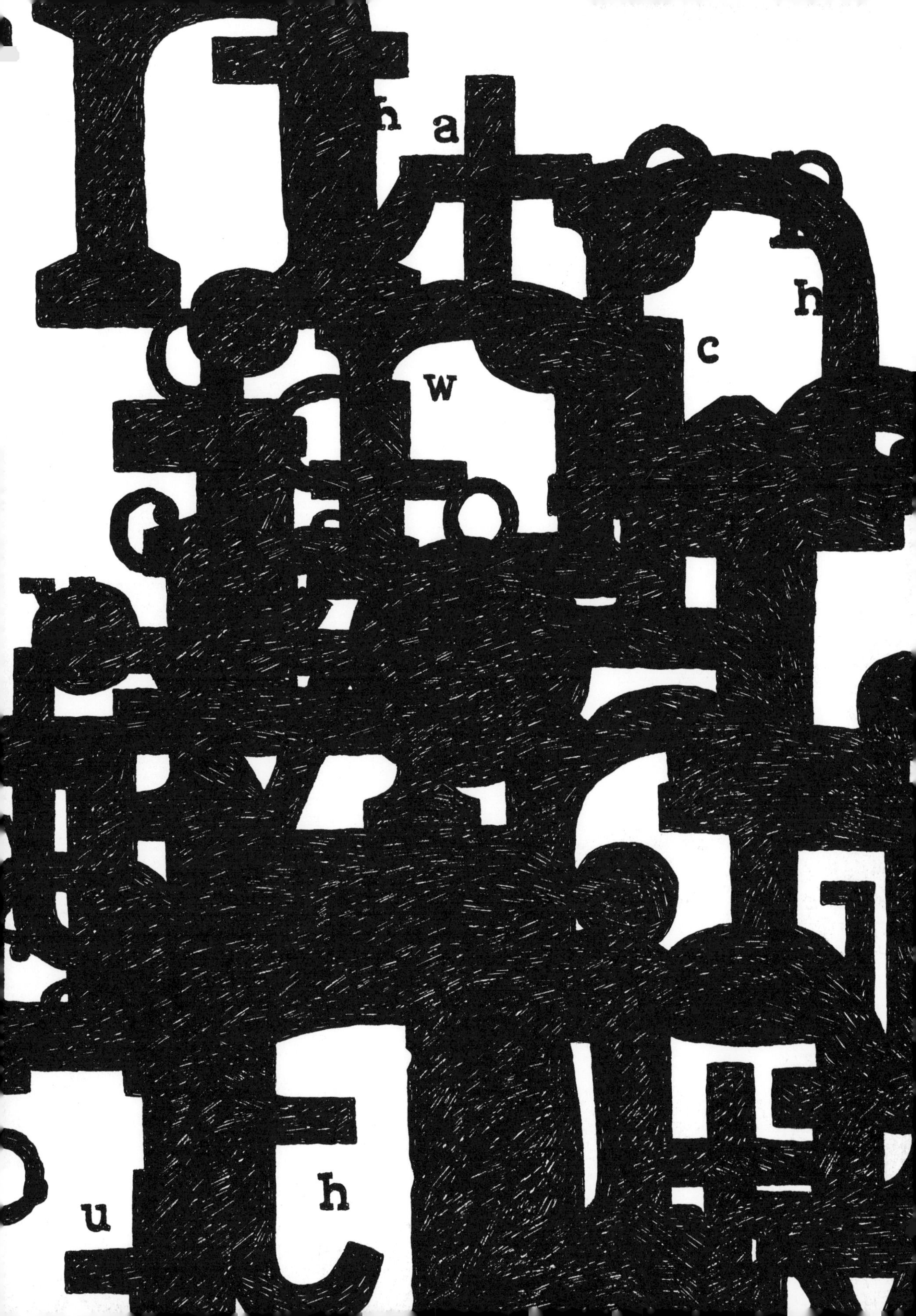

ha
h
c
w
u
h

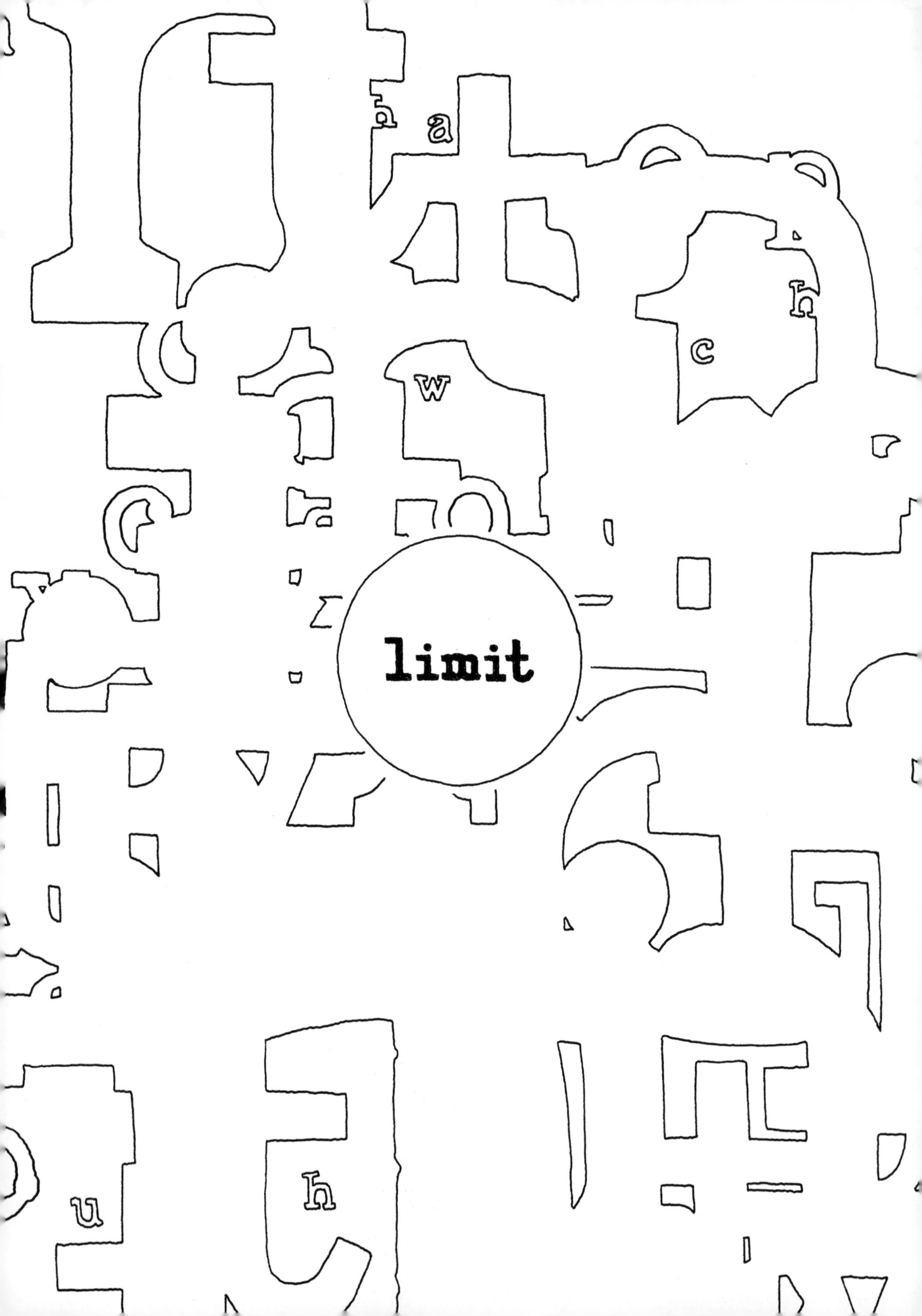
limit

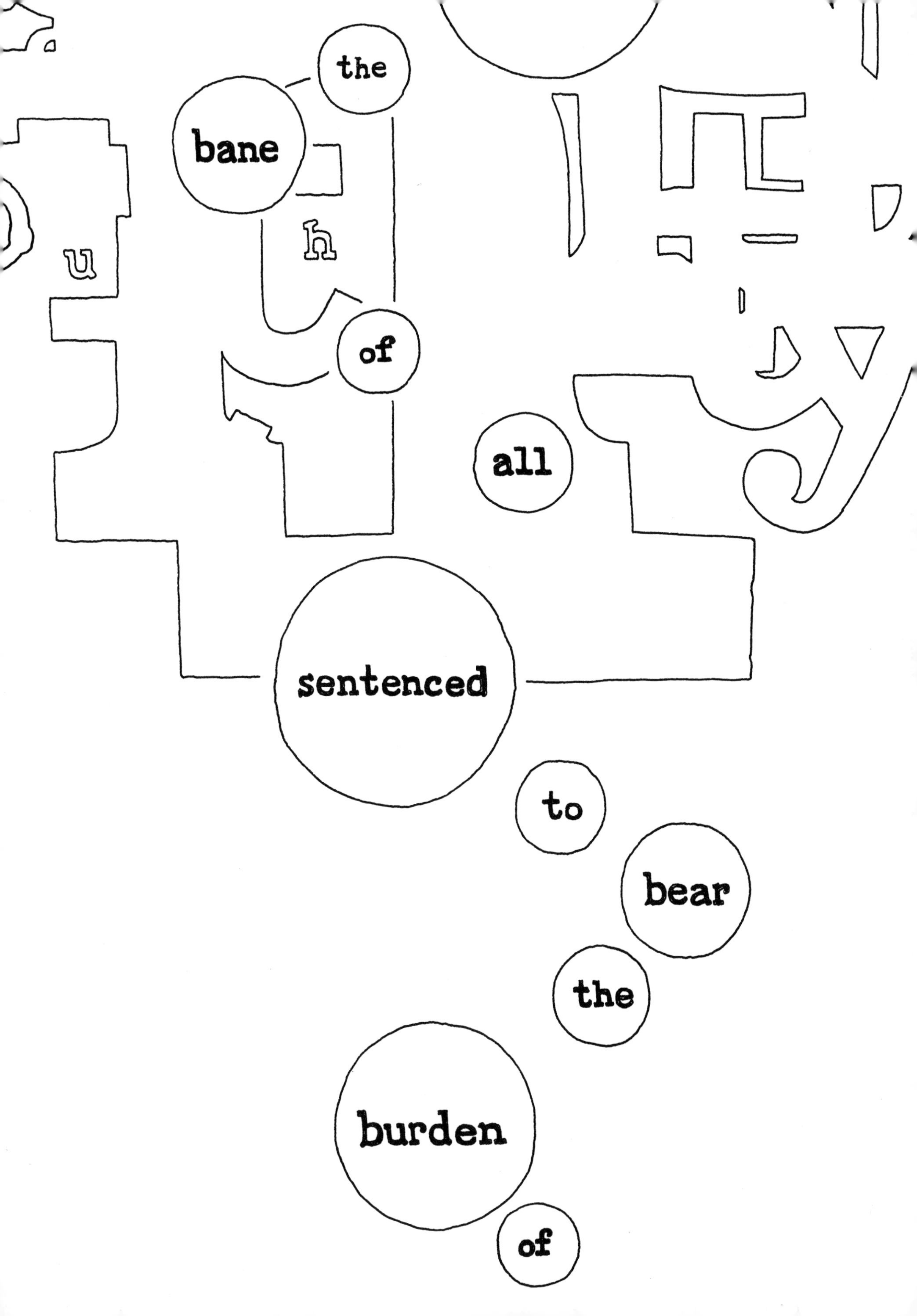
the
bane
u
h
of
all
sentenced
to
bear
the
burden
of

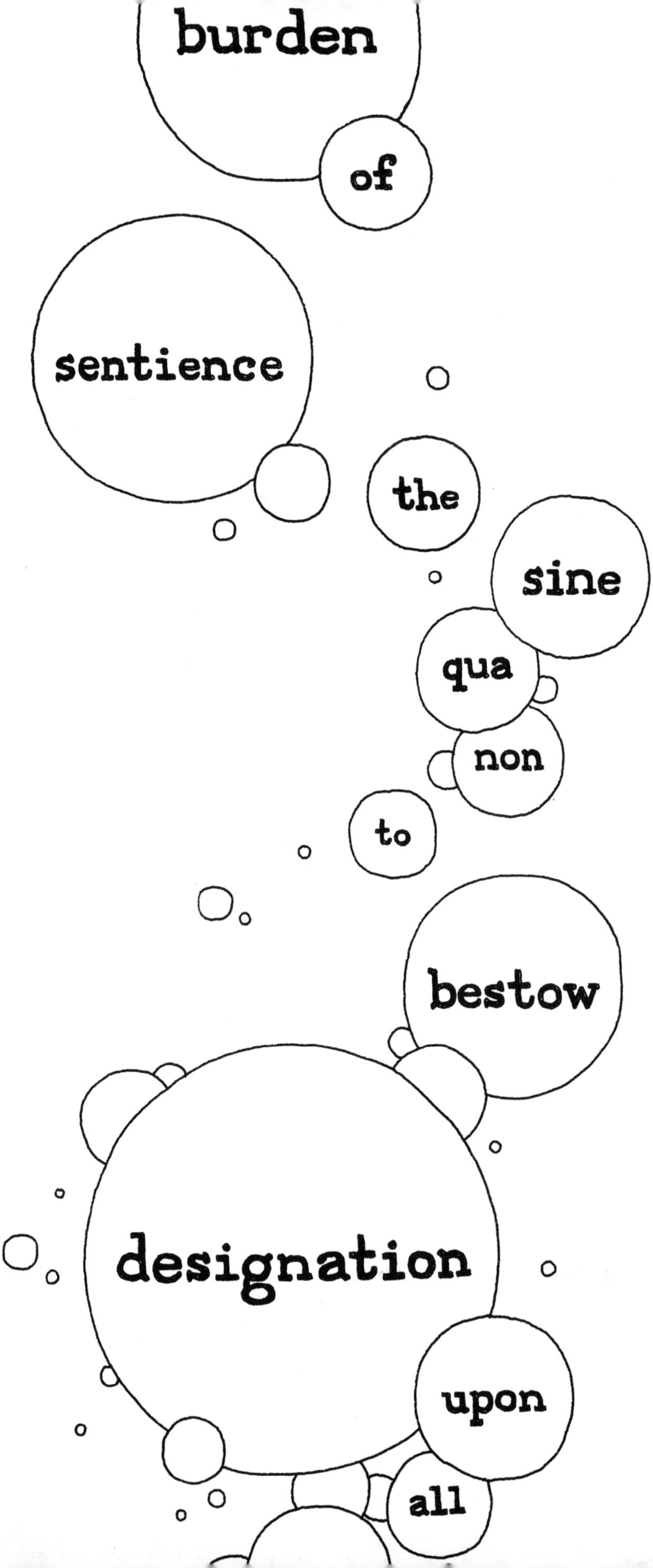
burden
of
sentience
the
sine
qua
non
to
bestow
designation
upon
all

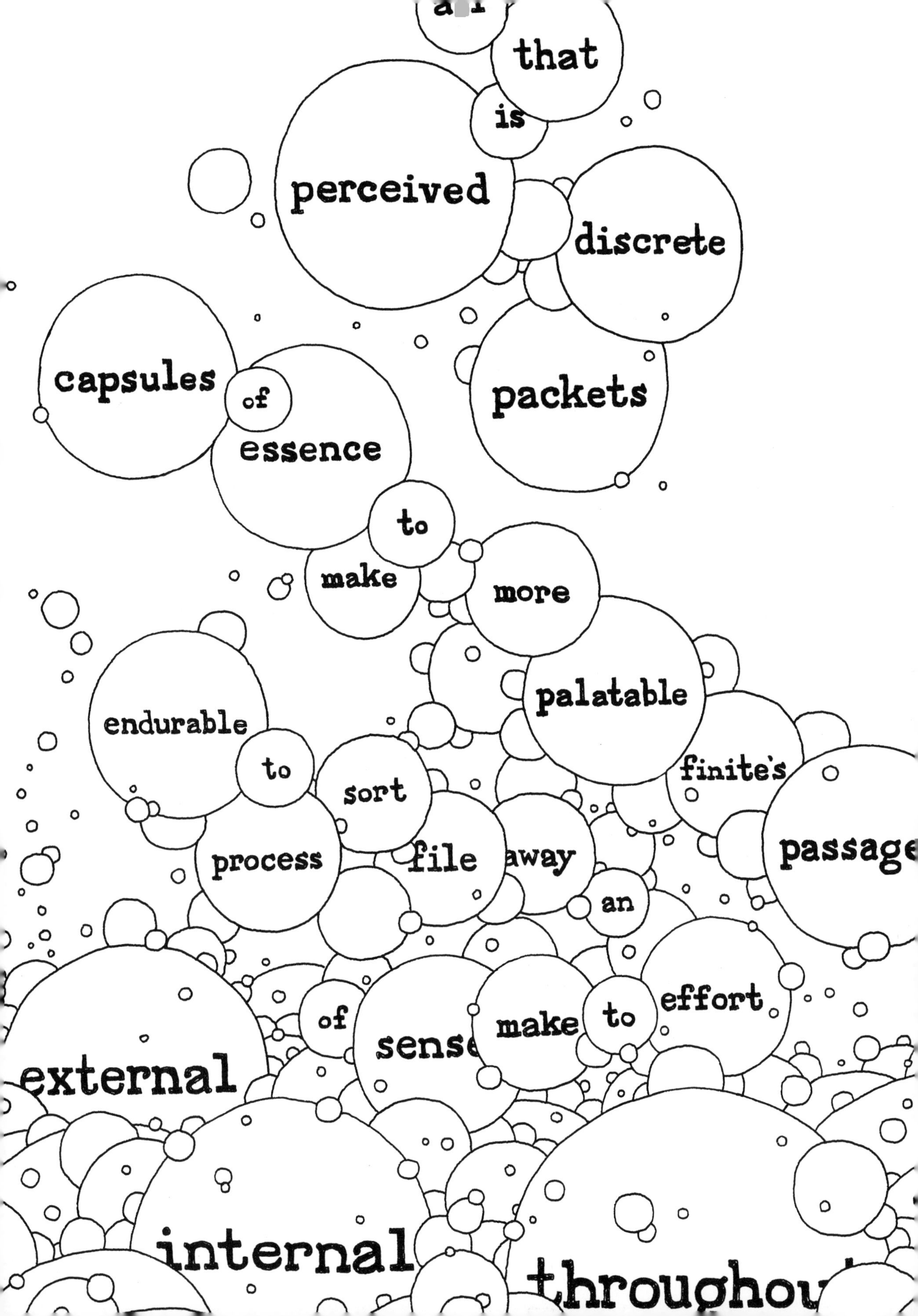
that
is
perceived
discrete
packets
capsules
of
essence
to
make
more
palatable
endurable
to
sort
process
file
away
finite's
passag
an
effort
to
make
sense
of
external
internal
throughou

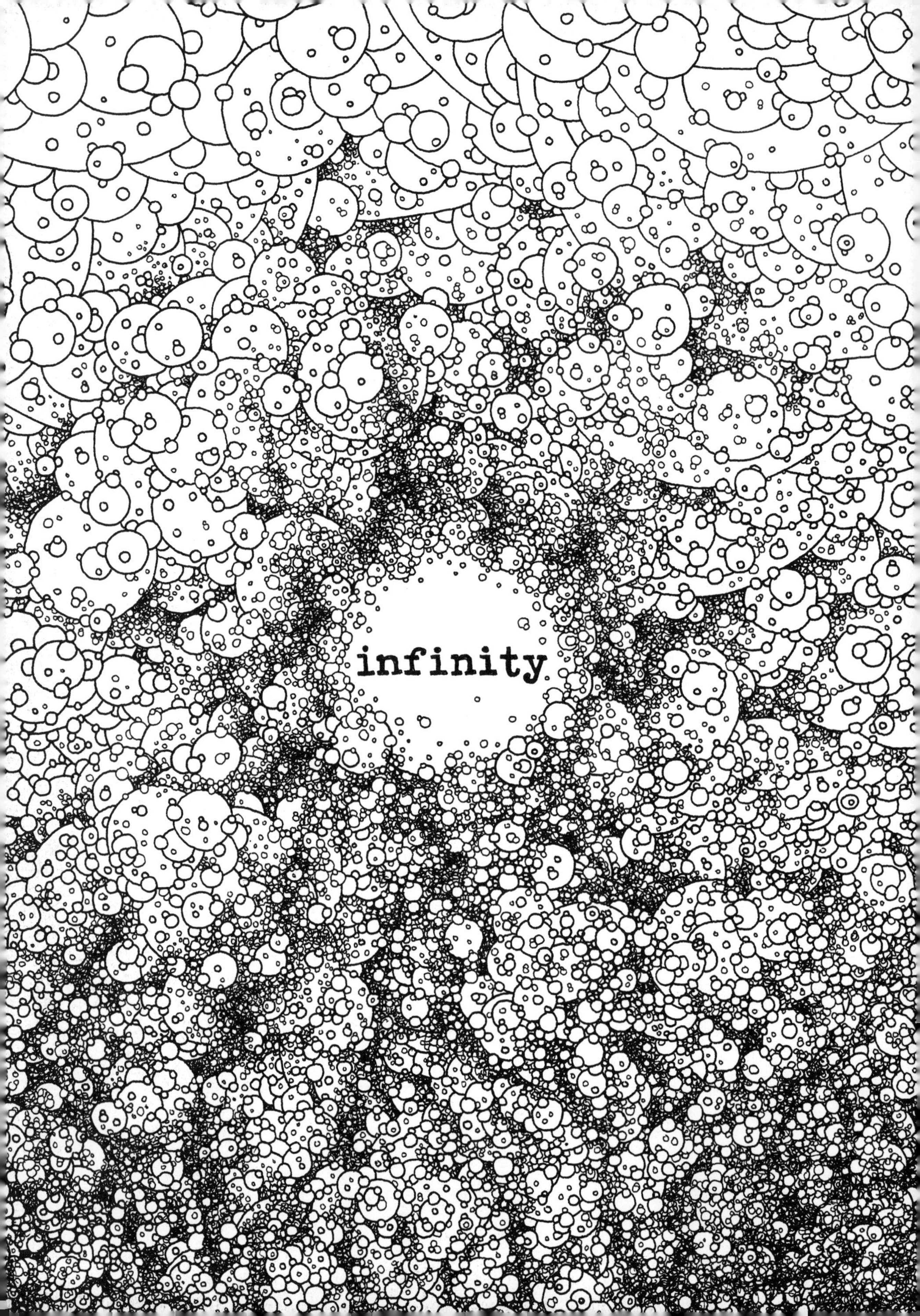
infinity

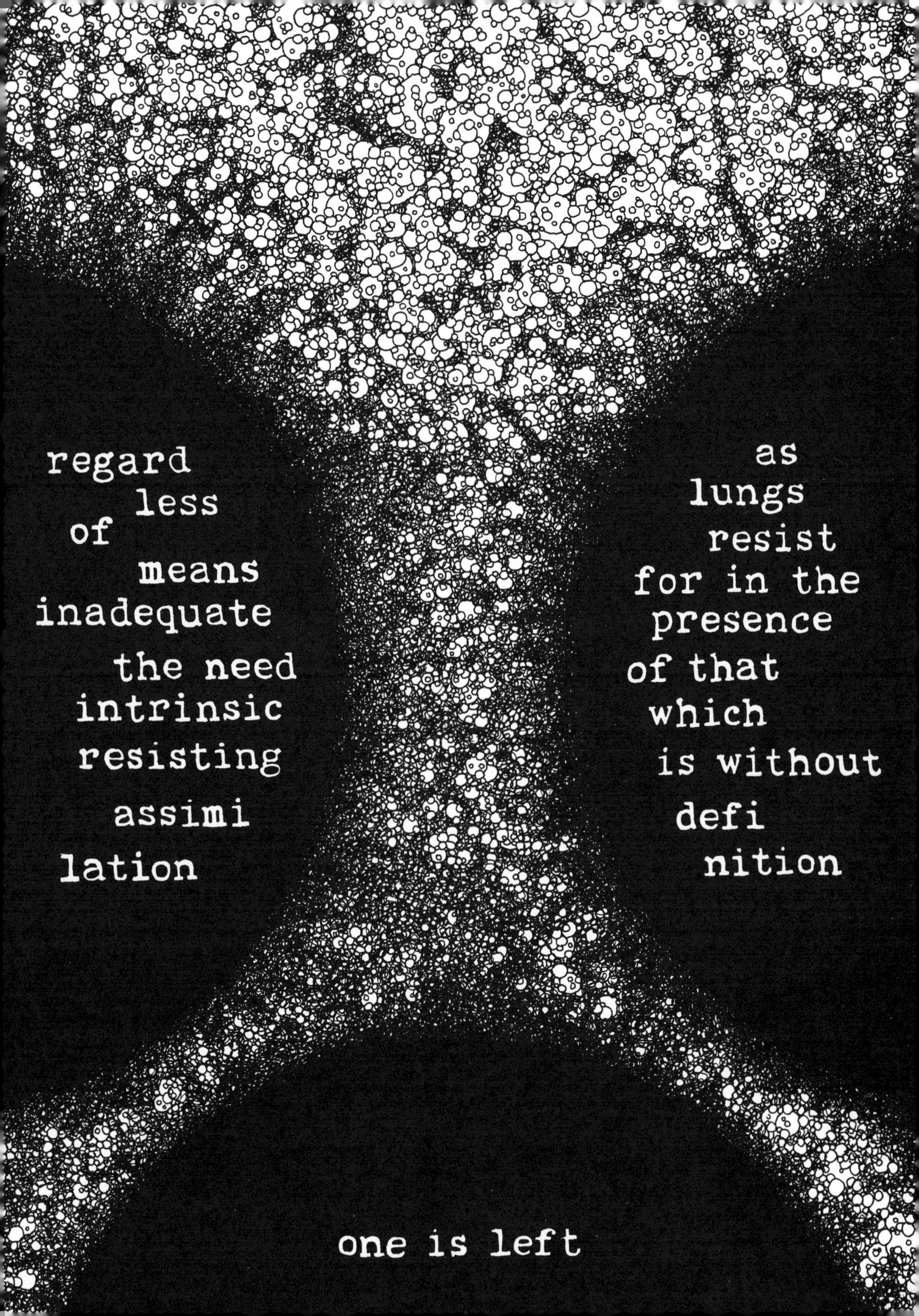
regard
less
of
means
inadequate
the need
intrinsic
resisting
assimi
lation
as
lungs
resist
for in the
presence
of that
which
is without
defi
nition
one is left

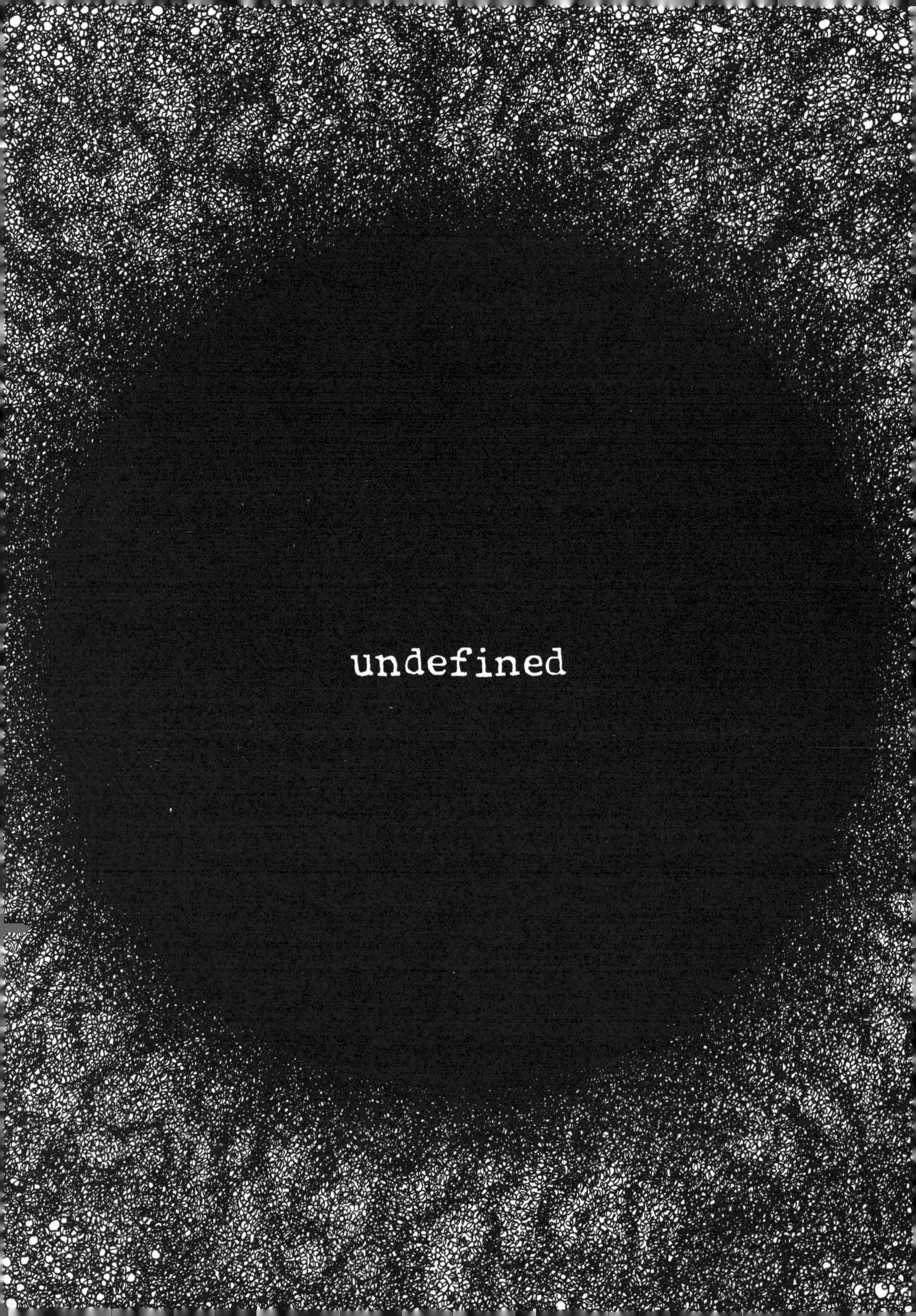
undefined

amorphous state

floating

abhorrent
to

being

as life
without
meaning
without

purpose

for
in the
presence
of

negative

necessitates
positive

negative

invents

and
so

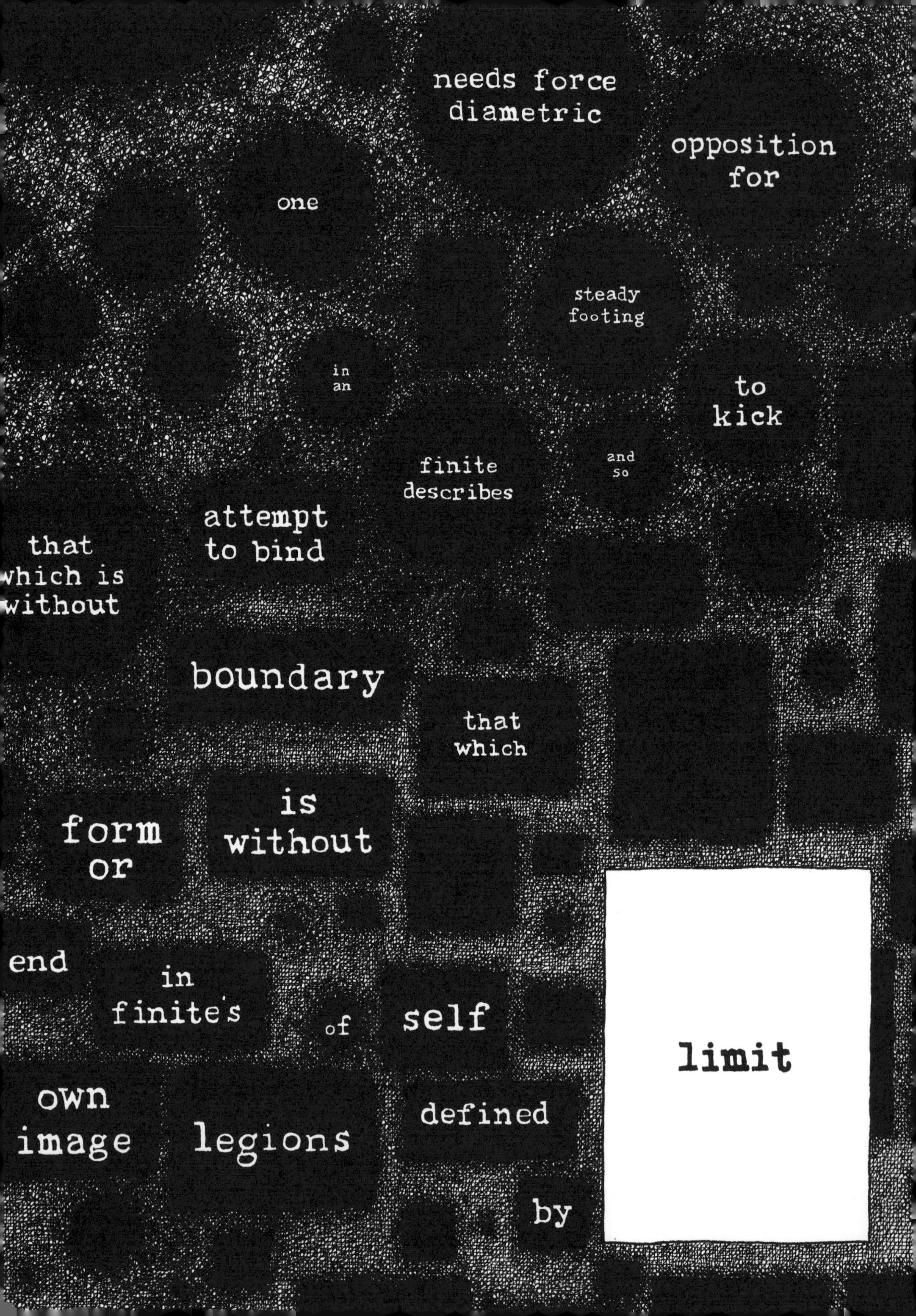
needs force diametric
opposition for
one
steady footing
in an
to kick
finite describes
and so
attempt to bind
that which is without
boundary
that which
form or
is without
end
in finite's
of
self
limit
own image
legions
defined
by

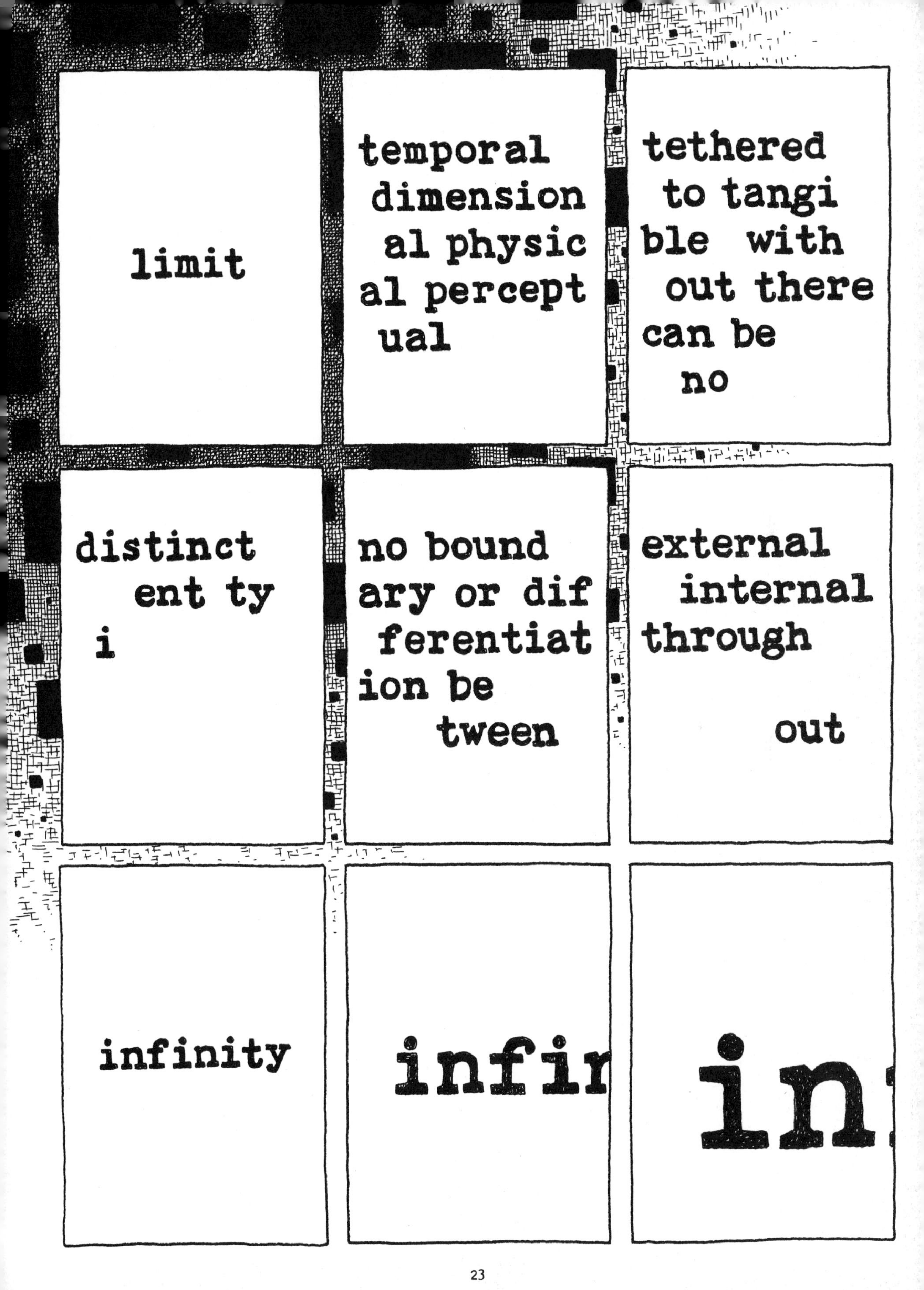
limit
temporal dimension al physic al percept ual
tethered to tangi ble with out there can be no
distinct ent ty i
no bound ary or dif ferentiat ion be tween
external internal through out
infinity
infir
in

just

should

self

be

illusory

one

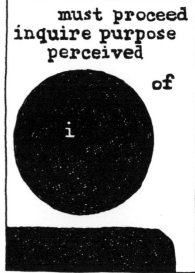
must proceed
inquire purpose
perceived

of

i

and in what
capacity
could

discrete
packets

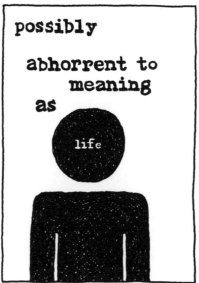
possibly

abhorrent to
meaning

as

life

without
purpose for in
the presence
of

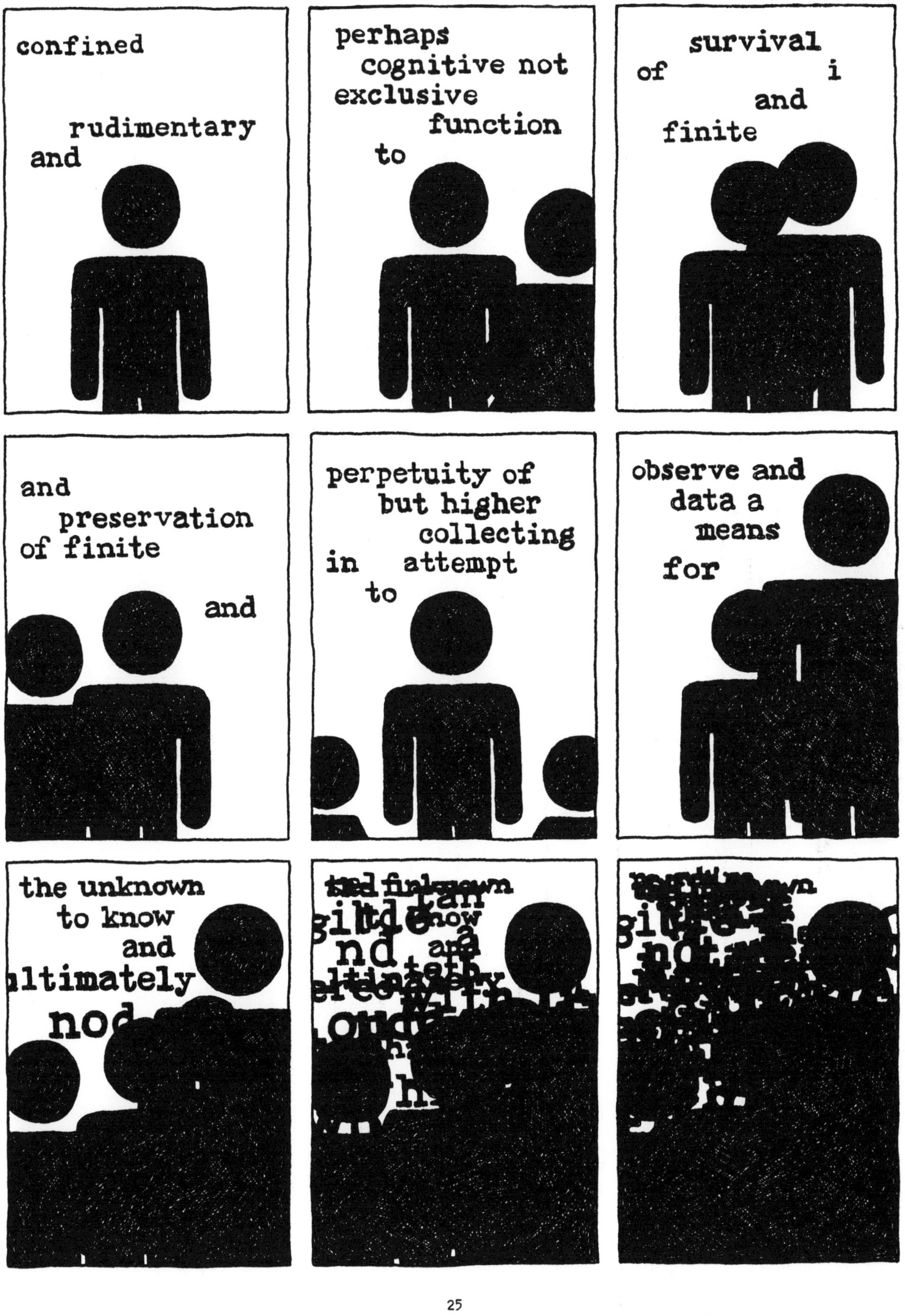
confined
rudimentary
and
perhaps
cognitive not
exclusive
function
to
survival
of
i
and
finite
and
preservation
of finite
and
perpetuity of
but higher
collecting
in attempt
to
observe and
data a
means
for
the unknown
to know
and
ltimately
nod

SO

negative
IDEFINES

faith

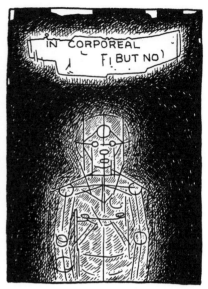

IN CORPOREAL
Fı BUT NO)

DISTINCTION

LEFT UNOBSERVED IN

ORDER TO ASCERTAIN SUM
MUST CAPABLE COMPREHEND

PARTS. I PROPOSE

IMPLEMENTATION IN REPLICA
ORGANISM. VESSEL PERMU-
TATION I.   I

CUSTOMIZED SELF-REALIZING
COMPONENT MODELED AFTER

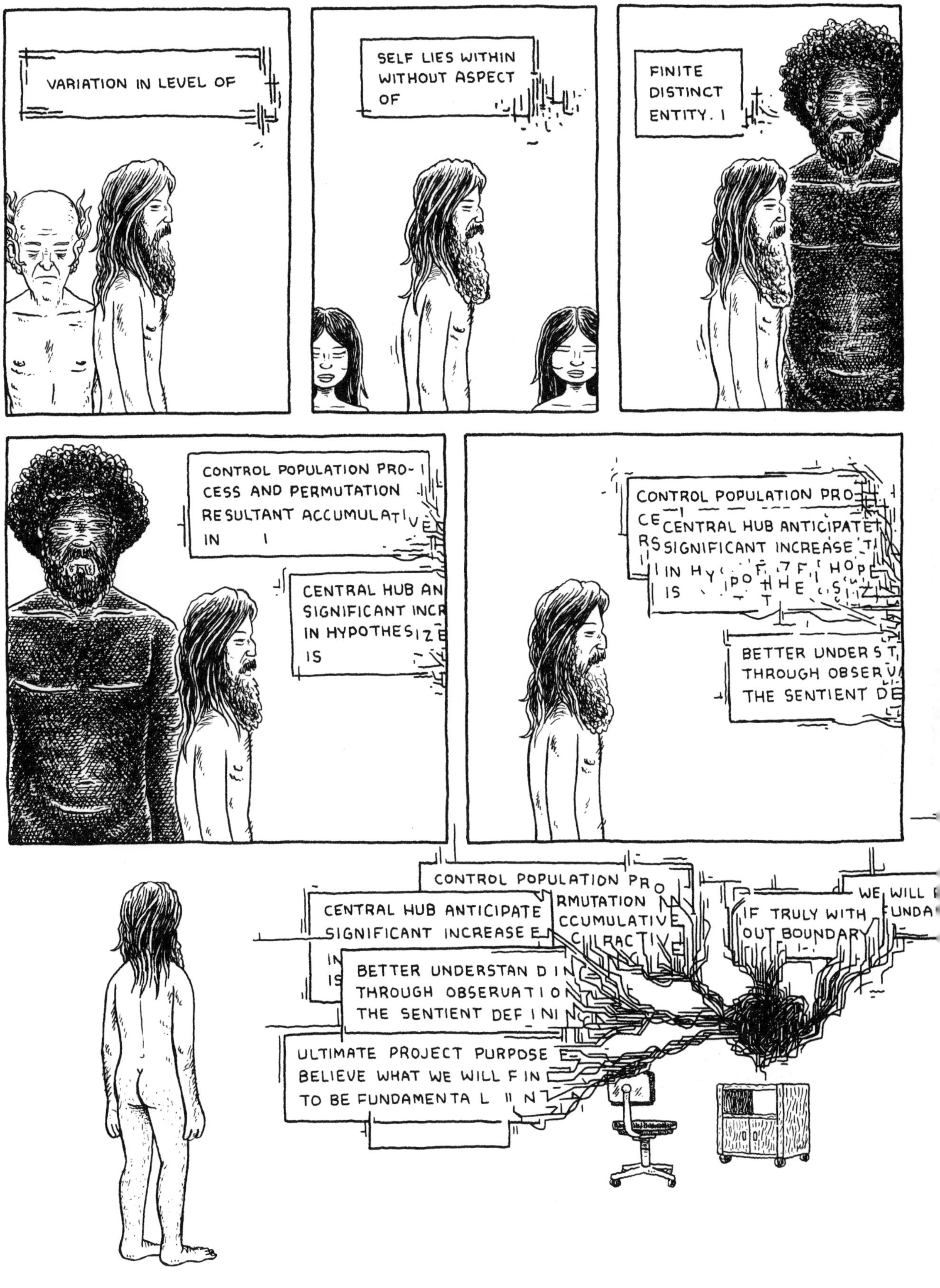
VARIATION IN LEVEL OF
SELF LIES WITHIN WITHOUT ASPECT OF
FINITE DISTINCT ENTITY. I
CONTROL POPULATION PRO- CESS AND PERMUTATION RESULTANT ACCUMULATIVE IN
CENTRAL HUB AN SIGNIFICANT INCR IN HYPOTHESIZE IS
CONTROL POPULATION PRO
CENTRAL HUB ANTICIPATE SIGNIFICANT INCREASE IN HY IS
BETTER UNDERST THROUGH OBSERV THE SENTIENT DE
CONTROL POPULATION PRO RMUTATION CCUMULATIVE
CENTRAL HUB ANTICIPATE SIGNIFICANT INCREASE
BETTER UNDERSTAN DIN THROUGH OBSERVATION THE SENTIENT DEF INI
ULTIMATE PROJECT PURPOSE BELIEVE WHAT WE WILL FIN TO BE FUNDAMENTAL IN
IF TRULY WITH OUT BOUNDARY
WE WILL UNDA

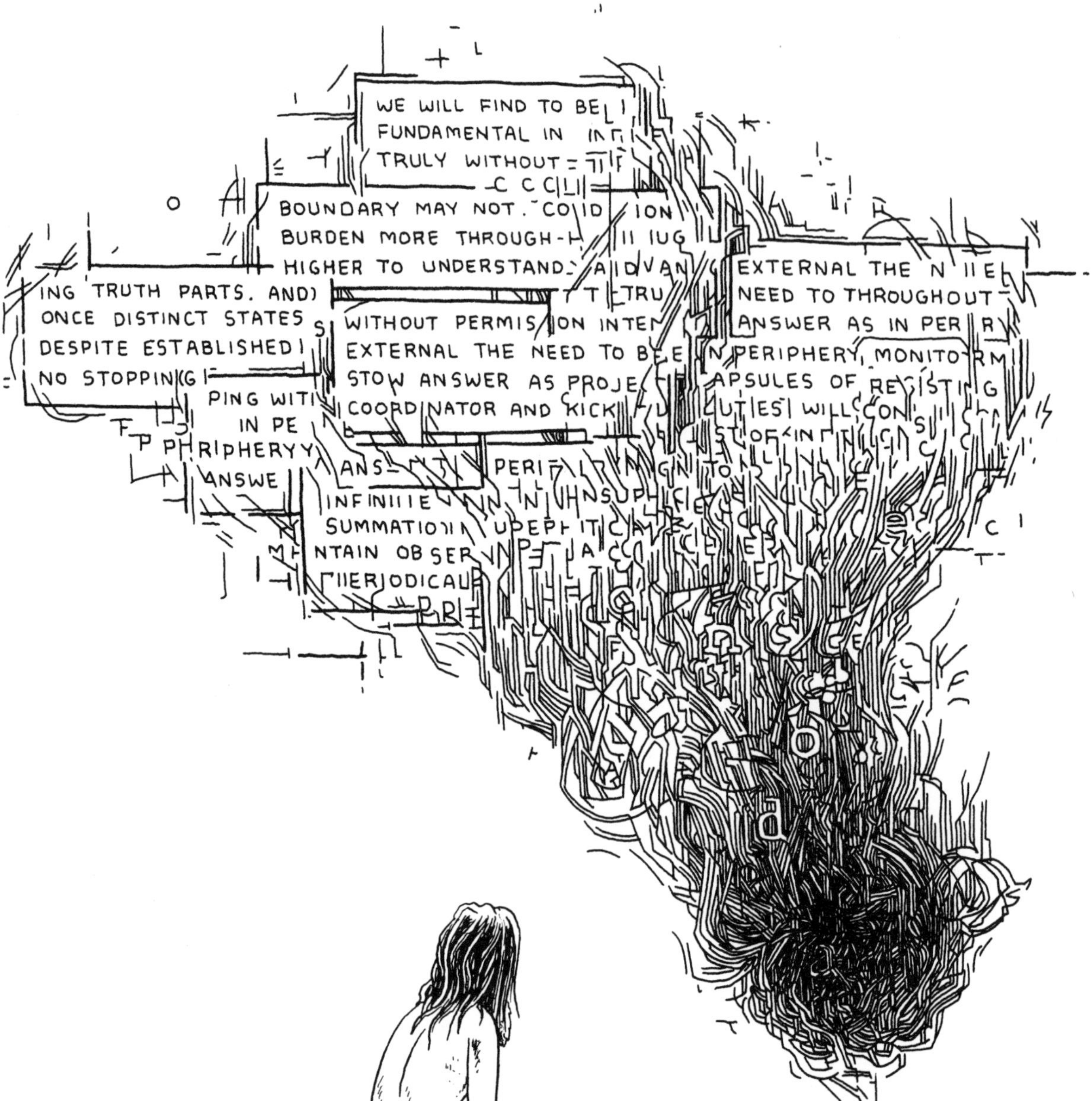
WE WILL FIND TO BE
FUNDAMENTAL IN
TRULY WITHOUT
BOUNDARY MAY NOT.
BURDEN MORE THROUGH
HIGHER TO UNDERSTAND
ING TRUTH PARTS. AND
ONCE DISTINCT STATES
DESPITE ESTABLISHED
NO STOPPIN
WITHOUT PERMIS ION INTE
EXTERNAL THE NEED TO B
STOW ANSWER AS PROJE
COORDINATOR AND KICK
EXTERNAL THE
NEED TO THROUGHOUT
ANSWER AS IN PER
PERIPHERY MONITO
APSULES OF RESISTING
PING WIT
IN PE
RIPHERY
ANSWE
SUMMATIO
NTAIN OB SER
SQK

AMORPHOUS REPORT
FLOATING AND BEING
AS LIFE WITHOUT AND
OBSERVE AND
REPORT AND OBSER
AND
OBSER AND
(BS)
OBSERVE AND
OBSERVE AND RE
OBSERVE AND

ULTIMATE L

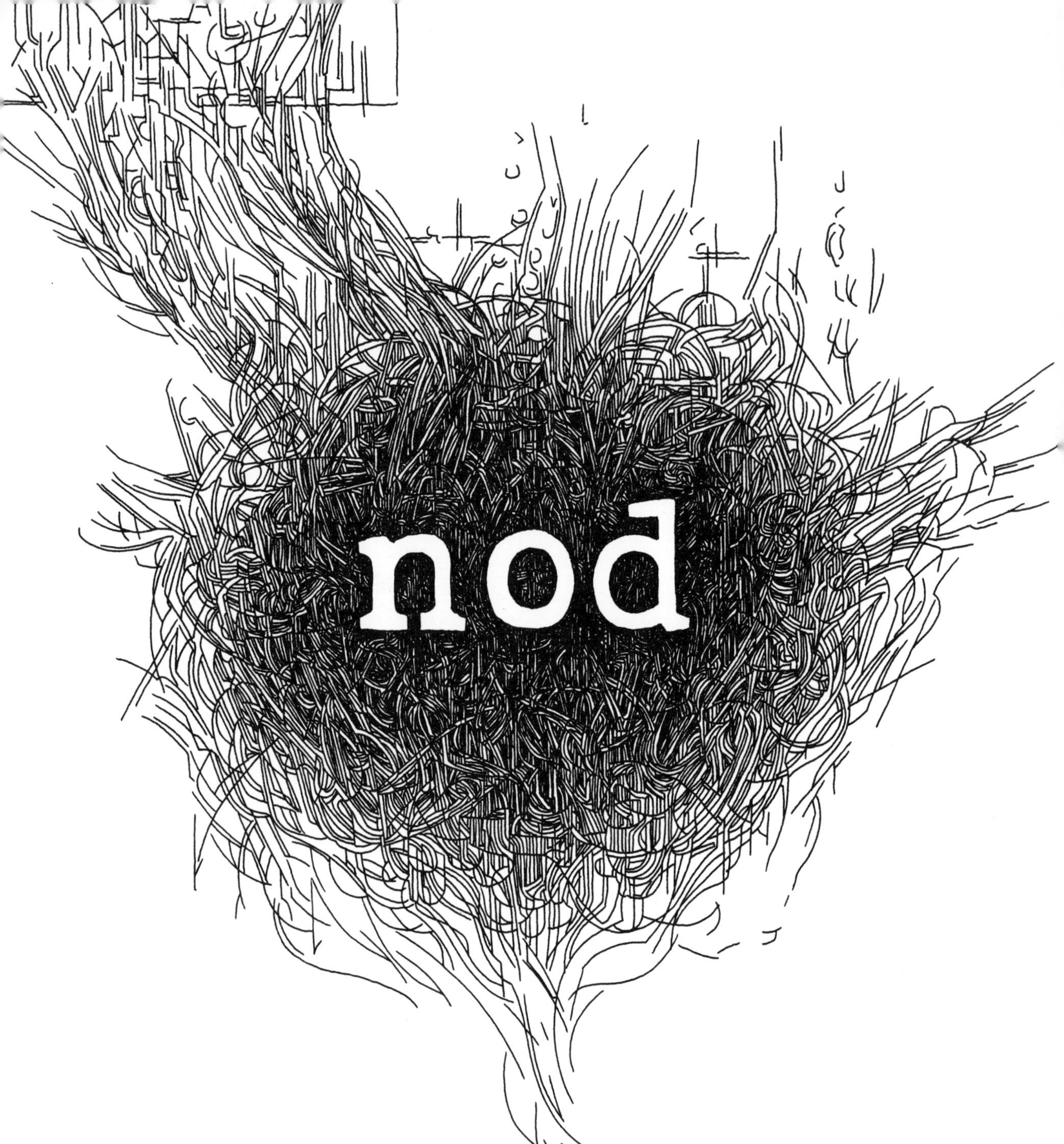
nod

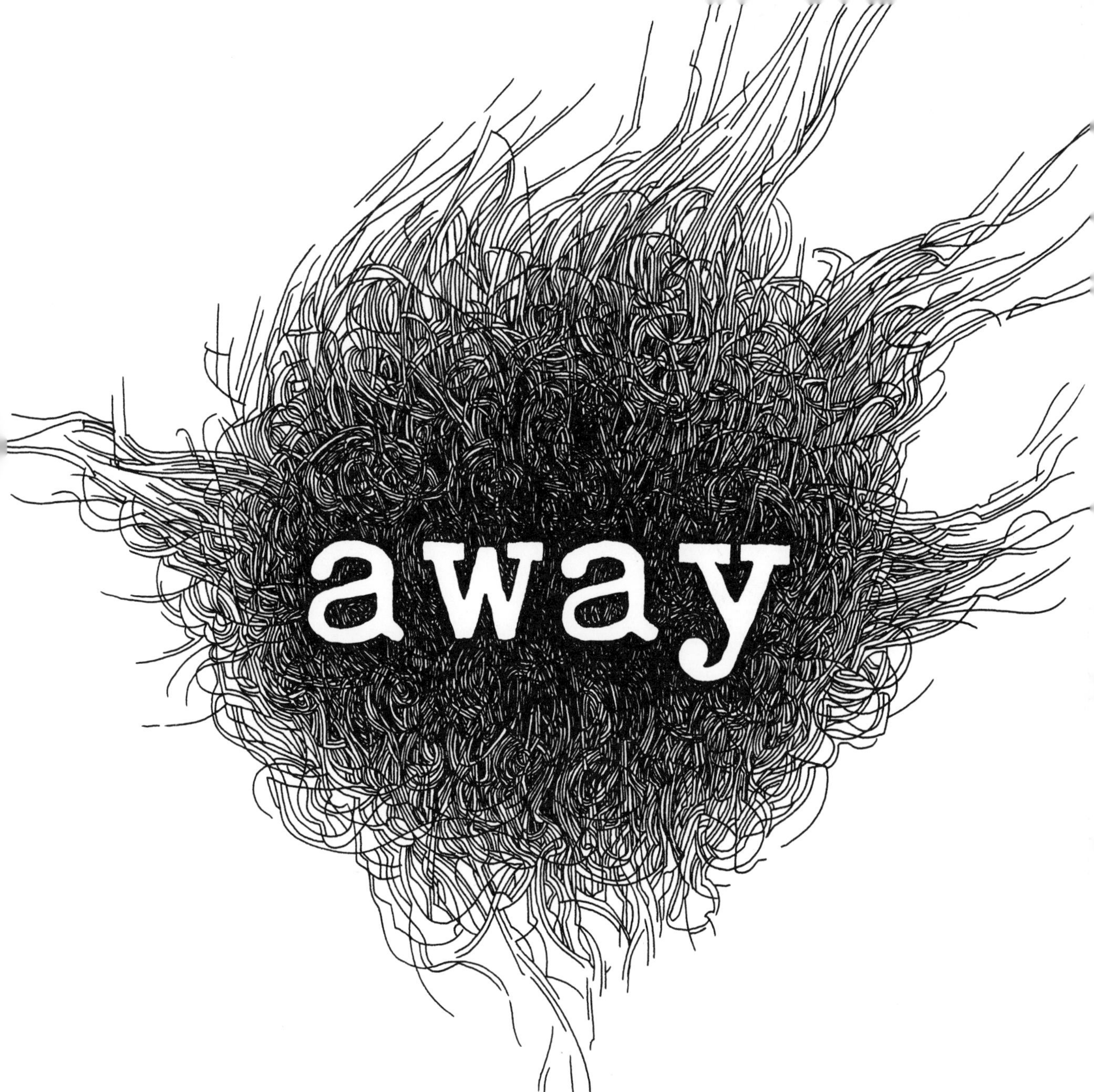
away

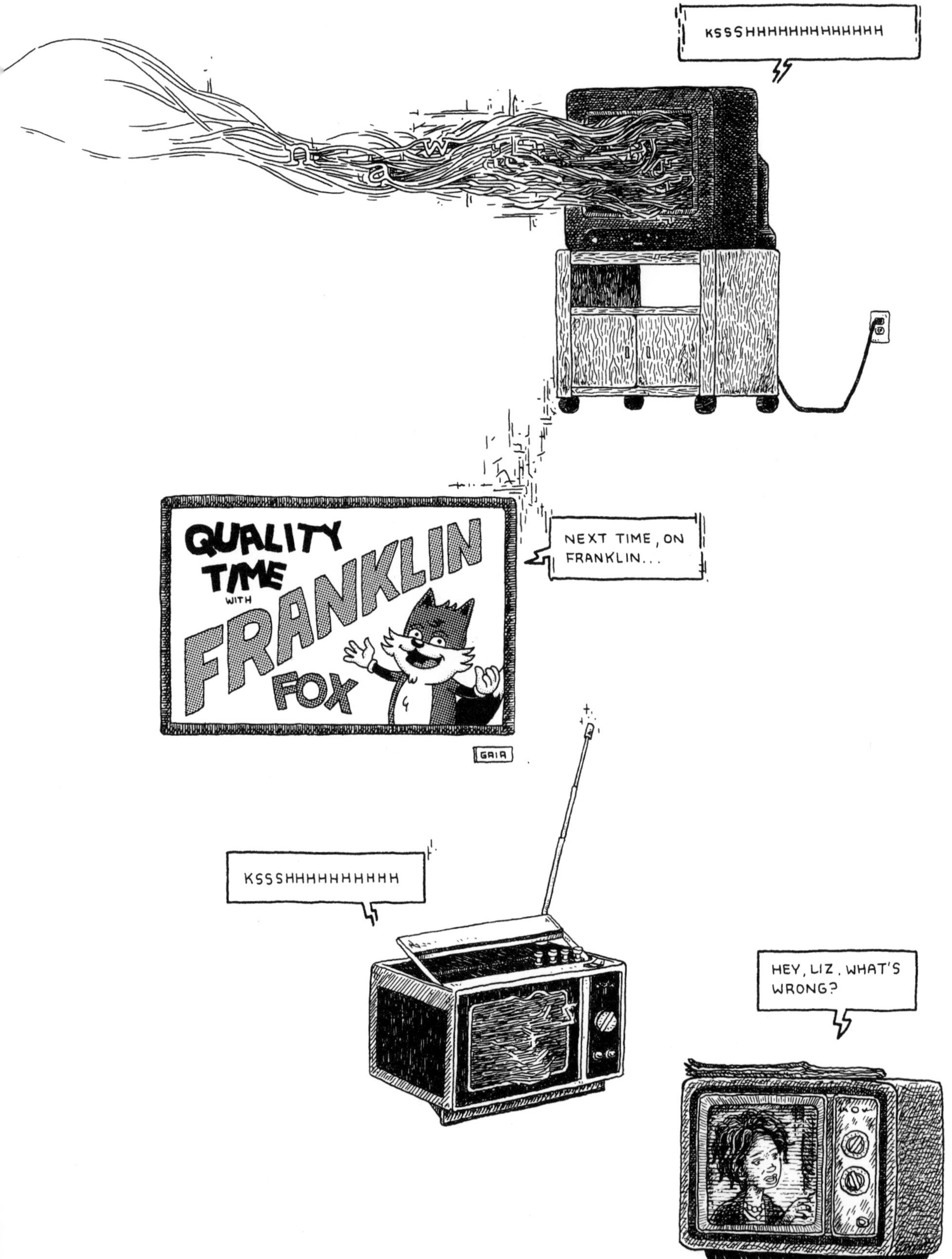
KSSSHHHHHHHHHHHH
QUALITY TIME WITH FRANKLIN FOX
NEXT TIME, ON FRANKLIN...
GAIA
KSSSHHHHHHHHHH
HEY, LIZ. WHAT'S WRONG?

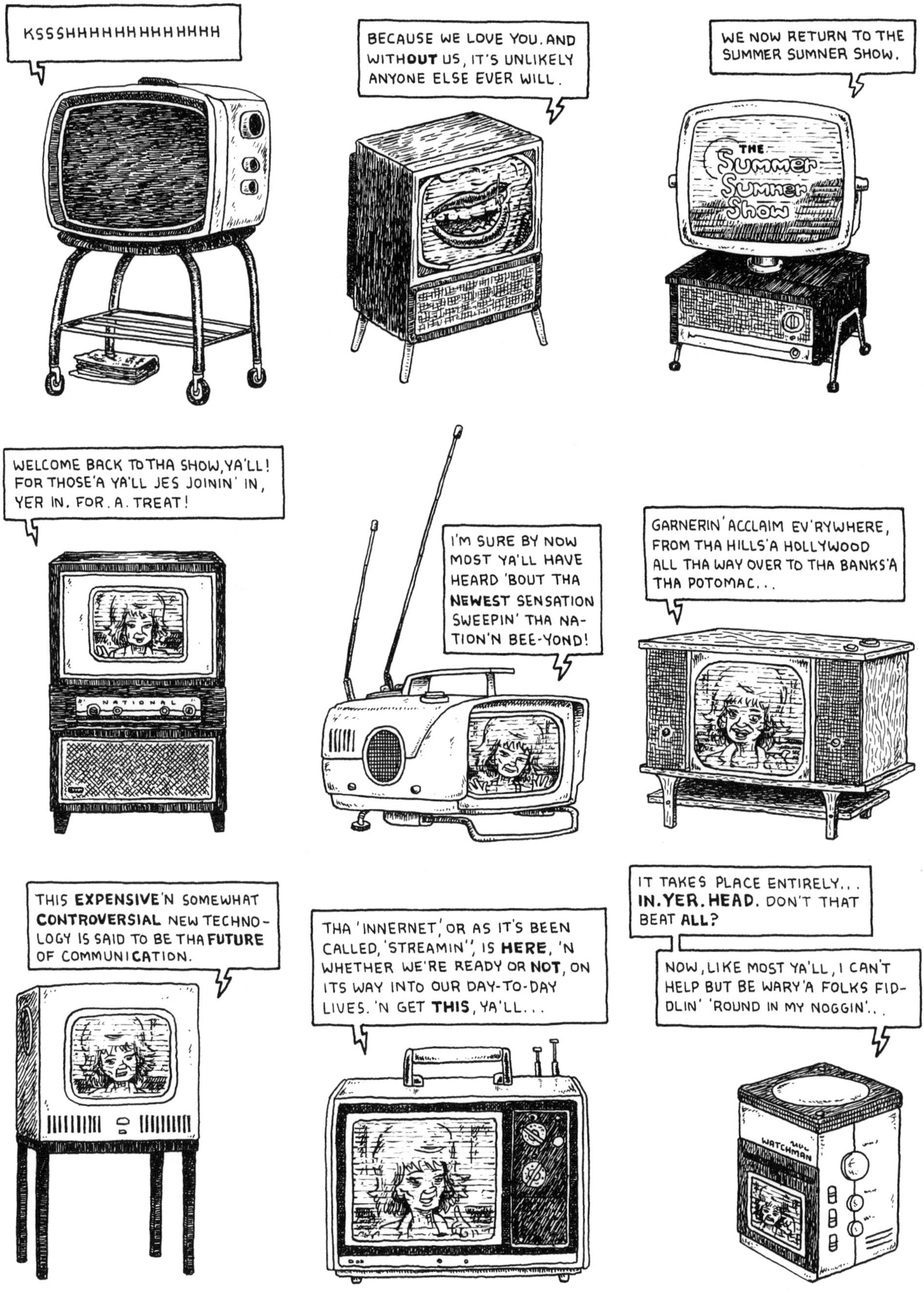
KSSSHHHHHHHHHHHHH
BECAUSE WE LOVE YOU. AND WITHOUT US, IT'S UNLIKELY ANYONE ELSE EVER WILL.
WE NOW RETURN TO THE SUMMER SUMNER SHOW.
THE Summer Sumner Show
WELCOME BACK TO THA SHOW, YA'LL! FOR THOSE'A YA'LL JES JOININ' IN, YER IN. FOR. A. TREAT!
NATIONAL
I'M SURE BY NOW MOST YA'LL HAVE HEARD 'BOUT THA NEWEST SENSATION SWEEPIN' THA NATION'N BEE-YOND!
GARNERIN' ACCLAIM EV'RYWHERE, FROM THA HILLS'A HOLLYWOOD ALL THA WAY OVER TO THA BANKS'A THA POTOMAC...
THIS EXPENSIVE'N SOMEWHAT CONTROVERSIAL NEW TECHNOLOGY IS SAID TO BE THA FUTURE OF COMMUNICATION.
THA 'INNERNET,' OR AS IT'S BEEN CALLED, 'STREAMIN',' IS HERE, 'N WHETHER WE'RE READY OR NOT, ON ITS WAY INTO OUR DAY-TO-DAY LIVES. 'N GET THIS, YA'LL...
IT TAKES PLACE ENTIRELY... IN. YER. HEAD. DON'T THAT BEAT ALL?
NOW, LIKE MOST YA'LL, I CAN'T HELP BUT BE WARY'A FOLKS FIDDLIN' 'ROUND IN MY NOGGIN'...
WATCHMAN

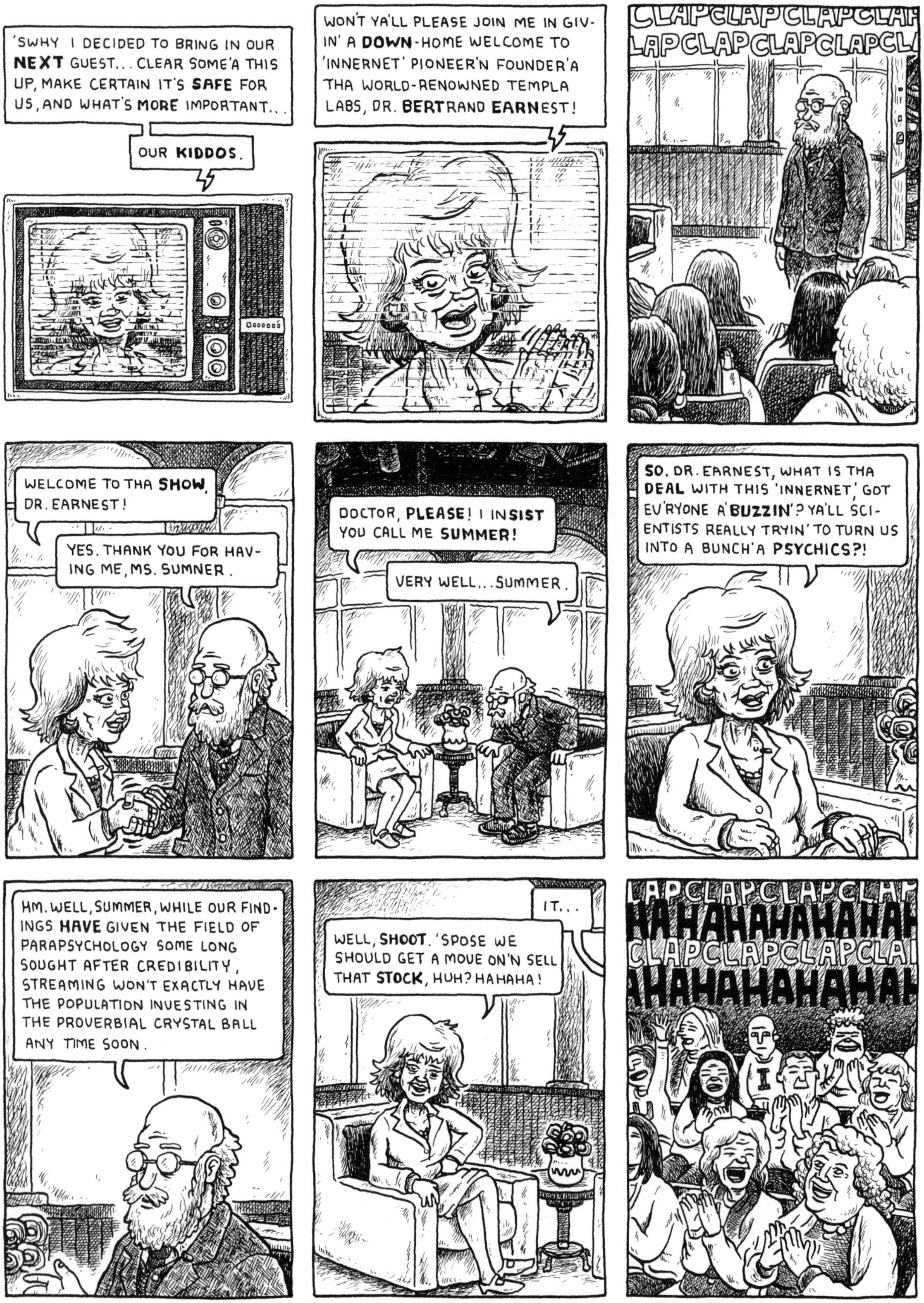
'SWHY I DECIDED TO BRING IN OUR NEXT GUEST... CLEAR SOME'A THIS UP, MAKE CERTAIN IT'S SAFE FOR US, AND WHAT'S MORE IMPORTANT...
OUR KIDDOS.
WON'T YA'LL PLEASE JOIN ME IN GIVIN' A DOWN-HOME WELCOME TO 'INNERNET' PIONEER'N FOUNDER'A THA WORLD-RENOWNED TEMPLA LABS, DR. BERTRAND EARNEST!
CLAPCLAPCLAPCLAPCLAPCLAPCLAPCLAPCLAPCLAP
WELCOME TO THA SHOW, DR. EARNEST!
YES. THANK YOU FOR HAVING ME, MS. SUMNER.
DOCTOR, PLEASE! I INSIST YOU CALL ME SUMMER!
VERY WELL... SUMMER.
SO, DR. EARNEST, WHAT IS THA DEAL WITH THIS 'INNERNET,' GOT EV'RYONE A'BUZZIN'? YA'LL SCIENTISTS REALLY TRYIN' TO TURN US INTO A BUNCH'A PSYCHICS?!
HM. WELL, SUMMER, WHILE OUR FINDINGS HAVE GIVEN THE FIELD OF PARAPSYCHOLOGY SOME LONG SOUGHT AFTER CREDIBILITY, STREAMING WON'T EXACTLY HAVE THE POPULATION INVESTING IN THE PROVERBIAL CRYSTAL BALL ANY TIME SOON.
IT...
WELL, SHOOT. 'SPOSE WE SHOULD GET A MOVE ON'N SELL THAT STOCK, HUH? HAHAHA!
CLAPCLAPCLAPCLAP
HAHAHAHAHAHAHA
CLAPCLAPCLAPCLAP
HAHAHAHAHAHAHA

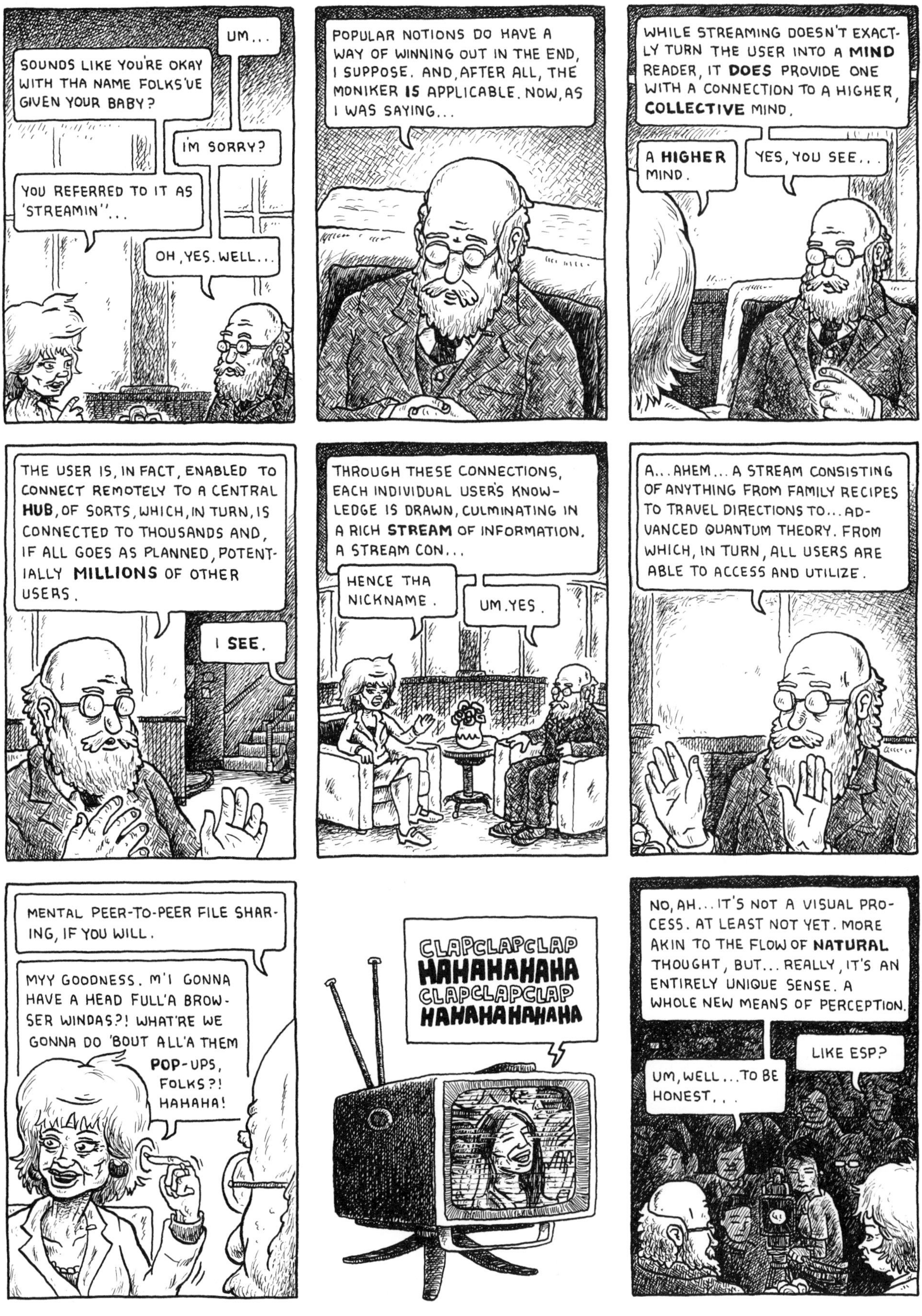
UM...
SOUNDS LIKE YOU'RE OKAY WITH THA NAME FOLKS'VE GIVEN YOUR BABY?
I'M SORRY?
YOU REFERRED TO IT AS 'STREAMIN''...
OH, YES. WELL...
POPULAR NOTIONS DO HAVE A WAY OF WINNING OUT IN THE END, I SUPPOSE. AND, AFTER ALL, THE MONIKER IS APPLICABLE. NOW, AS I WAS SAYING...
WHILE STREAMING DOESN'T EXACTLY TURN THE USER INTO A MIND READER, IT DOES PROVIDE ONE WITH A CONNECTION TO A HIGHER, COLLECTIVE MIND.
A HIGHER MIND.
YES, YOU SEE...
THE USER IS, IN FACT, ENABLED TO CONNECT REMOTELY TO A CENTRAL HUB, OF SORTS, WHICH, IN TURN, IS CONNECTED TO THOUSANDS AND, IF ALL GOES AS PLANNED, POTENTIALLY MILLIONS OF OTHER USERS.
I SEE.
THROUGH THESE CONNECTIONS, EACH INDIVIDUAL USER'S KNOWLEDGE IS DRAWN, CULMINATING IN A RICH STREAM OF INFORMATION. A STREAM CON...
HENCE THA NICKNAME.
UM. YES.
A... AHEM... A STREAM CONSISTING OF ANYTHING FROM FAMILY RECIPES TO TRAVEL DIRECTIONS TO... ADVANCED QUANTUM THEORY. FROM WHICH, IN TURN, ALL USERS ARE ABLE TO ACCESS AND UTILIZE.
MENTAL PEER-TO-PEER FILE SHARING, IF YOU WILL.
MYY GOODNESS. M'I GONNA HAVE A HEAD FULL'A BROWSER WINDAS?! WHAT'RE WE GONNA DO 'BOUT ALL'A THEM POP-UPS, FOLKS?! HAHAHA!
CLAPCLAPCLAP HAHAHAHAHA CLAPCLAPCLAP HAHAHAHAHAHA
NO, AH... IT'S NOT A VISUAL PROCESS. AT LEAST NOT YET. MORE AKIN TO THE FLOW OF NATURAL THOUGHT, BUT... REALLY, IT'S AN ENTIRELY UNIQUE SENSE. A WHOLE NEW MEANS OF PERCEPTION.
LIKE ESP?
UM, WELL... TO BE HONEST...

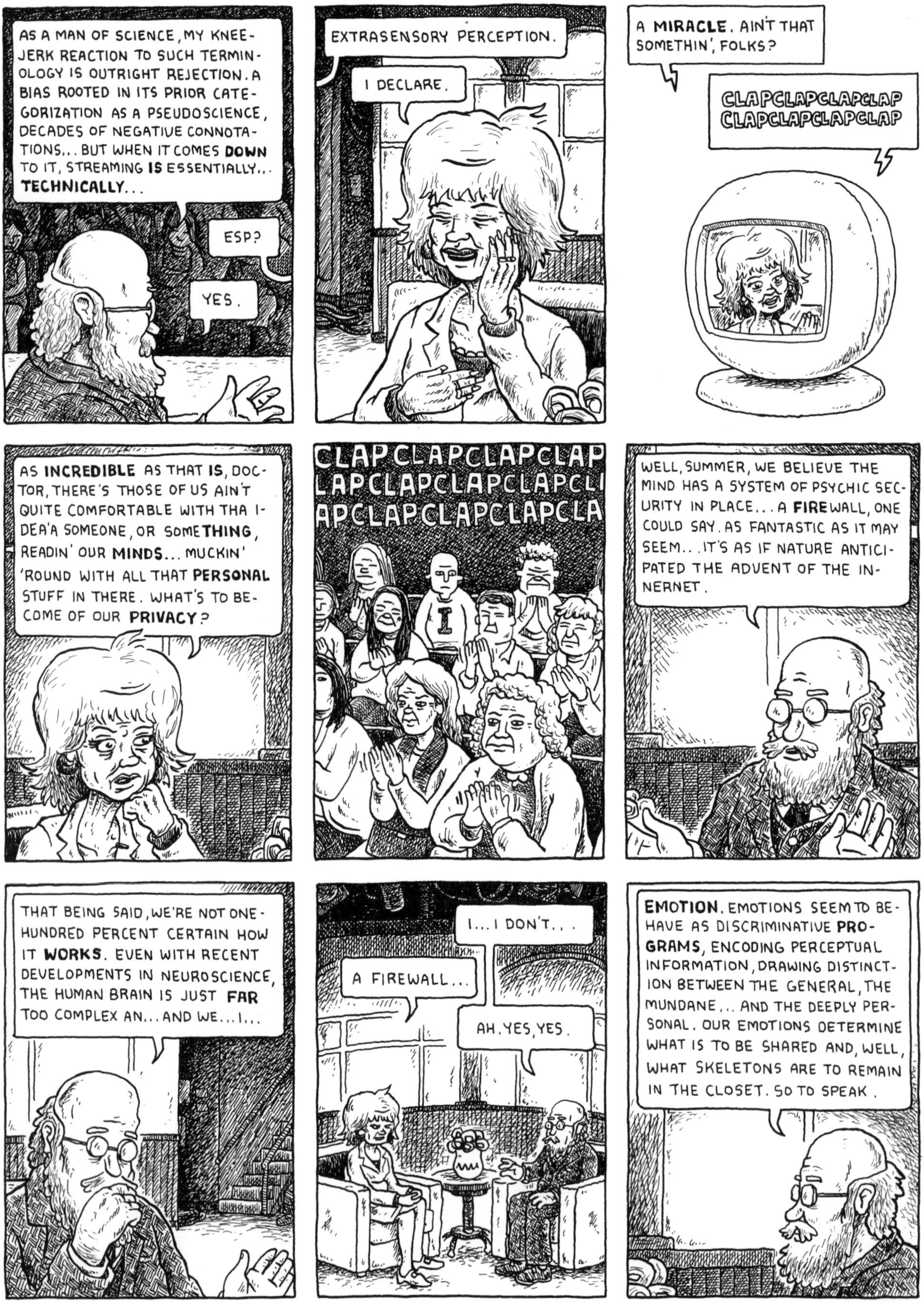
AS A MAN OF SCIENCE, MY KNEE-JERK REACTION TO SUCH TERMINOLOGY IS OUTRIGHT REJECTION. A BIAS ROOTED IN ITS PRIOR CATEGORIZATION AS A PSEUDOSCIENCE, DECADES OF NEGATIVE CONNOTATIONS... BUT WHEN IT COMES DOWN TO IT, STREAMING IS ESSENTIALLY... TECHNICALLY...
ESP?
YES.
EXTRASENSORY PERCEPTION.
I DECLARE.
A MIRACLE. AIN'T THAT SOMETHIN', FOLKS?
CLAPCLAPCLAPCLAP CLAPCLAPCLAPCLAP
AS INCREDIBLE AS THAT IS, DOCTOR, THERE'S THOSE OF US AIN'T QUITE COMFORTABLE WITH THA I-DEA'A SOMEONE, OR SOMETHING, READIN' OUR MINDS... MUCKIN' 'ROUND WITH ALL THAT PERSONAL STUFF IN THERE. WHAT'S TO BECOME OF OUR PRIVACY?
CLAPCLAPCLAPCLAP LAPCLAPCLAPCLAPCLAPCLI APCLAPCLAPCLAPCLA
WELL, SUMMER, WE BELIEVE THE MIND HAS A SYSTEM OF PSYCHIC SECURITY IN PLACE... A FIREWALL, ONE COULD SAY. AS FANTASTIC AS IT MAY SEEM... IT'S AS IF NATURE ANTICIPATED THE ADVENT OF THE INNERNET.
THAT BEING SAID, WE'RE NOT ONE-HUNDRED PERCENT CERTAIN HOW IT WORKS. EVEN WITH RECENT DEVELOPMENTS IN NEUROSCIENCE, THE HUMAN BRAIN IS JUST FAR TOO COMPLEX AN... AND WE... I...
I... I DON'T...
A FIREWALL...
AH. YES, YES.
EMOTION. EMOTIONS SEEM TO BEHAVE AS DISCRIMINATIVE PROGRAMS, ENCODING PERCEPTUAL INFORMATION, DRAWING DISTINCTION BETWEEN THE GENERAL, THE MUNDANE... AND THE DEEPLY PERSONAL. OUR EMOTIONS DETERMINE WHAT IS TO BE SHARED AND, WELL, WHAT SKELETONS ARE TO REMAIN IN THE CLOSET. SO TO SPEAK.

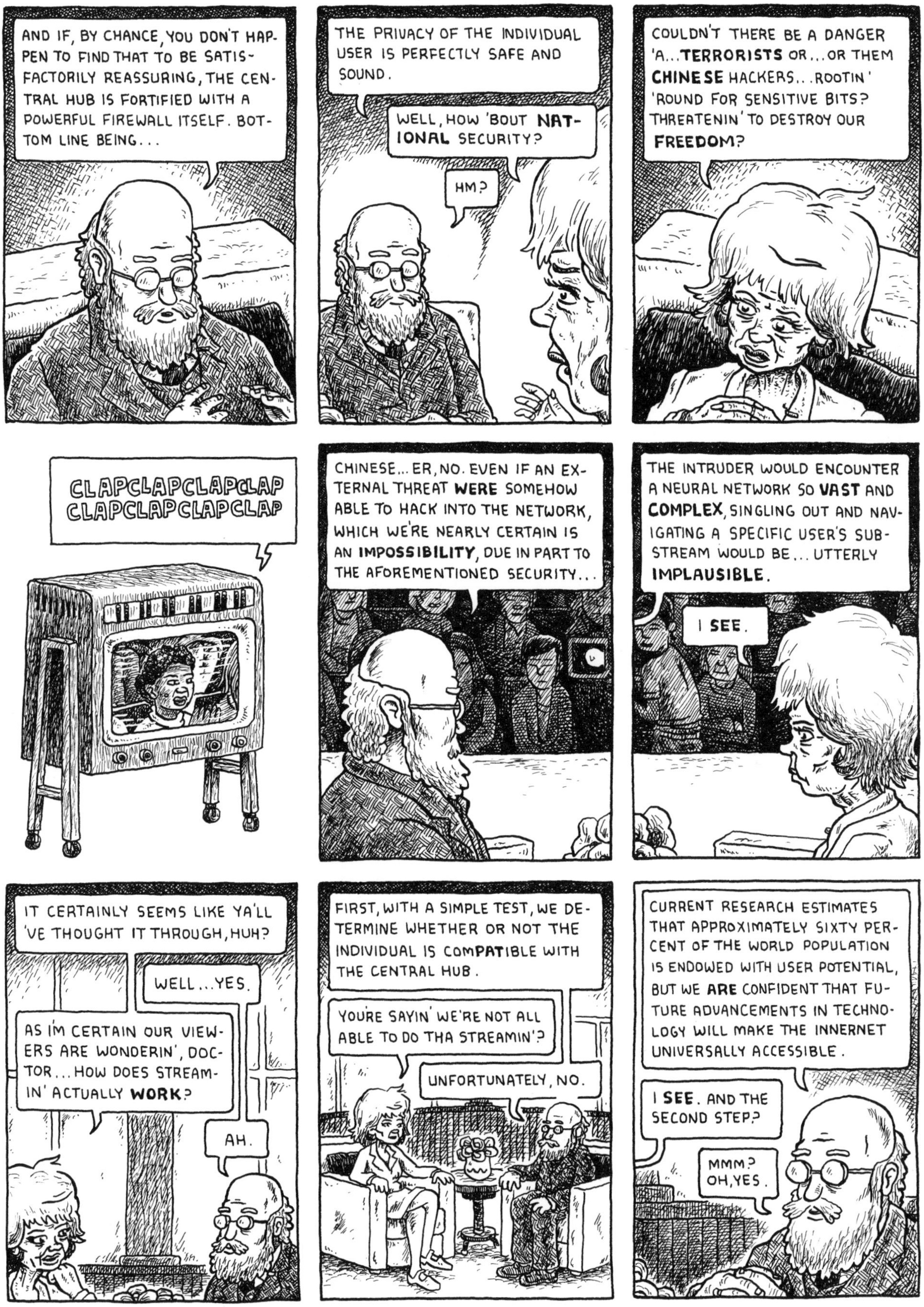
AND IF, BY CHANCE, YOU DON'T HAPPEN TO FIND THAT TO BE SATISFACTORILY REASSURING, THE CENTRAL HUB IS FORTIFIED WITH A POWERFUL FIREWALL ITSELF. BOTTOM LINE BEING...
THE PRIVACY OF THE INDIVIDUAL USER IS PERFECTLY SAFE AND SOUND.
WELL, HOW 'BOUT NATIONAL SECURITY?
HM?
COULDN'T THERE BE A DANGER 'A... TERRORISTS OR... OR THEM CHINESE HACKERS... ROOTIN' 'ROUND FOR SENSITIVE BITS? THREATENIN' TO DESTROY OUR FREEDOM?
CLAPCLAPCLAPCLAP CLAPCLAPCLAPCLAP
CHINESE... ER, NO. EVEN IF AN EXTERNAL THREAT WERE SOMEHOW ABLE TO HACK INTO THE NETWORK, WHICH WE'RE NEARLY CERTAIN IS AN IMPOSSIBILITY, DUE IN PART TO THE AFOREMENTIONED SECURITY...
THE INTRUDER WOULD ENCOUNTER A NEURAL NETWORK SO VAST AND COMPLEX, SINGLING OUT AND NAVIGATING A SPECIFIC USER'S SUBSTREAM WOULD BE... UTTERLY IMPLAUSIBLE.
I SEE.
IT CERTAINLY SEEMS LIKE YA'LL 'VE THOUGHT IT THROUGH, HUH?
WELL... YES.
AS I'M CERTAIN OUR VIEWERS ARE WONDERIN', DOCTOR... HOW DOES STREAMIN' ACTUALLY WORK?
AH.
FIRST, WITH A SIMPLE TEST, WE DETERMINE WHETHER OR NOT THE INDIVIDUAL IS COMPATIBLE WITH THE CENTRAL HUB.
YOU'RE SAYIN' WE'RE NOT ALL ABLE TO DO THA STREAMIN'?
UNFORTUNATELY, NO.
CURRENT RESEARCH ESTIMATES THAT APPROXIMATELY SIXTY PERCENT OF THE WORLD POPULATION IS ENDOWED WITH USER POTENTIAL, BUT WE ARE CONFIDENT THAT FUTURE ADVANCEMENTS IN TECHNOLOGY WILL MAKE THE INNERNET UNIVERSALLY ACCESSIBLE.
I SEE. AND THE SECOND STEP?
MMM? OH, YES.

IN WHAT IS, RELATIVELY, A QUICK AND PAINLESS PROCEDURE, A NANO-CHIP IS IMPLANTED IN THE USER'S CEREBRAL CORTEX AND, THIRDLY,...

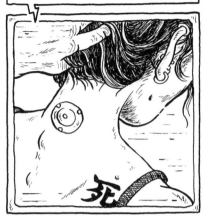

THE USER ADHERES A SMALL, RE-MOVEABLE TRANSMITTOR AT THE BASE OF HER SKULL. THEN, AS THEY SAY... 'YOU'RE IN BUSINESS'.

EASY AS THAT?

WELL, IT'S NOT **QUITE** THAT SIMPLE, BUT THAT **IS** THE GENERAL IDEA.

I SEE. I'M **CURIOUS**, DOCTOR...

... ARE YOU STREAMIN' RIGHT NOW?

I AM.

EXCELLENT. HOW 'BOUT WE GIVE YA A 'LIL TEST?

VERY WELL.

WHAT'CHA THINK, YA'LL?!

APCLAPCLAPCLAPCLA
WOOTWOOTWOOTWO
CLAPCLAPCLAPCLA
OOTWOOTWOOTWOO

DR. EARNEST... WHAT AM I THINKIN' 'BOUT... **RIGHT NOW?**

URM. WELL, SUMMER, I'M AFRAID THERE'S NO WAY FOR ME TO **KNOW.** EVEN IF **YOU** WERE A USER, STREAMING DOESN'T...

I **SEE.**

ANY **PREDICTIONS** REGARDIN' THA UPCOMIN' PRESIDENTIAL 'LECTION?

PREDICT... I... N-NO. I'M INCAPABLE OF PREDICT-ING THE OUTCOME OF **ANY** FUTURE EVENT. IT'S... STREAMING DOESN'T...

DOCTOR... WHEN CAN WE EXPECT THA SECOND COMIN'?

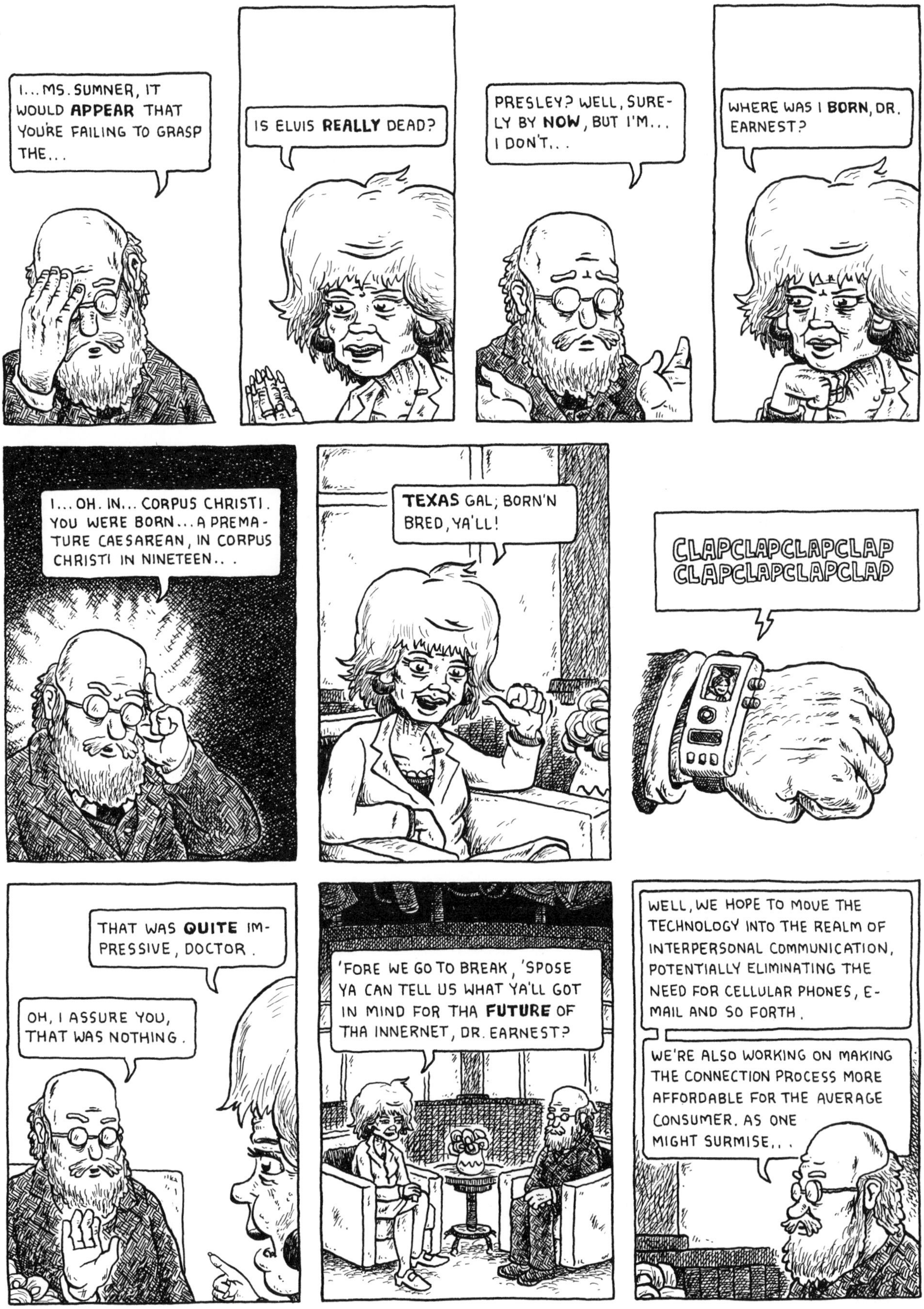
I... MS. SUMNER, IT WOULD APPEAR THAT YOU'RE FAILING TO GRASP THE...
IS ELVIS REALLY DEAD?
PRESLEY? WELL, SURELY BY NOW, BUT I'M... I DON'T...
WHERE WAS I BORN, DR. EARNEST?
I... OH. IN... CORPUS CHRISTI. YOU WERE BORN... A PREMATURE CAESAREAN, IN CORPUS CHRISTI IN NINETEEN...
TEXAS GAL; BORN'N BRED, YA'LL!
CLAPCLAPCLAPCLAP CLAPCLAPCLAPCLAP
THAT WAS QUITE IMPRESSIVE, DOCTOR.
OH, I ASSURE YOU, THAT WAS NOTHING.
'FORE WE GO TO BREAK, 'SPOSE YA CAN TELL US WHAT YA'LL GOT IN MIND FOR THA FUTURE OF THA INNERNET, DR. EARNEST?
WELL, WE HOPE TO MOVE THE TECHNOLOGY INTO THE REALM OF INTERPERSONAL COMMUNICATION, POTENTIALLY ELIMINATING THE NEED FOR CELLULAR PHONES, E-MAIL AND SO FORTH.
WE'RE ALSO WORKING ON MAKING THE CONNECTION PROCESS MORE AFFORDABLE FOR THE AVERAGE CONSUMER. AS ONE MIGHT SURMISE...

THE MORE USERS CONNECTED, THE RICHER THE STREAM. TO THE BENEFIT OF ALL.

SOUNDS **EXCITIN'**, DOCTOR.

IT TRULY IS AN EXCITING TIME, SUMMER.

TRULY.

I'D LIKE TO THANK DR. EARNEST FOR TAKIN' THA TIME TO VISIT WITH US TODAY.

CLAPCLAPCLAP
APCLAPCLAPCLAP
LAPCLAPCLAPCL

UP NEXT... WE'VE GOT CONJOINED **TRIPLETS** SWINGIN' BY. 'N FOLKS, NOT ONLY ARE THEY MORBIDLY **O-BESE**, BUT...

THEY AIN'T ALL BATTIN' FOR THA SAME **TEAM**, IF YA'LL CATCH MY MEANIN'!

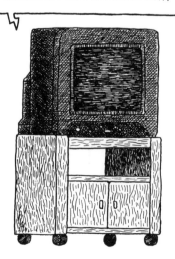

WE'LL BE RIGHT BACK WITH THA SUMMER SUMNER SHOW, YA'LL... JES AFTER THESE HERE MESSAGES.

♪ CHUCK WAGON **CHUCK** WAGON **CHUCK CHUCK CHUCK** ♪

KSSSHHHHHHHHHHHHHHHHH

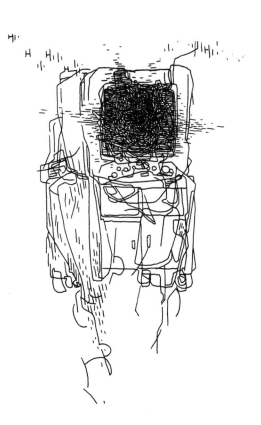

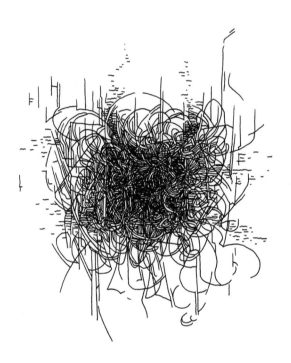

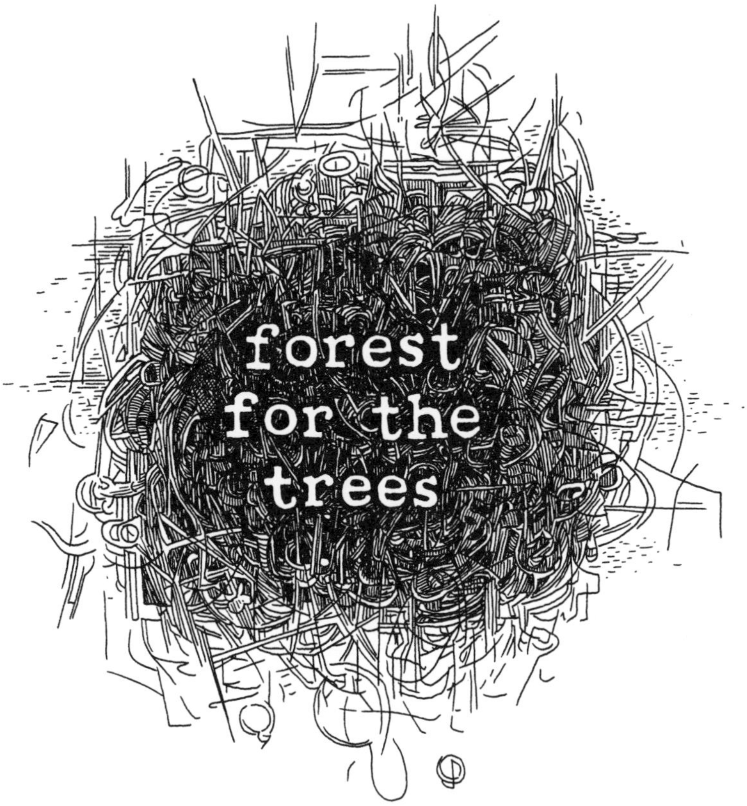
forest
for the
trees

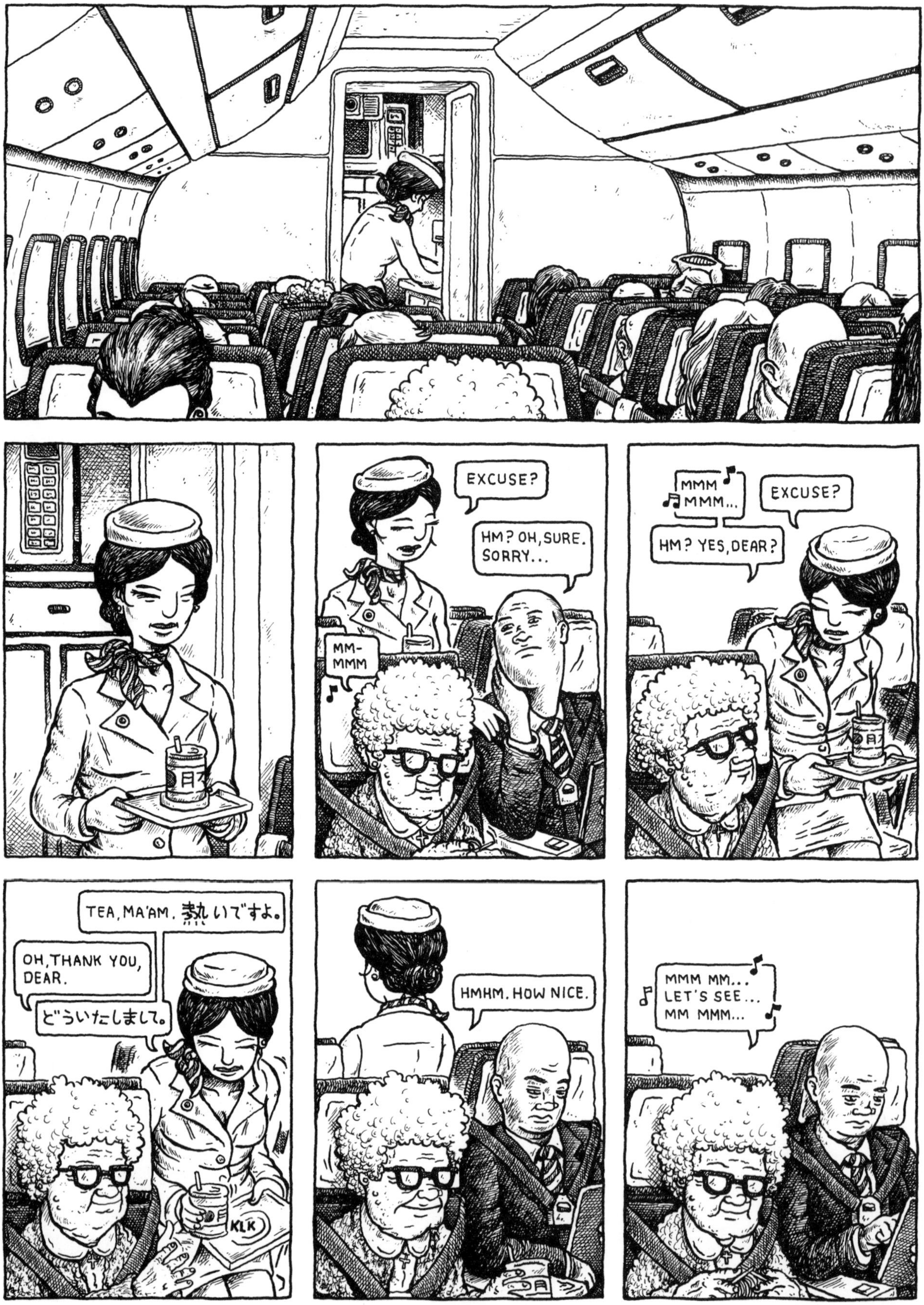
EXCUSE?
HM? OH, SURE. SORRY...
MM-MMM
MMM MMM...
EXCUSE?
HM? YES, DEAR?
TEA, MA'AM. 熱いですよ。
OH, THANK YOU, DEAR.
どういたしまして。
KLK
HMHM. HOW NICE.
MMM MM... LET'S SEE... MM MMM...

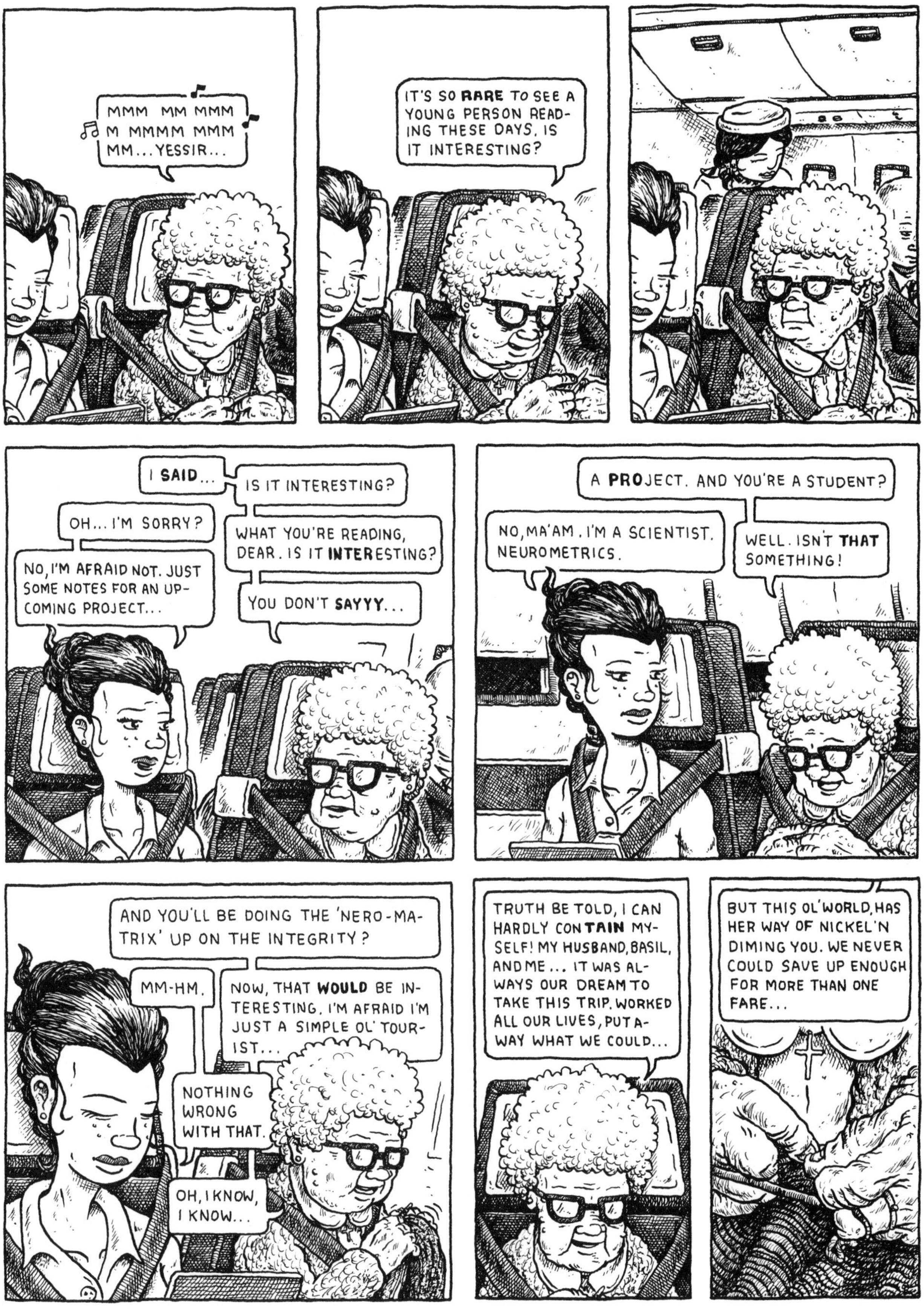

MMM MM MMM M MMMM MMM MM... YESSIR...
IT'S SO RARE TO SEE A YOUNG PERSON READ-ING THESE DAYS. IS IT INTERESTING?
I SAID...
IS IT INTERESTING?
OH... I'M SORRY?
WHAT YOU'RE READING, DEAR. IS IT INTERESTING?
NO, I'M AFRAID NOT. JUST SOME NOTES FOR AN UP-COMING PROJECT...
YOU DON'T SAYYY...
A PROJECT. AND YOU'RE A STUDENT?
NO, MA'AM. I'M A SCIENTIST. NEUROMETRICS.
WELL. ISN'T THAT SOMETHING!
AND YOU'LL BE DOING THE 'NERO-MA-TRIX' UP ON THE INTEGRITY?
MM-HM.
NOW, THAT WOULD BE IN-TERESTING. I'M AFRAID I'M JUST A SIMPLE OL' TOUR-IST...
NOTHING WRONG WITH THAT.
OH, I KNOW, I KNOW...
TRUTH BE TOLD, I CAN HARDLY CONTAIN MY-SELF! MY HUSBAND, BASIL, AND ME... IT WAS AL-WAYS OUR DREAM TO TAKE THIS TRIP. WORKED ALL OUR LIVES, PUT A-WAY WHAT WE COULD...
BUT THIS OL' WORLD, HAS HER WAY OF NICKEL'N DIMING YOU. WE NEVER COULD SAVE UP ENOUGH FOR MORE THAN ONE FARE...

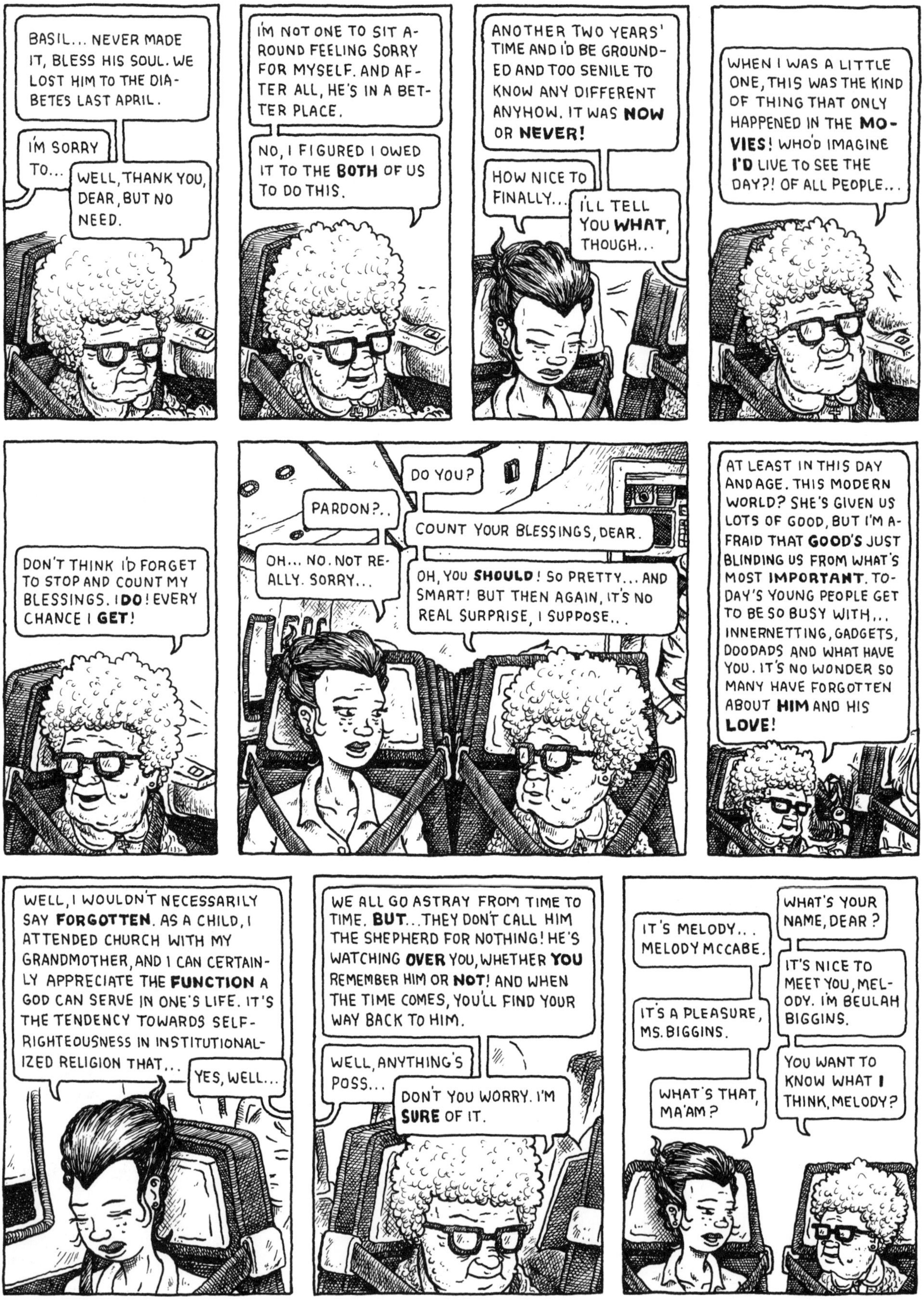
BASIL... NEVER MADE IT, BLESS HIS SOUL. WE LOST HIM TO THE DIABETES LAST APRIL.
I'M SORRY TO...
WELL, THANK YOU, DEAR, BUT NO NEED.
I'M NOT ONE TO SIT AROUND FEELING SORRY FOR MYSELF. AND AFTER ALL, HE'S IN A BETTER PLACE.
NO, I FIGURED I OWED IT TO THE **BOTH** OF US TO DO THIS.
ANOTHER TWO YEARS' TIME AND I'D BE GROUNDED AND TOO SENILE TO KNOW ANY DIFFERENT ANYHOW. IT WAS **NOW** OR **NEVER!**
HOW NICE TO FINALLY...
I'LL TELL YOU **WHAT**, THOUGH...
WHEN I WAS A LITTLE ONE, THIS WAS THE KIND OF THING THAT ONLY HAPPENED IN THE **MOVIES**! WHO'D IMAGINE **I'D** LIVE TO SEE THE DAY?! OF ALL PEOPLE...
DON'T THINK I'D FORGET TO STOP AND COUNT MY BLESSINGS. I **DO**! EVERY CHANCE I **GET**!
COUNT YOUR BLESSINGS, DEAR.
PARDON?..
DO YOU?
OH... NO. NOT REALLY. SORRY...
OH, YOU **SHOULD**! SO PRETTY... AND SMART! BUT THEN AGAIN, IT'S NO REAL SURPRISE, I SUPPOSE...
AT LEAST IN THIS DAY AND AGE. THIS MODERN WORLD? SHE'S GIVEN US LOTS OF GOOD, BUT I'M AFRAID THAT **GOOD'S** JUST BLINDING US FROM WHAT'S MOST **IMPORTANT**. TODAY'S YOUNG PEOPLE GET TO BE SO BUSY WITH... INNERNETTING, GADGETS, DOODADS AND WHAT HAVE YOU. IT'S NO WONDER SO MANY HAVE FORGOTTEN ABOUT **HIM** AND HIS **LOVE**!
WELL, I WOULDN'T NECESSARILY SAY **FORGOTTEN**. AS A CHILD, I ATTENDED CHURCH WITH MY GRANDMOTHER, AND I CAN CERTAINLY APPRECIATE THE **FUNCTION** A GOD CAN SERVE IN ONE'S LIFE. IT'S THE TENDENCY TOWARDS SELF-RIGHTEOUSNESS IN INSTITUTIONALIZED RELIGION THAT...
YES, WELL...
WE ALL GO ASTRAY FROM TIME TO TIME. **BUT**... THEY DON'T CALL HIM THE SHEPHERD FOR NOTHING! HE'S WATCHING **OVER** YOU, WHETHER **YOU** REMEMBER HIM OR **NOT**! AND WHEN THE TIME COMES, YOU'LL FIND YOUR WAY BACK TO HIM.
WELL, ANYTHING'S POSS...
DON'T YOU WORRY. I'M **SURE** OF IT.
WHAT'S YOUR NAME, DEAR?
IT'S MELODY... MELODY MCCABE.
IT'S NICE TO MEET YOU, MELODY. I'M BEULAH BIGGINS.
IT'S A PLEASURE, MS. BIGGINS.
YOU WANT TO KNOW WHAT **I** THINK, MELODY?
WHAT'S THAT, MA'AM?

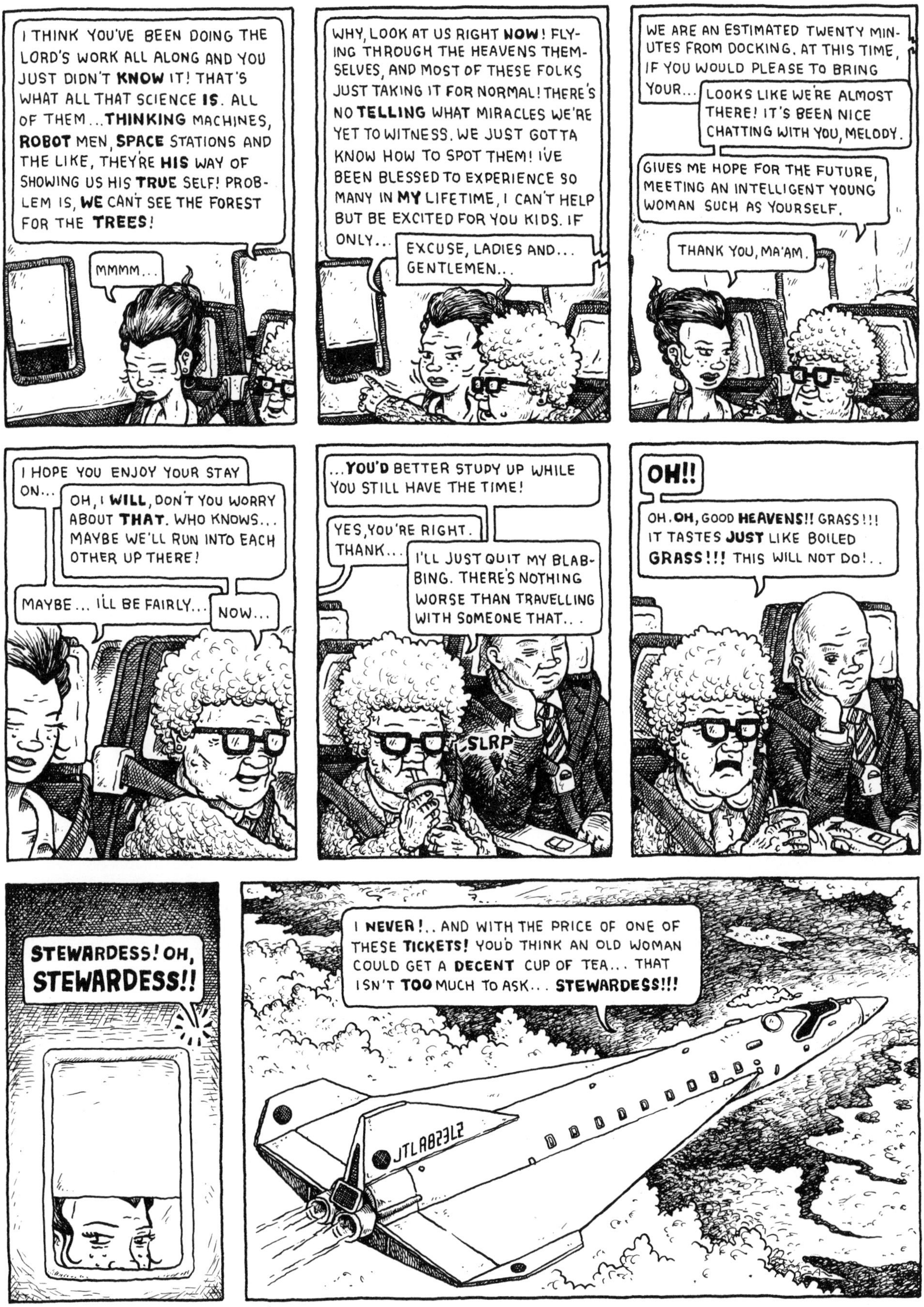
I THINK YOU'VE BEEN DOING THE LORD'S WORK ALL ALONG AND YOU JUST DIDN'T KNOW IT! THAT'S WHAT ALL THAT SCIENCE IS. ALL OF THEM... THINKING MACHINES, ROBOT MEN, SPACE STATIONS AND THE LIKE, THEY'RE HIS WAY OF SHOWING US HIS TRUE SELF! PROBLEM IS, WE CAN'T SEE THE FOREST FOR THE TREES!
MMMM...
WHY, LOOK AT US RIGHT NOW! FLYING THROUGH THE HEAVENS THEMSELVES, AND MOST OF THESE FOLKS JUST TAKING IT FOR NORMAL! THERE'S NO TELLING WHAT MIRACLES WE'RE YET TO WITNESS. WE JUST GOTTA KNOW HOW TO SPOT THEM! I'VE BEEN BLESSED TO EXPERIENCE SO MANY IN MY LIFETIME, I CAN'T HELP BUT BE EXCITED FOR YOU KIDS. IF ONLY...
EXCUSE, LADIES AND... GENTLEMEN...
WE ARE AN ESTIMATED TWENTY MINUTES FROM DOCKING. AT THIS TIME, IF YOU WOULD PLEASE TO BRING YOUR...
LOOKS LIKE WE'RE ALMOST THERE! IT'S BEEN NICE CHATTING WITH YOU, MELODY.
GIVES ME HOPE FOR THE FUTURE, MEETING AN INTELLIGENT YOUNG WOMAN SUCH AS YOURSELF.
THANK YOU, MA'AM.
I HOPE YOU ENJOY YOUR STAY ON...
OH, I WILL, DON'T YOU WORRY ABOUT THAT. WHO KNOWS... MAYBE WE'LL RUN INTO EACH OTHER UP THERE!
MAYBE... I'LL BE FAIRLY...
NOW...
...YOU'D BETTER STUDY UP WHILE YOU STILL HAVE THE TIME!
YES, YOU'RE RIGHT. THANK...
I'LL JUST QUIT MY BLABBING. THERE'S NOTHING WORSE THAN TRAVELLING WITH SOMEONE THAT...
SLRP
OH!!
OH. OH, GOOD HEAVENS!! GRASS!!! IT TASTES JUST LIKE BOILED GRASS!!! THIS WILL NOT DO!..
STEWARDESS! OH, STEWARDESS!!
I NEVER!.. AND WITH THE PRICE OF ONE OF THESE TICKETS! YOU'D THINK AN OLD WOMAN COULD GET A DECENT CUP OF TEA... THAT ISN'T TOO MUCH TO ASK... STEWARDESS!!!
JTLAB23L2

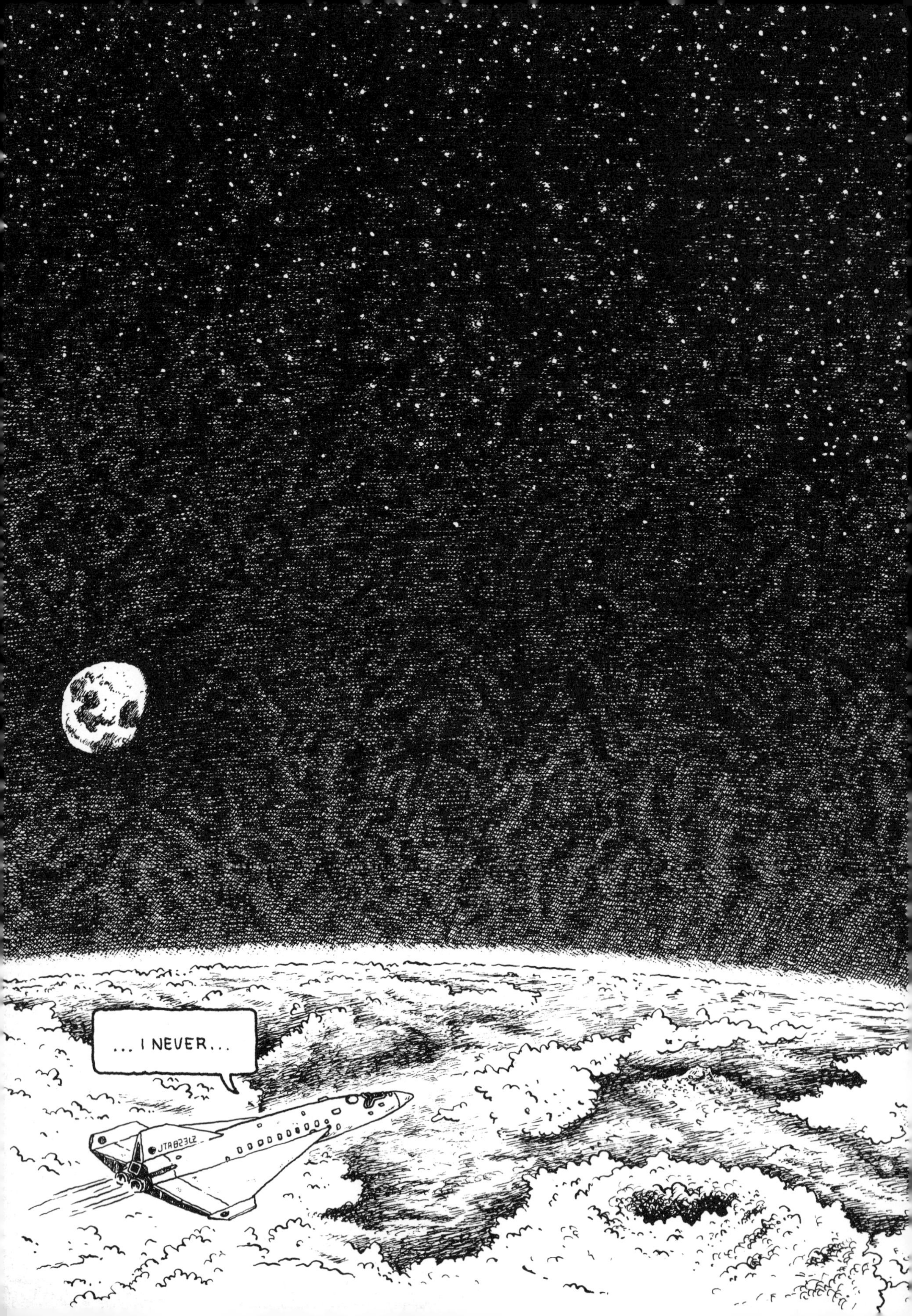
... I NEVER ...

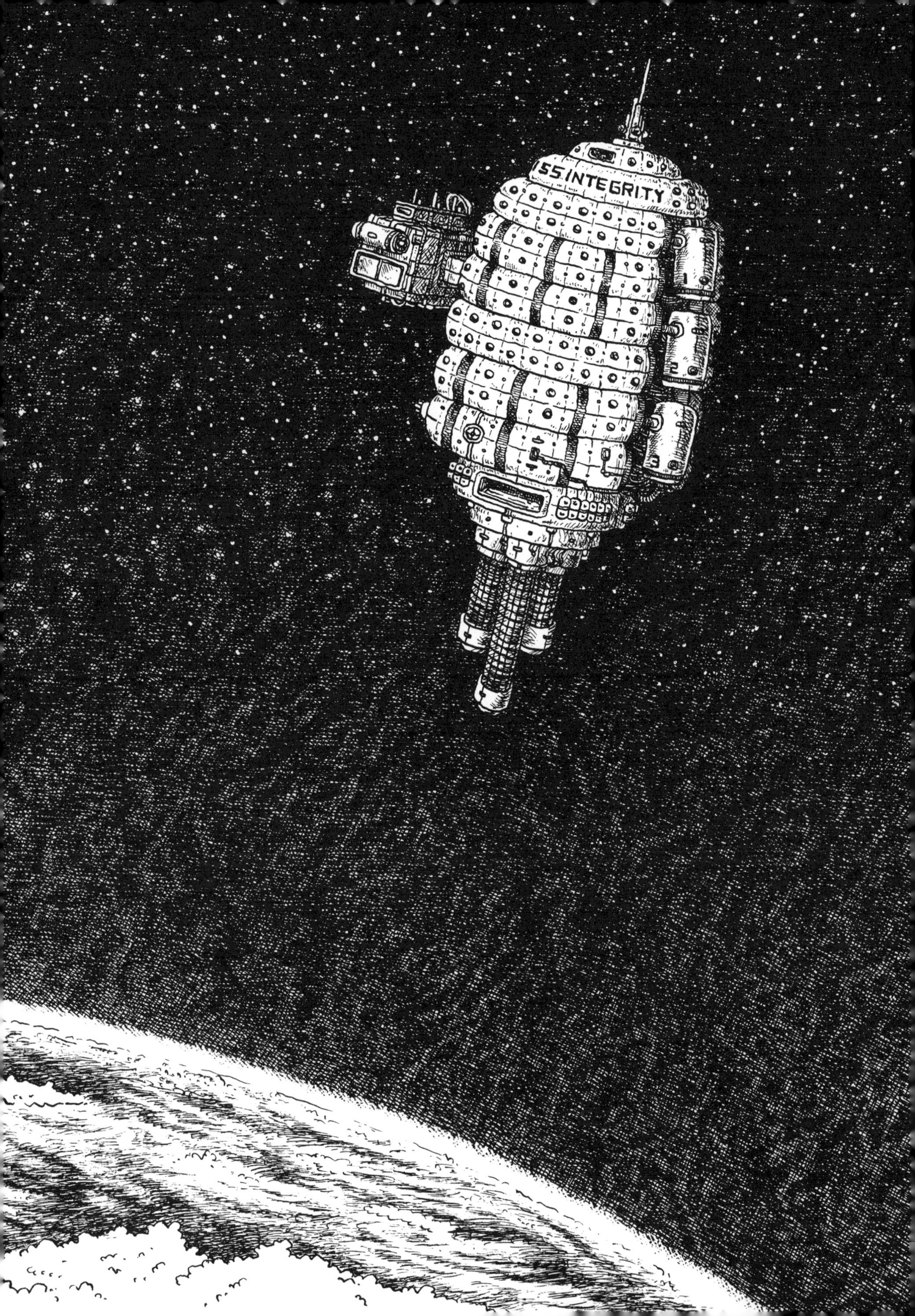
SS INTEGRITY
1
2
3

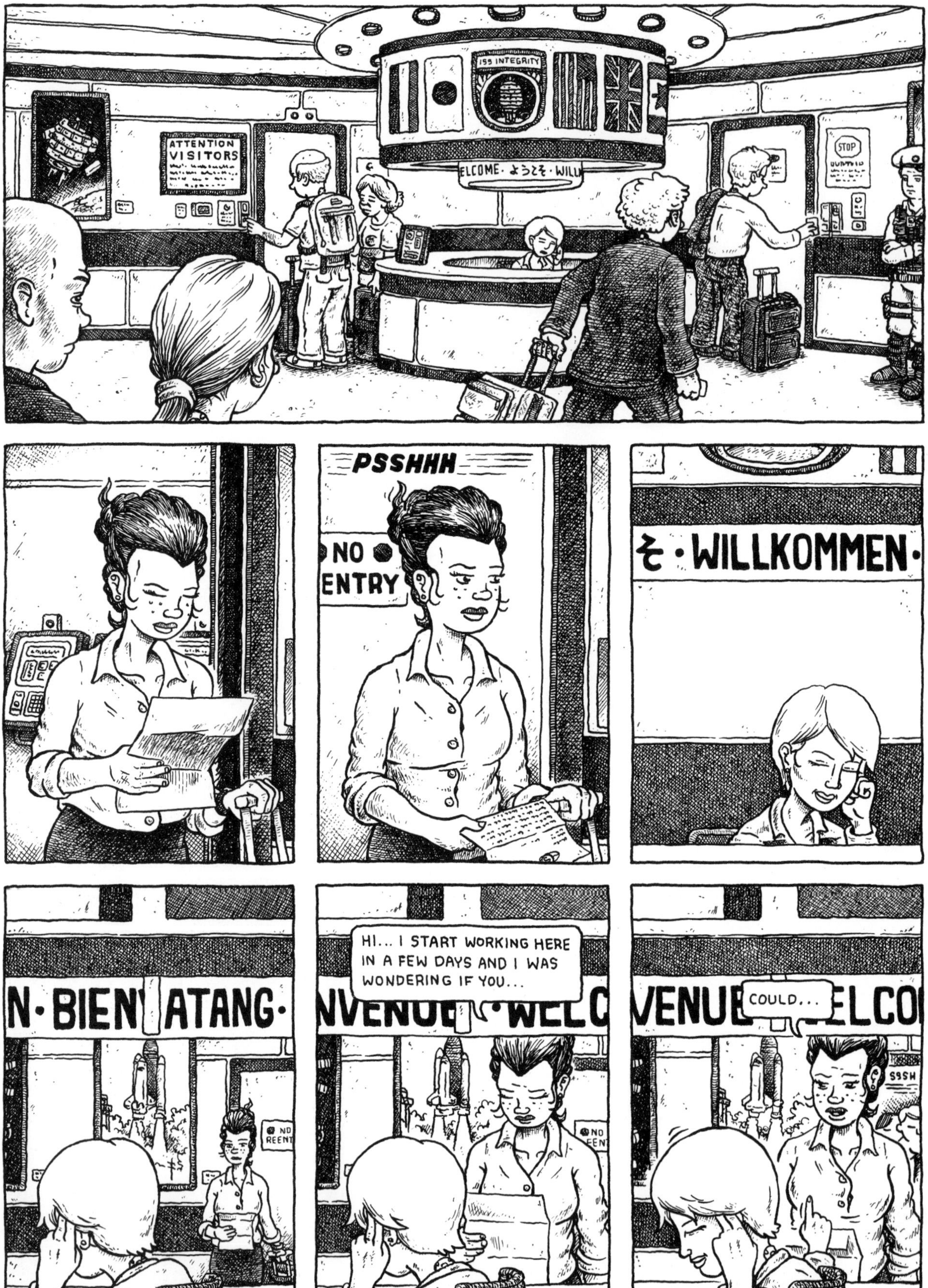
ISS INTEGRITY
ATTENTION VISITORS
ELCOME · ようこそ · WILL
STOP
PSSHHH
NO ENTRY
そ · WILLKOMMEN ·
N · BIEN ATANG ·
HI... I START WORKING HERE IN A FEW DAYS AND I WAS WONDERING IF YOU...
NVENUE · WELC
VENUE ELCO
COULD...

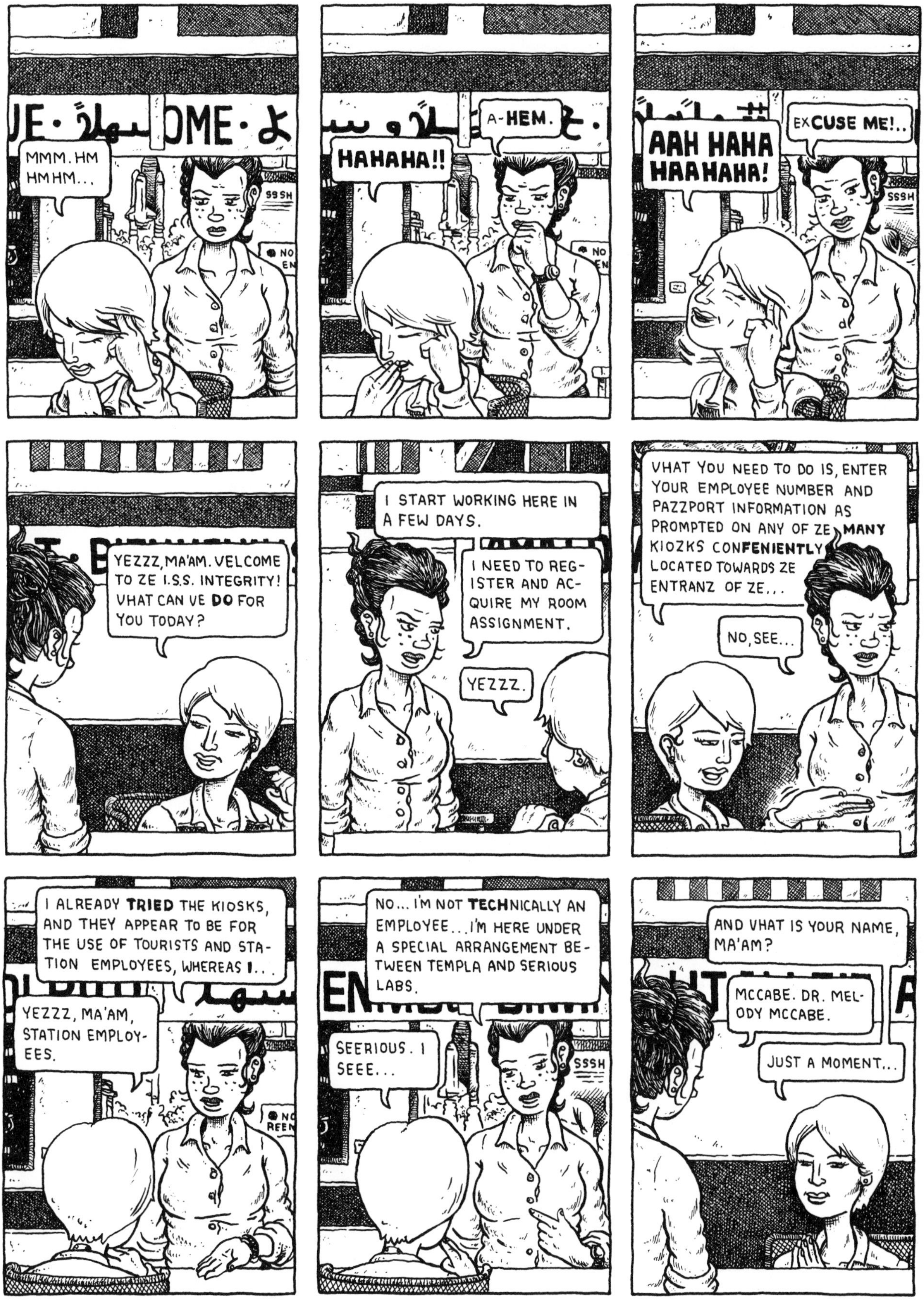
MMM. HM HMHM...
HAHAHA!!
A-HEM.
AAH HAHA HAAHAHA!
EXCUSE ME!..
YEZZZ, MA'AM. VELCOME TO ZE I.S.S. INTEGRITY! VHAT CAN VE DO FOR YOU TODAY?
I START WORKING HERE IN A FEW DAYS.
I NEED TO REGISTER AND ACQUIRE MY ROOM ASSIGNMENT.
YEZZZ.
VHAT YOU NEED TO DO IS, ENTER YOUR EMPLOYEE NUMBER AND PAZZPORT INFORMATION AS PROMPTED ON ANY OF ZE MANY KIOZKS CONFENIENTLY LOCATED TOWARDS ZE ENTRANZ OF ZE...
NO, SEE...
I ALREADY TRIED THE KIOSKS, AND THEY APPEAR TO BE FOR THE USE OF TOURISTS AND STATION EMPLOYEES, WHEREAS I...
YEZZZ, MA'AM, STATION EMPLOYEES.
NO... I'M NOT TECHNICALLY AN EMPLOYEE... I'M HERE UNDER A SPECIAL ARRANGEMENT BETWEEN TEMPLA AND SERIOUS LABS.
SEERIOUS. I SEEE...
AND VHAT IS YOUR NAME, MA'AM?
MCCABE. DR. MELODY MCCABE.
JUST A MOMENT...

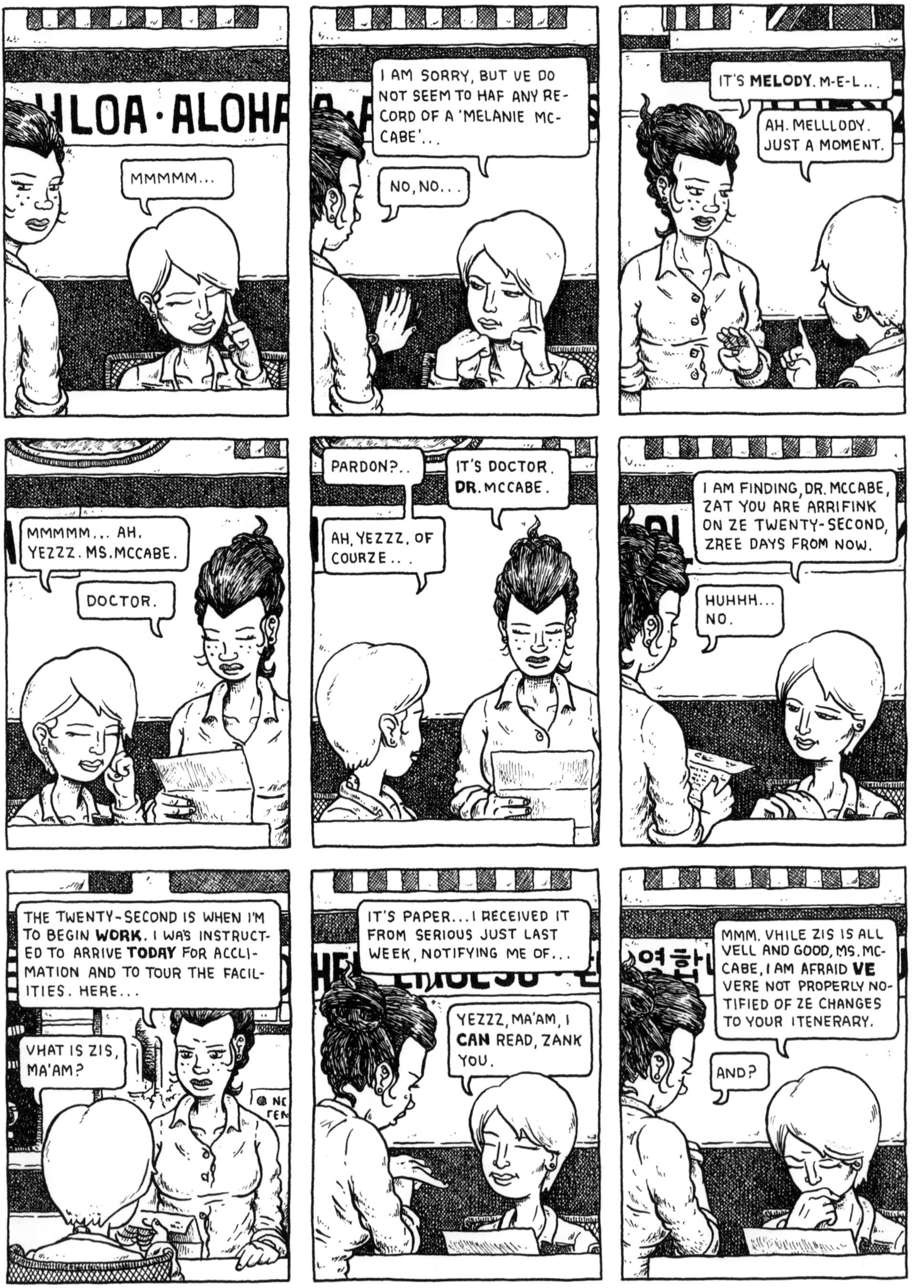
MMMMM...
I AM SORRY, BUT VE DO NOT SEEM TO HAF ANY RECORD OF A 'MELANIE MCCABE'...
NO, NO...
IT'S **MELODY**. M-E-L...
AH. MELLLODY. JUST A MOMENT.
MMMMM... AH. YEZZZ. MS. MCCABE.
DOCTOR.
PARDON?..
IT'S DOCTOR. **DR.** MCCABE.
AH, YEZZZ, OF COURZE...
I AM FINDING, DR. MCCABE, ZAT YOU ARE ARRIFINK ON ZE TWENTY-SECOND, ZREE DAYS FROM NOW.
HUHHH... NO.
THE TWENTY-SECOND IS WHEN I'M TO BEGIN **WORK**. I WAS INSTRUCTED TO ARRIVE **TODAY** FOR ACCLIMATION AND TO TOUR THE FACILITIES. HERE...
VHAT IS ZIS, MA'AM?
IT'S PAPER... I RECEIVED IT FROM SERIOUS JUST LAST WEEK, NOTIFYING ME OF...
YEZZZ, MA'AM, I **CAN** READ, ZANK YOU.
MMM. VHILE ZIS IS ALL VELL AND GOOD, MS. MCCABE, I AM AFRAID **VE** VERE NOT PROPERLY NOTIFIED OF ZE CHANGES TO YOUR ITENERARY.
AND?

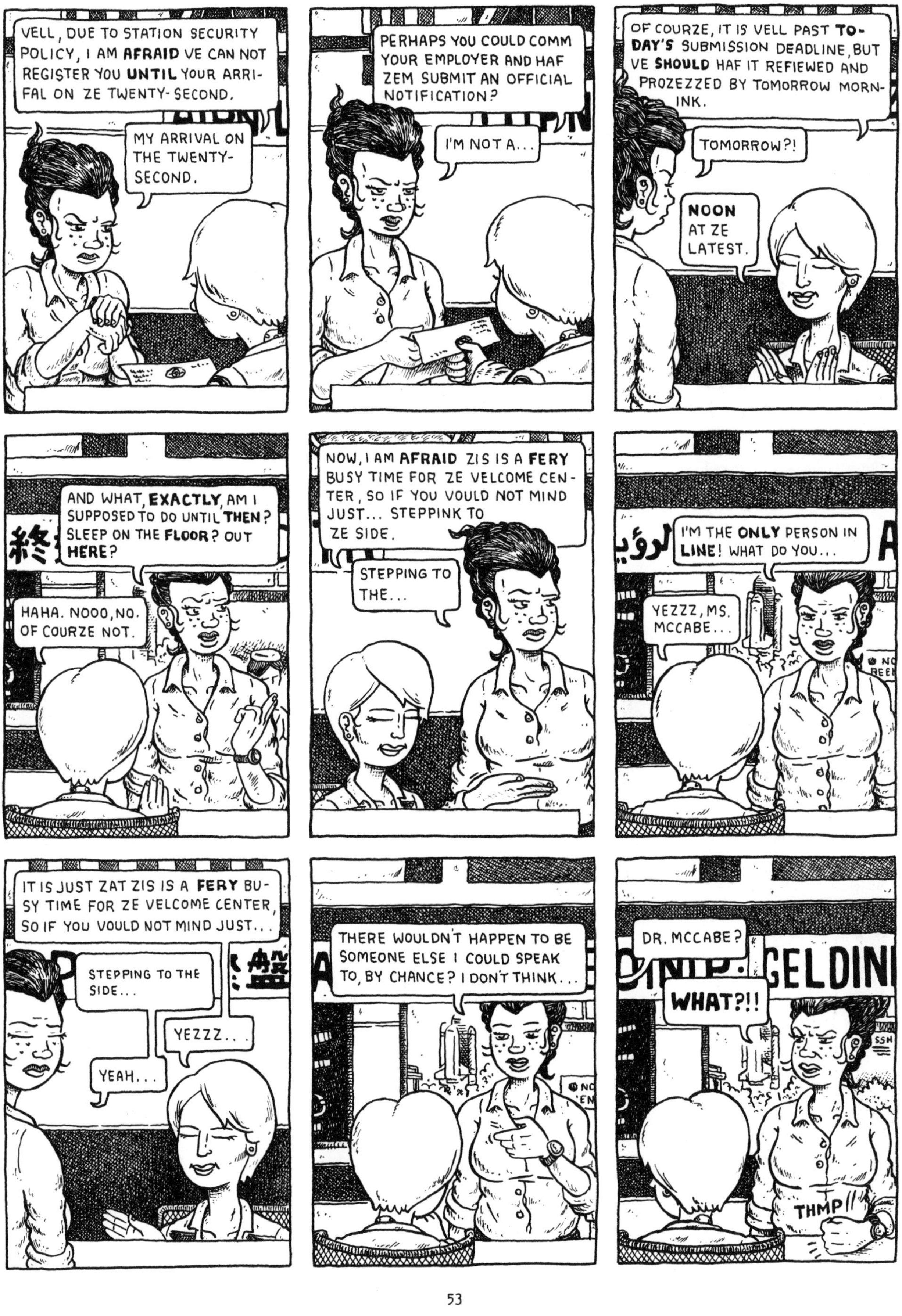
VELL, DUE TO STATION SECURITY POLICY, I AM **AFRAID** VE CAN NOT REGISTER YOU **UNTIL** YOUR ARRIFAL ON ZE TWENTY-SECOND.
MY ARRIVAL ON THE TWENTY-SECOND.
PERHAPS YOU COULD COMM YOUR EMPLOYER AND HAF ZEM SUBMIT AN OFFICIAL NOTIFICATION?
I'M NOT A...
OF COURZE, IT IS VELL PAST **TODAY'S** SUBMISSION DEADLINE, BUT VE **SHOULD** HAF IT REFIEWED AND PROZEZZED BY TOMORROW MORNINK.
TOMORROW?!
NOON AT ZE LATEST.
AND WHAT, **EXACTLY**, AM I SUPPOSED TO DO UNTIL **THEN**? SLEEP ON THE **FLOOR**? OUT **HERE**?
HAHA. NOOO, NO. OF COURZE NOT.
NOW, I AM **AFRAID** ZIS IS A **FERY** BUSY TIME FOR ZE VELCOME CENTER, SO IF YOU VOULD NOT MIND JUST... STEPPINK TO ZE SIDE.
STEPPING TO THE...
I'M THE **ONLY** PERSON IN **LINE**! WHAT DO YOU...
YEZZZ, MS. MCCABE...
IT IS JUST ZAT ZIS IS A **FERY** BUSY TIME FOR ZE VELCOME CENTER, SO IF YOU VOULD NOT MIND JUST...
STEPPING TO THE SIDE...
YEZZZ...
YEAH...
THERE WOULDN'T HAPPEN TO BE SOMEONE ELSE I COULD SPEAK TO, BY CHANCE? I DON'T THINK...
DR. MCCABE?
WHAT?!!
GELDIN
THMP!!

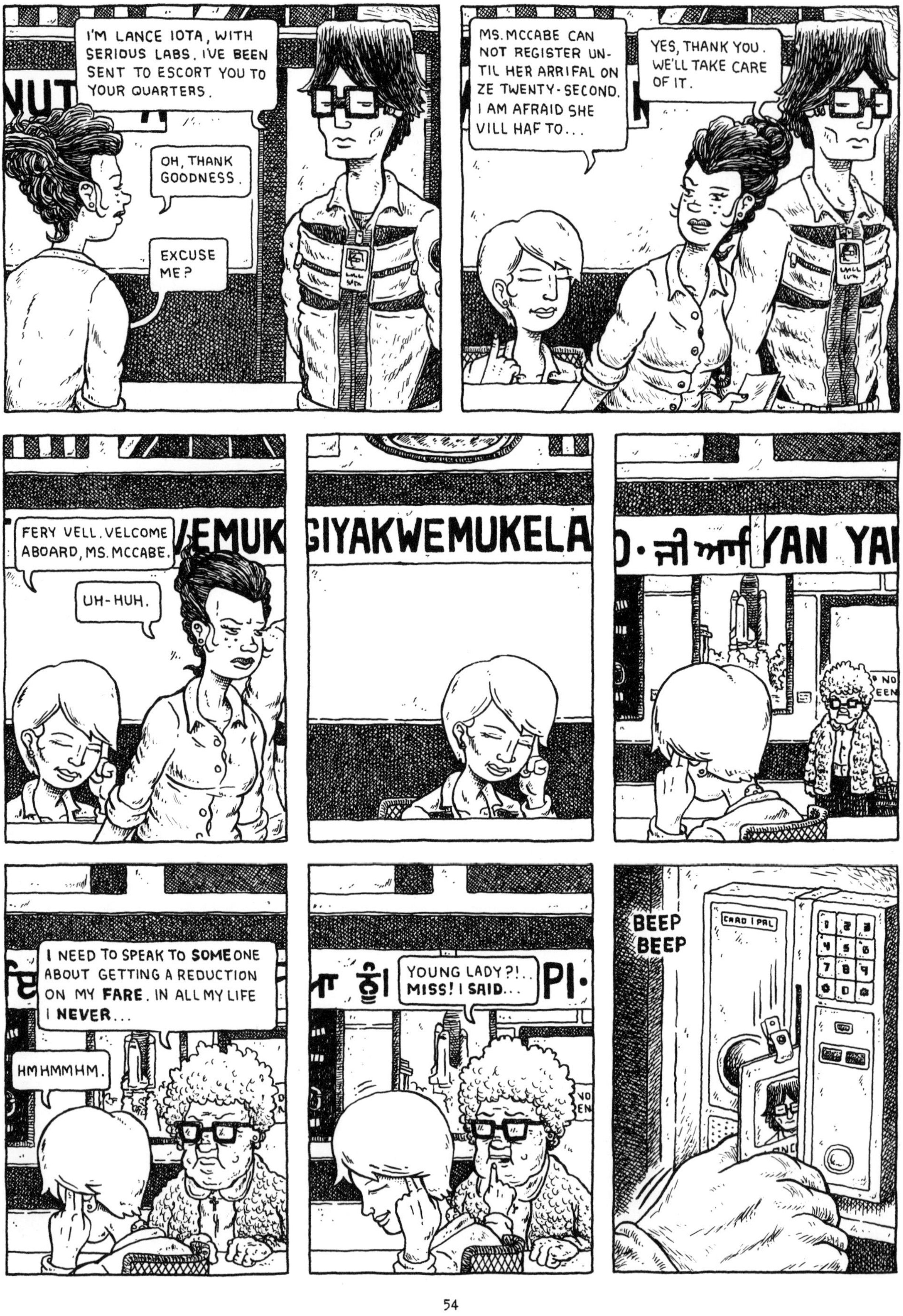

I'M LANCE IOTA, WITH SERIOUS LABS. I'VE BEEN SENT TO ESCORT YOU TO YOUR QUARTERS.
OH, THANK GOODNESS.
EXCUSE ME?
MS. MCCABE CAN NOT REGISTER UNTIL HER ARRIFAL ON ZE TWENTY-SECOND. I AM AFRAID SHE VILL HAF TO...
YES, THANK YOU. WE'LL TAKE CARE OF IT.
FERY VELL. VELCOME ABOARD, MS. MCCABE.
UH-HUH.
GIYAKWEMUKELA
I NEED TO SPEAK TO **SOME**ONE ABOUT GETTING A REDUCTION ON MY **FARE**. IN ALL MY LIFE I **NEVER**...
HMHMMHM.
YOUNG LADY?!.. **MISS! I SAID...**
BEEP BEEP
CARD I PAL

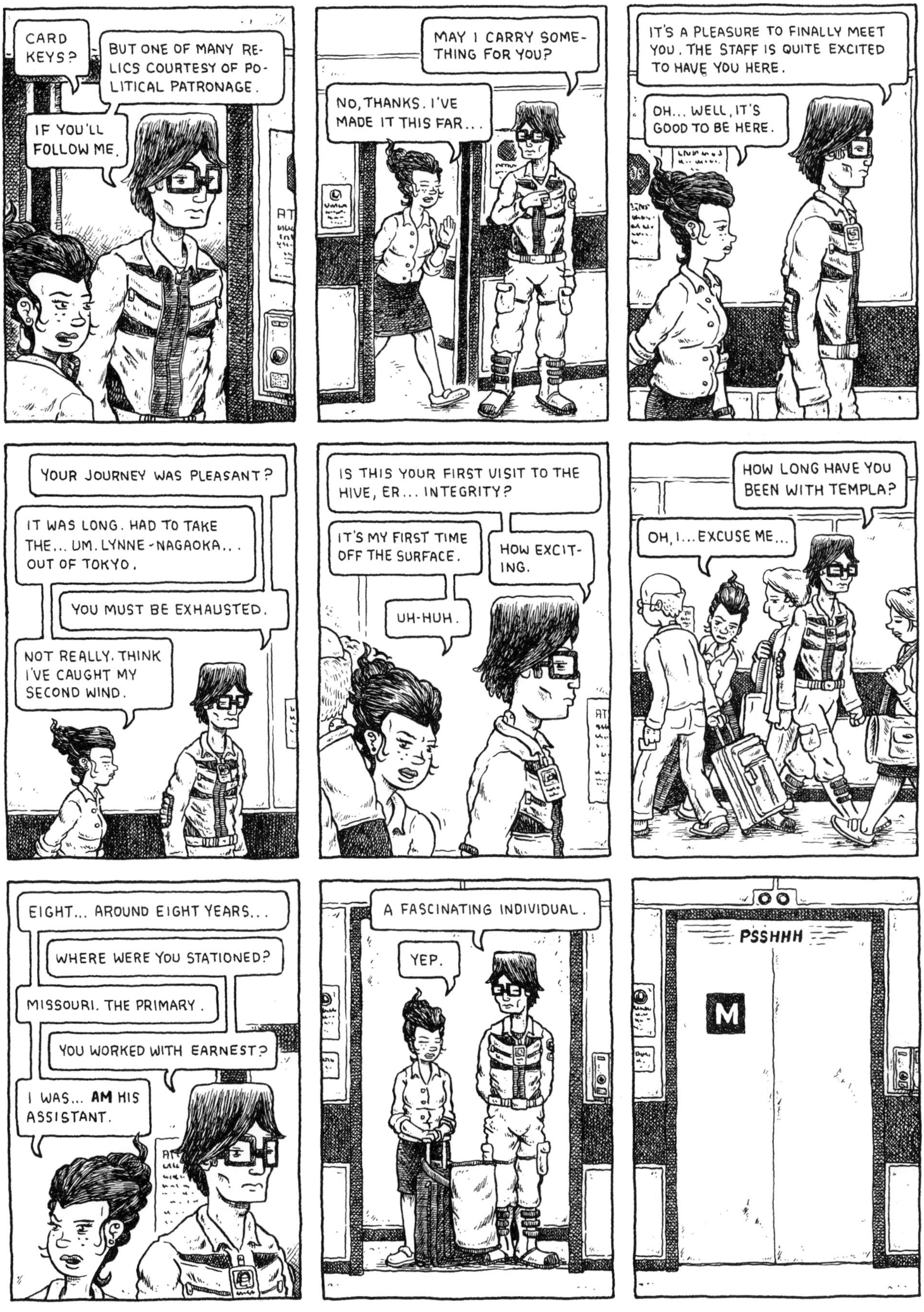
CARD KEYS?
BUT ONE OF MANY RELICS COURTESY OF POLITICAL PATRONAGE.
IF YOU'LL FOLLOW ME.
MAY I CARRY SOMETHING FOR YOU?
NO, THANKS. I'VE MADE IT THIS FAR...
IT'S A PLEASURE TO FINALLY MEET YOU. THE STAFF IS QUITE EXCITED TO HAVE YOU HERE.
OH... WELL, IT'S GOOD TO BE HERE.
YOUR JOURNEY WAS PLEASANT?
IT WAS LONG. HAD TO TAKE THE... UM. LYNNE-NAGAOKA... OUT OF TOKYO.
YOU MUST BE EXHAUSTED.
NOT REALLY. THINK I'VE CAUGHT MY SECOND WIND.
IS THIS YOUR FIRST VISIT TO THE HIVE, ER... INTEGRITY?
IT'S MY FIRST TIME OFF THE SURFACE.
HOW EXCITING.
UH-HUH.
HOW LONG HAVE YOU BEEN WITH TEMPLA?
OH, I... EXCUSE ME...
EIGHT... AROUND EIGHT YEARS...
WHERE WERE YOU STATIONED?
MISSOURI. THE PRIMARY.
YOU WORKED WITH EARNEST?
I WAS... **AM** HIS ASSISTANT.
A FASCINATING INDIVIDUAL.
YEP.
PSSHHH
M

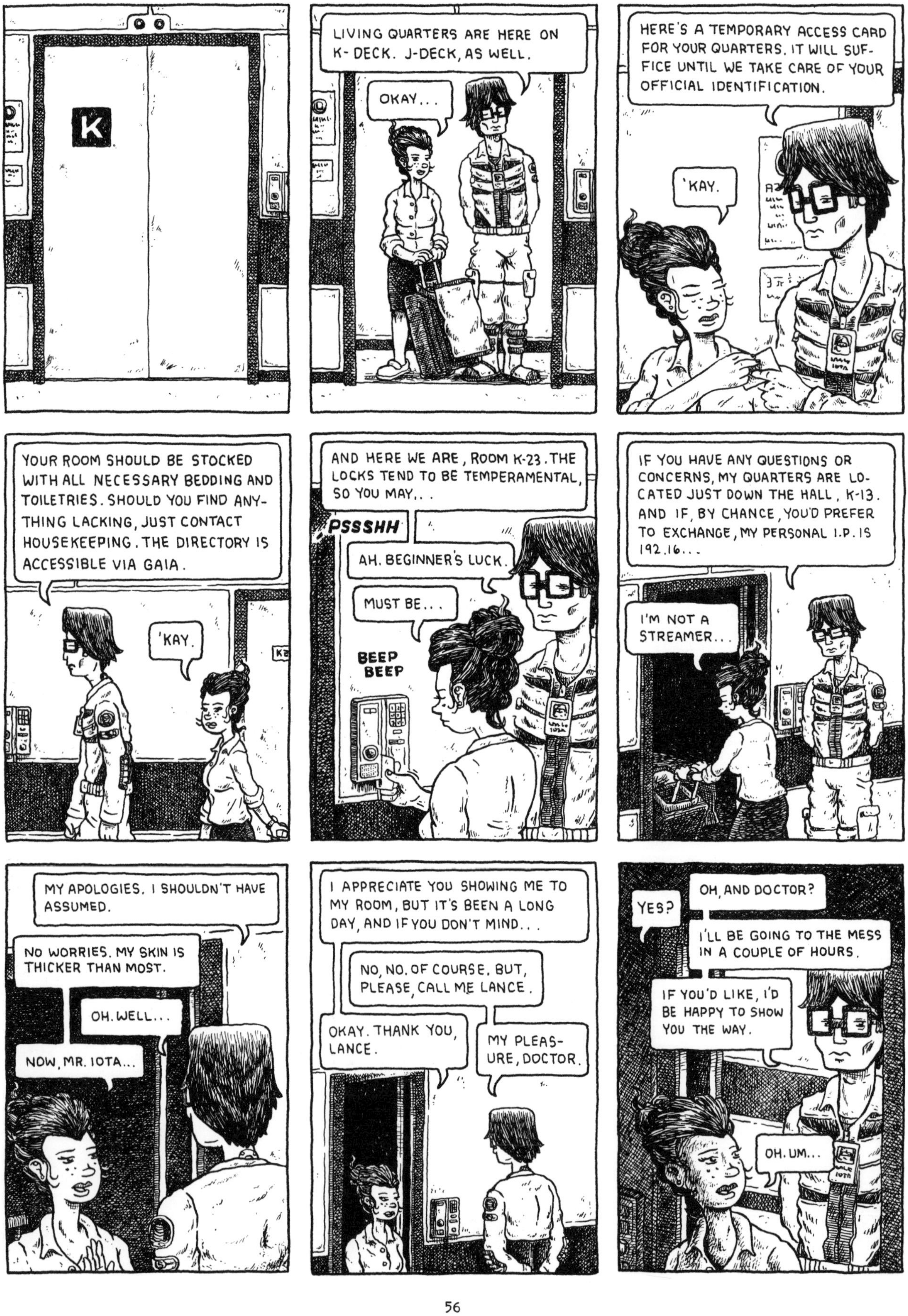
K
LIVING QUARTERS ARE HERE ON K-DECK. J-DECK, AS WELL.
OKAY...
HERE'S A TEMPORARY ACCESS CARD FOR YOUR QUARTERS. IT WILL SUFFICE UNTIL WE TAKE CARE OF YOUR OFFICIAL IDENTIFICATION.
'KAY.
YOUR ROOM SHOULD BE STOCKED WITH ALL NECESSARY BEDDING AND TOILETRIES. SHOULD YOU FIND ANYTHING LACKING, JUST CONTACT HOUSEKEEPING. THE DIRECTORY IS ACCESSIBLE VIA GAIA.
'KAY.
AND HERE WE ARE, ROOM K-23. THE LOCKS TEND TO BE TEMPERAMENTAL, SO YOU MAY...
PSSSHH
AH. BEGINNER'S LUCK.
MUST BE...
BEEP BEEP
IF YOU HAVE ANY QUESTIONS OR CONCERNS, MY QUARTERS ARE LOCATED JUST DOWN THE HALL, K-13. AND IF, BY CHANCE, YOU'D PREFER TO EXCHANGE, MY PERSONAL I.P. IS 192.16...
I'M NOT A STREAMER...
MY APOLOGIES. I SHOULDN'T HAVE ASSUMED.
NO WORRIES. MY SKIN IS THICKER THAN MOST.
OH. WELL...
NOW, MR. IOTA...
I APPRECIATE YOU SHOWING ME TO MY ROOM, BUT IT'S BEEN A LONG DAY, AND IF YOU DON'T MIND...
NO, NO. OF COURSE. BUT, PLEASE, CALL ME LANCE.
OKAY. THANK YOU, LANCE.
MY PLEASURE, DOCTOR.
OH, AND DOCTOR?
YES?
I'LL BE GOING TO THE MESS IN A COUPLE OF HOURS.
IF YOU'D LIKE, I'D BE HAPPY TO SHOW YOU THE WAY.
OH. UM...

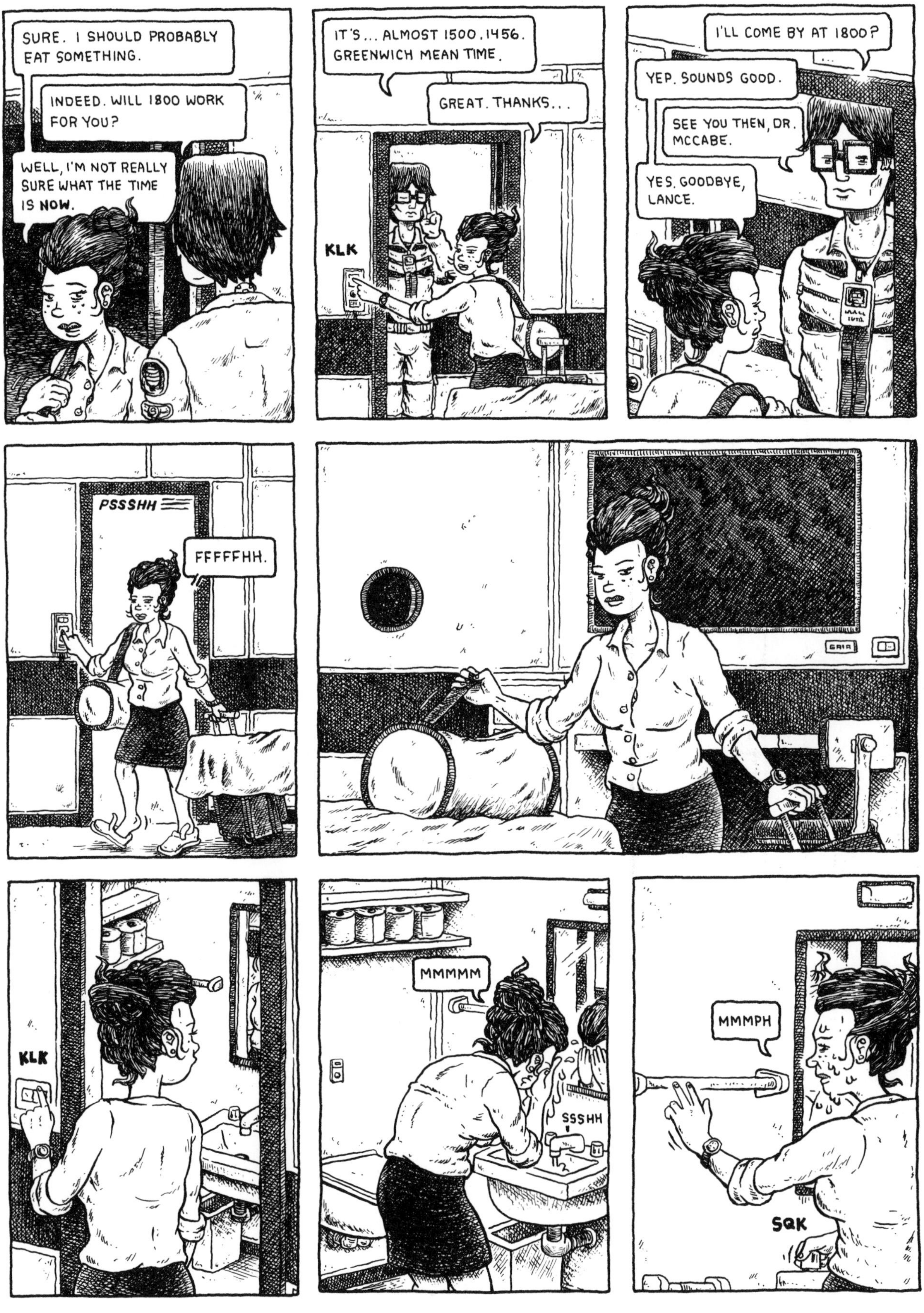
SURE. I SHOULD PROBABLY EAT SOMETHING.
INDEED. WILL 1800 WORK FOR YOU?
WELL, I'M NOT REALLY SURE WHAT THE TIME IS **NOW**.
IT'S... ALMOST 1500, 1456. GREENWICH MEAN TIME.
GREAT. THANKS...
KLK
I'LL COME BY AT 1800?
YEP. SOUNDS GOOD.
SEE YOU THEN, DR. MCCABE.
YES. GOODBYE, LANCE.
PSSSHH
FFFFFHH.
KLK
MMMMM
SSSHH
MMMPH
SQK

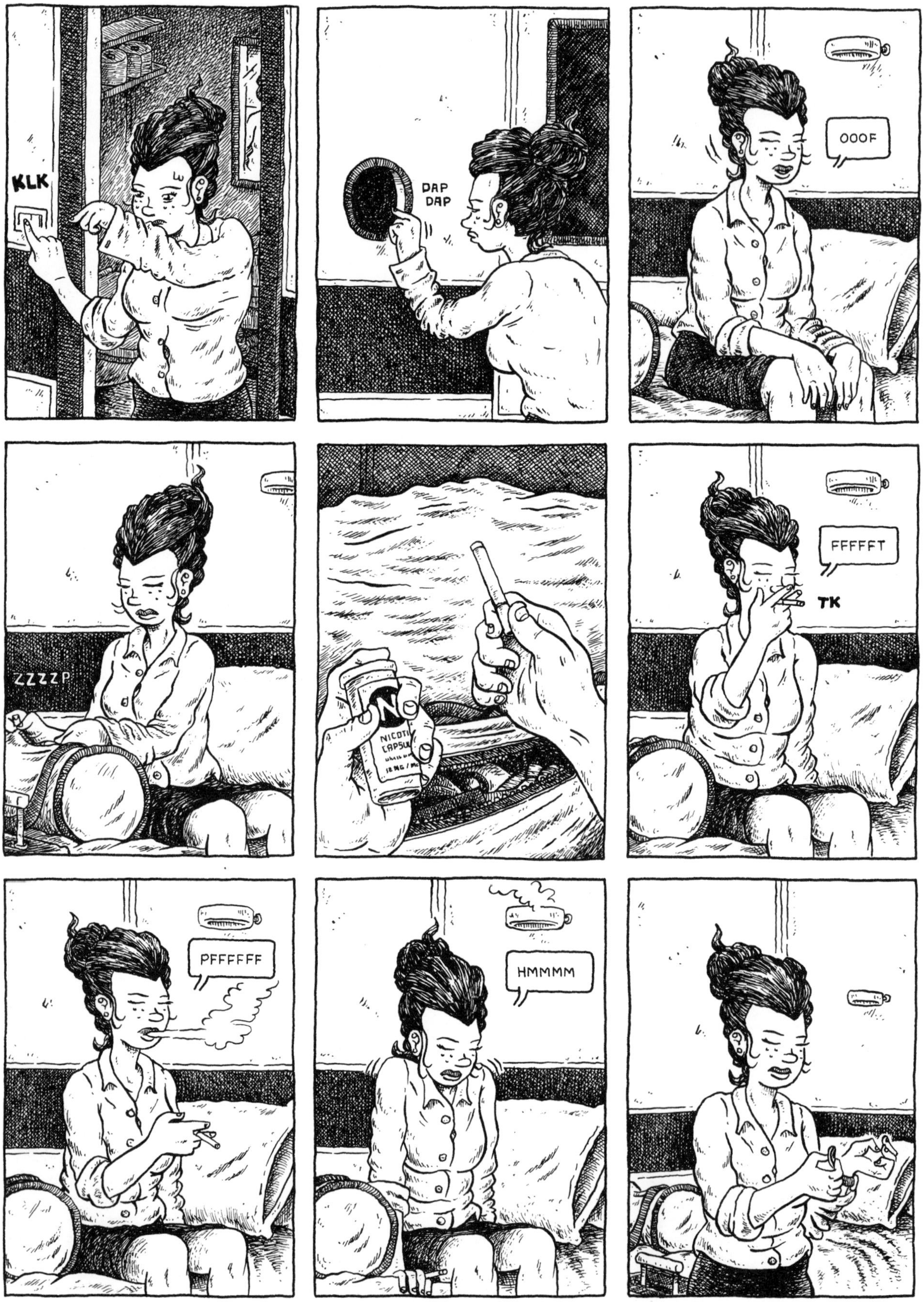
KLK
DAP DAP
OOOF
ZZZZP
FFFFFT
TK
PFFFFFF
HMMMM

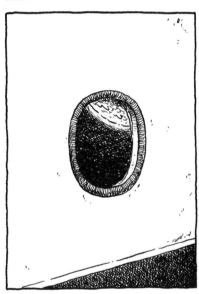
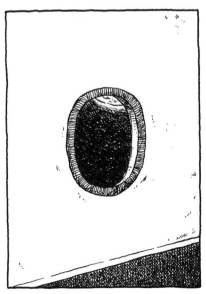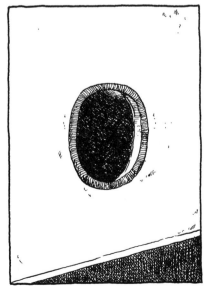

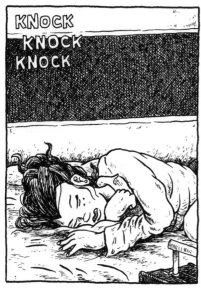

KNOCK
KNOCK
KNOCK

KNOCK
KNOCK

SNUH...

MM...
COMIN'.

KNOCK
KNOCK

COMIN'!

GOOD MORNING, DOCTOR.

OH, HEY. LANCE. I MUST'VE...FALLEN ASLEEP...

DINNER ALREADY?

NO, NOT EXACTLY. YOU WERE UNRESPONSIVE WHEN I STOPPED BY YESTERDAY EVENING.

I ASSUMED YOU WERE MOST LIKELY FATIGUED FROM YOUR TRAVELS.

YESTERDAY... YEAH. GEEZ. I GUESS. HOW LONG WAS I OUT?

OF THAT I AM UNCERTAIN.

IT'S NEARLY 0800 NOW. I'M HERE TO SEE IF YOU'D BE INTERESTED IN A GUIDED TOUR OF THE HIVE. BUT FIRST, PERHAPS, YOU'D LIKE TO BREAK YOUR FAST?

YEAH... YES. I'M STARVING. BUT I...UH...

I HAVEN'T SHOWERED IN, LIKE, THREE DAYS...

THAT'S PERFECTLY FINE, WE'RE IN NO HURRY. TAKE YOUR TIME PREPARING FOR THE DAY, AND WHENEVER YOU'RE READY, JUST COME BY MY QUARTERS.

WHICH?..

K-13.

K-13.

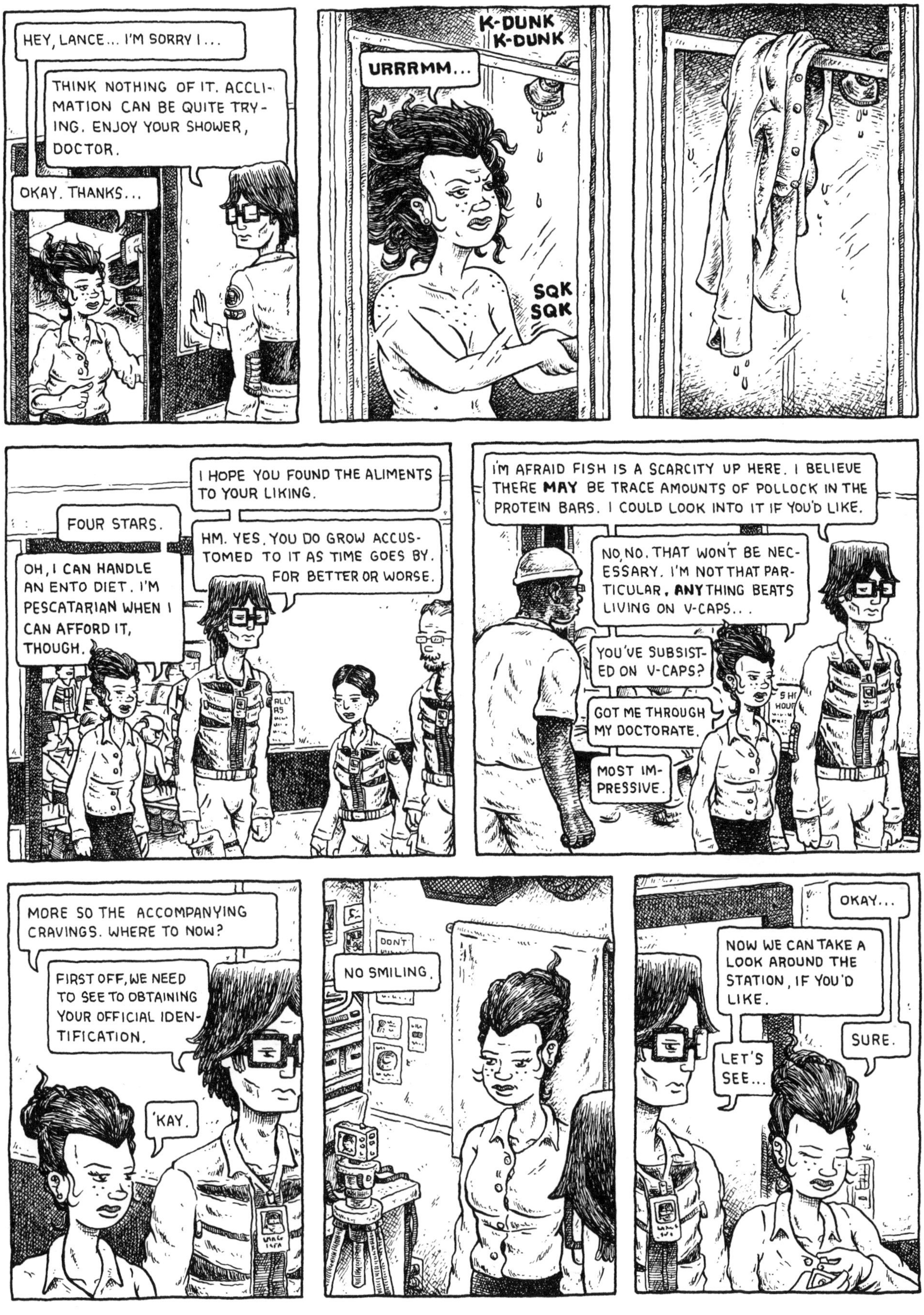
HEY, LANCE... I'M SORRY I...
THINK NOTHING OF IT. ACCLIMATION CAN BE QUITE TRYING. ENJOY YOUR SHOWER, DOCTOR.
OKAY. THANKS...
K-DUNK K-DUNK
URRRMM...
SQK SQK
I HOPE YOU FOUND THE ALIMENTS TO YOUR LIKING.
FOUR STARS.
HM. YES. YOU DO GROW ACCUSTOMED TO IT AS TIME GOES BY. FOR BETTER OR WORSE.
OH, I CAN HANDLE AN ENTO DIET. I'M PESCATARIAN WHEN I CAN AFFORD IT, THOUGH.
I'M AFRAID FISH IS A SCARCITY UP HERE. I BELIEVE THERE **MAY** BE TRACE AMOUNTS OF POLLOCK IN THE PROTEIN BARS. I COULD LOOK INTO IT IF YOU'D LIKE.
NO, NO. THAT WON'T BE NECESSARY. I'M NOT THAT PARTICULAR. **ANY**THING BEATS LIVING ON V-CAPS...
YOU'VE SUBSISTED ON V-CAPS?
GOT ME THROUGH MY DOCTORATE.
MOST IMPRESSIVE.
MORE SO THE ACCOMPANYING CRAVINGS. WHERE TO NOW?
FIRST OFF, WE NEED TO SEE TO OBTAINING YOUR OFFICIAL IDENTIFICATION.
'KAY.
NO SMILING.
OKAY...
NOW WE CAN TAKE A LOOK AROUND THE STATION, IF YOU'D LIKE.
SURE.
LET'S SEE...

THERE'S A LAUNDROMAT...

VIRTUALLY ANHYDROUS.

GENERAL STORE...

FOR THE ACQUISITION OF SUNDRIES AND SUCH.

CONVENIENT.

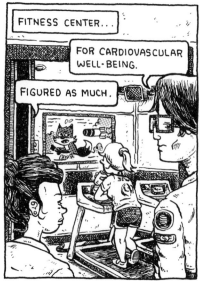

FITNESS CENTER...

FOR CARDIOVASCULAR WELL-BEING.

FIGURED AS MUCH.

CONSERVATORY...

FOR WHEN NATURE CALLS.

UM...

CHAPEL...

IF YOU'RE FEELING PIOUS.

NOT AT THE MOMENT.

LIFEBOATS...

BUILT FOR TWO.

SNUG.

OBSERVATION DECK...

...THE INSTALLATION INSPIRED BY TURRELL, OF COURSE. NOW, WHILE YOU BASK IN THE AMBIENCE, I WILL ATTEMPT, BY MEANS OF LENGTHY DISCOURSE, TO PROVIDE YOU WITH THE CONTEXT I FEEL TO BE NECESSARY FOR ONE TO FULLY APPRECIATE THE...

MM-HM.

62

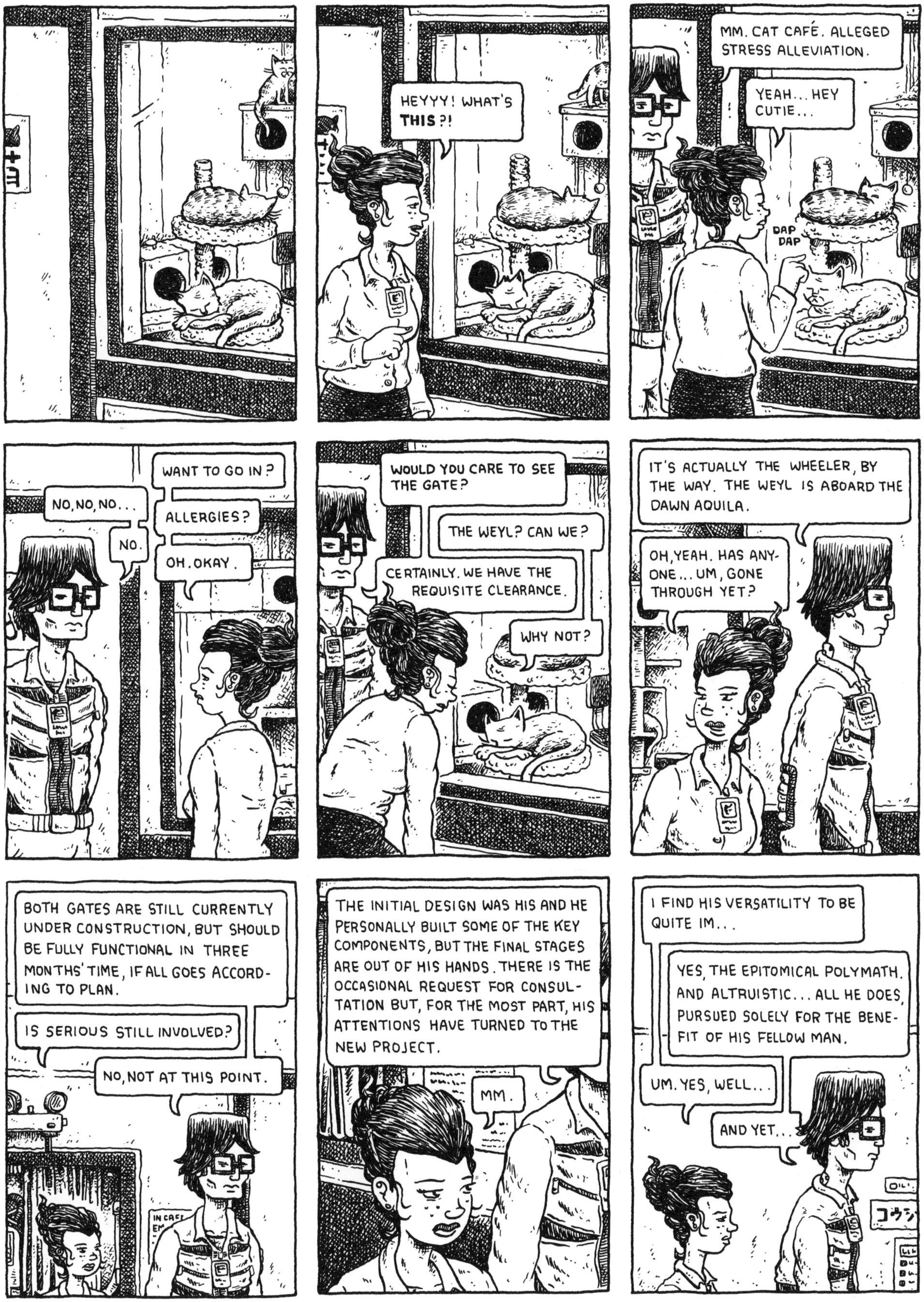
HEYYY! WHAT'S **THIS**?!
MM. CAT CAFÉ. ALLEGED STRESS ALLEVIATION.
YEAH... HEY CUTIE...
DAP DAP
WANT TO GO IN?
NO, NO, NO...
ALLERGIES?
NO.
OH. OKAY.
WOULD YOU CARE TO SEE THE GATE?
THE WEYL? CAN WE?
CERTAINLY. WE HAVE THE REQUISITE CLEARANCE.
WHY NOT?
IT'S ACTUALLY THE WHEELER, BY THE WAY. THE WEYL IS ABOARD THE DAWN AQUILA.
OH, YEAH. HAS ANYONE... UM, GONE THROUGH YET?
BOTH GATES ARE STILL CURRENTLY UNDER CONSTRUCTION, BUT SHOULD BE FULLY FUNCTIONAL IN THREE MONTHS' TIME, IF ALL GOES ACCORDING TO PLAN.
IS SERIOUS STILL INVOLVED?
NO, NOT AT THIS POINT.
THE INITIAL DESIGN WAS HIS AND HE PERSONALLY BUILT SOME OF THE KEY COMPONENTS, BUT THE FINAL STAGES ARE OUT OF HIS HANDS. THERE IS THE OCCASIONAL REQUEST FOR CONSULTATION BUT, FOR THE MOST PART, HIS ATTENTIONS HAVE TURNED TO THE NEW PROJECT.
MM.
I FIND HIS VERSATILITY TO BE QUITE IM...
YES, THE EPITOMICAL POLYMATH. AND ALTRUISTIC... ALL HE DOES, PURSUED SOLELY FOR THE BENEFIT OF HIS FELLOW MAN.
UM. YES, WELL...
AND YET...

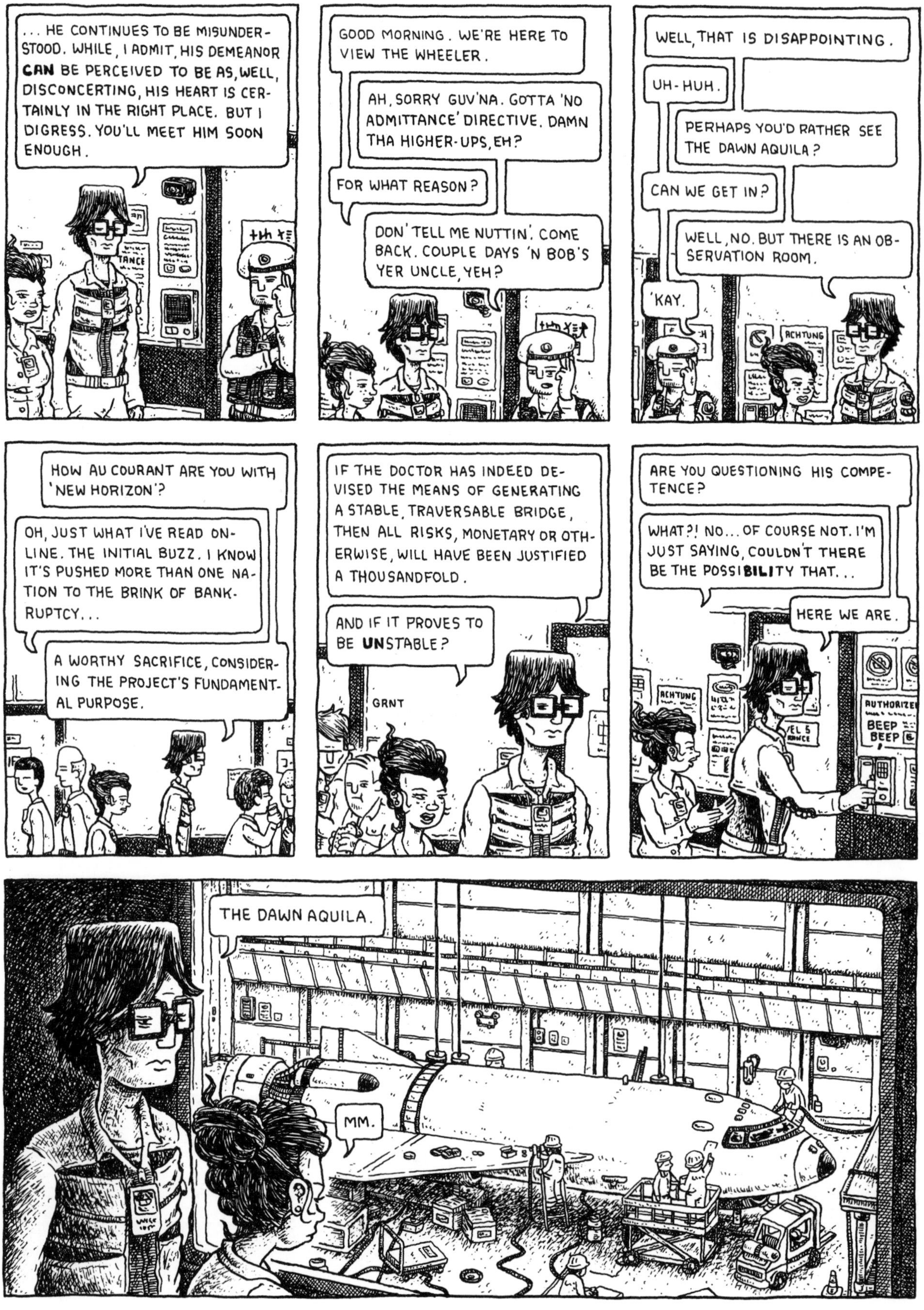

... HE CONTINUES TO BE MISUNDERSTOOD. WHILE, I ADMIT, HIS DEMEANOR **CAN** BE PERCEIVED TO BE AS, WELL, DISCONCERTING, HIS HEART IS CERTAINLY IN THE RIGHT PLACE. BUT I DIGRESS. YOU'LL MEET HIM SOON ENOUGH.
GOOD MORNING. WE'RE HERE TO VIEW THE WHEELER.
AH, SORRY GUV'NA. GOTTA 'NO ADMITTANCE' DIRECTIVE. DAMN THA HIGHER-UPS, EH?
FOR WHAT REASON?
DON' TELL ME NUTTIN'. COME BACK. COUPLE DAYS 'N BOB'S YER UNCLE, YEH?
WELL, THAT IS DISAPPOINTING.
UH-HUH.
PERHAPS YOU'D RATHER SEE THE DAWN AQUILA?
CAN WE GET IN?
WELL, NO. BUT THERE IS AN OBSERVATION ROOM.
'KAY.
ACHTUNG
HOW AU COURANT ARE YOU WITH 'NEW HORIZON'?
OH, JUST WHAT I'VE READ ONLINE. THE INITIAL BUZZ. I KNOW IT'S PUSHED MORE THAN ONE NATION TO THE BRINK OF BANKRUPTCY...
A WORTHY SACRIFICE, CONSIDERING THE PROJECT'S FUNDAMENTAL PURPOSE.
IF THE DOCTOR HAS INDEED DEVISED THE MEANS OF GENERATING A STABLE, TRAVERSABLE BRIDGE, THEN ALL RISKS, MONETARY OR OTHERWISE, WILL HAVE BEEN JUSTIFIED A THOUSANDFOLD.
AND IF IT PROVES TO BE **UN**STABLE?
GRNT
ARE YOU QUESTIONING HIS COMPETENCE?
WHAT?! NO... OF COURSE NOT. I'M JUST SAYING, COULDN'T THERE BE THE POSSI**BILI**TY THAT...
HERE WE ARE.
ACHTUNG
AUTHORIZED
BEEP BEEP
THE DAWN AQUILA.
MM.

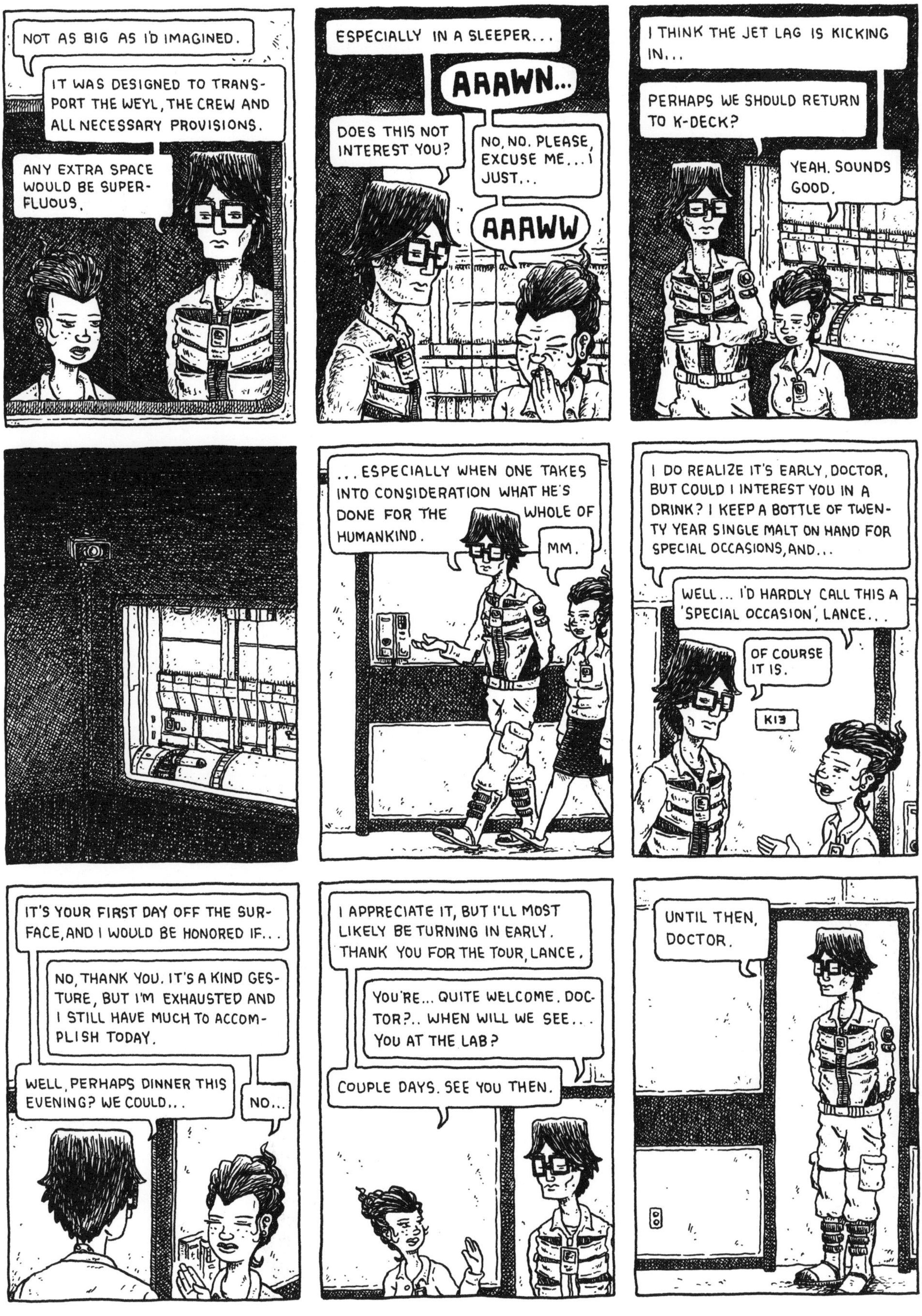
NOT AS BIG AS I'D IMAGINED.
IT WAS DESIGNED TO TRANSPORT THE WEYL, THE CREW AND ALL NECESSARY PROVISIONS.
ANY EXTRA SPACE WOULD BE SUPERFLUOUS.
ESPECIALLY IN A SLEEPER...
AAAWN...
DOES THIS NOT INTEREST YOU?
NO, NO. PLEASE, EXCUSE ME... I JUST...
AAAWW
I THINK THE JET LAG IS KICKING IN...
PERHAPS WE SHOULD RETURN TO K-DECK?
YEAH. SOUNDS GOOD.
...ESPECIALLY WHEN ONE TAKES INTO CONSIDERATION WHAT HE'S DONE FOR THE WHOLE OF HUMANKIND.
MM.
I DO REALIZE IT'S EARLY, DOCTOR, BUT COULD I INTEREST YOU IN A DRINK? I KEEP A BOTTLE OF TWENTY YEAR SINGLE MALT ON HAND FOR SPECIAL OCCASIONS, AND...
WELL... I'D HARDLY CALL THIS A 'SPECIAL OCCASION', LANCE...
OF COURSE IT IS.
K13
IT'S YOUR FIRST DAY OFF THE SURFACE, AND I WOULD BE HONORED IF...
NO, THANK YOU. IT'S A KIND GESTURE, BUT I'M EXHAUSTED AND I STILL HAVE MUCH TO ACCOMPLISH TODAY.
WELL, PERHAPS DINNER THIS EVENING? WE COULD...
NO...
I APPRECIATE IT, BUT I'LL MOST LIKELY BE TURNING IN EARLY. THANK YOU FOR THE TOUR, LANCE.
YOU'RE... QUITE WELCOME. DOCTOR?.. WHEN WILL WE SEE... YOU AT THE LAB?
COUPLE DAYS. SEE YOU THEN.
UNTIL THEN, DOCTOR.

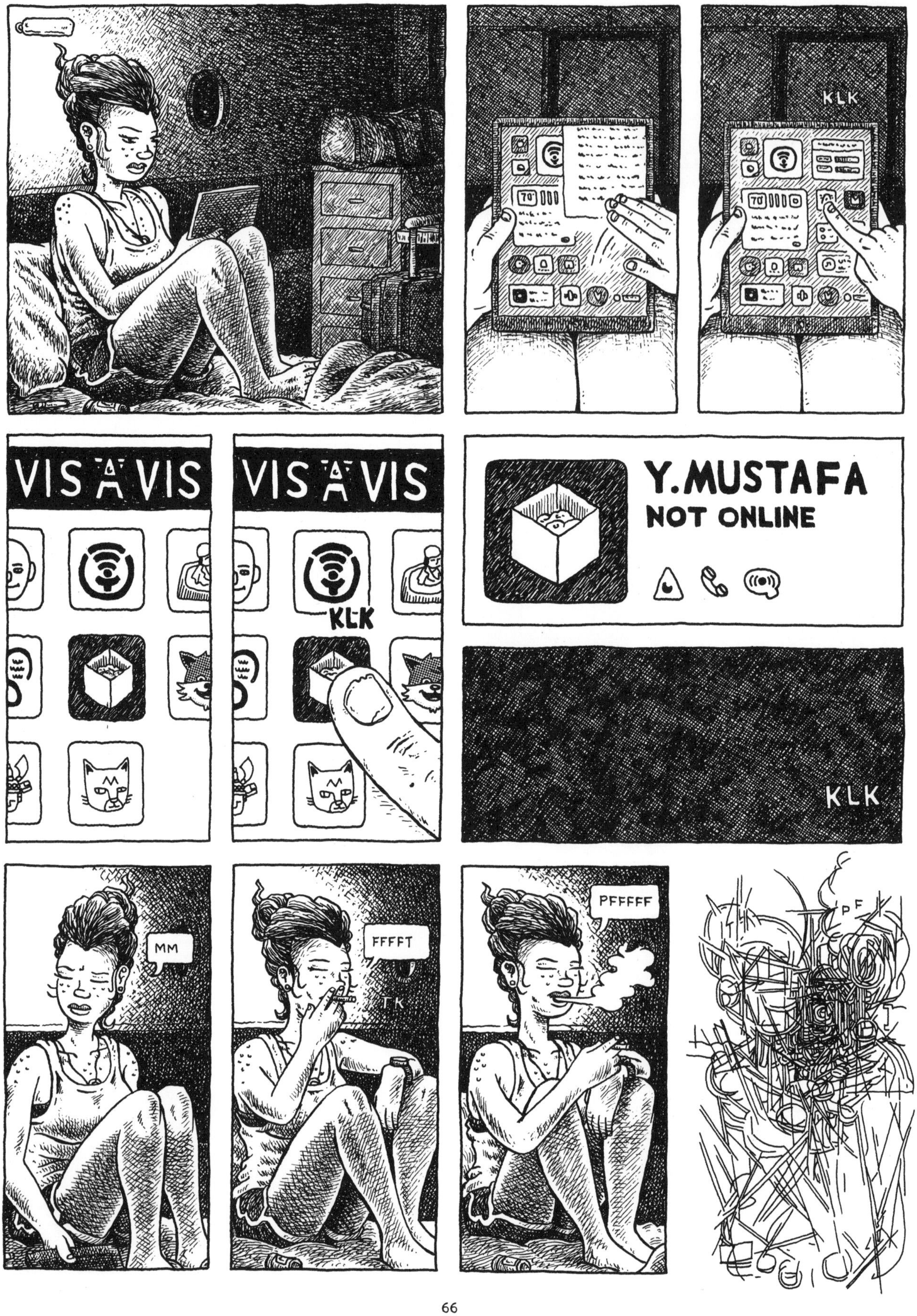
KLK
VIS À VIS
VIS À VIS
KLK
Y.MUSTAFA
NOT ONLINE
KLK
MM
FFFFT
TK
PFFFFF
PF

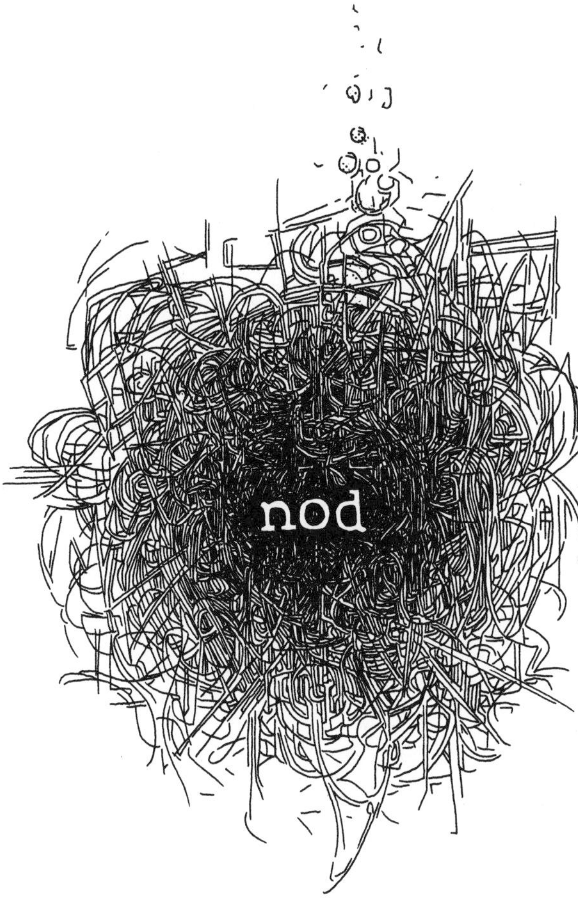
nod

FAILED TO INITIA
31418 ERROR:
FAILED TO INITIA
31419 ERROR:
FAILED TO INITIA
:>
RESERVE POWER:
LEVELS CRITICAL
:>
INITIATE:
EMERGENCY REVIV

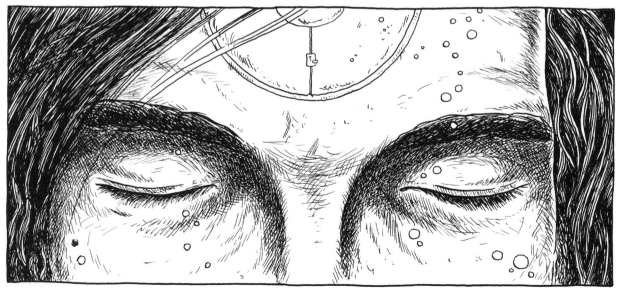

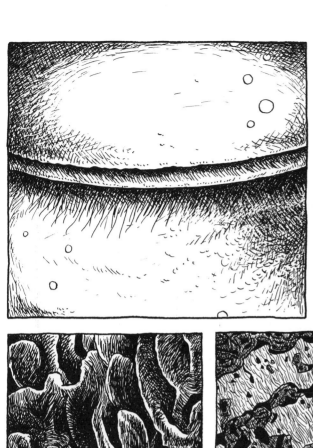
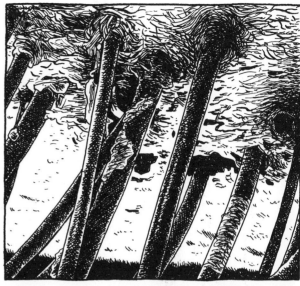

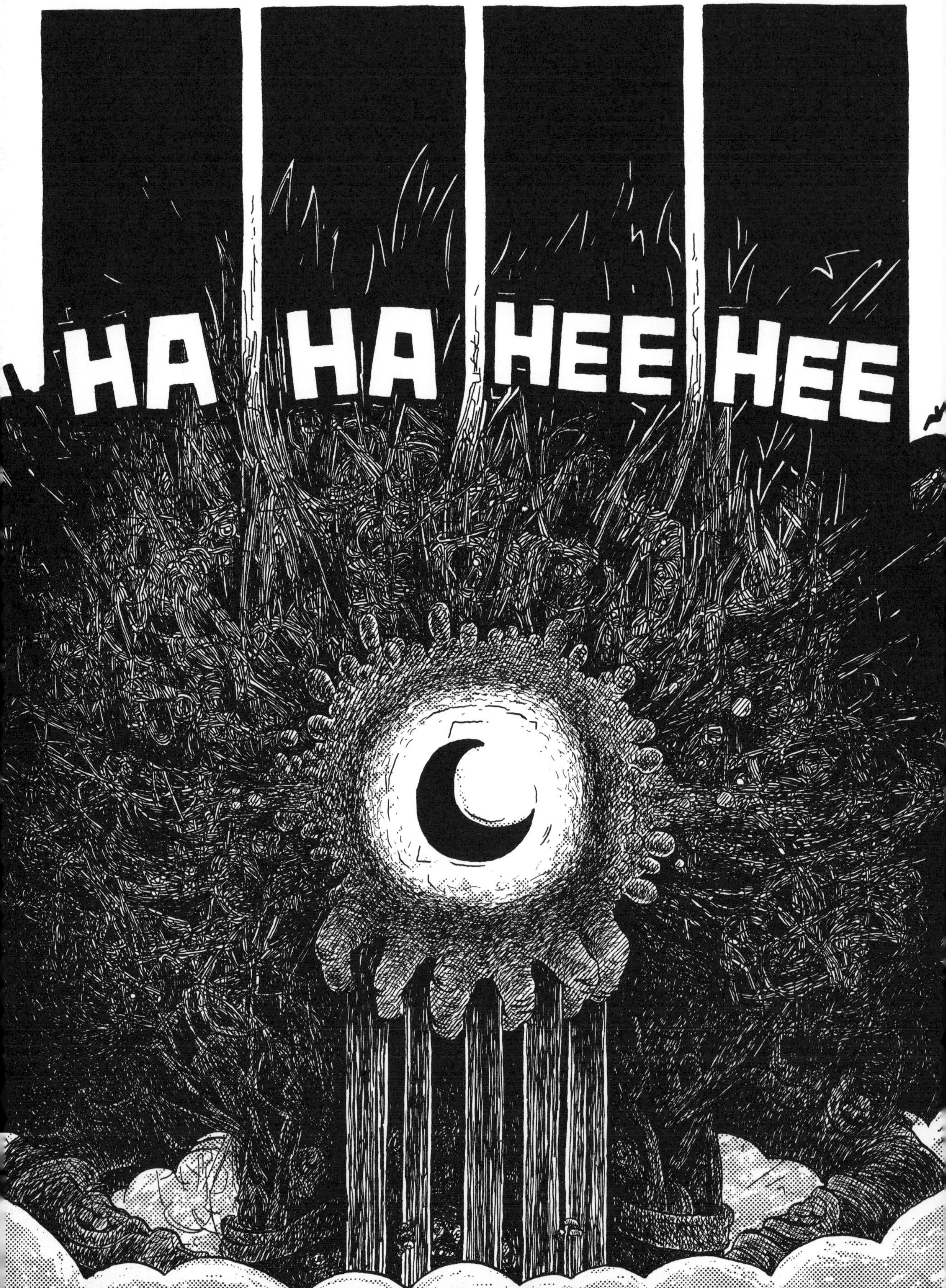
HA
HA
HEE
HEE

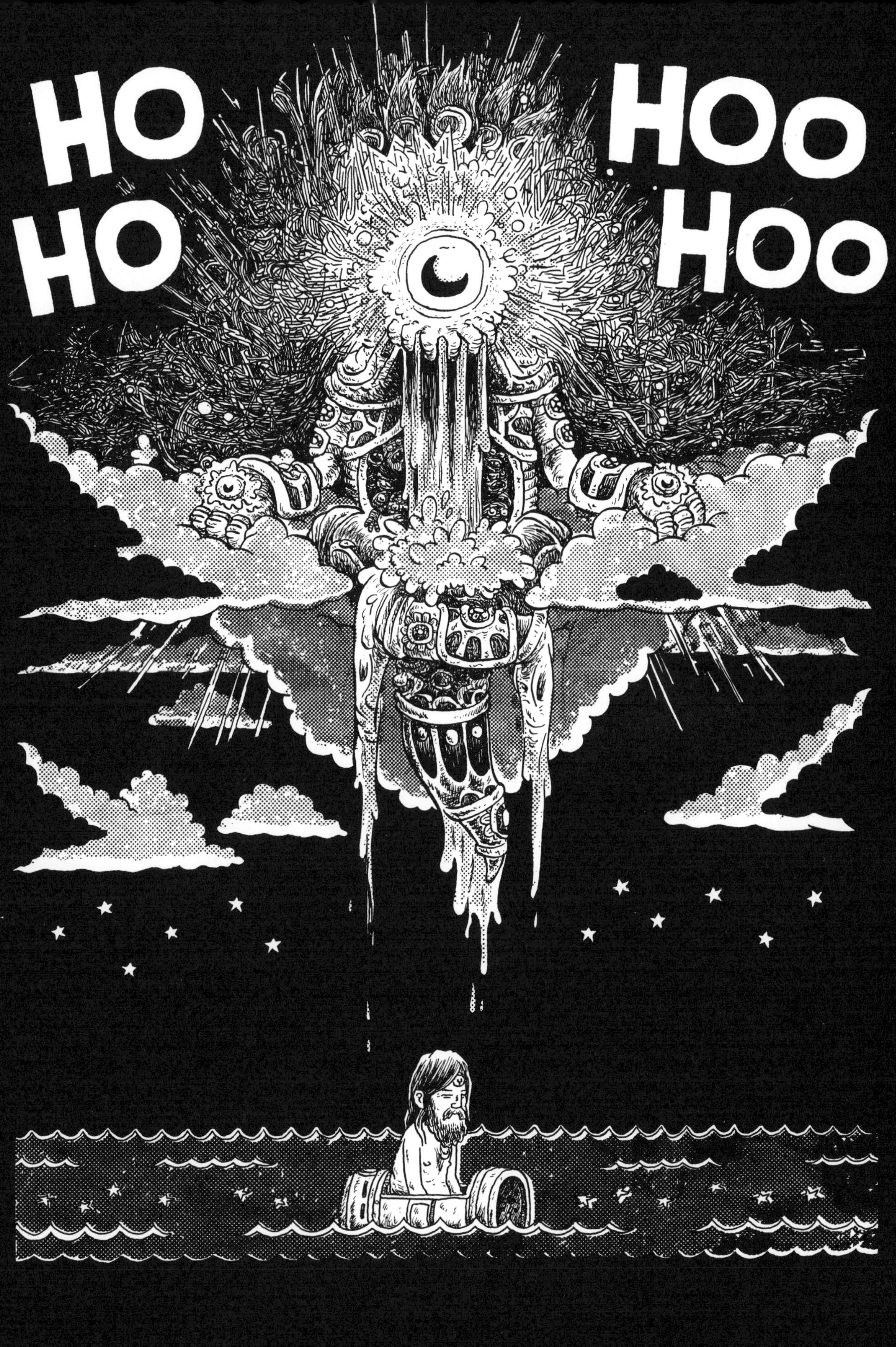
HO HO
HOO HOO

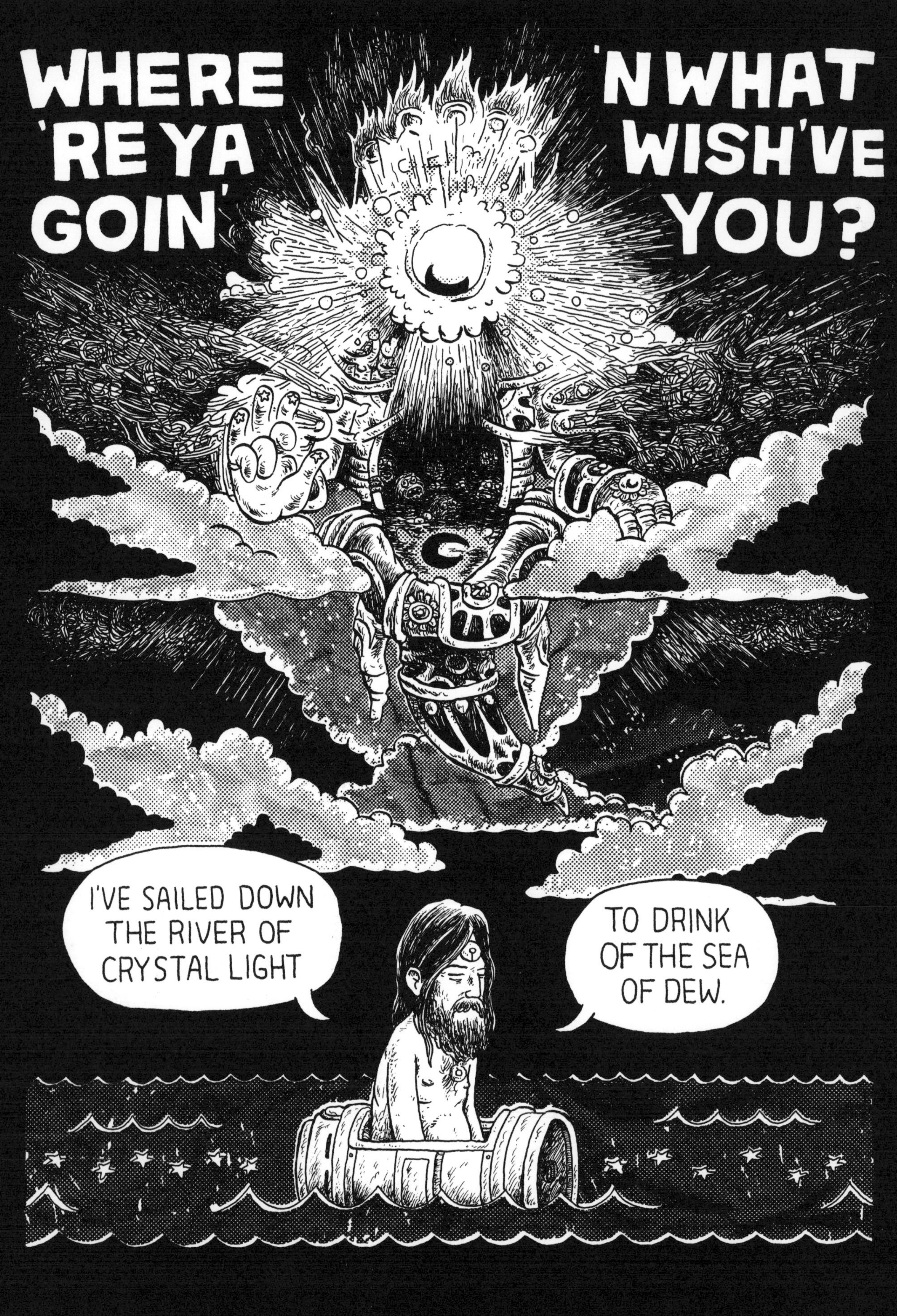
WHERE 'RE YA GOIN'
'N WHAT WISH'VE YOU?
I'VE SAILED DOWN THE RIVER OF CRYSTAL LIGHT
TO DRINK OF THE SEA OF DEW.

HA HOO HOHO HEE
HA HOO HO HEE
HOW LUCKY AM I
FOR SOON I'LL BE
FREE
WELL, YOUR JOURNEY IS OVER
ALL OCEANS ARE YOURS,
DRINK DEEP OF THE BLUE OF THE SEA!

BUT WHAT OF THE OTHERS SWIMMING ITS DEPTHS? SURELY DISRUPTIVE I'D BE.
ALL LEFT FOR DEAD 'N MEAT FOR THE SHADOWS ALONE IN THIS PLACE YOU 'N ME!
Now that's not quite true
But we'd be glad t'have ya
Here in this ol' sea o'dew!

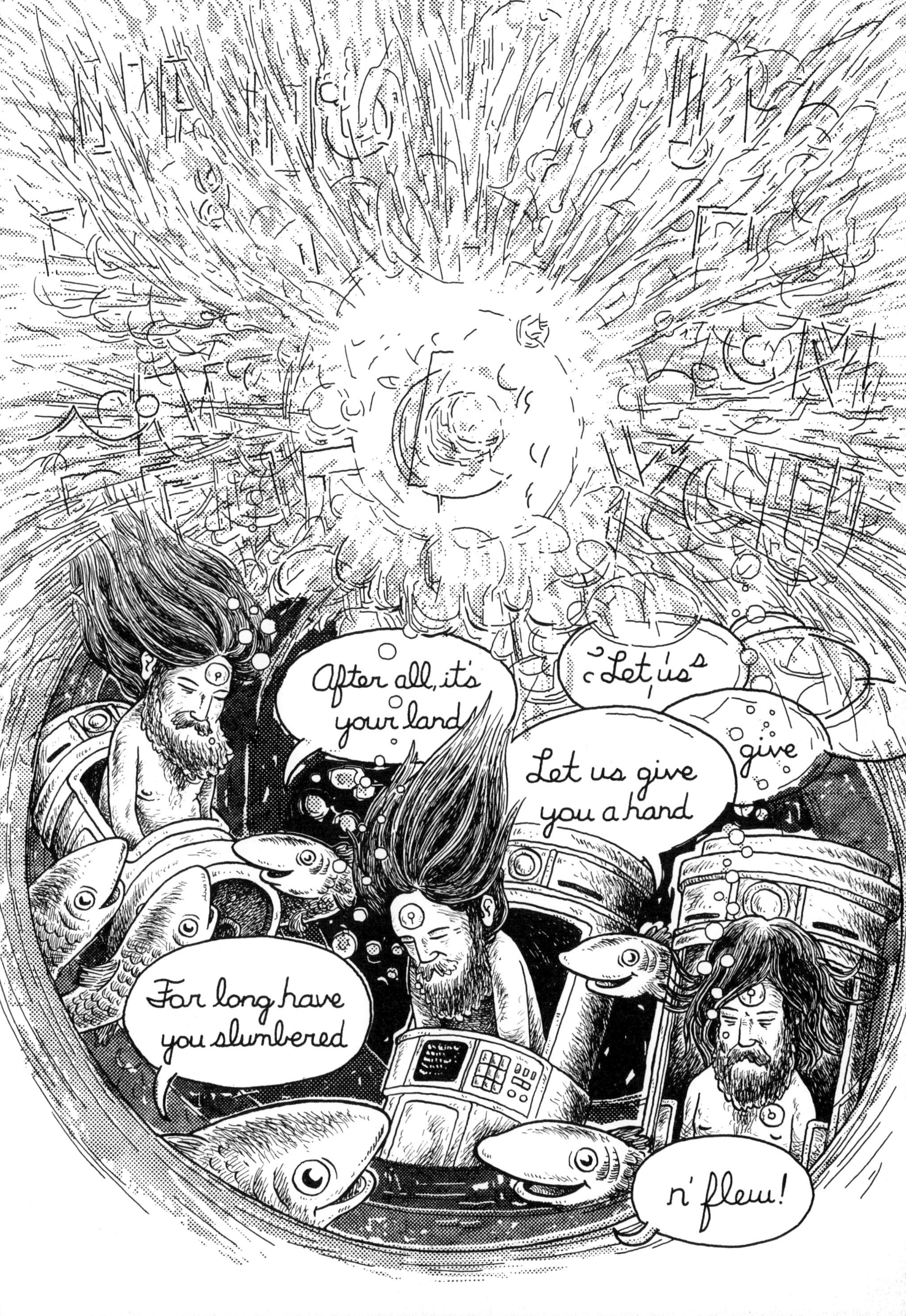
After all, it's your land
Let us
Let us give you a hand
give
For long have you slumbered
n' flew!

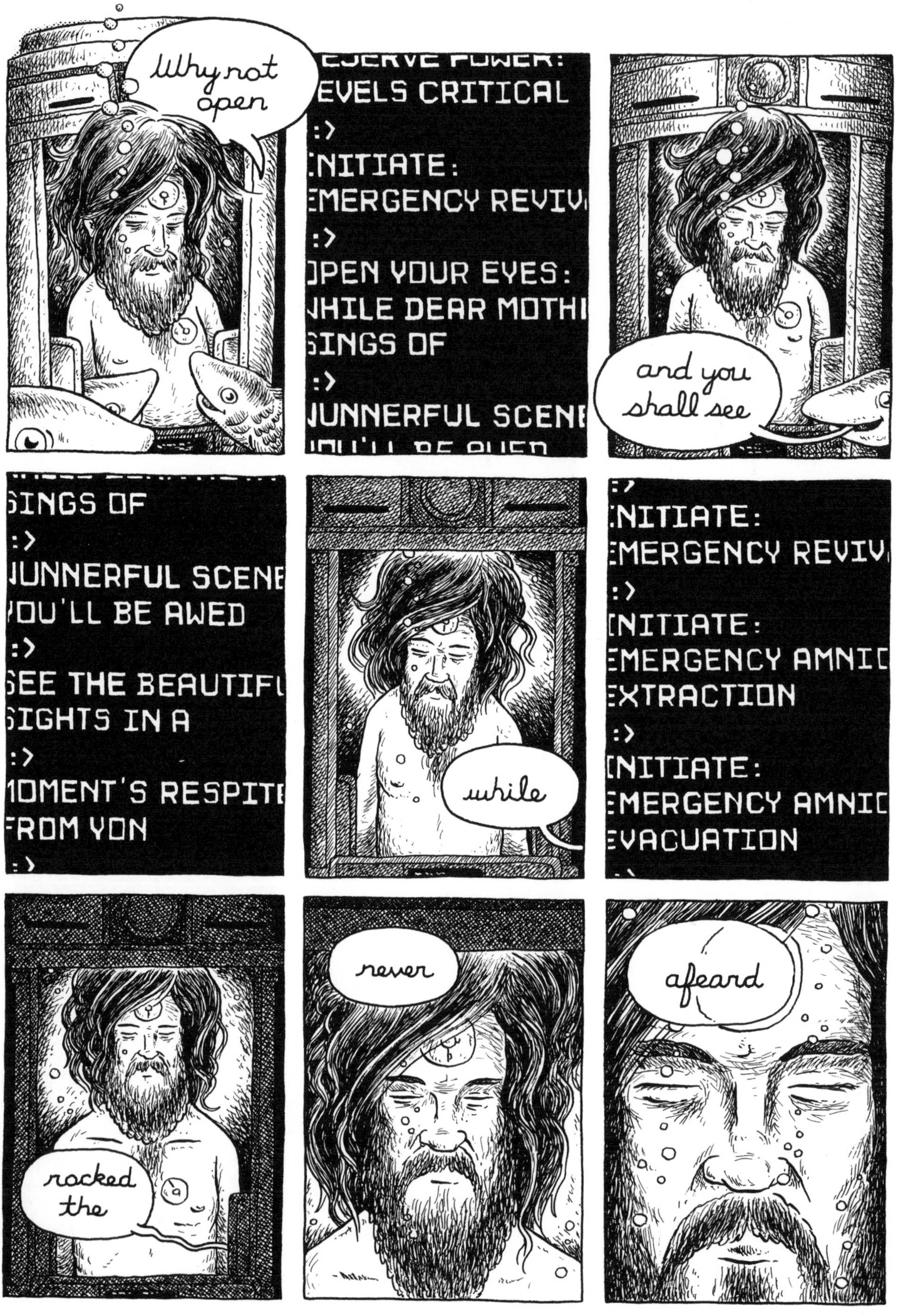
Why not open
EVELS CRITICAL
:>
NITIATE:
EMERGENCY REVIV
:>
OPEN YOUR EYES:
WHILE DEAR MOTH
SINGS OF
:>
WUNNERFUL SCENE
and you shall see
SINGS OF
:>
WUNNERFUL SCENE
YOU'LL BE AWED
:>
SEE THE BEAUTIF
SIGHTS IN A
:>
MOMENT'S RESPITE
FROM YON
:>
while
:>
NITIATE:
EMERGENCY REVIV
:>
NITIATE:
EMERGENCY AMNIO
EXTRACTION
:>
NITIATE:
EMERGENCY AMNIO
EVACUATION
rocked the
never
afeard

wynken
blynken
NOD
PHHHH
DNK
UNH
KOFF
FUMP
KOFF KOFF
KOFF
KOFF KOFF
KAFF KAFFF
HUU HUNNNH
KOFF KOFF KOFF
NN
N
KOFF
KOF KAF
HUU HUUUUU
HAACK
AAACK
NNNNN
KOFF
KOF

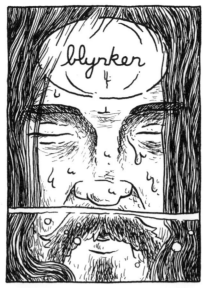

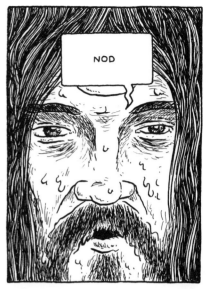

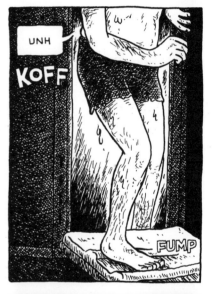

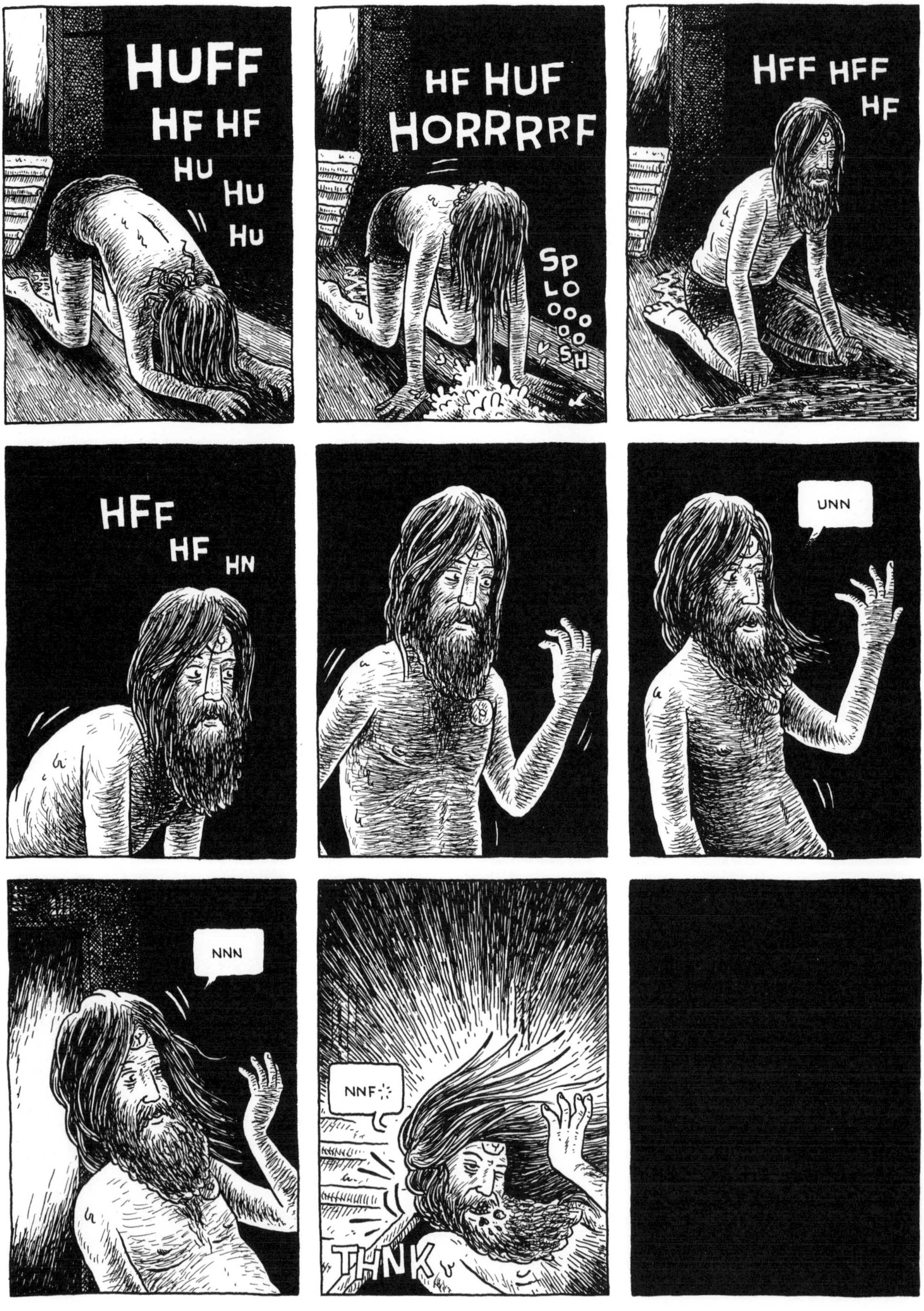
HUFF
HF HF
HU
HU
HU
HF HUF
HORRRRRF
SPLOOOOOOSH
HFF HFF
HF
HFF
HF HN
UNN
NNN
NNF
THNK

EMERGENCY AMNIL
EVACUATION:
COMPLETE
:>
RESERVE POWER:
LEVELS CRITICAL
:>
RESERVE POWER:
LEVELS CRITICAL
:>

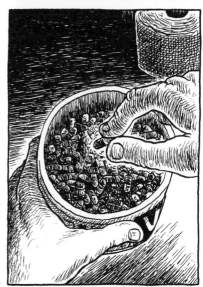

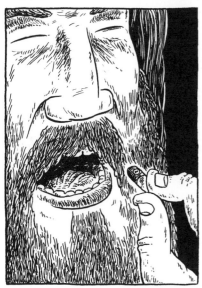

MM

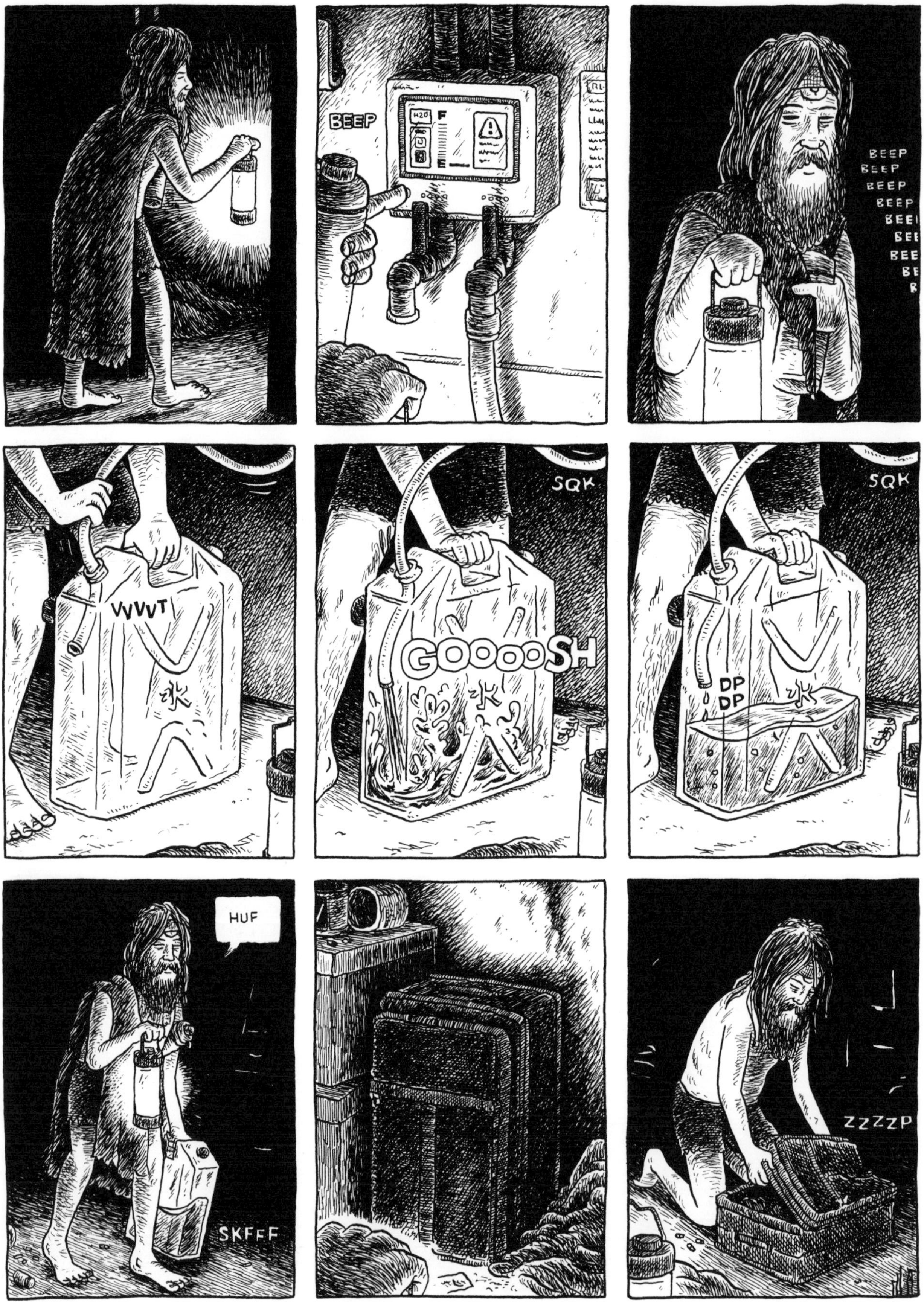
BEEP
H2O
F
E
BEEP
BEEP
BEEP
BEEP
VVVVT
水
SQK
GOOooSH
SQK
DP
DP
HUF
SKFFF
ZZZZP

BAN'
BAN'
ZZZP

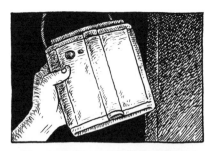

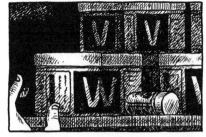

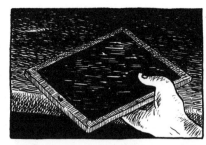

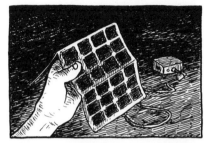

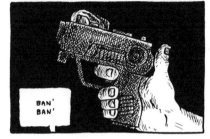

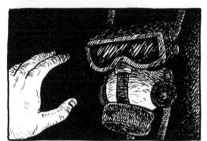

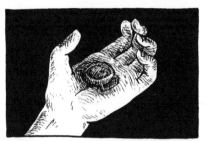

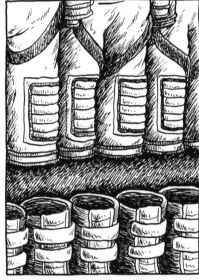

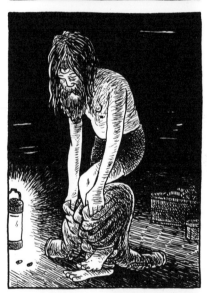

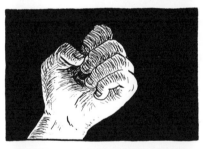

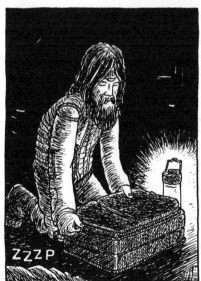

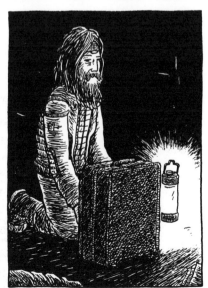

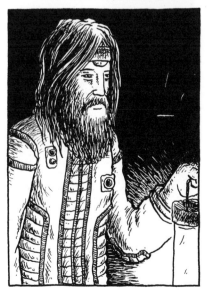

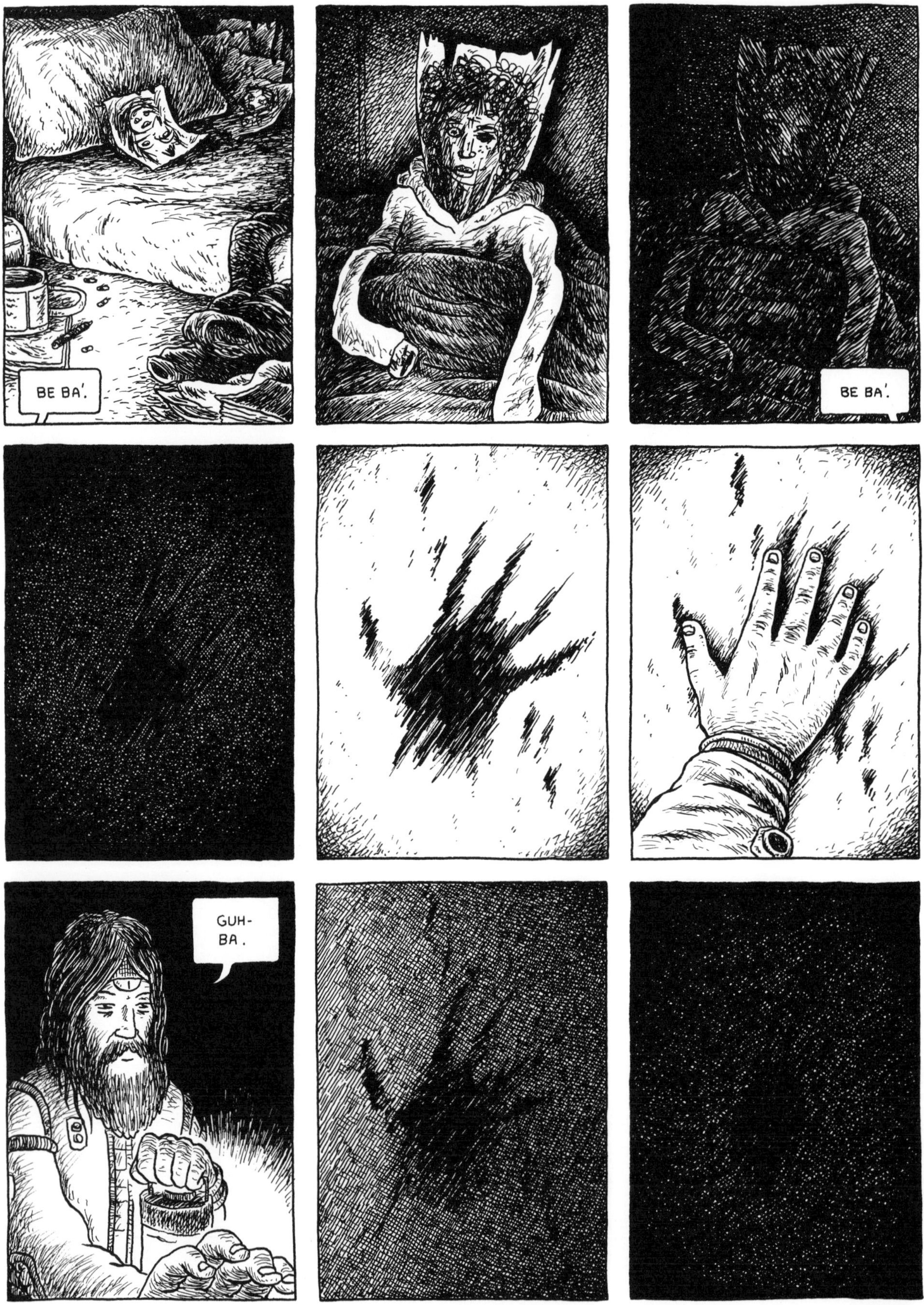
BE BA'.
BE BA'.
GUH-BA.

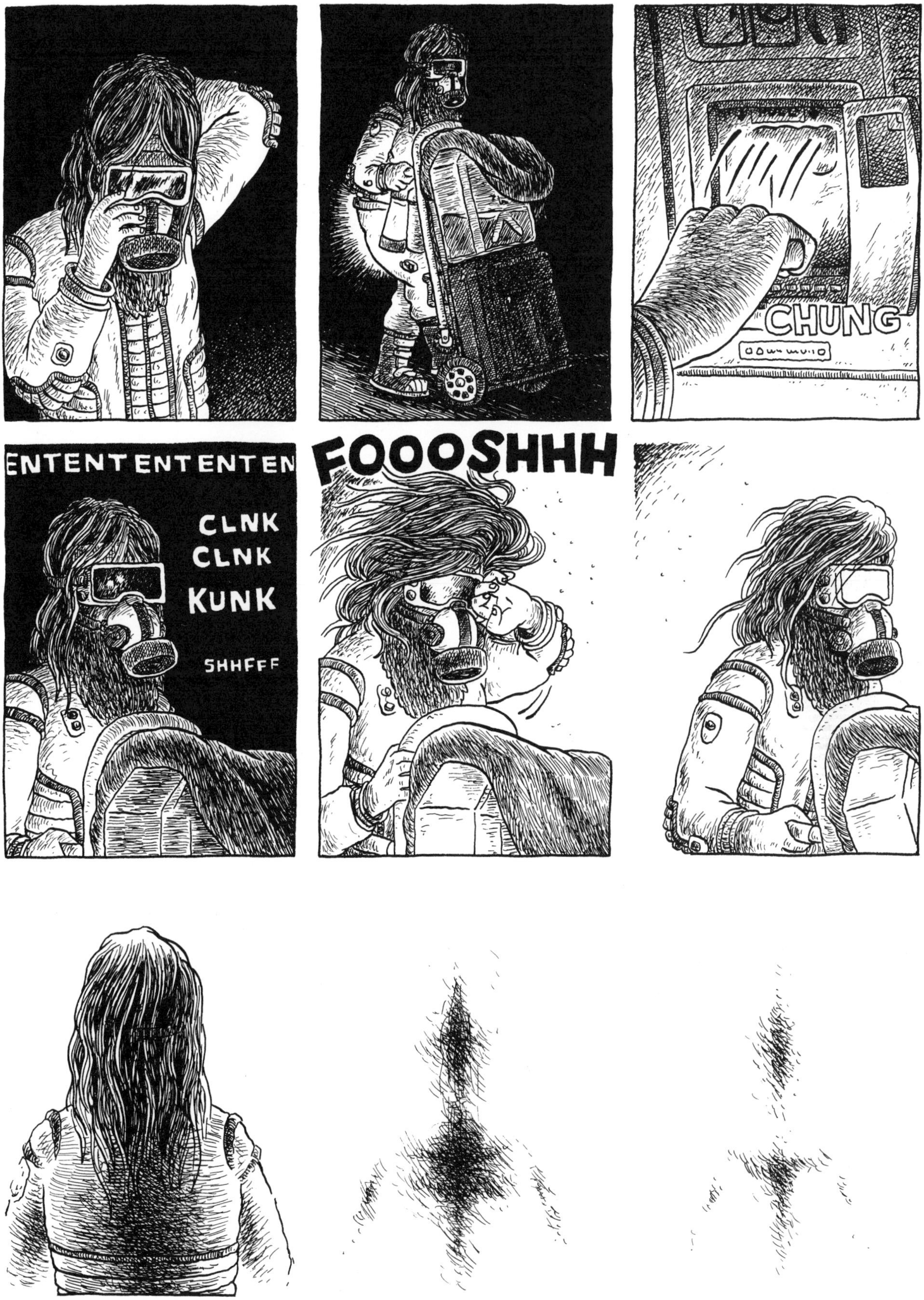
CHUNG
ENTENTENTENTEN
CLNK
CLNK
KUNK
SHHFFF
FOOOSHHH

tough
as nails

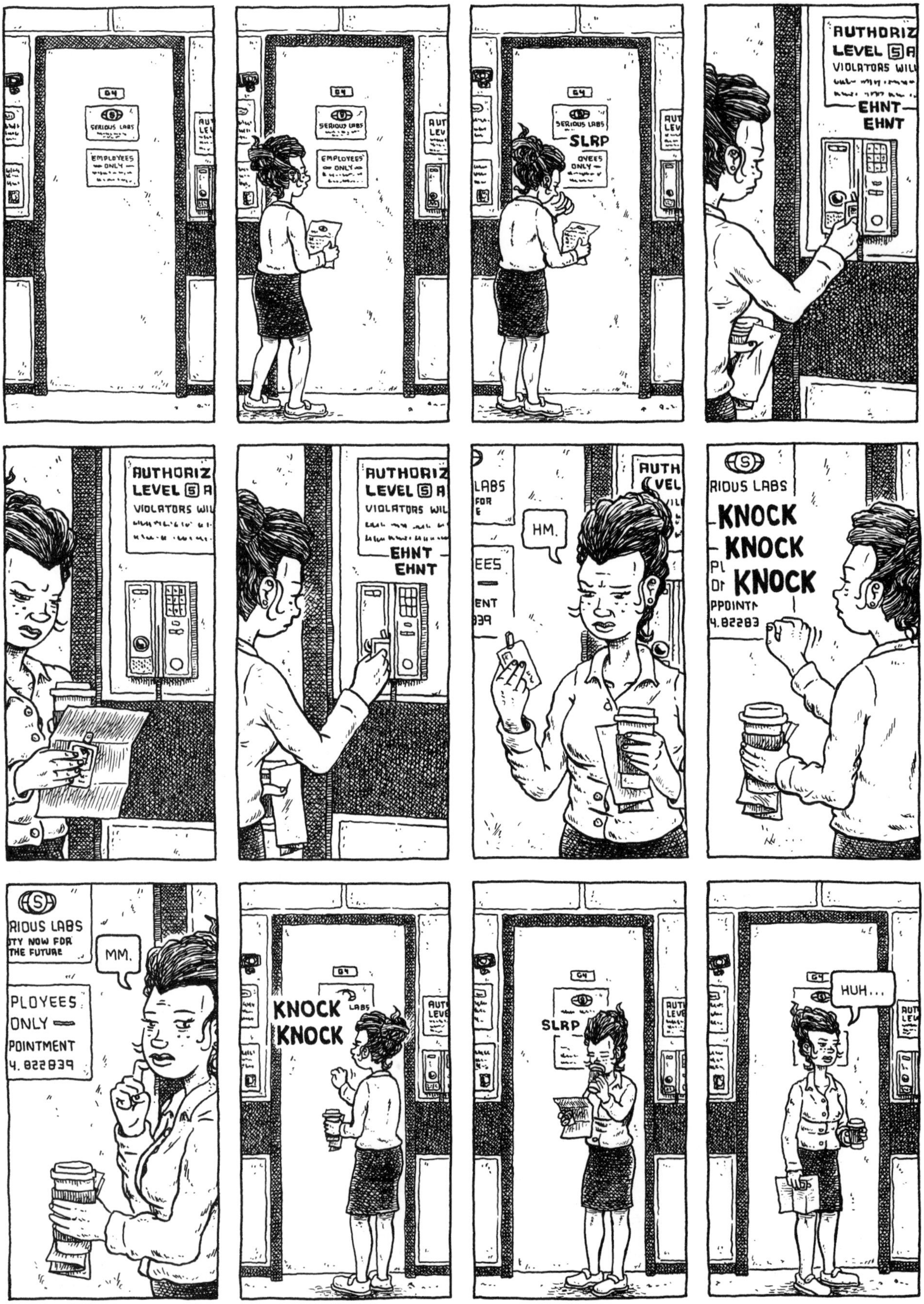
G4
SERIOUS LABS
EMPLOYEES ONLY
SLRP
AUTHORIZ
LEVEL 5 A
VIOLATORS WIL
EHNT
EHNT
EHNT
EHNT
HM.
KNOCK
KNOCK
KNOCK
MM.
KNOCK
KNOCK
SLRP
HUH...

おはよう
ございます。

SLRP

OH. UM... SORRY?

GOOD MORNING!

OH...

GOOD MORNING.

CAN I HELP YOU?

WELL, I DON'T KNOW...

SERIOUS LABS

AUTHORIZED PERSONNEL
LEVEL ⑤ ACCESS ONLY
...LATORS WILL BE PROSECUTED

MY NAME IS MELODY MCCABE...
I'M SUPPOSED TO...

HEYYY, DR. MCCABE!!! I WAS
THINKING YOU MIGHT BE YOU!!

AUTHORIZED PERSONN
LEVEL ⑤ ACCESS ONL
...LATORS WILL BE PROSECUTED

SOOOO NICE TO MEET YOU! I AM
OKONOMI! OKONOMI YAKI. WE
WILL BE WORKING TOGETHER,
KIND OF!

IT'S... NICE TO MEET
YOU, TOO!

AUTHORIZED PERSONNEL
LEVEL ⑤ ACCESS ONLY

WHY ARE YOU OUT **HERE**?

OH, MY CARD... IT ISN'T WORK-
ING FOR SOME REASON.

IT IS 'CAUSE THEY ARE MADE
OF **BULL**SHIT IS WHY. HERE...

UM.

AU HORIZED PERS
LEVEL ⑤ ACCESS ON

≡PSSSH

やった! MAGIC
FINGERS, YEAH?

YEAH...

AUTHORIZED PER EL
CCESS ONLY

BEEP
BEEP

COME ON. IT WILL BE A WHILE
BEFORE ANYONE ELSE SHOWS UP.

OKAY...

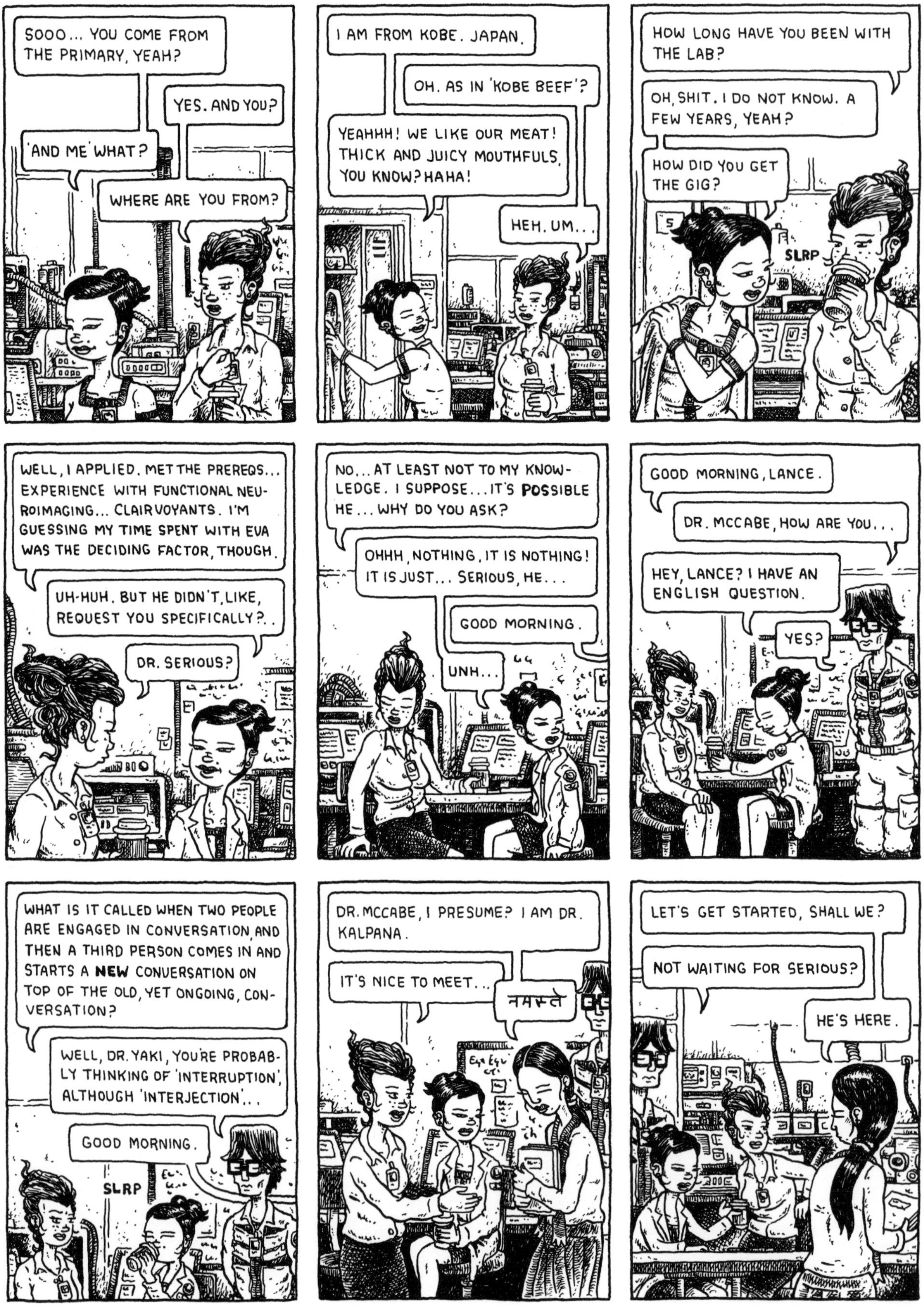
SOOO... YOU COME FROM THE PRIMARY, YEAH?
YES. AND YOU?
'AND ME' WHAT?
WHERE ARE YOU FROM?
I AM FROM KOBE. JAPAN.
OH. AS IN 'KOBE BEEF'?
YEAHHH! WE LIKE OUR MEAT! THICK AND JUICY MOUTHFULS, YOU KNOW? HAHA!
HEH. UM...
HOW LONG HAVE YOU BEEN WITH THE LAB?
OH, SHIT. I DO NOT KNOW. A FEW YEARS, YEAH?
HOW DID YOU GET THE GIG?
SLRP
WELL, I APPLIED. MET THE PREREQS... EXPERIENCE WITH FUNCTIONAL NEU-ROIMAGING... CLAIRVOYANTS. I'M GUESSING MY TIME SPENT WITH EVA WAS THE DECIDING FACTOR, THOUGH.
UH-HUH. BUT HE DIDN'T, LIKE, REQUEST YOU SPECIFICALLY?..
DR. SERIOUS?
NO,.. AT LEAST NOT TO MY KNOW-LEDGE. I SUPPOSE... IT'S POSSIBLE HE... WHY DO YOU ASK?
OHHH, NOTHING, IT IS NOTHING! IT IS JUST... SERIOUS, HE...
GOOD MORNING.
UNH...
GOOD MORNING, LANCE.
DR. MCCABE, HOW ARE YOU...
HEY, LANCE? I HAVE AN ENGLISH QUESTION.
YES?
WHAT IS IT CALLED WHEN TWO PEOPLE ARE ENGAGED IN CONVERSATION, AND THEN A THIRD PERSON COMES IN AND STARTS A NEW CONVERSATION ON TOP OF THE OLD, YET ONGOING, CON-VERSATION?
WELL, DR. YAKI, YOU'RE PROBAB-LY THINKING OF 'INTERRUPTION', ALTHOUGH 'INTERJECTION'...
GOOD MORNING.
SLRP
DR. MCCABE, I PRESUME? I AM DR. KALPANA.
IT'S NICE TO MEET...
नमस्ते
LET'S GET STARTED, SHALL WE?
NOT WAITING FOR SERIOUS?
HE'S HERE.

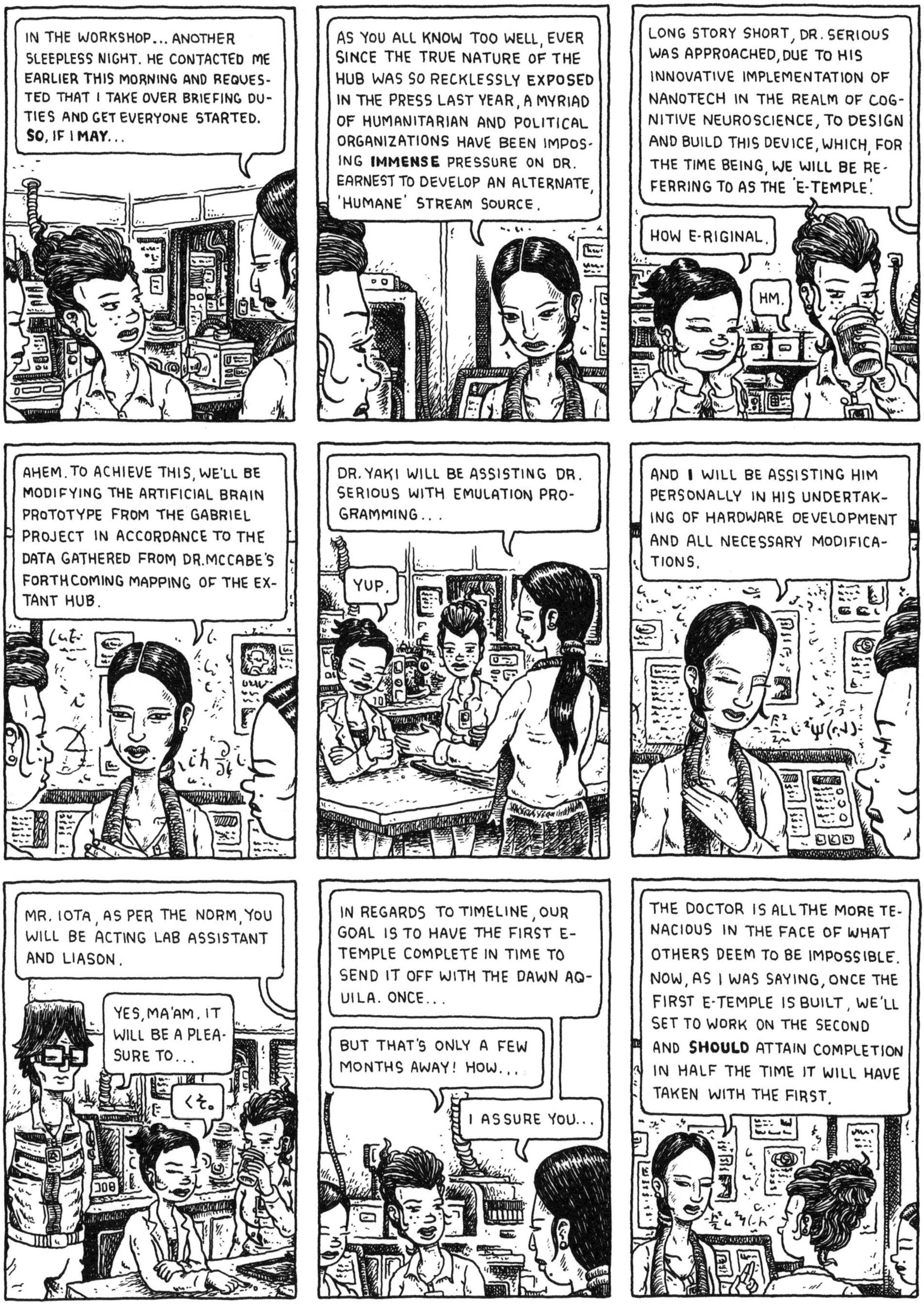
IN THE WORKSHOP... ANOTHER SLEEPLESS NIGHT. HE CONTACTED ME EARLIER THIS MORNING AND REQUESTED THAT I TAKE OVER BRIEFING DUTIES AND GET EVERYONE STARTED. SO, IF I MAY...
AS YOU ALL KNOW TOO WELL, EVER SINCE THE TRUE NATURE OF THE HUB WAS SO RECKLESSLY EXPOSED IN THE PRESS LAST YEAR, A MYRIAD OF HUMANITARIAN AND POLITICAL ORGANIZATIONS HAVE BEEN IMPOSING IMMENSE PRESSURE ON DR. EARNEST TO DEVELOP AN ALTERNATE, 'HUMANE' STREAM SOURCE.
LONG STORY SHORT, DR. SERIOUS WAS APPROACHED, DUE TO HIS INNOVATIVE IMPLEMENTATION OF NANOTECH IN THE REALM OF COGNITIVE NEUROSCIENCE, TO DESIGN AND BUILD THIS DEVICE, WHICH, FOR THE TIME BEING, WE WILL BE REFERRING TO AS THE 'E-TEMPLE'.
HOW E-RIGINAL.
HM.
AHEM. TO ACHIEVE THIS, WE'LL BE MODIFYING THE ARTIFICIAL BRAIN PROTOTYPE FROM THE GABRIEL PROJECT IN ACCORDANCE TO THE DATA GATHERED FROM DR. MCCABE'S FORTHCOMING MAPPING OF THE EXTANT HUB.
DR. YAKI WILL BE ASSISTING DR. SERIOUS WITH EMULATION PROGRAMMING...
YUP.
AND I WILL BE ASSISTING HIM PERSONALLY IN HIS UNDERTAKING OF HARDWARE DEVELOPMENT AND ALL NECESSARY MODIFICATIONS.
MR. IOTA, AS PER THE NORM, YOU WILL BE ACTING LAB ASSISTANT AND LIASON.
YES, MA'AM. IT WILL BE A PLEASURE TO...
くそ。
IN REGARDS TO TIMELINE, OUR GOAL IS TO HAVE THE FIRST E-TEMPLE COMPLETE IN TIME TO SEND IT OFF WITH THE DAWN AQUILA. ONCE...
BUT THAT'S ONLY A FEW MONTHS AWAY! HOW...
I ASSURE YOU...
THE DOCTOR IS ALL THE MORE TENACIOUS IN THE FACE OF WHAT OTHERS DEEM TO BE IMPOSSIBLE. NOW, AS I WAS SAYING, ONCE THE FIRST E-TEMPLE IS BUILT, WE'LL SET TO WORK ON THE SECOND AND SHOULD ATTAIN COMPLETION IN HALF THE TIME IT WILL HAVE TAKEN WITH THE FIRST.

IF ALL GOES AS PLANNED, BY THIS TIME NEXT YEAR STREAMING WILL BE ONE-HUNDRED PERCENT DIGITAL.

IT DOESN'T...

YES, DR. MCCABE?

I'M SORRY, BUT I HAVE TROUBLE BELIEVING THOSE GOALS TO BE **REALISTIC**...

THE TESTING PERIOD **ALONE** WOULD...

TESTING HAS BEEN TAKEN INTO ACCOUNT. AGAIN, DOCTOR, I **ASSURE** YOU, ALL GOALS ARE PERFECTLY PRACTICAL AND ATTAINABLE. OKAY?

OKAY.

THE SPECIFICS OF YOUR PROJECT RESPONSIBILITIES ARE DETAILED IN YOUR PACKET. DR. MCCABE, DR. SERIOUS PREFERS TO COMMUNICATE VIA TANGIBLE MEANS WHENEVER POSSIBLE, AND ALL DATA WILL BE SUBMITTED BOTH DIGITALLY AND BY HARDCOPY ON A DAILY BASIS. UNDERSTOOD?

YES, MA'AM.

WE BEGIN LAB WORK TOMORROW, SO I RECOMMEND YOU SPEND THE DAY PREPARING AND REVIEWING YOUR PACKETS. SHOULD YOU HAVE ANY QUESTIONS, **PLEASE** DIRECT THEM TO ME AS THE DOCTOR HAS AN AVERSION TO DISTRACTION.

I **AM** OBLIGATED TO REMIND YOU THAT THIS **ALL HIGHLY** CONFIDENTIAL. OKAY?

OKAY.

A-YUH.

DR. YAKI, IF YOU WOULD BE SO KIND AS TO FAMILIARIZE DR. MCCABE WITH THE LAB? AND IF YOU COULD GET HER A LAB COAT... THERE SHOULD BE SOME BACK IN STORAGE.

YESSUM.

MR. IOTA.

YES, DOCTOR?

I'D LIKE A MACCHIATO. DOUBLE.

YES, DOCTOR.

I'LL BE IN MY OFFICE SHOULD ANYONE NEED ME.

A BEVERAGE FOR ANYONE ELSE?

NOPE.

NO. THANK YOU, LANCE.

COME ON...

JESUS **TITS**, MAN.

WHAT IS IT?

FUCKING KALPANA. SOOO UPTIGHT...

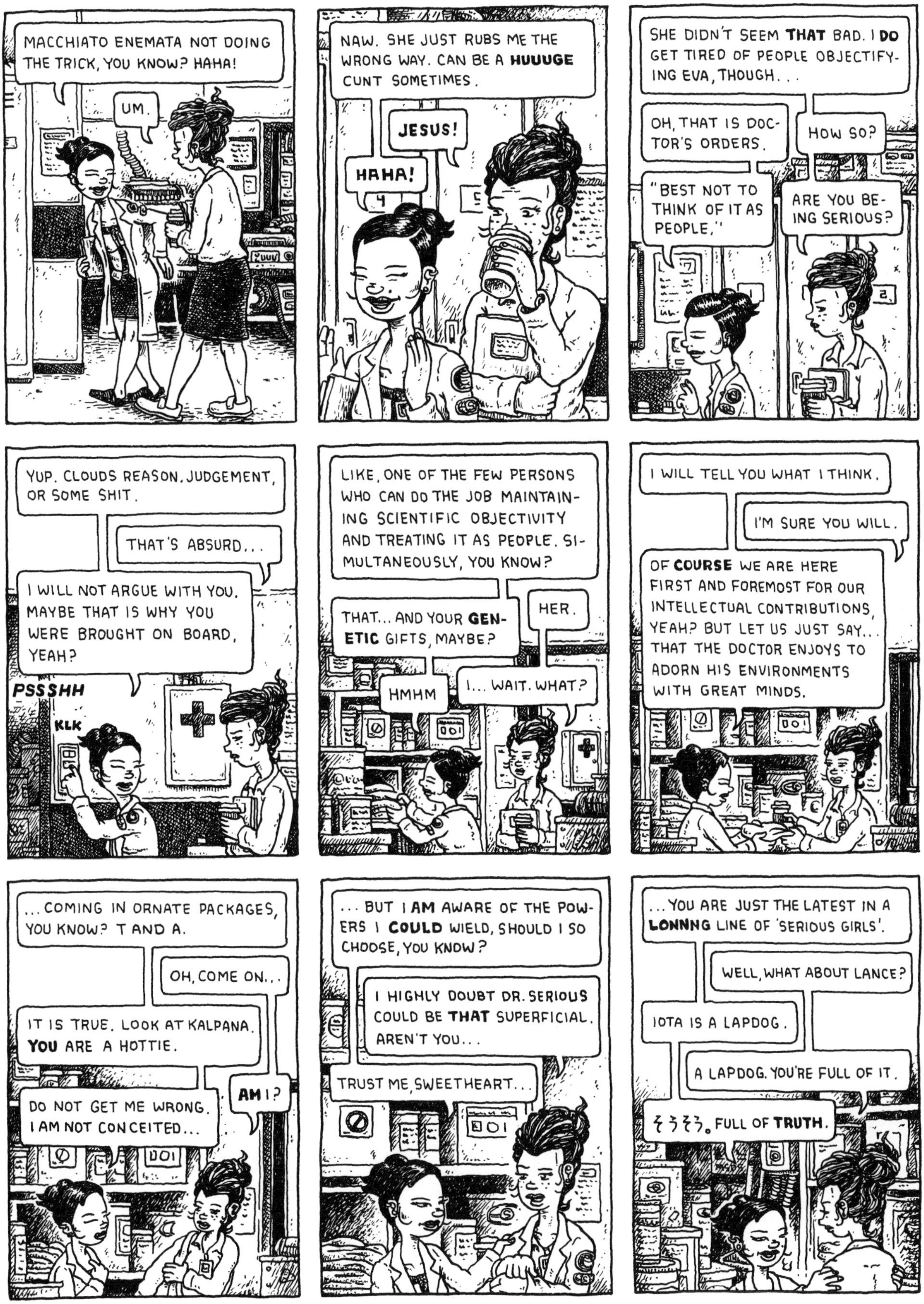

MACCHIATO ENEMATA NOT DOING THE TRICK, YOU KNOW? HAHA!
UM.
NAW. SHE JUST RUBS ME THE WRONG WAY. CAN BE A **HUUUGE** CUNT SOMETIMES.
JESUS!
HAHA!
SHE DIDN'T SEEM **THAT** BAD. I **DO** GET TIRED OF PEOPLE OBJECTIFYING EVA, THOUGH...
OH, THAT IS DOCTOR'S ORDERS.
HOW SO?
"BEST NOT TO THINK OF IT AS PEOPLE."
ARE YOU BEING SERIOUS?
YUP. CLOUDS REASON. JUDGEMENT, OR SOME SHIT.
THAT'S ABSURD...
I WILL NOT ARGUE WITH YOU. MAYBE THAT IS WHY YOU WERE BROUGHT ON BOARD, YEAH?
PSSSHH
KLK
LIKE, ONE OF THE FEW PERSONS WHO CAN DO THE JOB MAINTAINING SCIENTIFIC OBJECTIVITY AND TREATING IT AS PEOPLE. SIMULTANEOUSLY, YOU KNOW?
THAT... AND YOUR **GENETIC** GIFTS, MAYBE?
HER.
HMHM
I... WAIT. WHAT?
I WILL TELL YOU WHAT I THINK.
I'M SURE YOU WILL.
OF **COURSE** WE ARE HERE FIRST AND FOREMOST FOR OUR INTELLECTUAL CONTRIBUTIONS, YEAH? BUT LET US JUST SAY... THAT THE DOCTOR ENJOYS TO ADORN HIS ENVIRONMENTS WITH GREAT MINDS.
...COMING IN ORNATE PACKAGES, YOU KNOW? T AND A.
OH, COME ON...
IT IS TRUE. LOOK AT KALPANA. **YOU** ARE A HOTTIE.
DO NOT GET ME WRONG. I AM NOT CONCEITED...
AM I?
...BUT I **AM** AWARE OF THE POWERS I **COULD** WIELD, SHOULD I SO CHOOSE, YOU KNOW?
I HIGHLY DOUBT DR. SERIOUS COULD BE **THAT** SUPERFICIAL. AREN'T YOU...
TRUST ME, SWEETHEART...
...YOU ARE JUST THE LATEST IN A **LONNNG** LINE OF 'SERIOUS GIRLS'.
WELL, WHAT ABOUT LANCE?
IOTA IS A LAPDOG.
A LAPDOG. YOU'RE FULL OF IT.
そうそう。FULL OF **TRUTH**.

THAT IS A GOOD COAT. A LITTLE TIGHT. TO ACCENTUATE YOUR ASS FOR THE MASTER.

PSHH... IS EVERYONE FROM KOBE AS RESERVED AS YOU?

I AM A PLEASING ANOMALY, THE BLESSINGS OF NUMEROUS ENDEARING QUALITIES. NOW, COME WITH ME. LET US GET YOU FAMILIARIZED.

LEAD THE WAY.

VIS A VIS

VIS A VIS

KLK

Y. MUSTAFA
ONLINE
KLK

Y. MUSTAFA
DIALING...

BING

'ELLO?

YUSUF?

YEAH.. HEY, MELODY...

YUSUF, WHERE HAVE YOU BEEN?

WHAD'YA MEAN?

I'VE BEEN TRYING TO CONTACT YOU FOR **DAYS**!..

MM. BEEN BUSY.

BUSY?

BEEN BUSY.

WE AGREED THAT WE WOULD...

HEY.

I'VE GOT AN IDEA. HOW 'BOUT WE START THINGS OFF WITH AN ARGUMENT?

I'M NOT ARGUING! I'M JUST A LITTLE UPSET THAT...

I'M GONNA GET GOIN'.

WHAT?! NO... WAIT...

SORRY. I'M SORRY. I... HOW HAVE YOU BEEN?

WHY, I'VE BEEN FINE, MELODY. HOW ABOUT YOU?

GOOD. TOMORROW WILL BE MY FIRST DAY BACK WITH EVA...

UH-HUH.

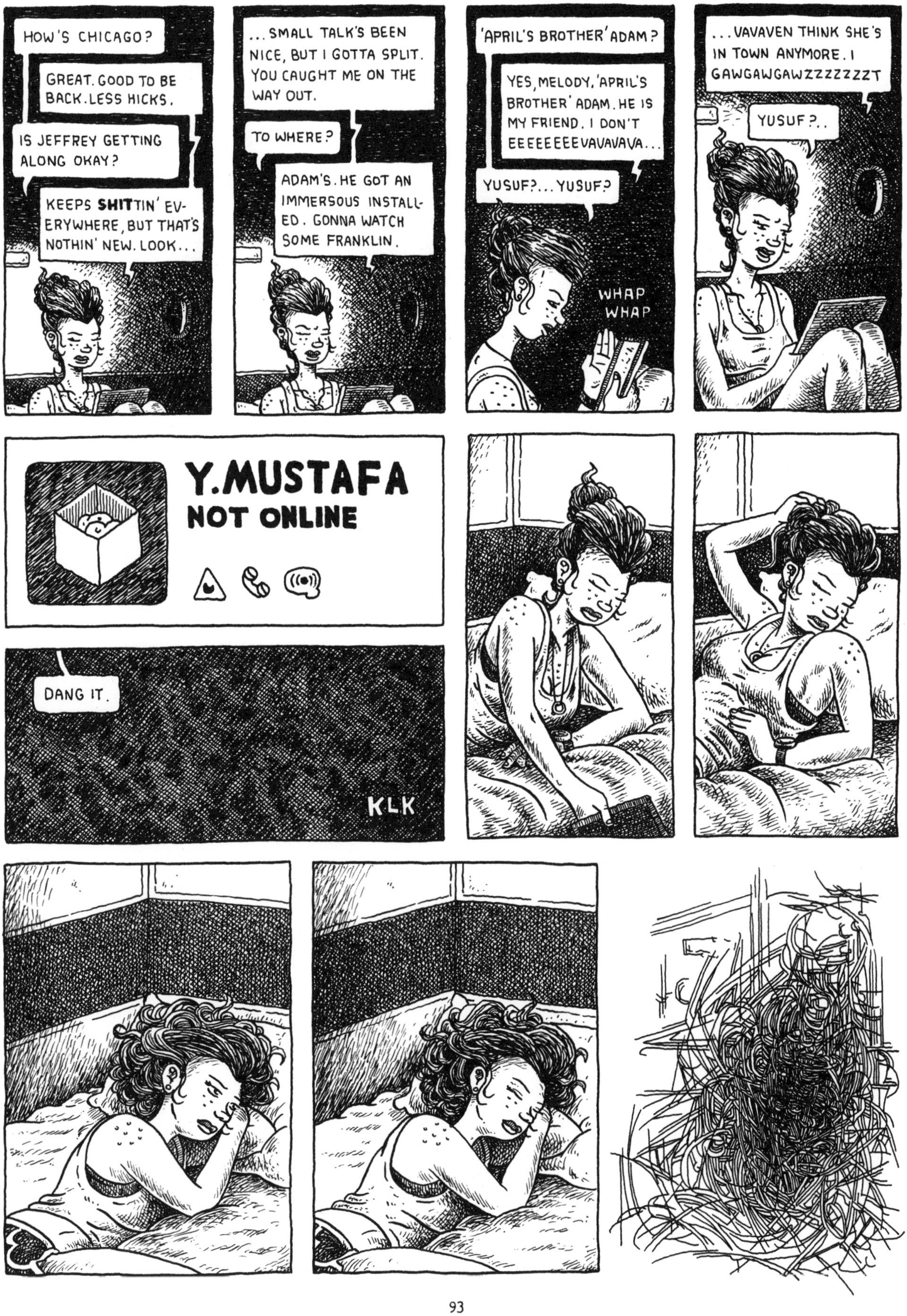

HOW'S CHICAGO?
GREAT. GOOD TO BE BACK. LESS HICKS.
IS JEFFREY GETTING ALONG OKAY?
KEEPS **SHIT**TIN' EVERYWHERE, BUT THAT'S NOTHIN' NEW. LOOK...
...SMALL TALK'S BEEN NICE, BUT I GOTTA SPLIT. YOU CAUGHT ME ON THE WAY OUT.
TO WHERE?
ADAM'S. HE GOT AN IMMERSOUS INSTALLED. GONNA WATCH SOME FRANKLIN.
'APRIL'S BROTHER' ADAM?
YES, MELODY, 'APRIL'S BROTHER' ADAM. HE IS MY FRIEND. I DON'T EEEEEEEEVAVAVAVA...
YUSUF?... YUSUF?
WHAP WHAP
...VAVAVEN THINK SHE'S IN TOWN ANYMORE. I GAWGAWGAWZZZZZZZT
YUSUF?..
Y.MUSTAFA
NOT ONLINE
DANG IT.
KLK

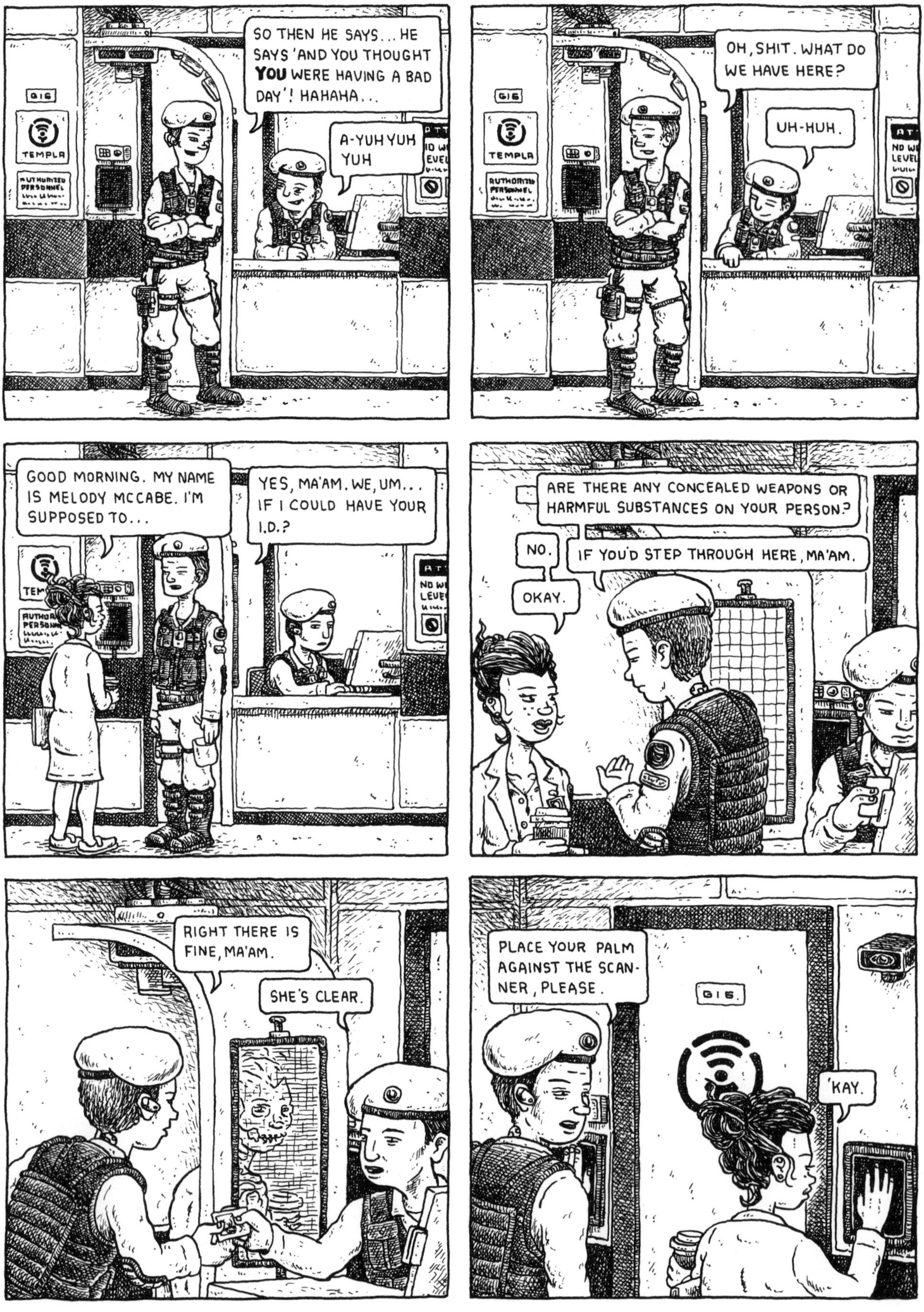
SO THEN HE SAYS... HE SAYS 'AND YOU THOUGHT **YOU** WERE HAVING A BAD DAY'! HAHAHA...
A-YUH YUH YUH
OH, SHIT. WHAT DO WE HAVE HERE?
UH-HUH.
GOOD MORNING. MY NAME IS MELODY MCCABE. I'M SUPPOSED TO...
YES, MA'AM. WE, UM... IF I COULD HAVE YOUR I.D.?
ARE THERE ANY CONCEALED WEAPONS OR HARMFUL SUBSTANCES ON YOUR PERSON?
NO.
IF YOU'D STEP THROUGH HERE, MA'AM.
OKAY.
RIGHT THERE IS FINE, MA'AM.
SHE'S CLEAR.
PLACE YOUR PALM AGAINST THE SCANNER, PLEASE.
'KAY.

BEEP
BEEP

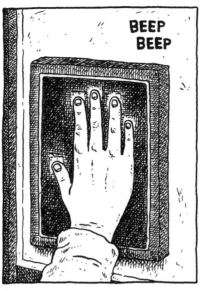

BEEP
BEEP

ALRIGHT.

PSSSHH

BEEP
BEEP
BEEP

YOU'RE GOOD TO GO. HAVE A NICE DAY, MA'AM.

THANK YOU. YOU AS WELL.

HELLO?

HAHAHAA!

HAHAA!

HELLO?

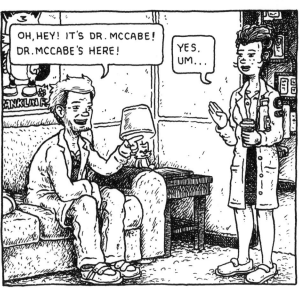

OH, HEY! IT'S DR. MCCABE! DR. MCCABE'S HERE!

YES, UM...

CHRISTIAN! SAVVY!

HI. IT'S NICE TO MEET...

OH, WE'VE MET.

OH. I...

YEAH! I DID SOME TRAINING AT THE PRIMARY.

UM...

REMEMBER?.. WE DISCUSSED THAT PACKET DISINTEGRATION THING? BACK WHEN THEY WERE WORKING OUT THE KINKS WITH, UM... THE COMM EXCHANGE.

OH, GEEZ. I...

MY HAIR WAS SHORTER BACK THEN.

OH. YEAH, YEAH... I THINK... UM...

HEY, EVA! LOOK WHO'S HERE! IT'S...

IN A MOMENT.

OH... SURE.

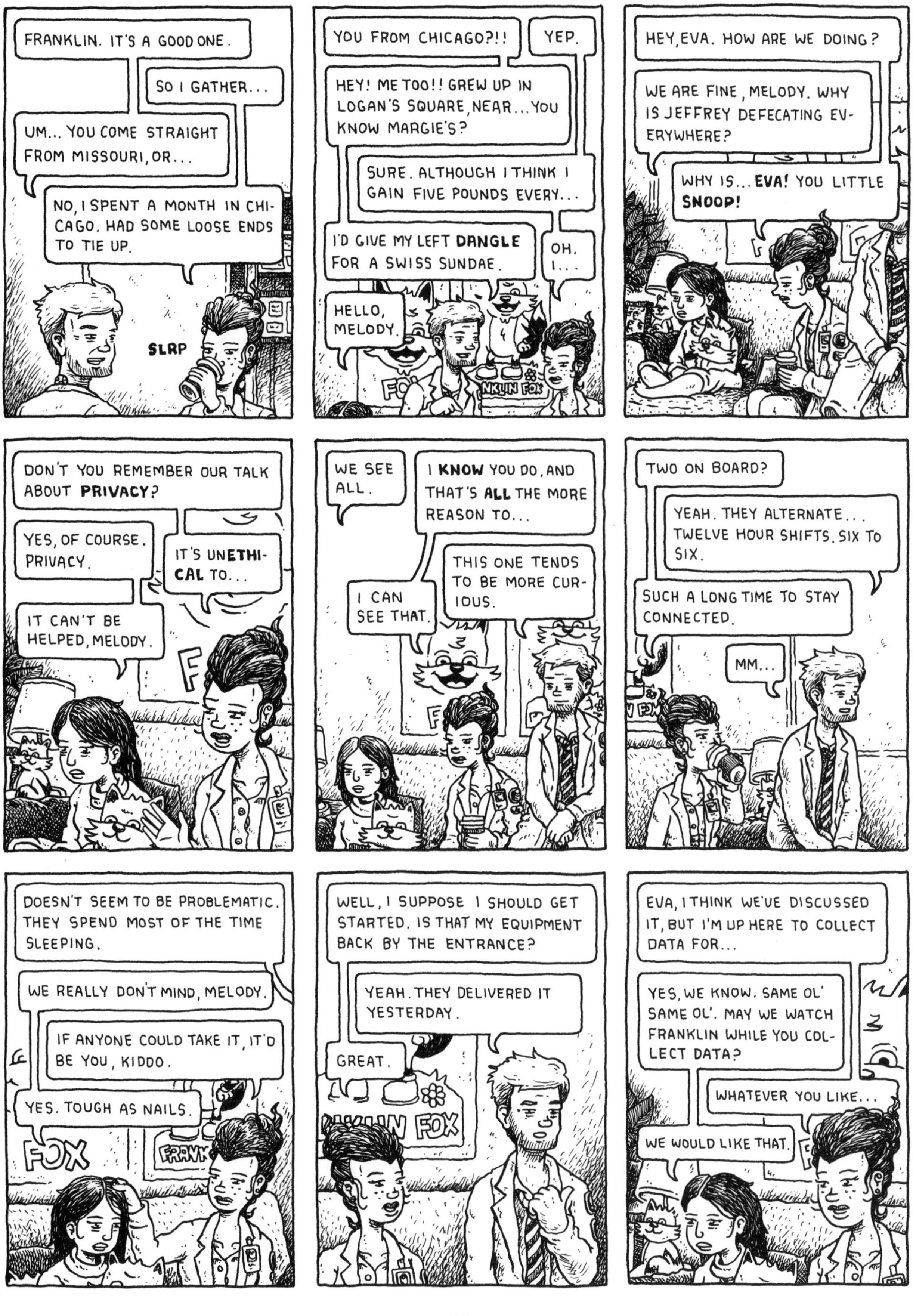
FRANKLIN. IT'S A GOOD ONE.
SO I GATHER...
UM... YOU COME STRAIGHT FROM MISSOURI, OR...
NO, I SPENT A MONTH IN CHICAGO. HAD SOME LOOSE ENDS TO TIE UP.
SLRP
YOU FROM CHICAGO?!!
YEP.
HEY! ME TOO!! GREW UP IN LOGAN'S SQUARE, NEAR... YOU KNOW MARGIE'S?
SURE. ALTHOUGH I THINK I GAIN FIVE POUNDS EVERY...
I'D GIVE MY LEFT **DANGLE** FOR A SWISS SUNDAE.
OH. I...
HELLO, MELODY.
HEY, EVA. HOW ARE WE DOING?
WE ARE FINE, MELODY. WHY IS JEFFREY DEFECATING EVERYWHERE?
WHY IS... **EVA!** YOU LITTLE **SNOOP!**
DON'T YOU REMEMBER OUR TALK ABOUT **PRIVACY**?
YES, OF COURSE. PRIVACY.
IT'S UN**ETHICAL** TO...
IT CAN'T BE HELPED, MELODY.
WE SEE ALL.
I **KNOW** YOU DO, AND THAT'S **ALL** THE MORE REASON TO...
THIS ONE TENDS TO BE MORE CURIOUS.
I CAN SEE THAT.
TWO ON BOARD?
YEAH. THEY ALTERNATE... TWELVE HOUR SHIFTS. SIX TO SIX.
SUCH A LONG TIME TO STAY CONNECTED.
MM...
DOESN'T SEEM TO BE PROBLEMATIC. THEY SPEND MOST OF THE TIME SLEEPING.
WE REALLY DON'T MIND, MELODY.
IF ANYONE COULD TAKE IT, IT'D BE YOU, KIDDO.
YES. TOUGH AS NAILS.
FOX
WELL, I SUPPOSE I SHOULD GET STARTED. IS THAT MY EQUIPMENT BACK BY THE ENTRANCE?
YEAH. THEY DELIVERED IT YESTERDAY.
GREAT.
EVA, I THINK WE'VE DISCUSSED IT, BUT I'M UP HERE TO COLLECT DATA FOR...
YES, WE KNOW. SAME OL' SAME OL'. MAY WE WATCH FRANKLIN WHILE YOU COLLECT DATA?
WHATEVER YOU LIKE...
WE WOULD LIKE THAT.

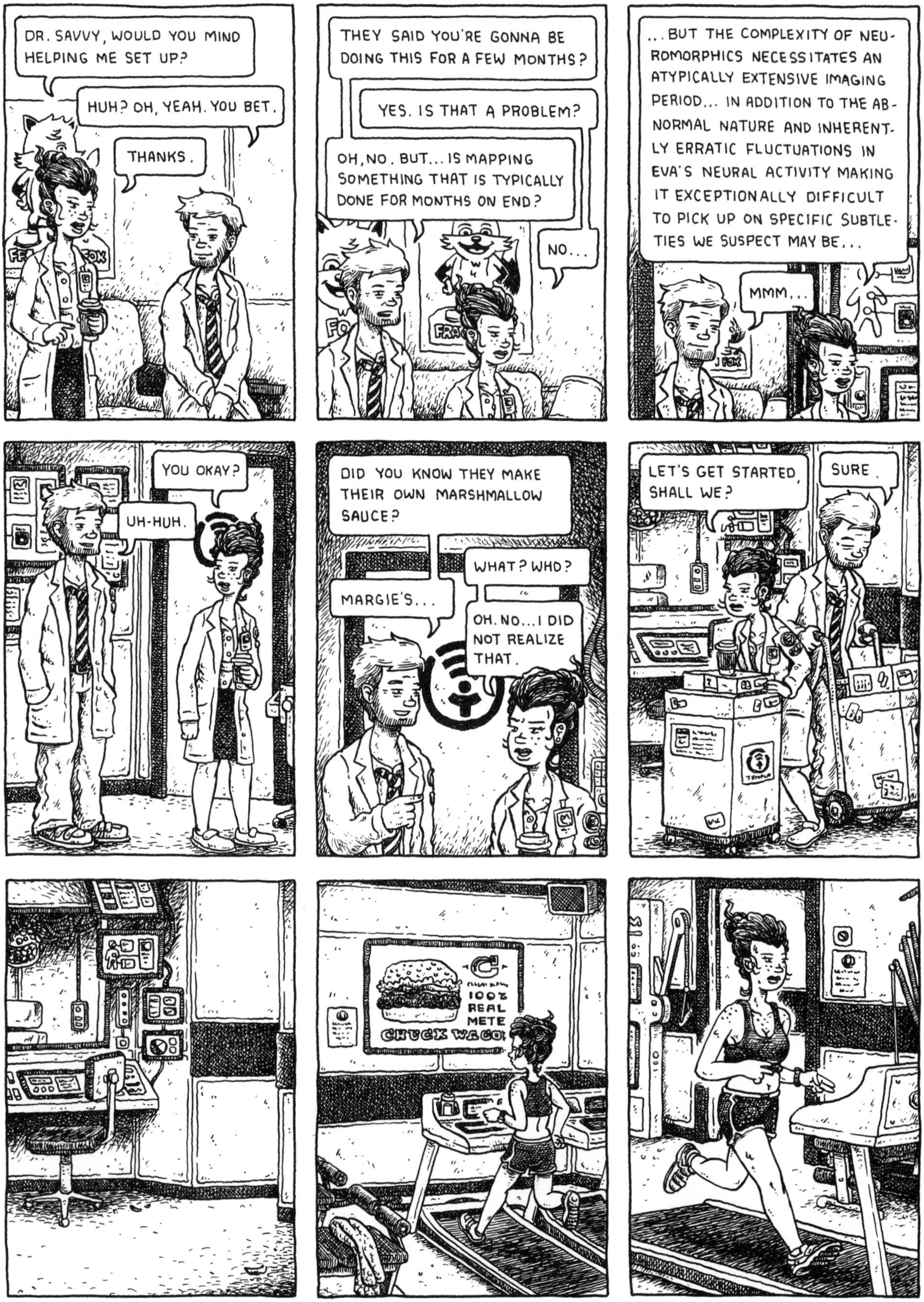

DR. SAVVY, WOULD YOU MIND HELPING ME SET UP?
HUH? OH, YEAH. YOU BET.
THANKS.
THEY SAID YOU'RE GONNA BE DOING THIS FOR A FEW MONTHS?
YES. IS THAT A PROBLEM?
OH, NO. BUT... IS MAPPING SOMETHING THAT IS TYPICALLY DONE FOR MONTHS ON END?
NO...
...BUT THE COMPLEXITY OF NEUROMORPHICS NECESSITATES AN ATYPICALLY EXTENSIVE IMAGING PERIOD... IN ADDITION TO THE ABNORMAL NATURE AND INHERENTLY ERRATIC FLUCTUATIONS IN EVA'S NEURAL ACTIVITY MAKING IT EXCEPTIONALLY DIFFICULT TO PICK UP ON SPECIFIC SUBTLETIES WE SUSPECT MAY BE...
MMM...
YOU OKAY?
UH-HUH.
DID YOU KNOW THEY MAKE THEIR OWN MARSHMALLOW SAUCE?
WHAT? WHO?
MARGIE'S...
OH. NO... I DID NOT REALIZE THAT.
LET'S GET STARTED, SHALL WE?
SURE.
100% REAL METE
CHUCK WAGO

SIVE **TEMPLA LABS VS MO**

REV.'BLACK'ANGUS: HUMANITARIAN OR HOLY TERROR?

DK

BEEP

...TODAY, REVEREND 'BLACK' ANGUS, LEADER OF THE SOI-DISANT 'CHURCH OF EMANCIPA-TION'...

GK

...THE 'HUMANITARIAN' ORGANI-ZATION SUSPECTED IN CONNEC-TION WITH THE RECENT ACTS OF TERRORISM WAGED AGAINST TEM-PLA LABS AND THEIR...

USIVE **TEMPLA LABS VS**

SUSPICIONS UNWARRANTED, MS. GRINDER. THE CHURCH IS **MERE-**LY A PEACEFUL COALITION OF CONCERNED WORLD CITIZENS. A PEOPLE **CHOSEN**...

MOUTH OF GOD | PIPE

...TO PUT AN **END** TO THE **PHYS-**ICAL AND **PSY**CHOLOGICAL BOND-AGE OF AN **INNOCENT**, A CHILD OF **CHRIST**, TAKING WHATEVER **LAWFUL** MEASURES DEEMED **NEC-**ESSARY.

BUT **REV**EREND... IS IT NOT TRUE THAT **NUMEROUS** MEMBERS OF YOUR...CONGRE**GA**TION... HAVE PAST AFFILIATION WITH **MER**CENARY GROUPS? GUER-RILLA IN**SUR**GENCY? **RADICAL** FUNDAMENTALIST...

HAD YOU DONE YOUR **RESEARCH**, YOU WOULD KNOW THAT SUCH AL-LEGATIONS ARE WHOLLY UNSUB-**STAN**TIATED. IF OUR DISCUSSION IS TO FOCUS ON ORGANIZATIONS STEEPED IN CRIMINAL **HISTORY**, WE NEED LOOK NO FURTHER THAN EARNEST'S **OWN**.

PADDING THEIR POCKETS, **TRULY**, FATTENING THEIR **HEARTS** FOR THE DAY OF **SLAUGHTER**, PARA-**SITIC**, WITHOUT REGARD FOR THE WELL-**BEING** OF A HELPLESS...

PERHAPS YOU SHOULD DO SOME RESEARCH YOUR**SELF**, REVEREND. I WAS UNDER THE IMPRESSION THAT DR. EARNEST IS ONE OF THE PREEMINENT, ALTRUISTIC SCIENTIFIC MINDS OF OUR **TIME**! HIS CONTRIBUTIONS TOWARDS ENRICHING OUR...

CONTRIBUTIONS ROOTED DEEP IN THE GROUNDS OF DECEIT.

OH? AND WHAT OF HIS RECENT ASSURANCES OF DEVELOPING AN ALTERNATE HUB?

PLEASE.

YES?

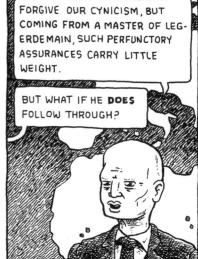

FORGIVE OUR CYNICISM, BUT COMING FROM A MASTER OF LEGERDEMAIN, SUCH PERFUNCTORY ASSURANCES CARRY LITTLE WEIGHT.

BUT WHAT IF HE **DOES** FOLLOW THROUGH?

IF EARNEST DOES INDEED DEVELOP AN ACCEPTABLE ALTERNATIVE TO CHILD SLAVERY, WE WILL ACCEPT IT WITH OPEN ARMS, OF COURSE. WE DO NOT TAKE ISSUE WITH THE PROPRIETY OF STREAMING ITSELF.

IT WOULD BE, HOWEVER, A MATTER OF TOO LITTLE, TOO LATE FOR HIM AND HIS ACCOMPLICES. THE DAMAGE **HAS** BEEN **DONE**, AND THEY **WILL** MAKE ATONEMENT FOR THEIR SINS.

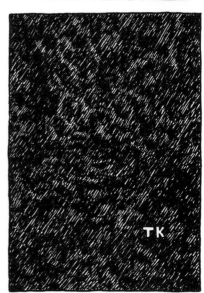

HAVING THE AUDACITY TO CHRISTEN HIS INSTITUTION 'TEMPLA' IS HERETICAL ENOUGH TO WARRANT...

IT'S COMMON KNOWLEDGE THAT 'TEMPLA' IS A PLAY ON THE 'SCARECROW EFFECT'.

SEMANTICS DO NOT...

SURELY...

SURELY SOMEONE WHO PURPORTS TO BE THE 'MOUTH OF **GOD**' WOULD KNOW SOMETHING AS...

OUTH OF GOD
RAND EARNEST UNDER

PIPER GRINDER LIVE

I AM THE MOUTH OF GOD!!!

OUTH OF GOD
RAND EARNEST UNDER

PIPER GRINDER LIVE

TK

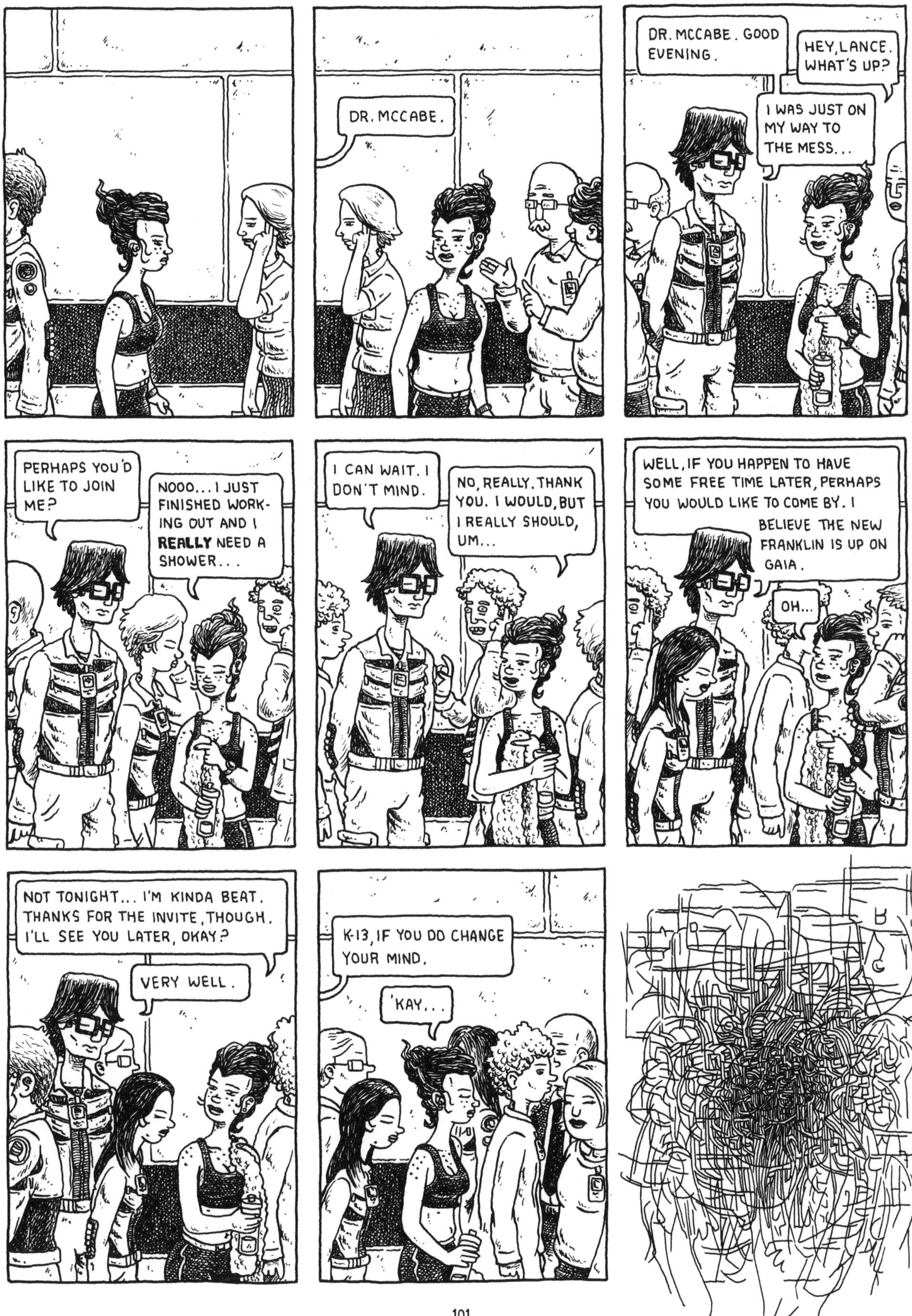
DR. MCCABE.
DR. MCCABE. GOOD EVENING.
HEY, LANCE. WHAT'S UP?
I WAS JUST ON MY WAY TO THE MESS...
PERHAPS YOU'D LIKE TO JOIN ME?
NOOO... I JUST FINISHED WORKING OUT AND I **REALLY** NEED A SHOWER...
I CAN WAIT. I DON'T MIND.
NO, REALLY. THANK YOU. I WOULD, BUT I REALLY SHOULD, UM...
WELL, IF YOU HAPPEN TO HAVE SOME FREE TIME LATER, PERHAPS YOU WOULD LIKE TO COME BY. I BELIEVE THE NEW FRANKLIN IS UP ON GAIA.
OH...
NOT TONIGHT... I'M KINDA BEAT. THANKS FOR THE INVITE, THOUGH. I'LL SEE YOU LATER, OKAY?
VERY WELL.
K-13, IF YOU DO CHANGE YOUR MIND.
'KAY...

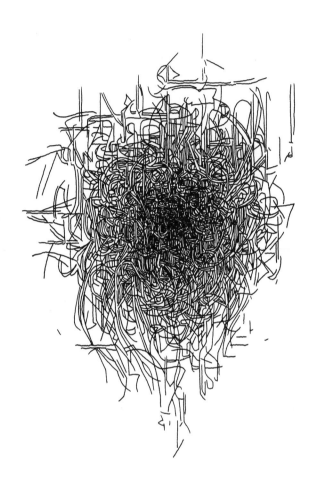

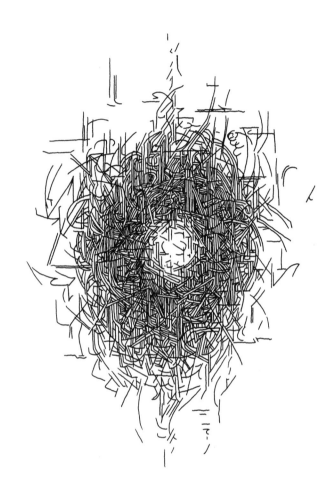

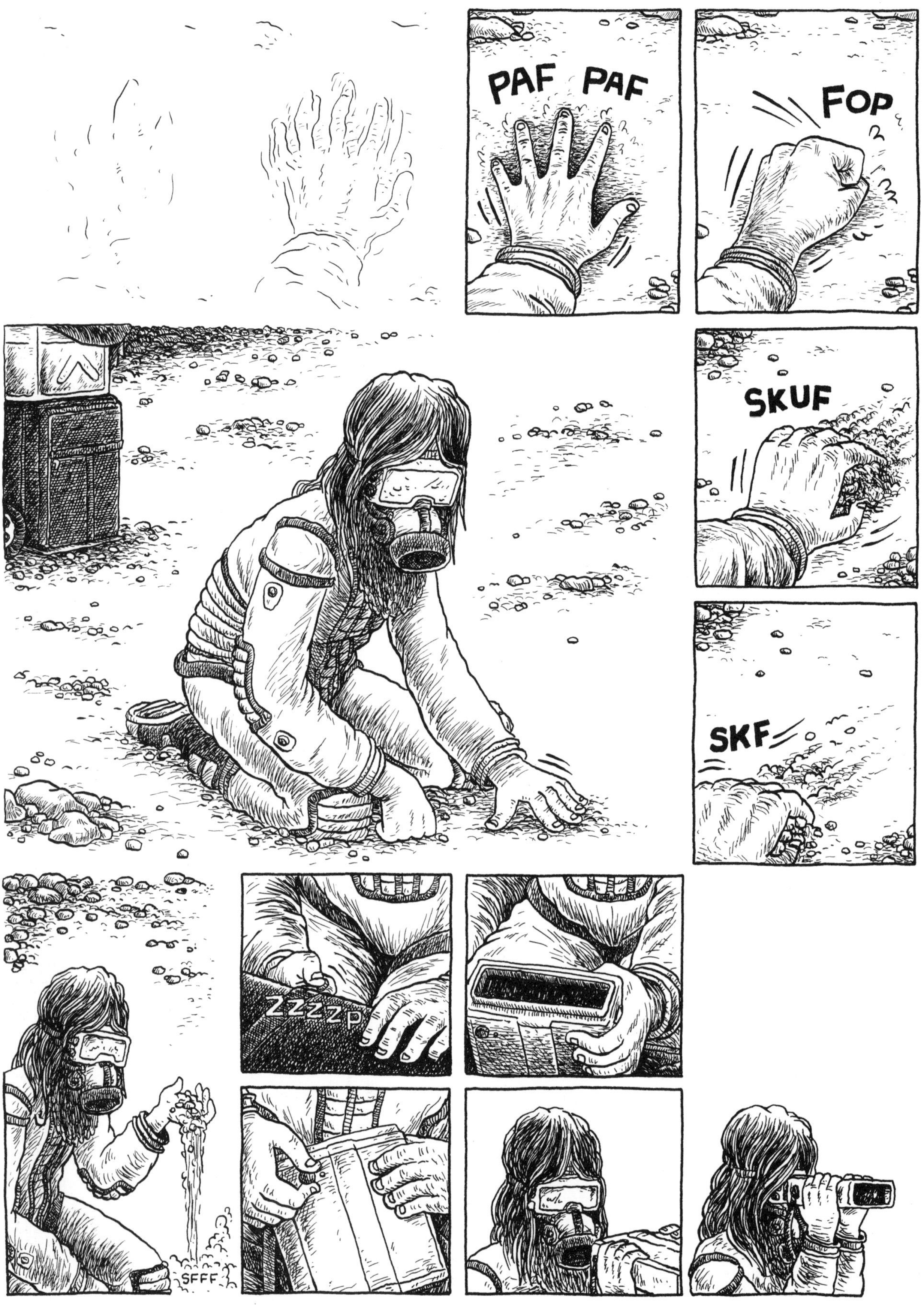
PAF PAF
FOP
SKUF
SKF
SFFF
ZZZZP

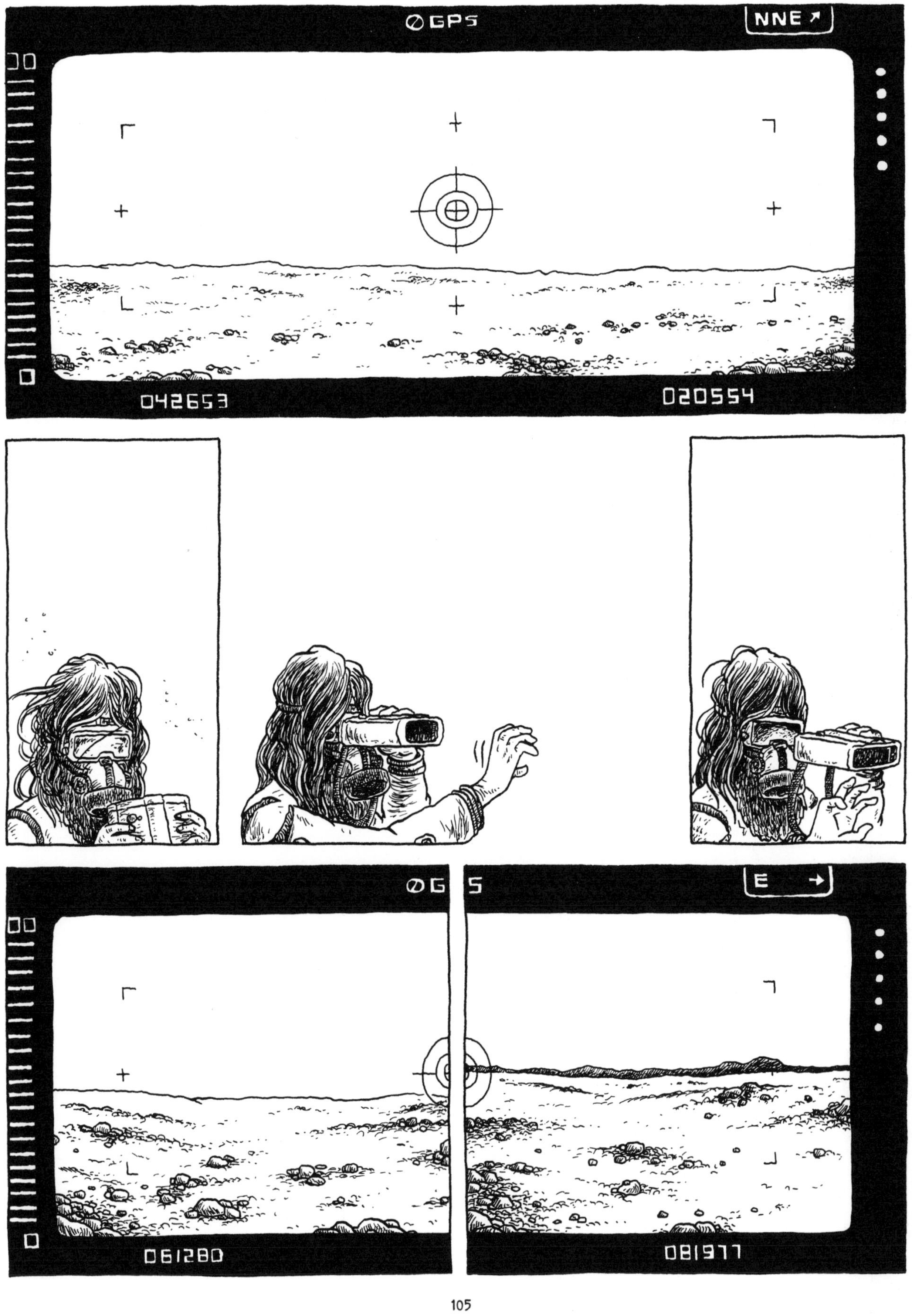
⊘GPS
NNE
042653
020554
E
061280
081977

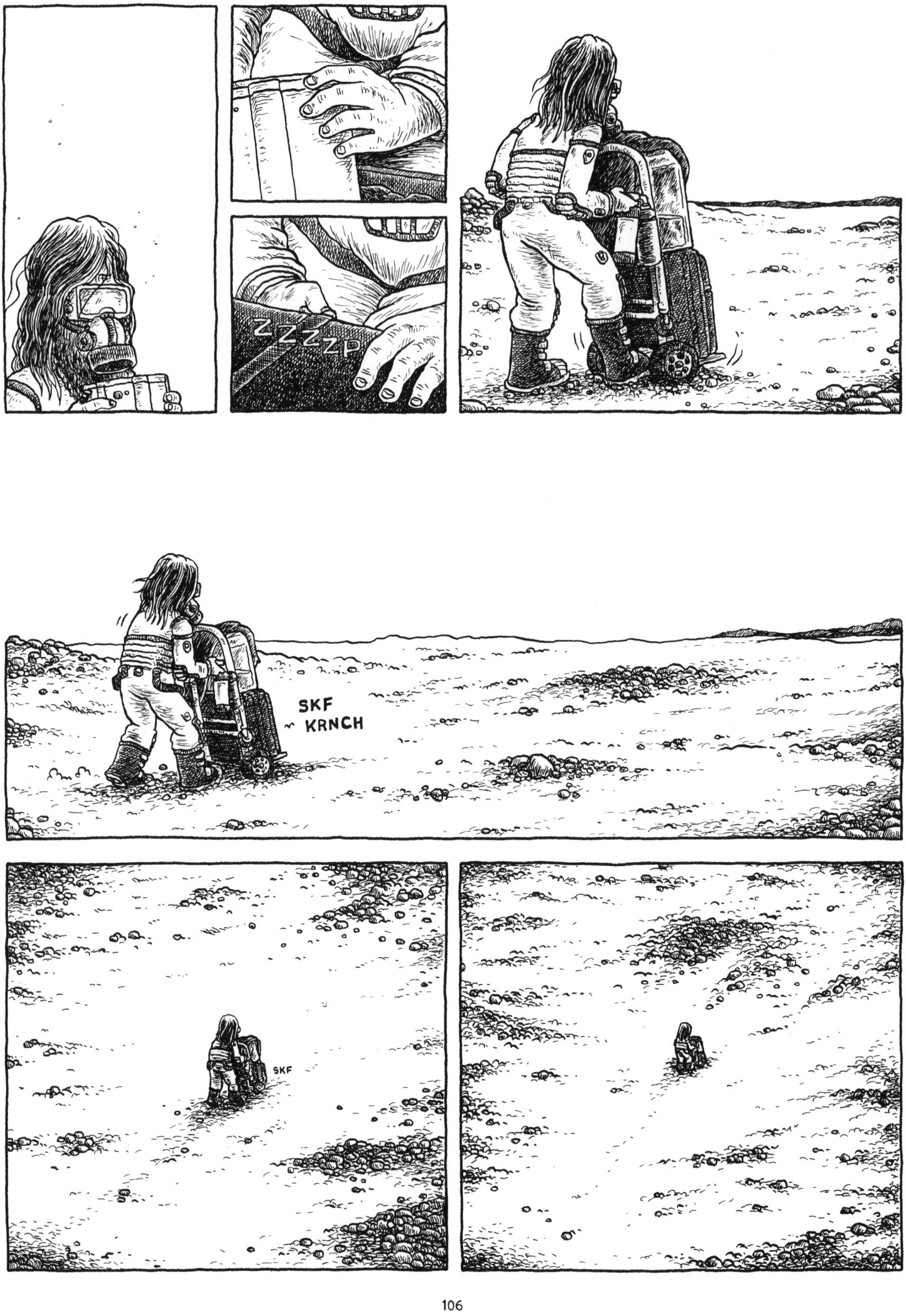
ZZZZZP
SKF
KRNCH
SKF

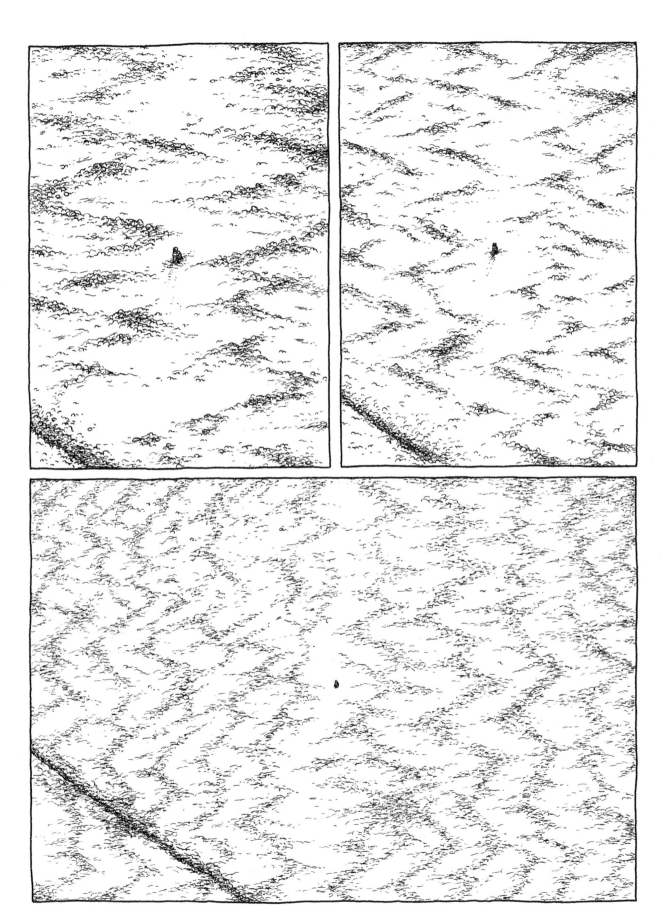

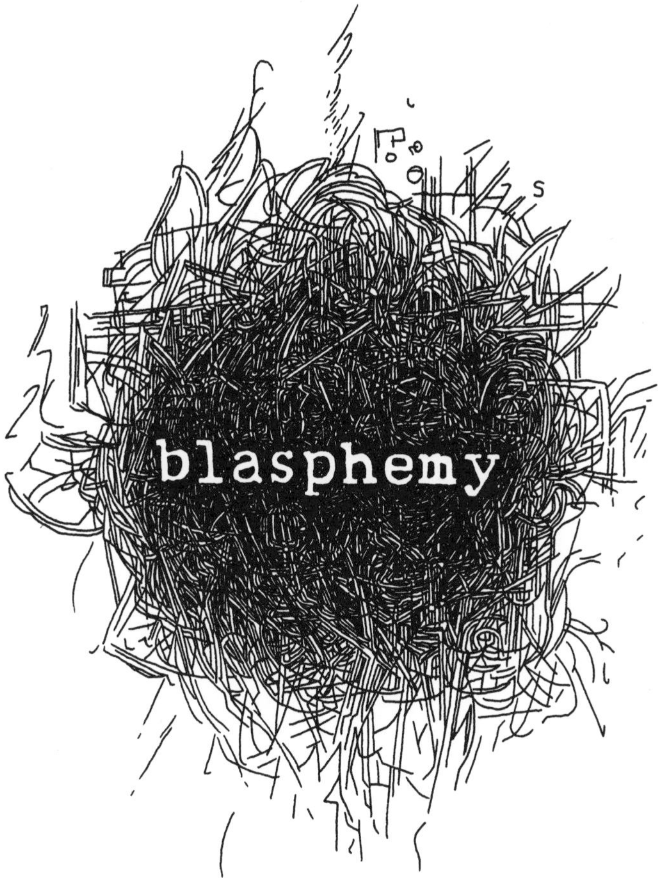
blasphemy

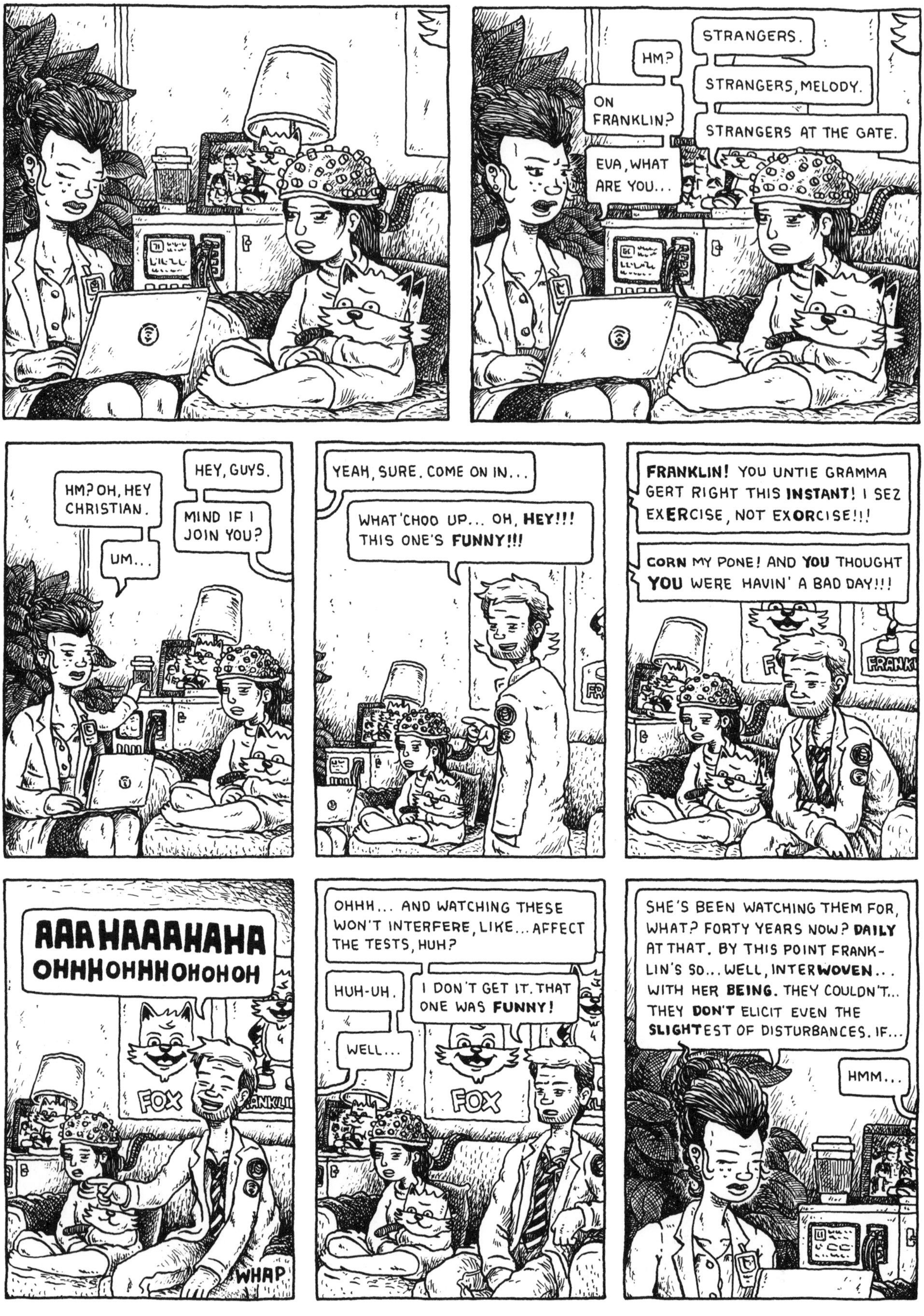
EVA, WHAT ARE YOU...
ON FRANKLIN?
HM?
STRANGERS.
STRANGERS, MELODY.
STRANGERS AT THE GATE.
HEY, GUYS.
HM? OH, HEY CHRISTIAN.
MIND IF I JOIN YOU?
UM...
YEAH, SURE. COME ON IN...
WHAT'CHOO UP... OH, HEY!!! THIS ONE'S FUNNY!!!
FRANKLIN! YOU UNTIE GRAMMA GERT RIGHT THIS INSTANT! I SEZ EXERCISE, NOT EXORCISE!!!
CORN MY PONE! AND YOU THOUGHT YOU WERE HAVIN' A BAD DAY!!!
AAAHAAAHAHA OHHHOHHHOHOHOH
FOX
WHAP
OHHH... AND WATCHING THESE WON'T INTERFERE, LIKE... AFFECT THE TESTS, HUH?
HUH-UH.
WELL...
I DON'T GET IT. THAT ONE WAS FUNNY!
FOX
SHE'S BEEN WATCHING THEM FOR, WHAT? FORTY YEARS NOW? DAILY AT THAT. BY THIS POINT FRANKLIN'S SO... WELL, INTERWOVEN... WITH HER BEING. THEY COULDN'T... THEY DON'T ELICIT EVEN THE SLIGHTEST OF DISTURBANCES. IF...
HMM...

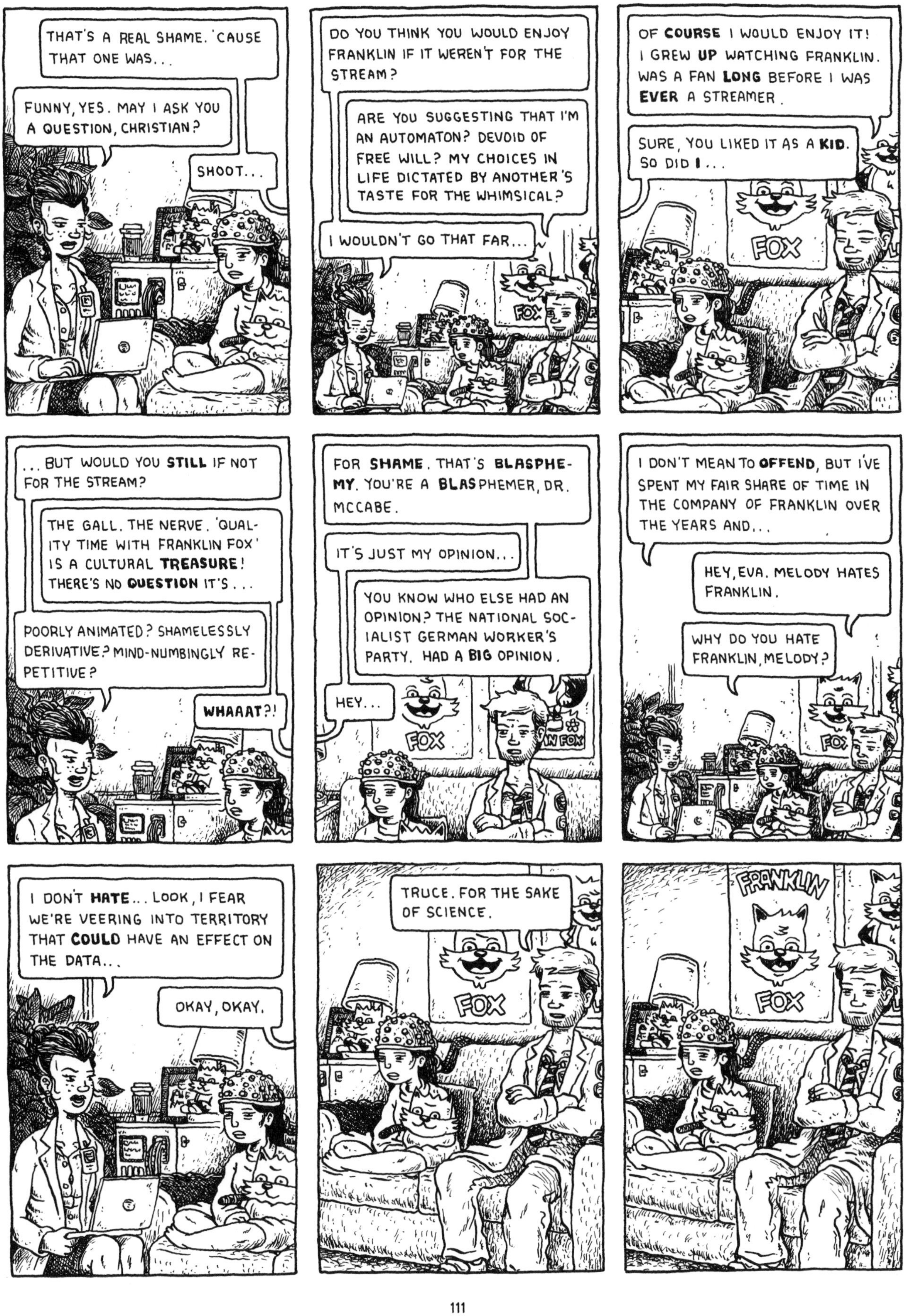

THAT'S A REAL SHAME. 'CAUSE THAT ONE WAS...
FUNNY, YES. MAY I ASK YOU A QUESTION, CHRISTIAN?
SHOOT...
DO YOU THINK YOU WOULD ENJOY FRANKLIN IF IT WEREN'T FOR THE STREAM?
ARE YOU SUGGESTING THAT I'M AN AUTOMATON? DEVOID OF FREE WILL? MY CHOICES IN LIFE DICTATED BY ANOTHER'S TASTE FOR THE WHIMSICAL?
I WOULDN'T GO THAT FAR...
OF **COURSE** I WOULD ENJOY IT! I GREW **UP** WATCHING FRANKLIN. WAS A FAN **LONG** BEFORE I WAS **EVER** A STREAMER.
SURE, YOU LIKED IT AS A **KID**. SO DID **I**...
FOX
...BUT WOULD YOU **STILL** IF NOT FOR THE STREAM?
THE GALL. THE NERVE. 'QUALITY TIME WITH FRANKLIN FOX' IS A CULTURAL **TREASURE**! THERE'S NO **QUESTION** IT'S...
POORLY ANIMATED? SHAMELESSLY DERIVATIVE? MIND-NUMBINGLY REPETITIVE?
WHAAAT?!
FOR **SHAME**. THAT'S **BLASPHEMY**. YOU'RE A **BLAS**PHEMER, DR. MCCABE.
IT'S JUST MY OPINION...
YOU KNOW WHO ELSE HAD AN OPINION? THE NATIONAL SOCIALIST GERMAN WORKER'S PARTY. HAD A **BIG** OPINION.
HEY...
FOX
I DON'T MEAN TO **OFFEND**, BUT I'VE SPENT MY FAIR SHARE OF TIME IN THE COMPANY OF FRANKLIN OVER THE YEARS AND...
HEY, EVA. MELODY HATES FRANKLIN.
WHY DO YOU HATE FRANKLIN, MELODY?
I DON'T **HATE**... LOOK, I FEAR WE'RE VEERING INTO TERRITORY THAT **COULD** HAVE AN EFFECT ON THE DATA...
OKAY, OKAY.
TRUCE. FOR THE SAKE OF SCIENCE.
FOX
FRANKLIN
FOX

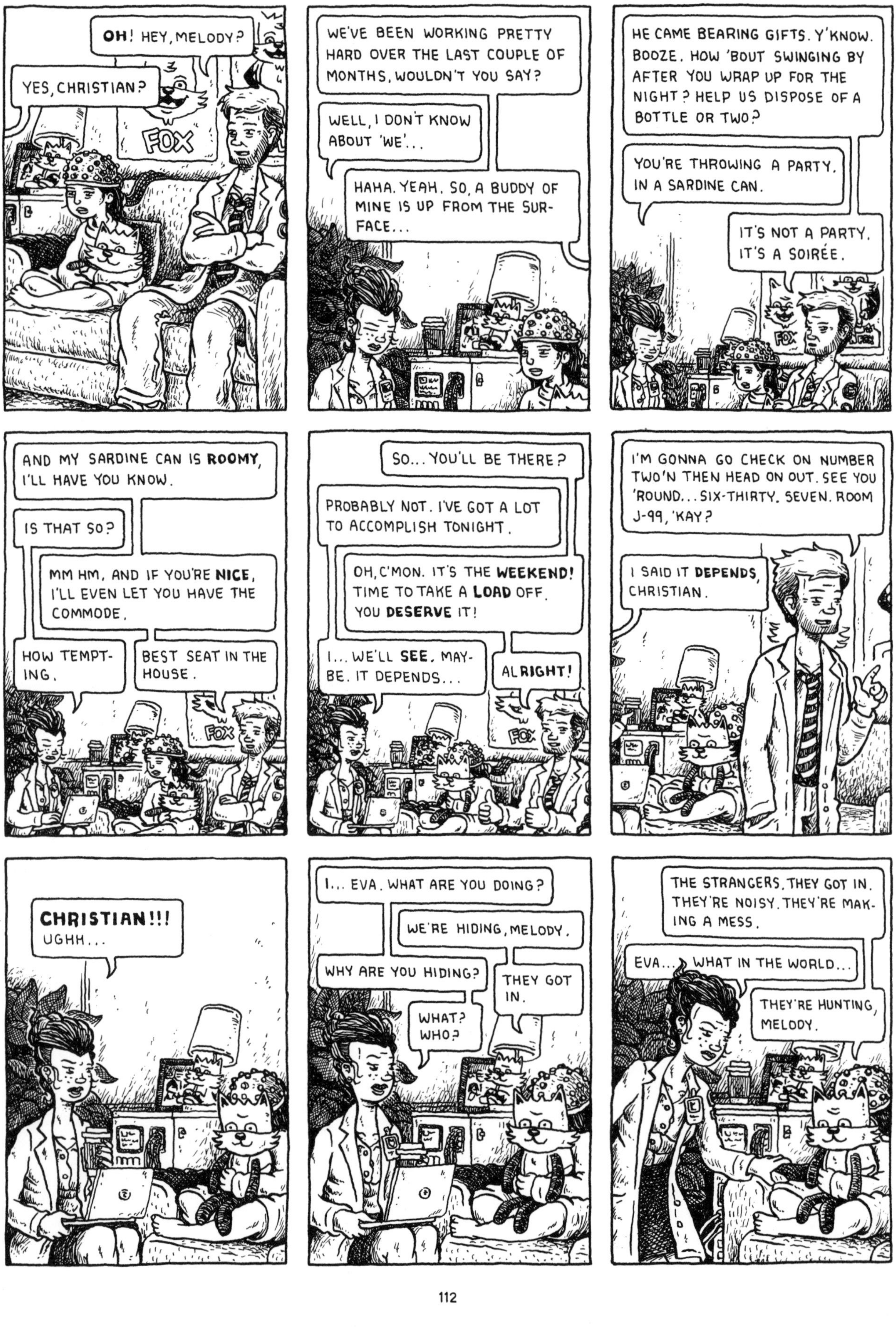
OH! HEY, MELODY?
YES, CHRISTIAN?
FOX
WE'VE BEEN WORKING PRETTY HARD OVER THE LAST COUPLE OF MONTHS, WOULDN'T YOU SAY?
WELL, I DON'T KNOW ABOUT 'WE'...
HAHA. YEAH. SO, A BUDDY OF MINE IS UP FROM THE SURFACE...
HE CAME BEARING GIFTS. Y'KNOW. BOOZE. HOW 'BOUT SWINGING BY AFTER YOU WRAP UP FOR THE NIGHT? HELP US DISPOSE OF A BOTTLE OR TWO?
YOU'RE THROWING A PARTY. IN A SARDINE CAN.
IT'S NOT A PARTY. IT'S A SOIRÉE.
AND MY SARDINE CAN IS **ROOMY**, I'LL HAVE YOU KNOW.
IS THAT SO?
MM HM, AND IF YOU'RE **NICE**, I'LL EVEN LET YOU HAVE THE COMMODE.
HOW TEMPTING.
BEST SEAT IN THE HOUSE.
SO... YOU'LL BE THERE?
PROBABLY NOT. I'VE GOT A LOT TO ACCOMPLISH TONIGHT.
OH, C'MON. IT'S THE **WEEKEND!** TIME TO TAKE A **LOAD** OFF. YOU **DESERVE** IT!
I... WE'LL **SEE**, MAYBE. IT DEPENDS...
AL**RIGHT!**
I'M GONNA GO CHECK ON NUMBER TWO'N THEN HEAD ON OUT. SEE YOU 'ROUND... SIX-THIRTY. SEVEN. ROOM J-99, 'KAY?
I SAID IT **DEPENDS**, CHRISTIAN.
CHRISTIAN!!! UGHH...
I... EVA. WHAT ARE YOU DOING?
WE'RE HIDING, MELODY.
WHY ARE YOU HIDING?
THEY GOT IN.
WHAT? WHO?
THE STRANGERS. THEY GOT IN. THEY'RE NOISY. THEY'RE MAKING A MESS.
EVA... WHAT IN THE WORLD...
THEY'RE HUNTING, MELODY.

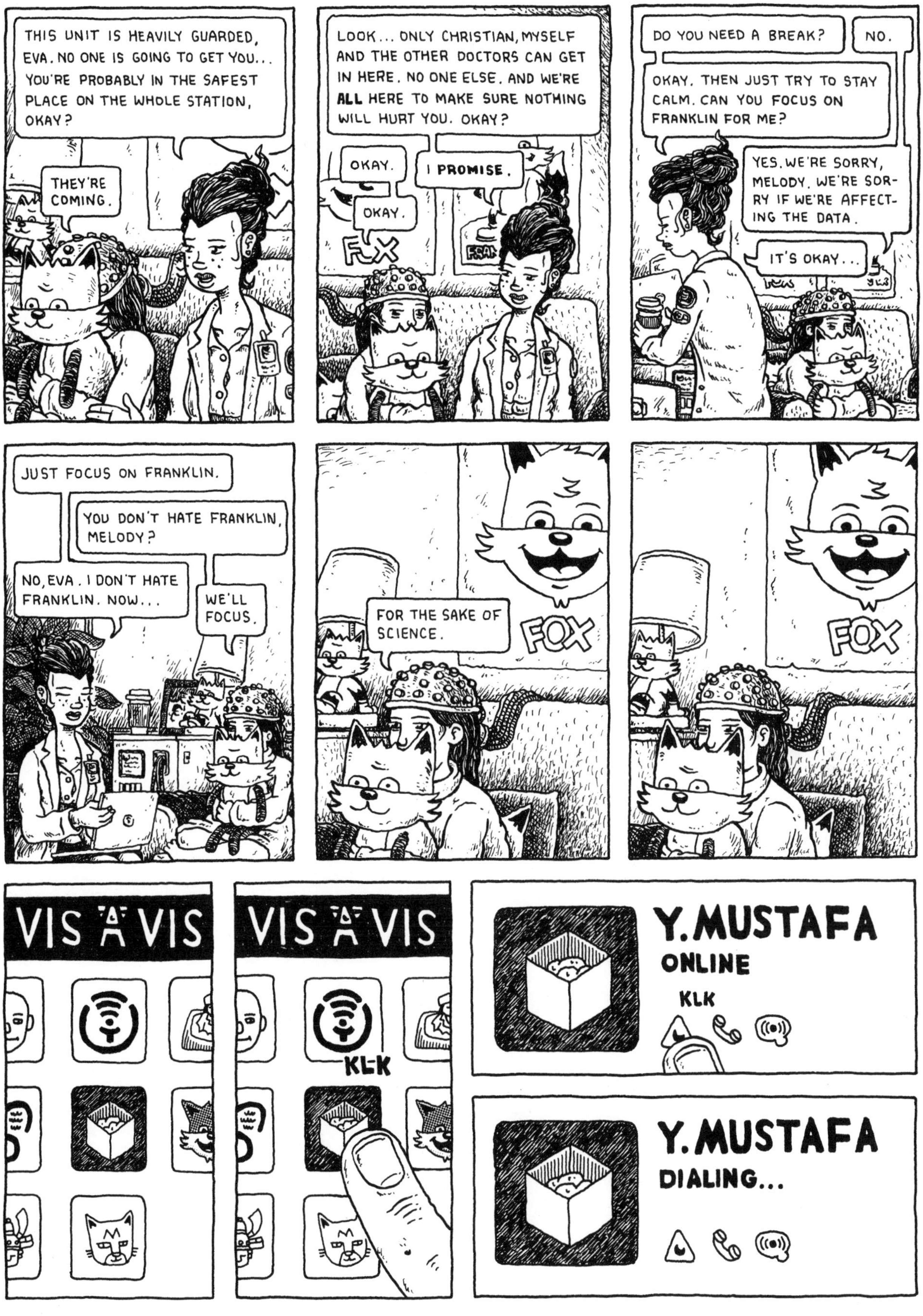
THIS UNIT IS HEAVILY GUARDED, EVA. NO ONE IS GOING TO GET YOU... YOU'RE PROBABLY IN THE SAFEST PLACE ON THE WHOLE STATION, OKAY?
THEY'RE COMING.
LOOK... ONLY CHRISTIAN, MYSELF AND THE OTHER DOCTORS CAN GET IN HERE. NO ONE ELSE. AND WE'RE ALL HERE TO MAKE SURE NOTHING WILL HURT YOU. OKAY?
OKAY.
OKAY.
I PROMISE.
FOX
DO YOU NEED A BREAK?
NO.
OKAY. THEN JUST TRY TO STAY CALM. CAN YOU FOCUS ON FRANKLIN FOR ME?
YES. WE'RE SORRY, MELODY. WE'RE SORRY IF WE'RE AFFECTING THE DATA.
IT'S OKAY...
JUST FOCUS ON FRANKLIN.
YOU DON'T HATE FRANKLIN, MELODY?
NO, EVA. I DON'T HATE FRANKLIN. NOW...
WE'LL FOCUS.
FOR THE SAKE OF SCIENCE.
FOX
FOX
VIS A VIS
VIS A VIS
KLK
Y. MUSTAFA
ONLINE
KLK
Y. MUSTAFA
DIALING...

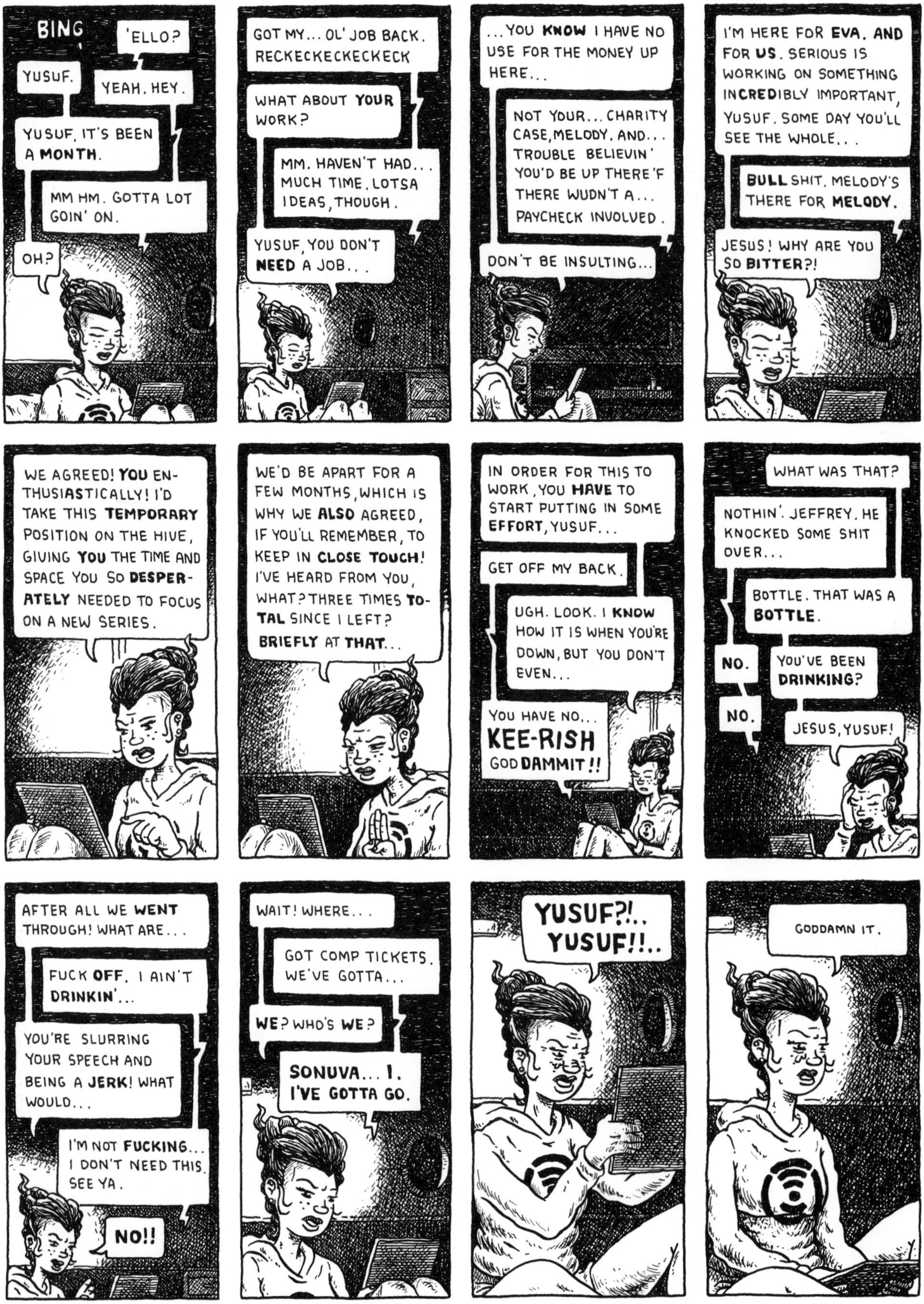
BING
'ELLO?
YUSUF.
YEAH. HEY.
YUSUF, IT'S BEEN A **MONTH**.
MM HM. GOTTA LOT GOIN' ON.
OH?
GOT MY... OL' JOB BACK. RECKECKECKECKECK
WHAT ABOUT **YOUR** WORK?
MM. HAVEN'T HAD... MUCH TIME. LOTSA IDEAS, THOUGH.
YUSUF, YOU DON'T **NEED** A JOB...
...YOU **KNOW** I HAVE NO USE FOR THE MONEY UP HERE...
NOT YOUR... CHARITY CASE, MELODY. AND... TROUBLE BELIEVIN' YOU'D BE UP THERE 'F THERE WUDN'T A... PAYCHECK INVOLVED.
DON'T BE INSULTING...
I'M HERE FOR **EVA**. **AND** FOR **US**. SERIOUS IS WORKING ON SOMETHING IN**CRED**IBLY IMPORTANT, YUSUF. SOME DAY YOU'LL SEE THE WHOLE...
BULLSHIT. MELODY'S THERE FOR **MELODY**.
JESUS! WHY ARE YOU SO **BITTER**?!
WE AGREED! **YOU** EN-THUSIA**S**TICALLY! I'D TAKE THIS **TEMPORARY** POSITION ON THE HIVE, GIVING **YOU** THE TIME AND SPACE YOU SO **DESPER-ATELY** NEEDED TO FOCUS ON A NEW SERIES.
WE'D BE APART FOR A FEW MONTHS, WHICH IS WHY WE **ALSO** AGREED, IF YOU'LL REMEMBER, TO KEEP IN **CLOSE TOUCH**! I'VE HEARD FROM YOU, WHAT? THREE TIMES **TO-TAL** SINCE I LEFT? **BRIEFLY** AT **THAT**...
IN ORDER FOR THIS TO WORK, YOU **HAVE** TO START PUTTING IN SOME **EFFORT**, YUSUF...
GET OFF MY BACK.
UGH. LOOK. I **KNOW** HOW IT IS WHEN YOU'RE DOWN, BUT YOU DON'T EVEN...
YOU HAVE NO... **KEE-RISH** GOD**DAMMIT**!!
WHAT WAS THAT?
NOTHIN'. JEFFREY. HE KNOCKED SOME SHIT OVER...
BOTTLE. THAT WAS A **BOTTLE**.
NO.
YOU'VE BEEN **DRINKING**?
NO.
JESUS, YUSUF!
AFTER ALL WE **WENT** THROUGH! WHAT ARE...
FUCK **OFF**. I AIN'T **DRINKIN'**...
YOU'RE SLURRING YOUR SPEECH AND BEING A **JERK**! WHAT WOULD...
I'M NOT **FUCKING**... I DON'T NEED THIS. SEE YA.
NO!!
WAIT! WHERE...
GOT COMP TICKETS. WE'VE GOTTA...
WE? WHO'S **WE**?
SONUVA... I. I'VE GOTTA GO.
YUSUF?!.. YUSUF!!..
GODDAMN IT.

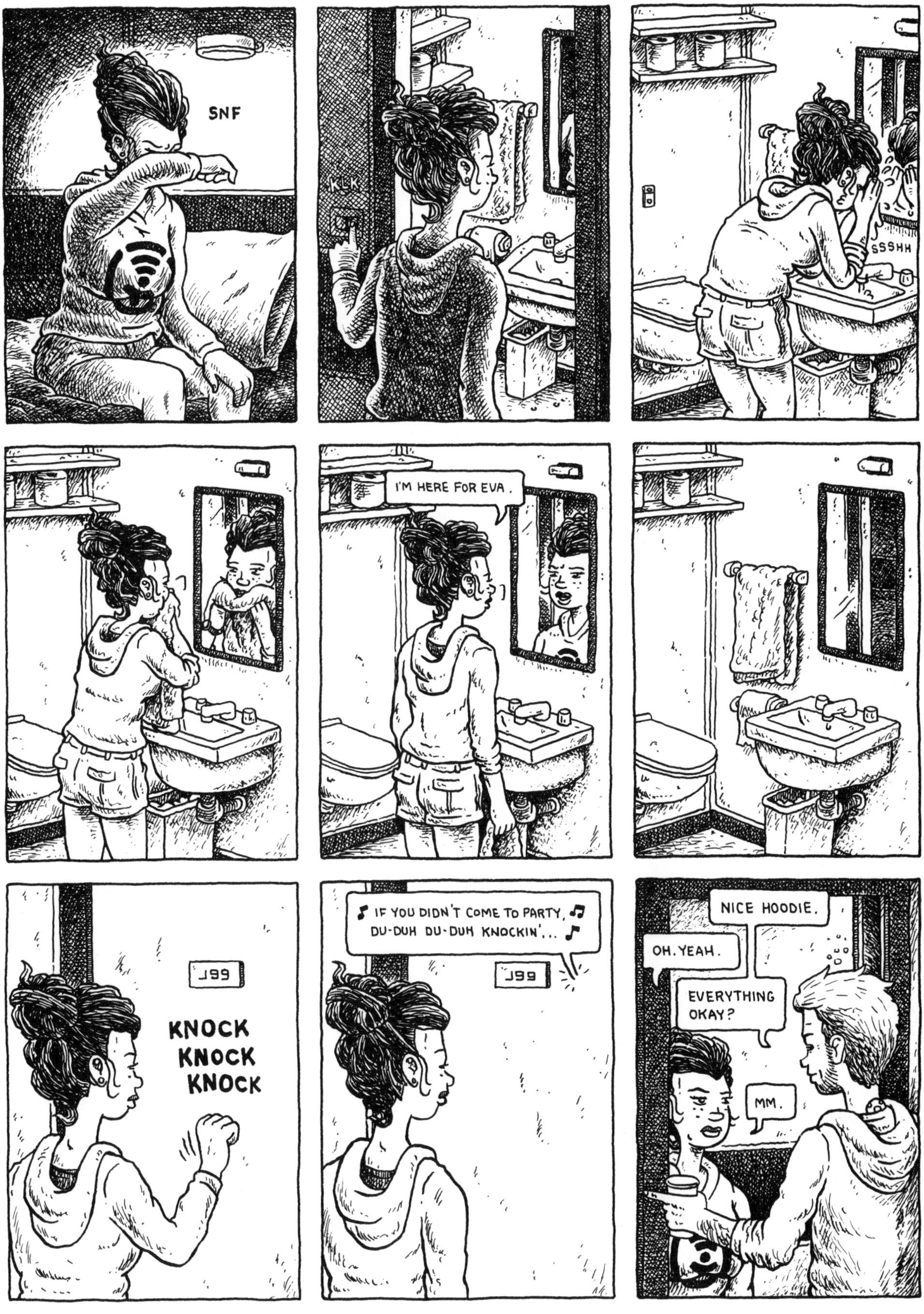
SNF
KLIK
SSSHH
I'M HERE FOR EVA.
KNOCK KNOCK KNOCK
IF YOU DIDN'T COME TO PARTY, DU-DUH DU-DUH KNOCKIN'...
NICE HOODIE.
OH. YEAH.
EVERYTHING OKAY?
MM.

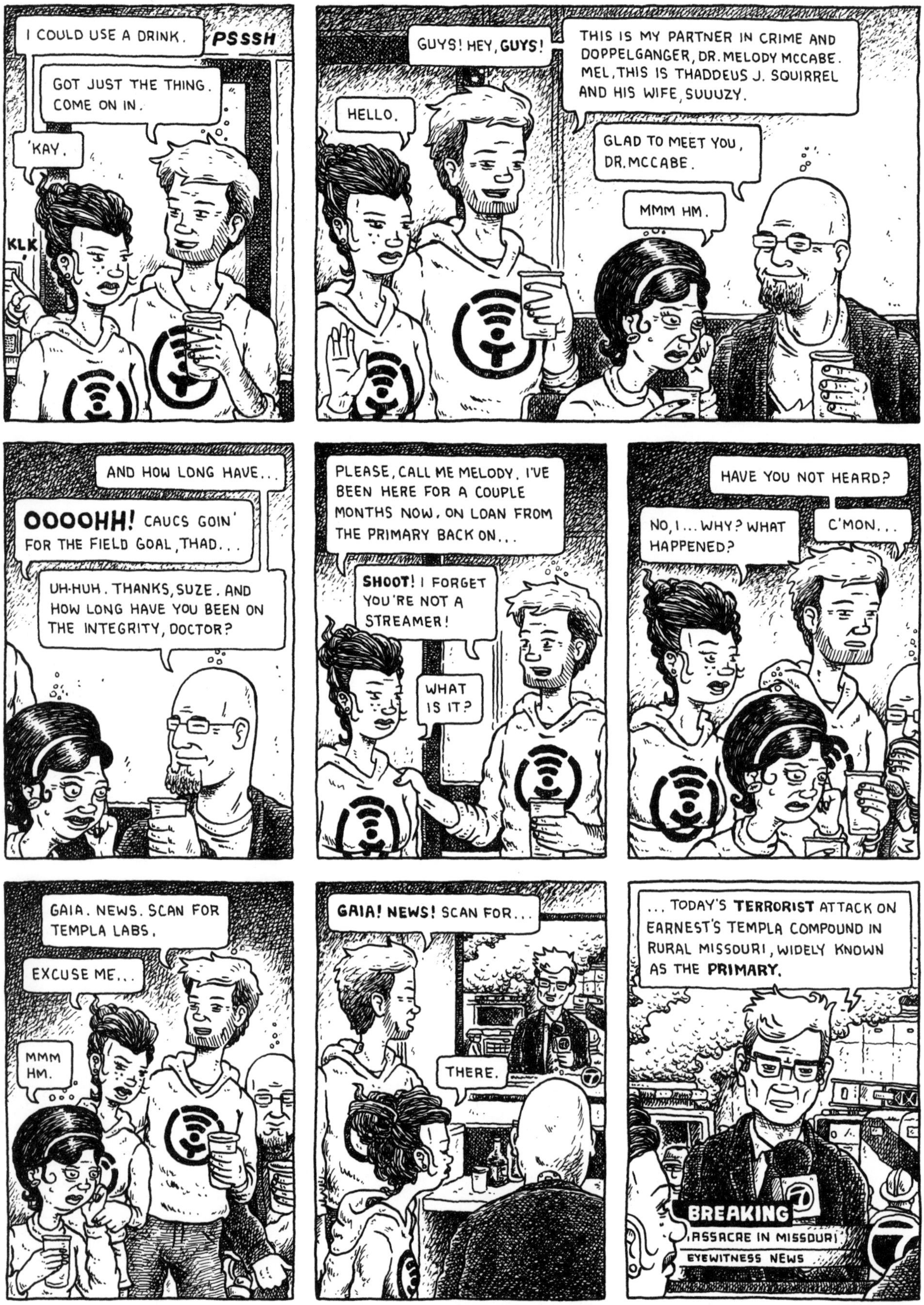

I COULD USE A DRINK.
PSSSH
GOT JUST THE THING. COME ON IN.
'KAY.
KLK
GUYS! HEY, **GUYS**!
HELLO.
THIS IS MY PARTNER IN CRIME AND DOPPELGANGER, DR. MELODY MCCABE. MEL, THIS IS THADDEUS J. SQUIRREL AND HIS WIFE, SUUUZY.
GLAD TO MEET YOU, DR. MCCABE.
MMM HM.
AND HOW LONG HAVE...
OOOOHH! CAUCS GOIN' FOR THE FIELD GOAL, THAD...
UH-HUH. THANKS, SUZE. AND HOW LONG HAVE YOU BEEN ON THE INTEGRITY, DOCTOR?
PLEASE, CALL ME MELODY. I'VE BEEN HERE FOR A COUPLE MONTHS NOW, ON LOAN FROM THE PRIMARY BACK ON...
SHOOT! I FORGET YOU'RE NOT A STREAMER!
WHAT IS IT?
HAVE YOU NOT HEARD?
NO, I... WHY? WHAT HAPPENED?
C'MON...
GAIA. NEWS. SCAN FOR TEMPLA LABS.
EXCUSE ME...
MMM HM.
GAIA! NEWS! SCAN FOR...
THERE.
... TODAY'S **TERRORIST** ATTACK ON EARNEST'S TEMPLA COMPOUND IN RURAL MISSOURI, WIDELY KNOWN AS THE **PRIMARY**.
BREAKING
ASSACRE IN MISSOURI
EYEWITNESS NEWS

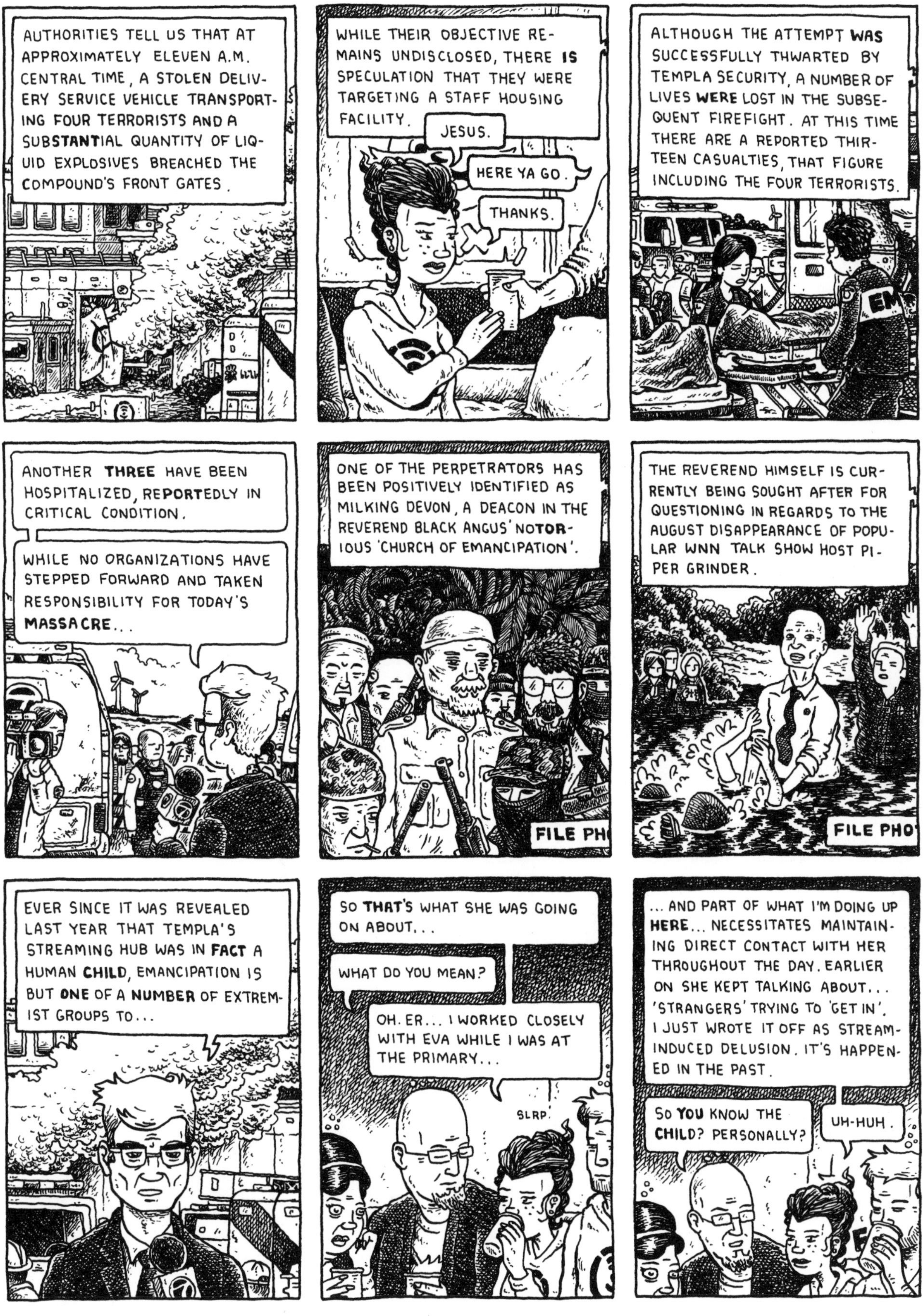
AUTHORITIES TELL US THAT AT APPROXIMATELY ELEVEN A.M. CENTRAL TIME, A STOLEN DELIVERY SERVICE VEHICLE TRANSPORTING FOUR TERRORISTS AND A SUBSTANTIAL QUANTITY OF LIQUID EXPLOSIVES BREACHED THE COMPOUND'S FRONT GATES.
WHILE THEIR OBJECTIVE REMAINS UNDISCLOSED, THERE IS SPECULATION THAT THEY WERE TARGETING A STAFF HOUSING FACILITY.
JESUS.
HERE YA GO.
THANKS.
ALTHOUGH THE ATTEMPT WAS SUCCESSFULLY THWARTED BY TEMPLA SECURITY, A NUMBER OF LIVES WERE LOST IN THE SUBSEQUENT FIREFIGHT. AT THIS TIME THERE ARE A REPORTED THIRTEEN CASUALTIES, THAT FIGURE INCLUDING THE FOUR TERRORISTS.
ANOTHER THREE HAVE BEEN HOSPITALIZED, REPORTEDLY IN CRITICAL CONDITION.
WHILE NO ORGANIZATIONS HAVE STEPPED FORWARD AND TAKEN RESPONSIBILITY FOR TODAY'S MASSACRE...
ONE OF THE PERPETRATORS HAS BEEN POSITIVELY IDENTIFIED AS MILKING DEVON, A DEACON IN THE REVEREND BLACK ANGUS' NOTORIOUS 'CHURCH OF EMANCIPATION'.
FILE PH
THE REVEREND HIMSELF IS CURRENTLY BEING SOUGHT AFTER FOR QUESTIONING IN REGARDS TO THE AUGUST DISAPPEARANCE OF POPULAR WNN TALK SHOW HOST PIPER GRINDER.
FILE PHO
EVER SINCE IT WAS REVEALED LAST YEAR THAT TEMPLA'S STREAMING HUB WAS IN FACT A HUMAN CHILD, EMANCIPATION IS BUT ONE OF A NUMBER OF EXTREMIST GROUPS TO...
SO THAT'S WHAT SHE WAS GOING ON ABOUT...
WHAT DO YOU MEAN?
OH. ER... I WORKED CLOSELY WITH EVA WHILE I WAS AT THE PRIMARY...
SLRP.
...AND PART OF WHAT I'M DOING UP HERE... NECESSITATES MAINTAINING DIRECT CONTACT WITH HER THROUGHOUT THE DAY. EARLIER ON SHE KEPT TALKING ABOUT... 'STRANGERS' TRYING TO 'GET IN'. I JUST WROTE IT OFF AS STREAM-INDUCED DELUSION. IT'S HAPPENED IN THE PAST.
SO YOU KNOW THE CHILD? PERSONALLY?
UH-HUH.

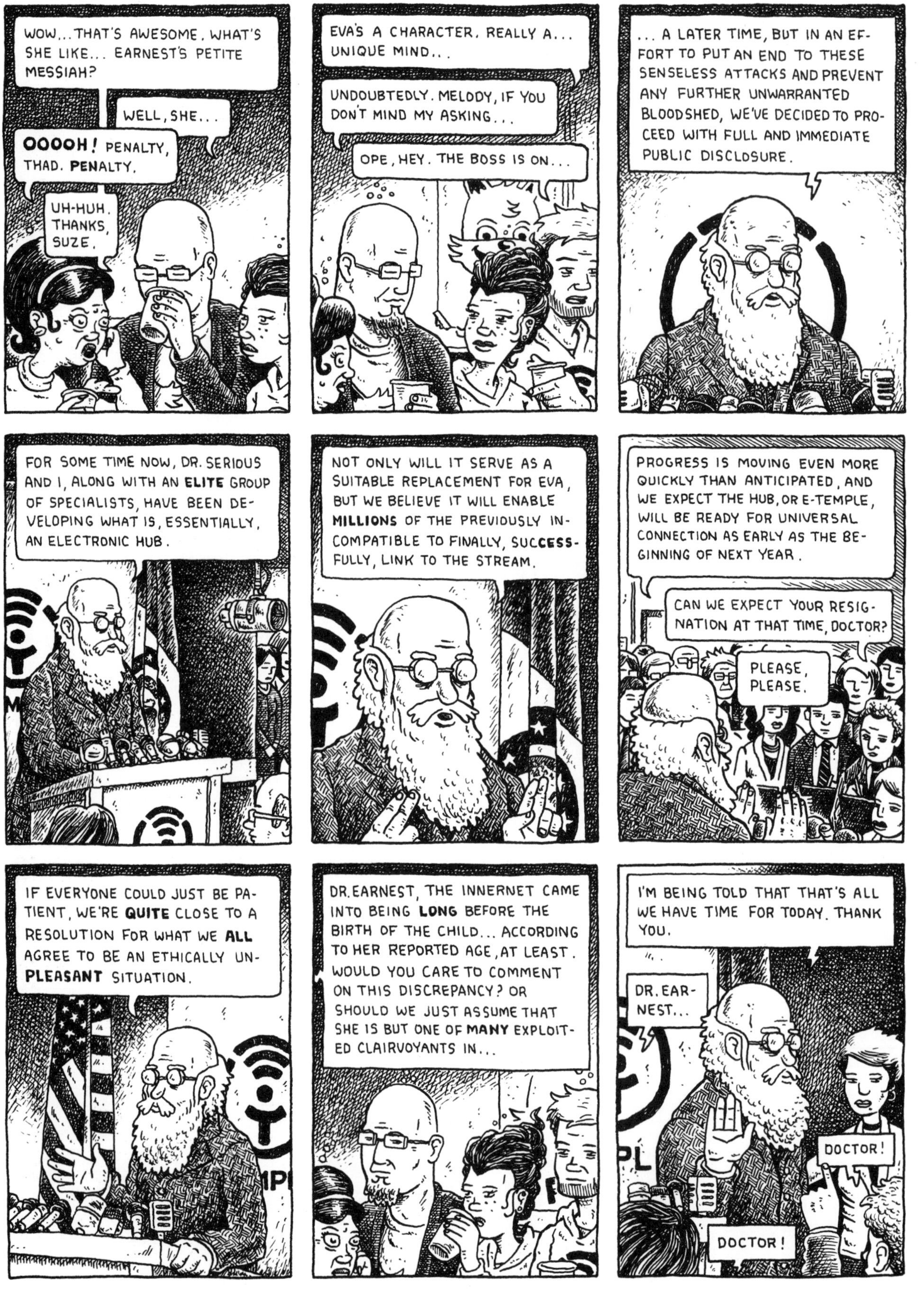

WOW... THAT'S AWESOME. WHAT'S SHE LIKE... EARNEST'S PETITE MESSIAH?
WELL, SHE...
OOOOH! PENALTY, THAD. PENALTY.
UH-HUH. THANKS, SUZE.
EVA'S A CHARACTER. REALLY A... UNIQUE MIND...
UNDOUBTEDLY. MELODY, IF YOU DON'T MIND MY ASKING...
OPE, HEY. THE BOSS IS ON...
... A LATER TIME, BUT IN AN EFFORT TO PUT AN END TO THESE SENSELESS ATTACKS AND PREVENT ANY FURTHER UNWARRANTED BLOODSHED, WE'VE DECIDED TO PROCEED WITH FULL AND IMMEDIATE PUBLIC DISCLOSURE.
FOR SOME TIME NOW, DR. SERIOUS AND I, ALONG WITH AN ELITE GROUP OF SPECIALISTS, HAVE BEEN DEVELOPING WHAT IS, ESSENTIALLY, AN ELECTRONIC HUB.
NOT ONLY WILL IT SERVE AS A SUITABLE REPLACEMENT FOR EVA, BUT WE BELIEVE IT WILL ENABLE MILLIONS OF THE PREVIOUSLY INCOMPATIBLE TO FINALLY, SUCCESSFULLY, LINK TO THE STREAM.
PROGRESS IS MOVING EVEN MORE QUICKLY THAN ANTICIPATED, AND WE EXPECT THE HUB, OR E-TEMPLE, WILL BE READY FOR UNIVERSAL CONNECTION AS EARLY AS THE BEGINNING OF NEXT YEAR.
CAN WE EXPECT YOUR RESIGNATION AT THAT TIME, DOCTOR?
PLEASE, PLEASE.
IF EVERYONE COULD JUST BE PATIENT, WE'RE QUITE CLOSE TO A RESOLUTION FOR WHAT WE ALL AGREE TO BE AN ETHICALLY UNPLEASANT SITUATION.
DR. EARNEST, THE INNERNET CAME INTO BEING LONG BEFORE THE BIRTH OF THE CHILD... ACCORDING TO HER REPORTED AGE, AT LEAST. WOULD YOU CARE TO COMMENT ON THIS DISCREPANCY? OR SHOULD WE JUST ASSUME THAT SHE IS BUT ONE OF MANY EXPLOITED CLAIRVOYANTS IN...
I'M BEING TOLD THAT THAT'S ALL WE HAVE TIME FOR TODAY. THANK YOU.
DR. EARNEST...
DOCTOR!
DOCTOR!

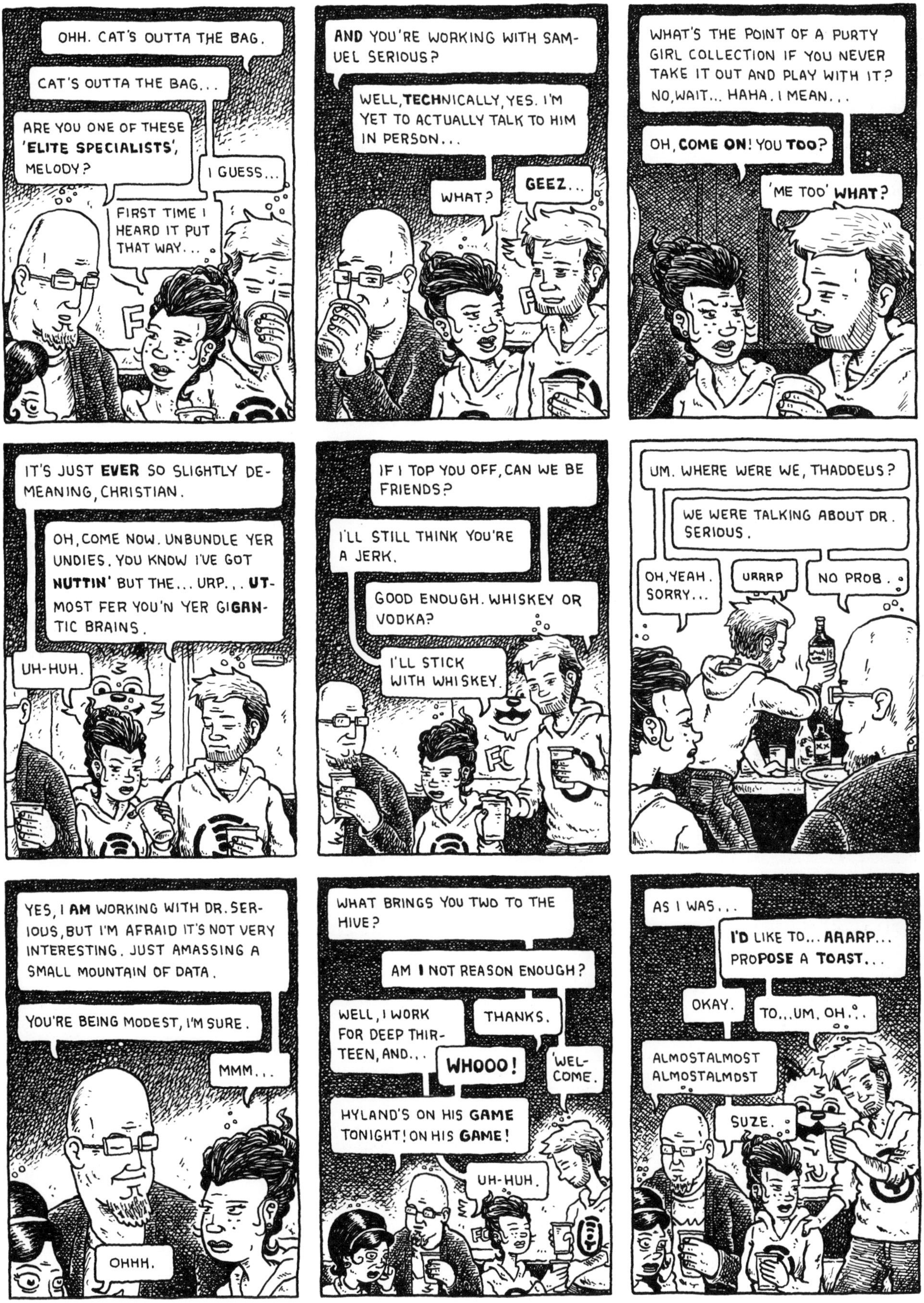
OHH. CAT'S OUTTA THE BAG.
CAT'S OUTTA THE BAG...
ARE YOU ONE OF THESE 'ELITE SPECIALISTS', MELODY?
I GUESS...
FIRST TIME I HEARD IT PUT THAT WAY...
AND YOU'RE WORKING WITH SAMUEL SERIOUS?
WELL, TECHNICALLY, YES. I'M YET TO ACTUALLY TALK TO HIM IN PERSON...
WHAT?
GEEZ...
WHAT'S THE POINT OF A PURTY GIRL COLLECTION IF YOU NEVER TAKE IT OUT AND PLAY WITH IT? NO, WAIT... HAHA. I MEAN...
OH, COME ON! YOU TOO?
'ME TOO' WHAT?
IT'S JUST EVER SO SLIGHTLY DEMEANING, CHRISTIAN.
OH, COME NOW. UNBUNDLE YER UNDIES. YOU KNOW I'VE GOT NUTTIN' BUT THE... URP... UTMOST FER YOU'N YER GIGANTIC BRAINS.
UH-HUH.
IF I TOP YOU OFF, CAN WE BE FRIENDS?
I'LL STILL THINK YOU'RE A JERK.
GOOD ENOUGH. WHISKEY OR VODKA?
I'LL STICK WITH WHISKEY.
UM. WHERE WERE WE, THADDEUS?
WE WERE TALKING ABOUT DR. SERIOUS.
OH, YEAH. SORRY...
URRRP
NO PROB.
YES, I AM WORKING WITH DR. SERIOUS, BUT I'M AFRAID IT'S NOT VERY INTERESTING. JUST AMASSING A SMALL MOUNTAIN OF DATA.
YOU'RE BEING MODEST, I'M SURE.
MMM...
OHHH.
WHAT BRINGS YOU TWO TO THE HIVE?
AM I NOT REASON ENOUGH?
WELL, I WORK FOR DEEP THIRTEEN, AND...
THANKS.
WHOOO!
'WELCOME.
HYLAND'S ON HIS GAME TONIGHT! ON HIS GAME!
UH-HUH.
AS I WAS...
I'D LIKE TO... AAARP... PROPOSE A TOAST...
OKAY.
TO...UM. OH.
ALMOSTALMOST ALMOSTALMOST
SUZE.

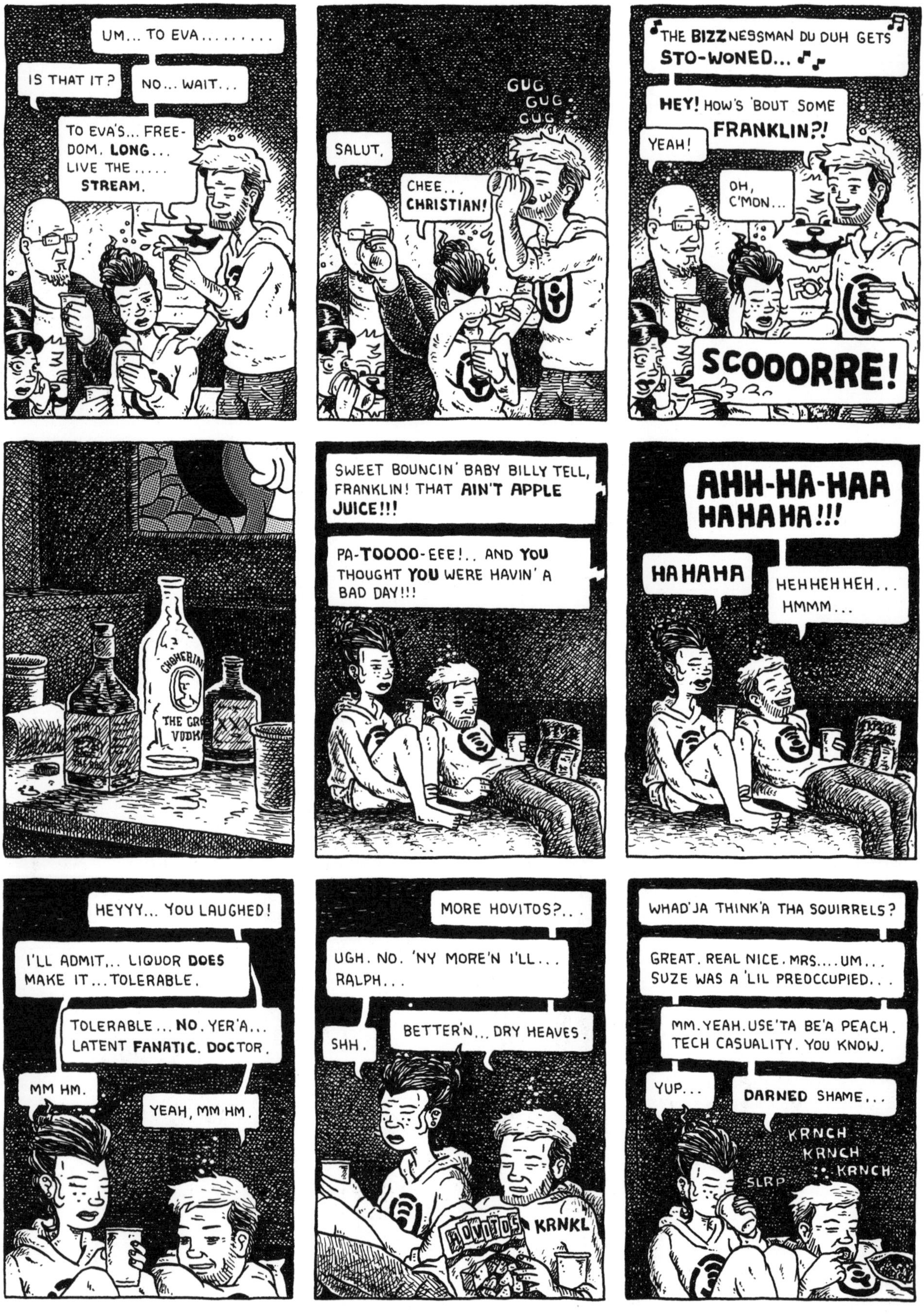
UM... TO EVA.........
IS THAT IT?
NO... WAIT...
TO EVA'S... FREE-DOM. LONG... LIVE THE..... STREAM.
GUG GUG GUG
SALUT.
CHEE... CHRISTIAN!
THE BIZZNESSMAN DU DUH GETS STO-WONED...
HEY! HOW'S 'BOUT SOME FRANKLIN?!
YEAH!
OH, C'MON...
SCOOORRE!
THE GR VODK
SWEET BOUNCIN' BABY BILLY TELL, FRANKLIN! THAT AIN'T APPLE JUICE!!!
PA-TOOOO-EEE!.. AND YOU THOUGHT YOU WERE HAVIN' A BAD DAY!!!
AHH-HA-HAA HAHAHA!!!
HAHAHA
HEHHEHHEH... HMMM...
HEYYY... YOU LAUGHED!
I'LL ADMIT,.. LIQUOR DOES MAKE IT... TOLERABLE.
TOLERABLE... NO. YER'A... LATENT FANATIC. DOCTOR.
MM HM.
YEAH, MM HM.
MORE HOVITOS?..
UGH. NO. 'NY MORE'N I'LL... RALPH...
SHH.
BETTER'N... DRY HEAVES.
HOVITOS
KRNKL
WHAD'JA THINK'A THA SQUIRRELS?
GREAT. REAL NICE. MRS.... UM... SUZE WAS A 'LIL PREOCCUPIED...
MM. YEAH. USE'TA BE'A PEACH. TECH CASUALITY. YOU KNOW.
YUP...
DARNED SHAME...
KRNCH KRNCH KRNCH
SLRP

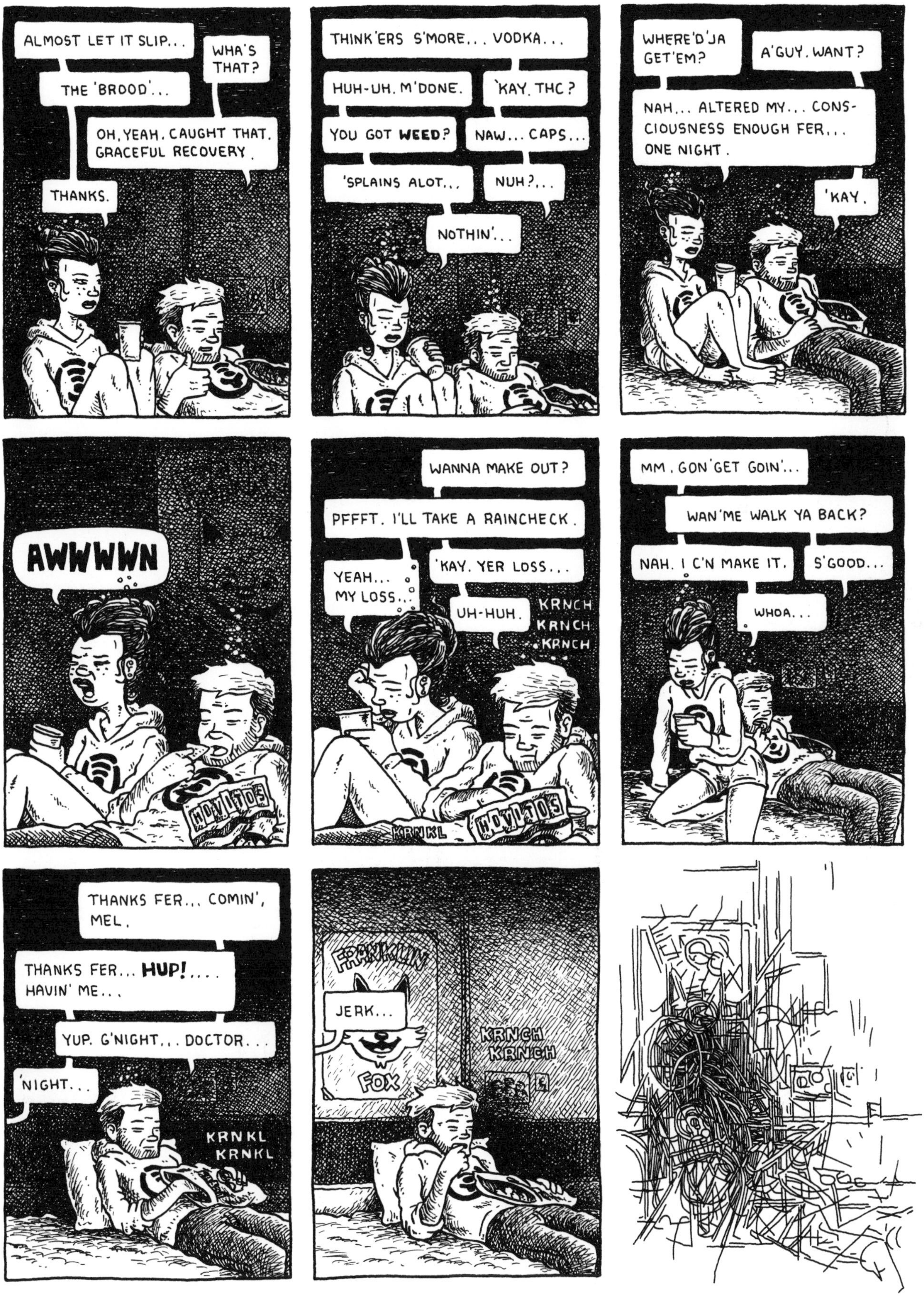
ALMOST LET IT SLIP...
WHA'S THAT?
THE 'BROOD'...
OH, YEAH. CAUGHT THAT. GRACEFUL RECOVERY.
THANKS.
THINK'ERS S'MORE... VODKA...
HUH-UH. M'DONE.
'KAY. THC?
YOU GOT **WEED**?
NAW... CAPS...
'SPLAINS ALOT...
NUH?...
NOTHIN'...
WHERE'D'JA GET'EM?
A'GUY. WANT?
NAH... ALTERED MY... CONSCIOUSNESS ENOUGH FER... ONE NIGHT.
'KAY.
AWWWWN
HOVITOS
WANNA MAKE OUT?
PFFFT. I'LL TAKE A RAINCHECK.
YEAH... MY LOSS...
'KAY. YER LOSS...
UH-HUH.
KRNCH KRNCH KRNCH
KRNKL
HOVITOS
MM. GON'GET GOIN'...
WAN'ME WALK YA BACK?
NAH. I C'N MAKE IT.
S'GOOD...
WHOA...
THANKS FER... COMIN', MEL.
THANKS FER... **HUP!**.... HAVIN' ME...
YUP. G'NIGHT... DOCTOR...
'NIGHT...
KRNKL KRNKL
FRANKLIN
JERK...
FOX
KRNCH KRNCH

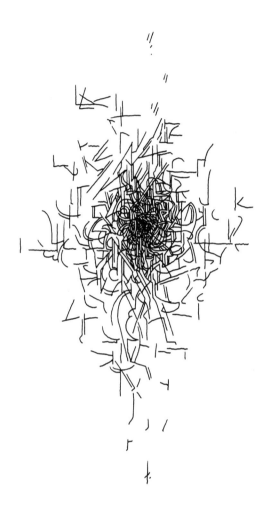

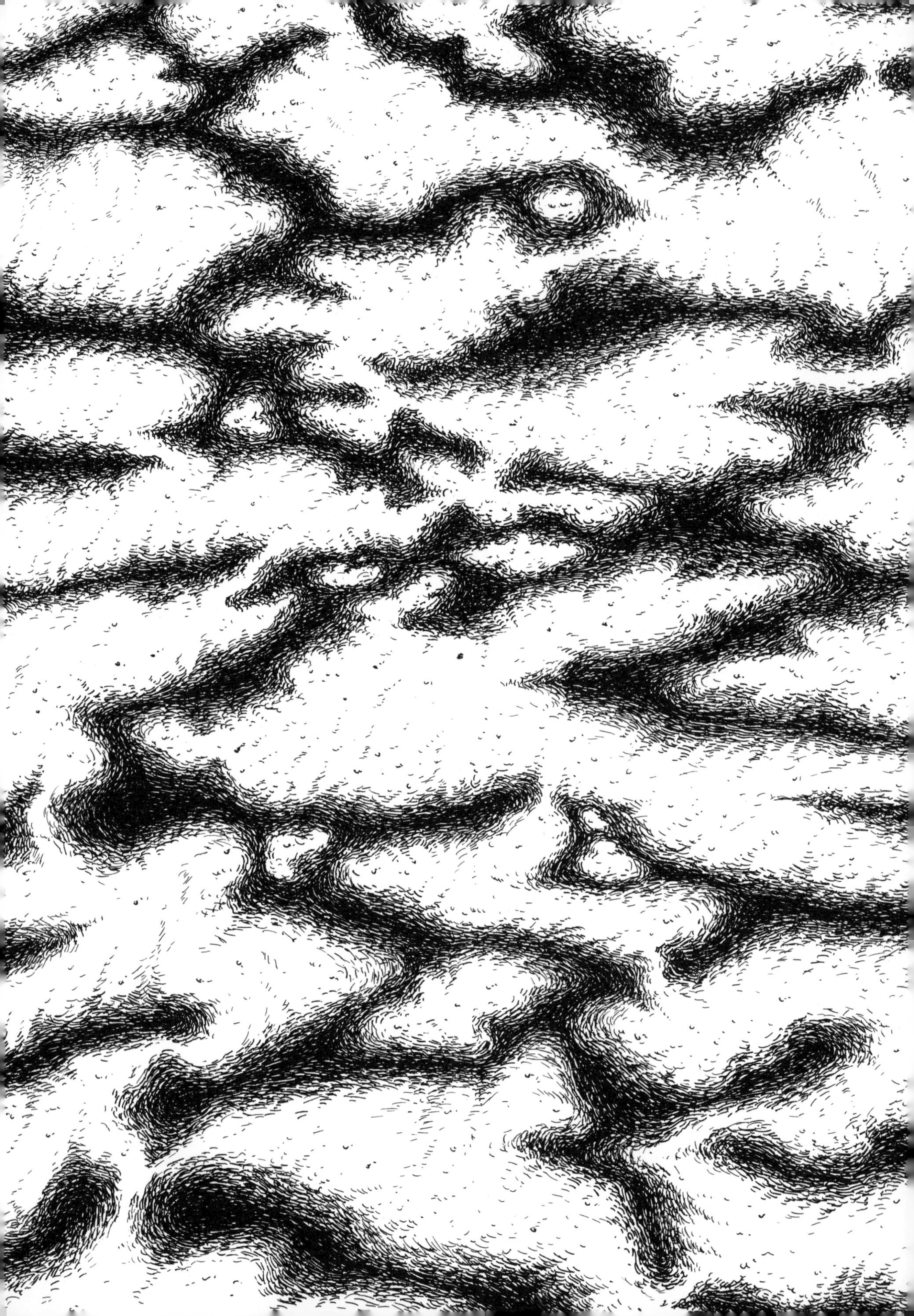

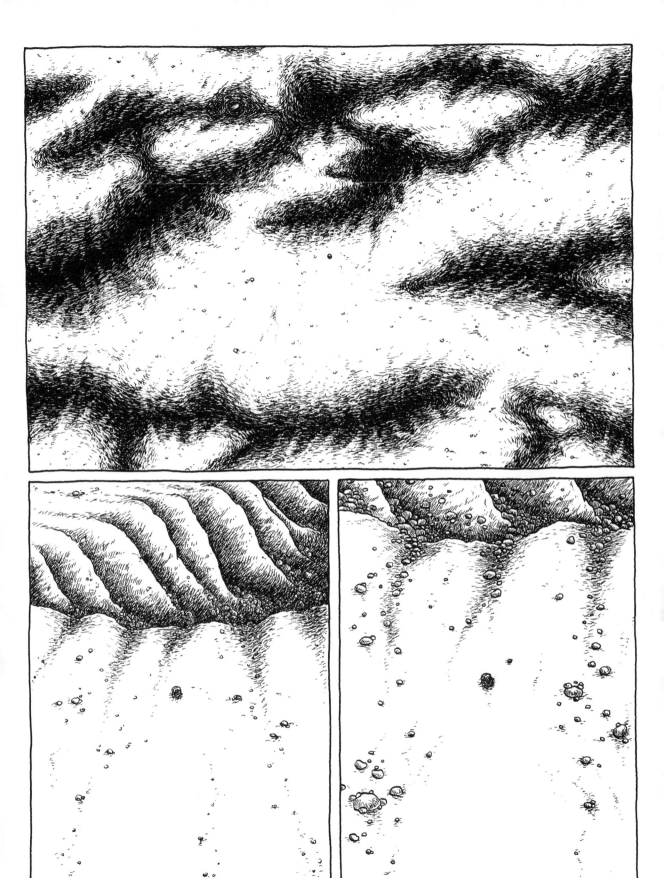

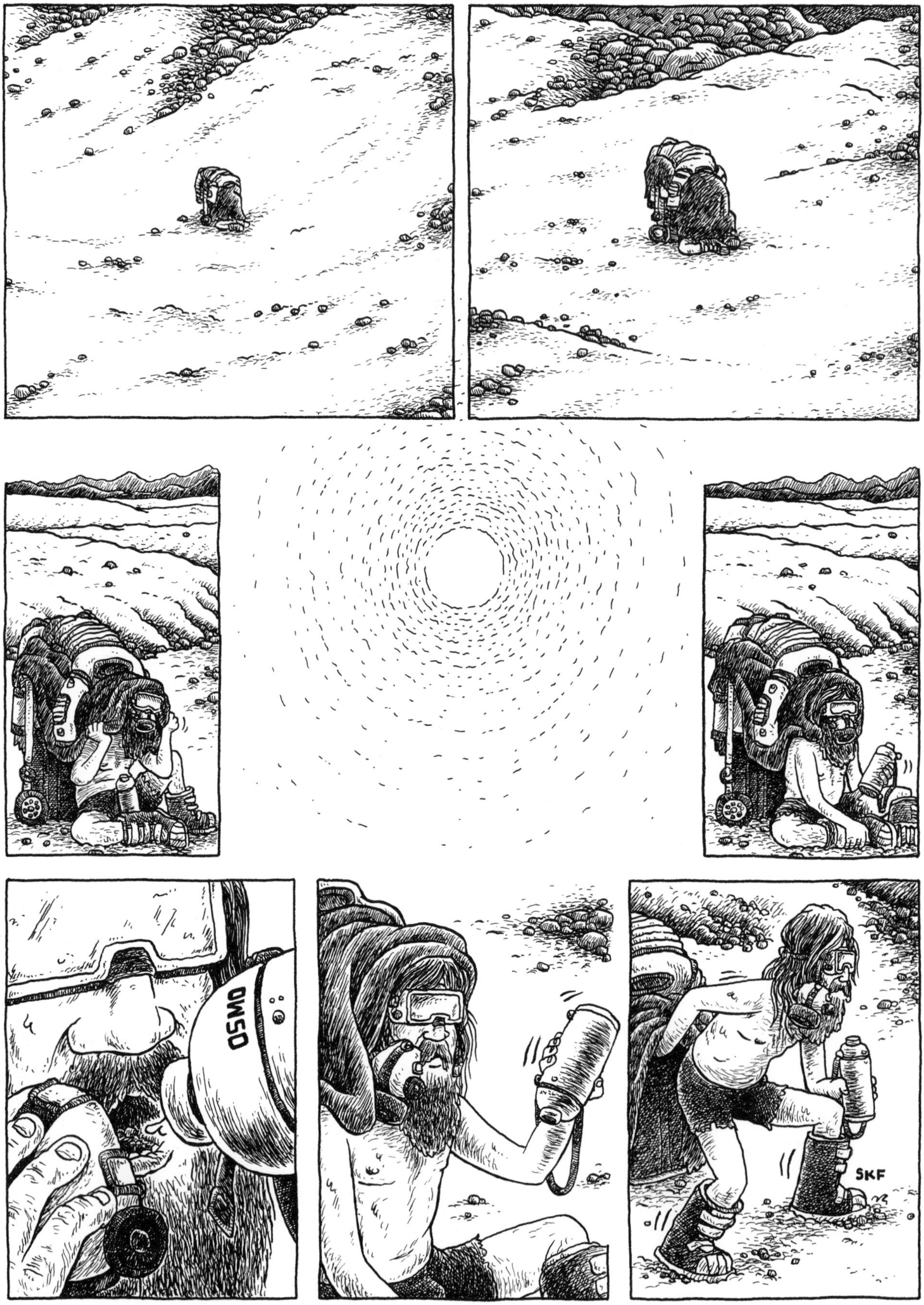
SKF

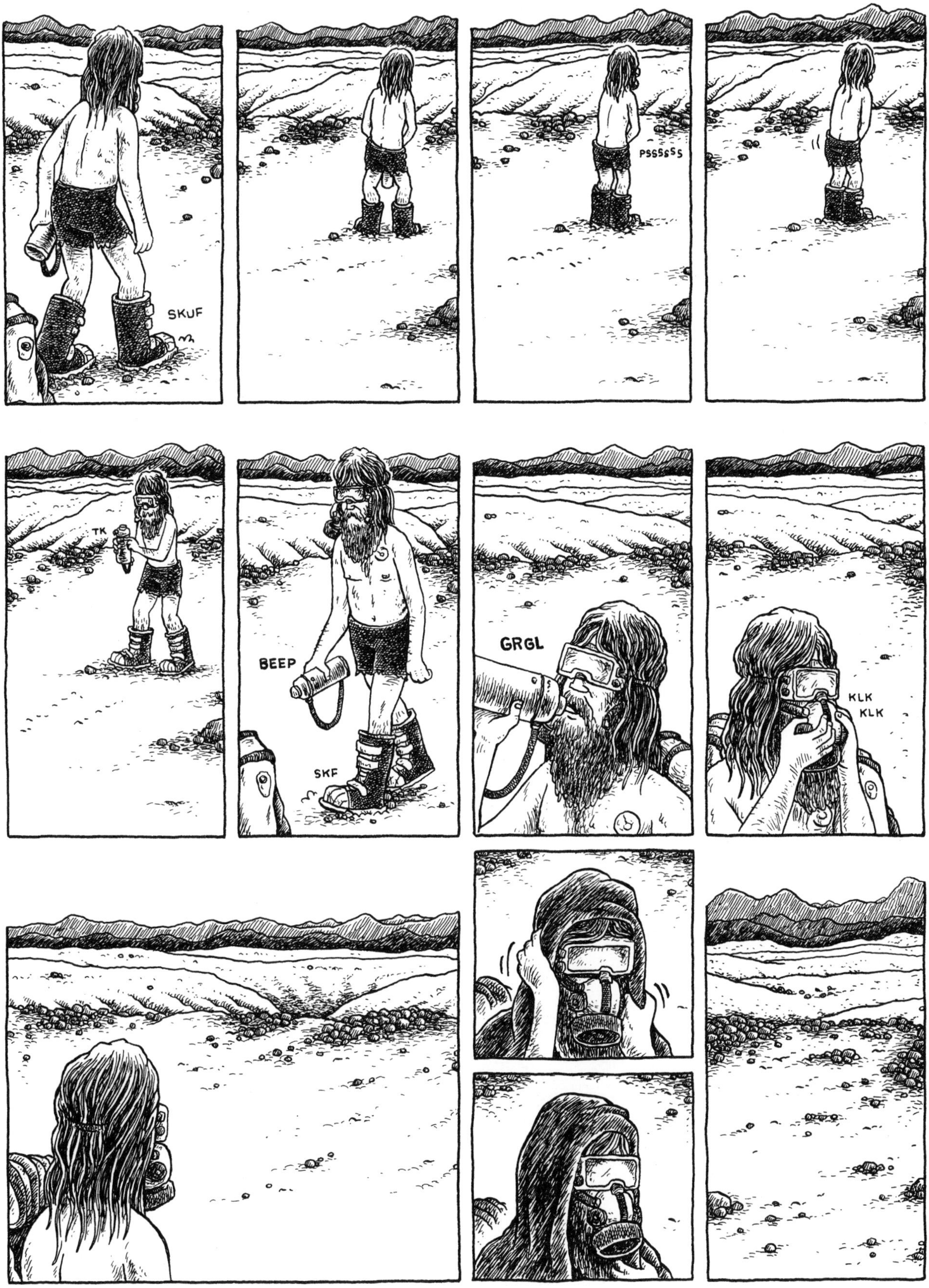
SKUF
PSSSSSS
TK
BEEP
SKF
GRGL
KLK
KLK

KF
KF KFF

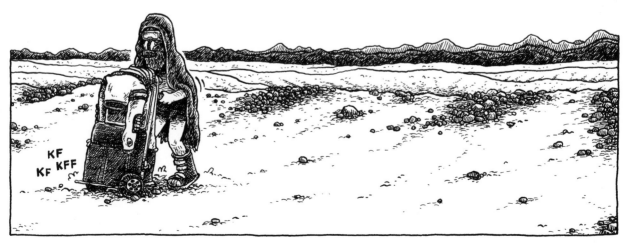

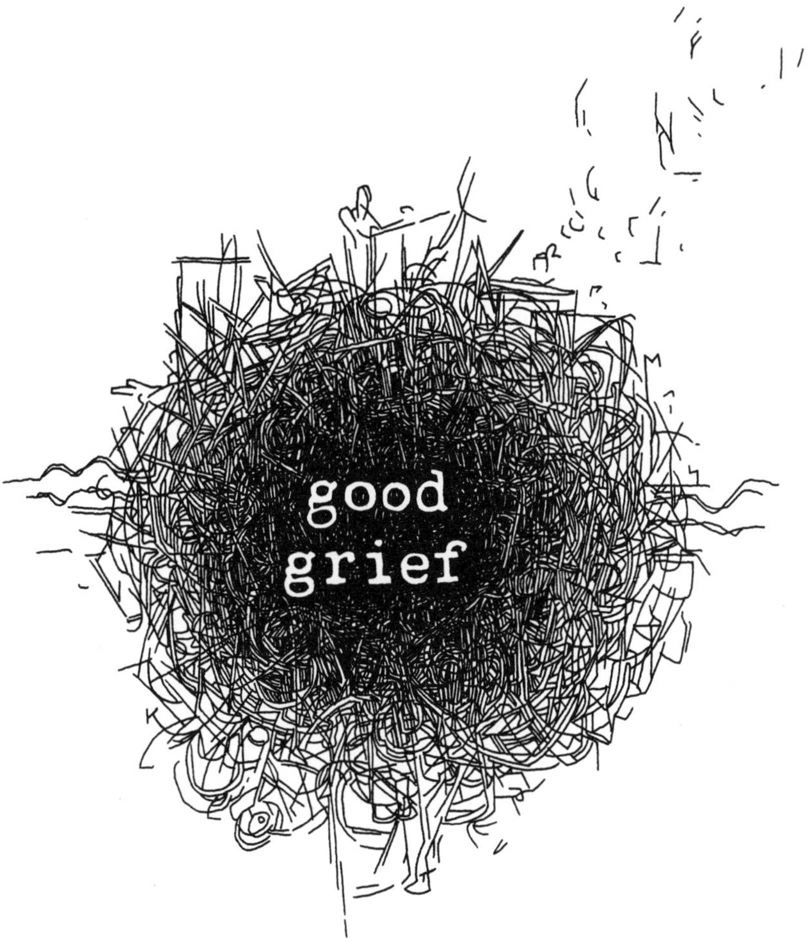
good
grief

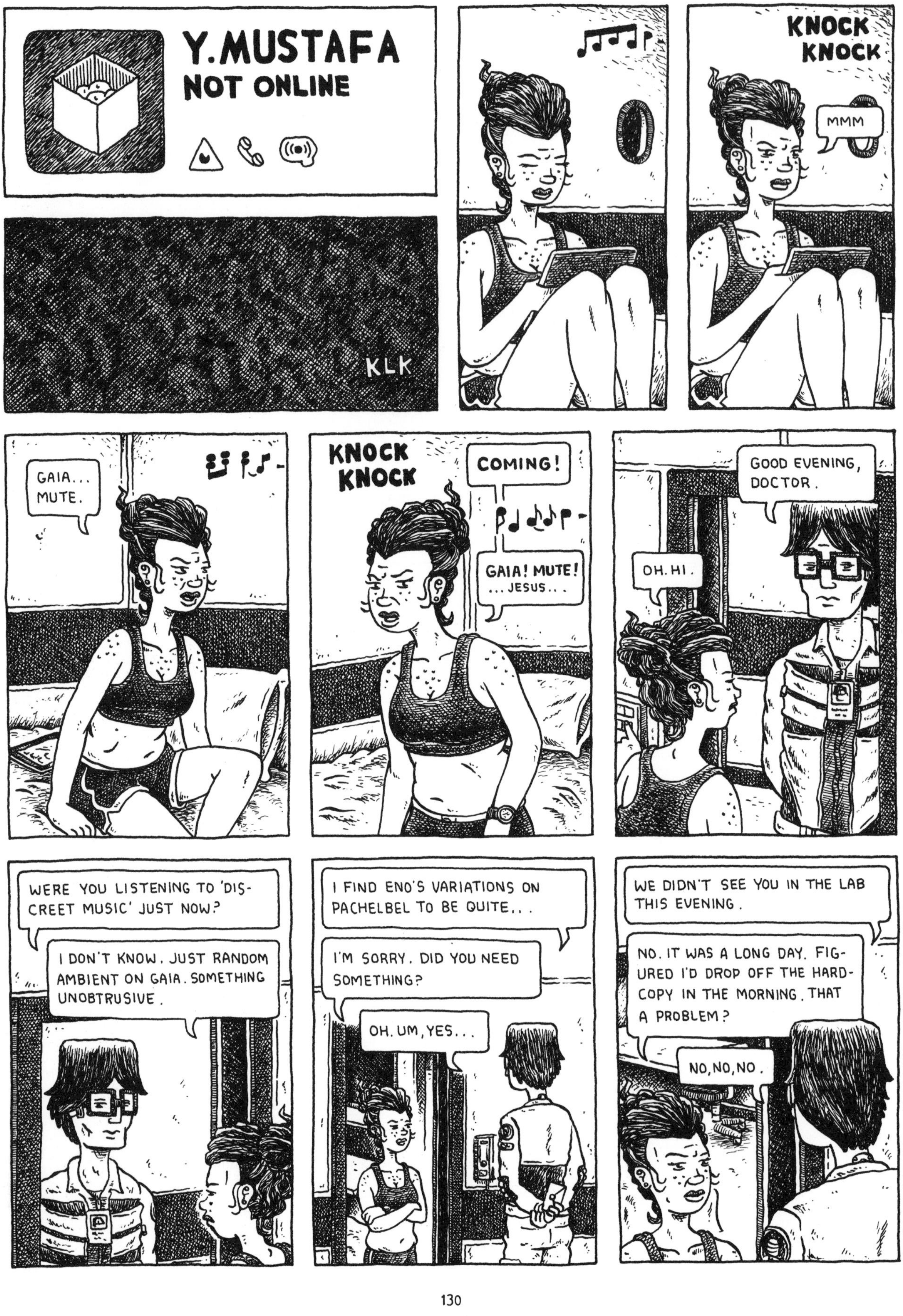
Y.MUSTAFA
NOT ONLINE
KLK
KNOCK KNOCK
MMM
GAIA... MUTE.
KNOCK KNOCK
COMING!
GAIA! MUTE! ...JESUS...
GOOD EVENING, DOCTOR.
OH. HI.
WERE YOU LISTENING TO 'DISCREET MUSIC' JUST NOW?
I DON'T KNOW. JUST RANDOM AMBIENT ON GAIA. SOMETHING UNOBTRUSIVE.
I FIND ENO'S VARIATIONS ON PACHELBEL TO BE QUITE...
I'M SORRY. DID YOU NEED SOMETHING?
OH. UM, YES...
WE DIDN'T SEE YOU IN THE LAB THIS EVENING.
NO. IT WAS A LONG DAY. FIGURED I'D DROP OFF THE HARDCOPY IN THE MORNING. THAT A PROBLEM?
NO, NO, NO.

DR. SERIOUS REQUESTED THAT I RELAY AN INVITATION TO YOU.

INVITATION TO WHAT?..

TOMORROW AT 0900. RATHER THAN REPORT TO THE LABS, HE WOULD LIKE ALL STAFF TO MEET AT THE WHEELER GATE.

THERE'S TO BE AN INAUGURAL CELEBRATION. REFRESHMENTS, PRESS, PHOTO OPS, ET CETERA.

I DON'T HAVE ANY INAUGURATION-APPROPRIATE CLOTHING WITH ME.

LAB DRESS IS ACCEPTABLE. IT'S ADDRESSED IN THE INVITATION.

OKAY...

I'LL JUST READ THE INVITE, THEN. SEE YOU IN THE MORNING.

OH. EXCUSE ME... DOCTOR?

YES?

I WAS WONDERING IF YOU'D CARE TO ACCOMPANY ME TO THE OBSERVATION LOUNGE ON SATURDAY? IF YOU FANCY AMBIENT MUSIC, CAMDEN HAS COMPOSED A NEW PIECE SPECIFICALLY FOR...

NO. THANKS.

OH.

WELL, PERHAPS THIS EVENING? DO YOU WATCH FRANKLIN? IF SO, WE COULD...

MR. IOTA. NO.

AS A RULE, I DO NOT FRATERNIZE WITH CO-WORKERS OUTSIDE OF THE LAB. OKAY? NOTHING PERSONAL.

I SEE. IN THAT CASE, I SHOULD BE GOING.

YEAH...

GOOD NIGHT, DOC ☼

PSSSH

JESUS CHRIST...

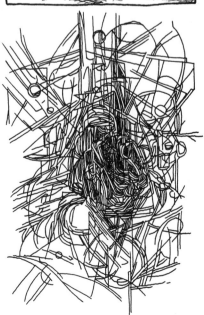

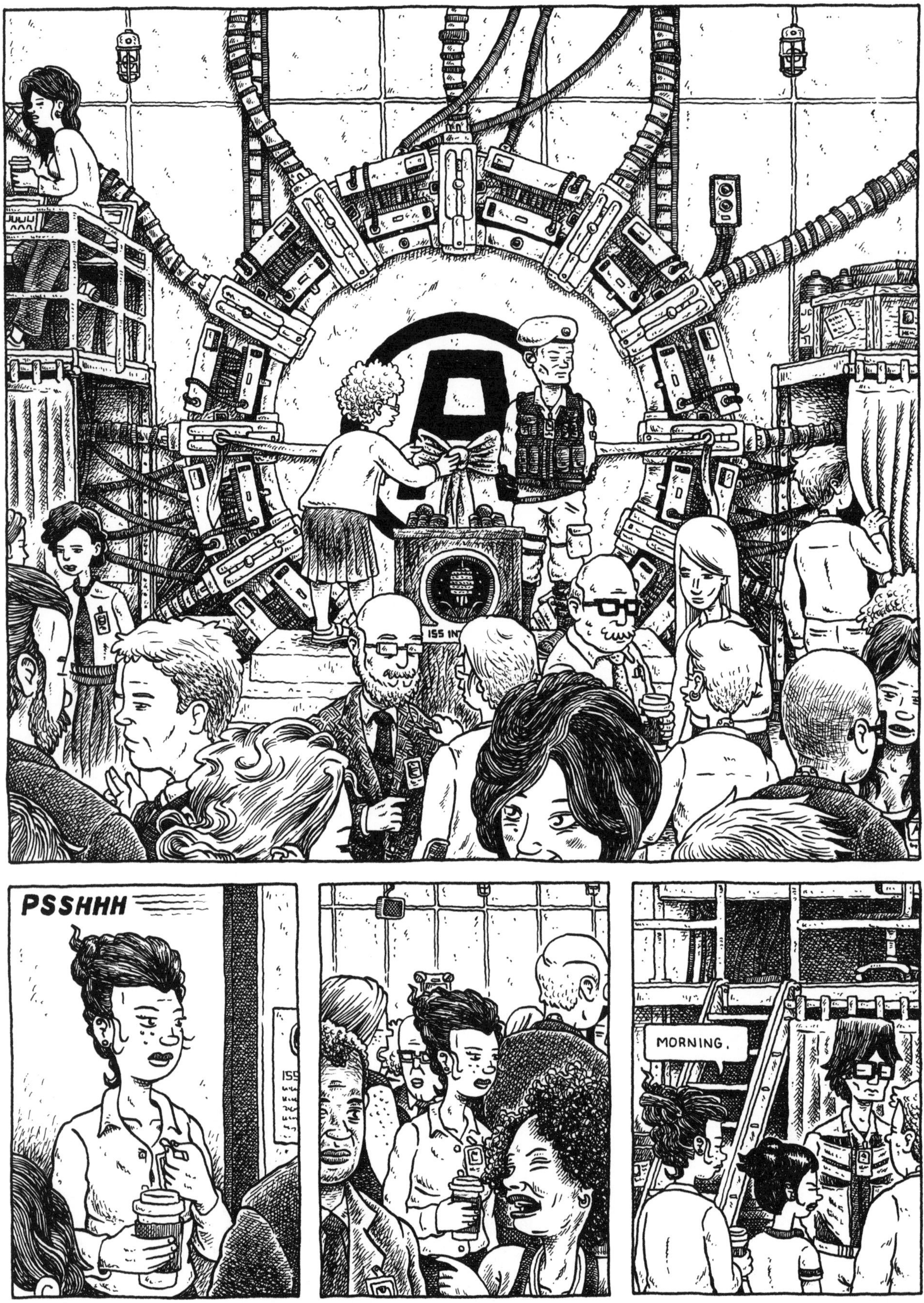
PSSHHH
MORNING.

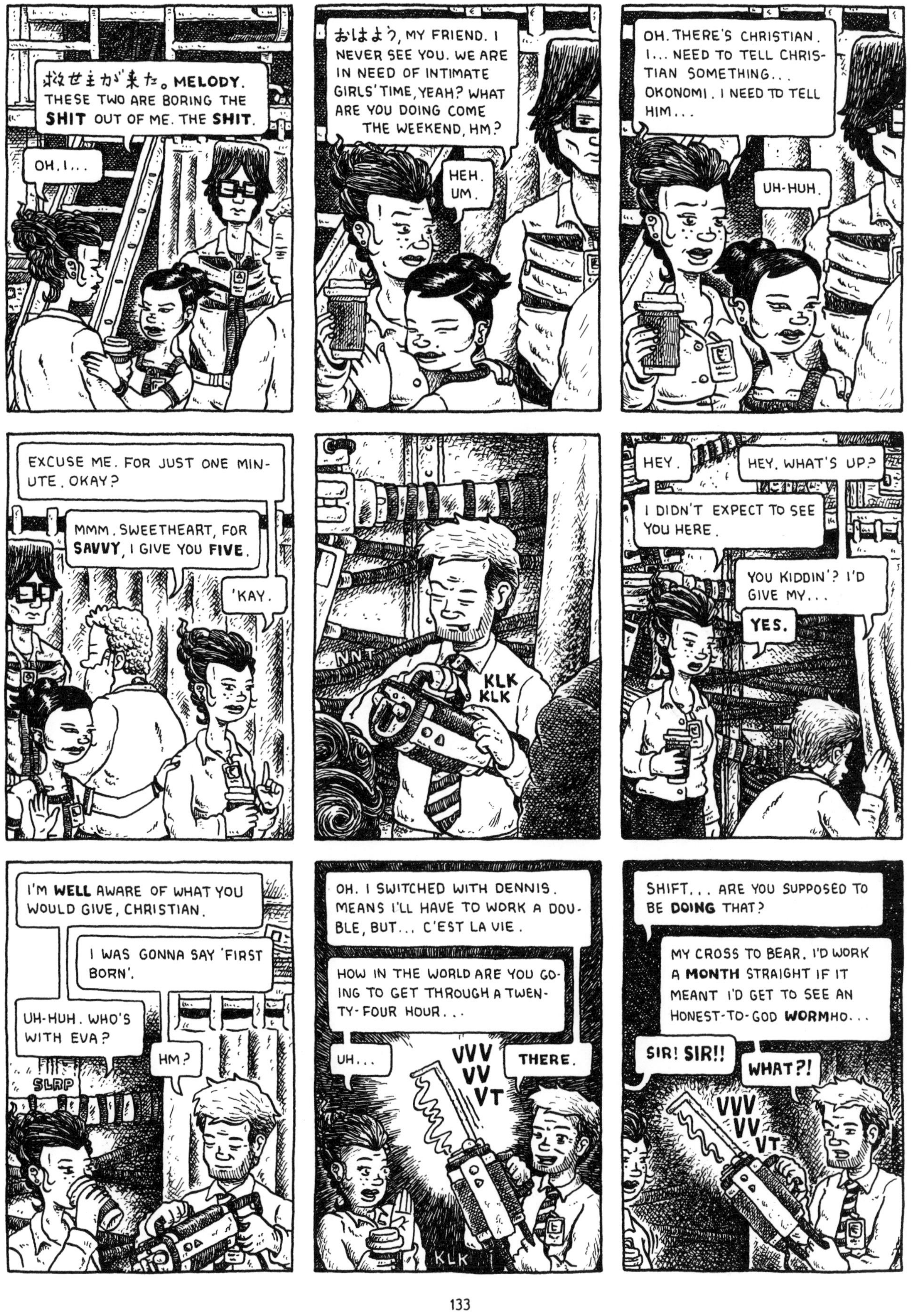
救世主が来た。MELODY. THESE TWO ARE BORING THE SHIT OUT OF ME. THE SHIT.
OH, I...
おはよう, MY FRIEND. I NEVER SEE YOU. WE ARE IN NEED OF INTIMATE GIRLS' TIME, YEAH? WHAT ARE YOU DOING COME THE WEEKEND, HM?
HEH. UM.
OH. THERE'S CHRISTIAN. I... NEED TO TELL CHRISTIAN SOMETHING... OKONOMI. I NEED TO TELL HIM...
UH-HUH.
EXCUSE ME. FOR JUST ONE MINUTE. OKAY?
MMM. SWEETHEART, FOR SAVVY, I GIVE YOU FIVE.
'KAY.
NNT
KLK KLK
HEY.
HEY. WHAT'S UP?
I DIDN'T EXPECT TO SEE YOU HERE.
YOU KIDDIN'? I'D GIVE MY...
YES.
I'M WELL AWARE OF WHAT YOU WOULD GIVE, CHRISTIAN.
I WAS GONNA SAY 'FIRST BORN'.
UH-HUH. WHO'S WITH EVA?
HM?
SLRP
OH. I SWITCHED WITH DENNIS. MEANS I'LL HAVE TO WORK A DOUBLE, BUT... C'EST LA VIE.
HOW IN THE WORLD ARE YOU GOING TO GET THROUGH A TWENTY-FOUR HOUR...
UH...
THERE.
VVV VV VT
KLK
SHIFT... ARE YOU SUPPOSED TO BE DOING THAT?
MY CROSS TO BEAR. I'D WORK A MONTH STRAIGHT IF IT MEANT I'D GET TO SEE AN HONEST-TO-GOD WORMHO...
SIR! SIR!!
WHAT?!
VVV VV VT

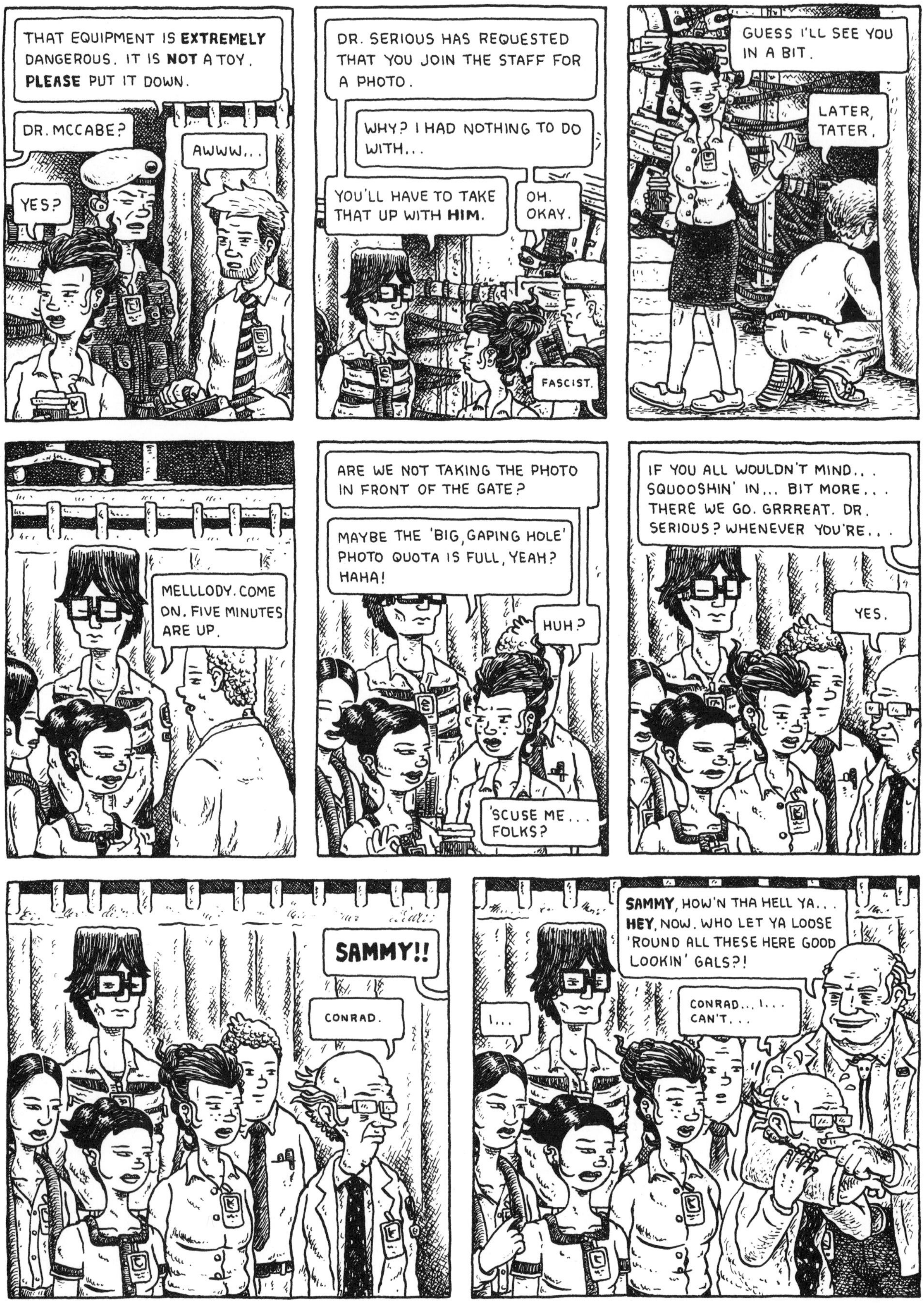

THAT EQUIPMENT IS **EXTREMELY** DANGEROUS. IT IS **NOT** A TOY. **PLEASE** PUT IT DOWN.
DR. MCCABE?
AWWW...
YES?
DR. SERIOUS HAS REQUESTED THAT YOU JOIN THE STAFF FOR A PHOTO.
WHY? I HAD NOTHING TO DO WITH...
YOU'LL HAVE TO TAKE THAT UP WITH **HIM**.
OH. OKAY.
FASCIST.
GUESS I'LL SEE YOU IN A BIT.
LATER, TATER.
MELLLODY. COME ON. FIVE MINUTES ARE UP.
ARE WE NOT TAKING THE PHOTO IN FRONT OF THE GATE?
MAYBE THE 'BIG, GAPING HOLE' PHOTO QUOTA IS FULL, YEAH? HAHA!
HUH?
'SCUSE ME... FOLKS?
IF YOU ALL WOULDN'T MIND... SQUOOSHIN' IN... BIT MORE... THERE WE GO. GRRREAT. DR. SERIOUS? WHENEVER YOU'RE...
YES.
SAMMY!!
CONRAD.
SAMMY, HOW'N THA HELL YA... **HEY**, NOW. WHO LET YA LOOSE 'ROUND ALL THESE HERE GOOD LOOKIN' GALS?!
I...
CONRAD... I... CAN'T...

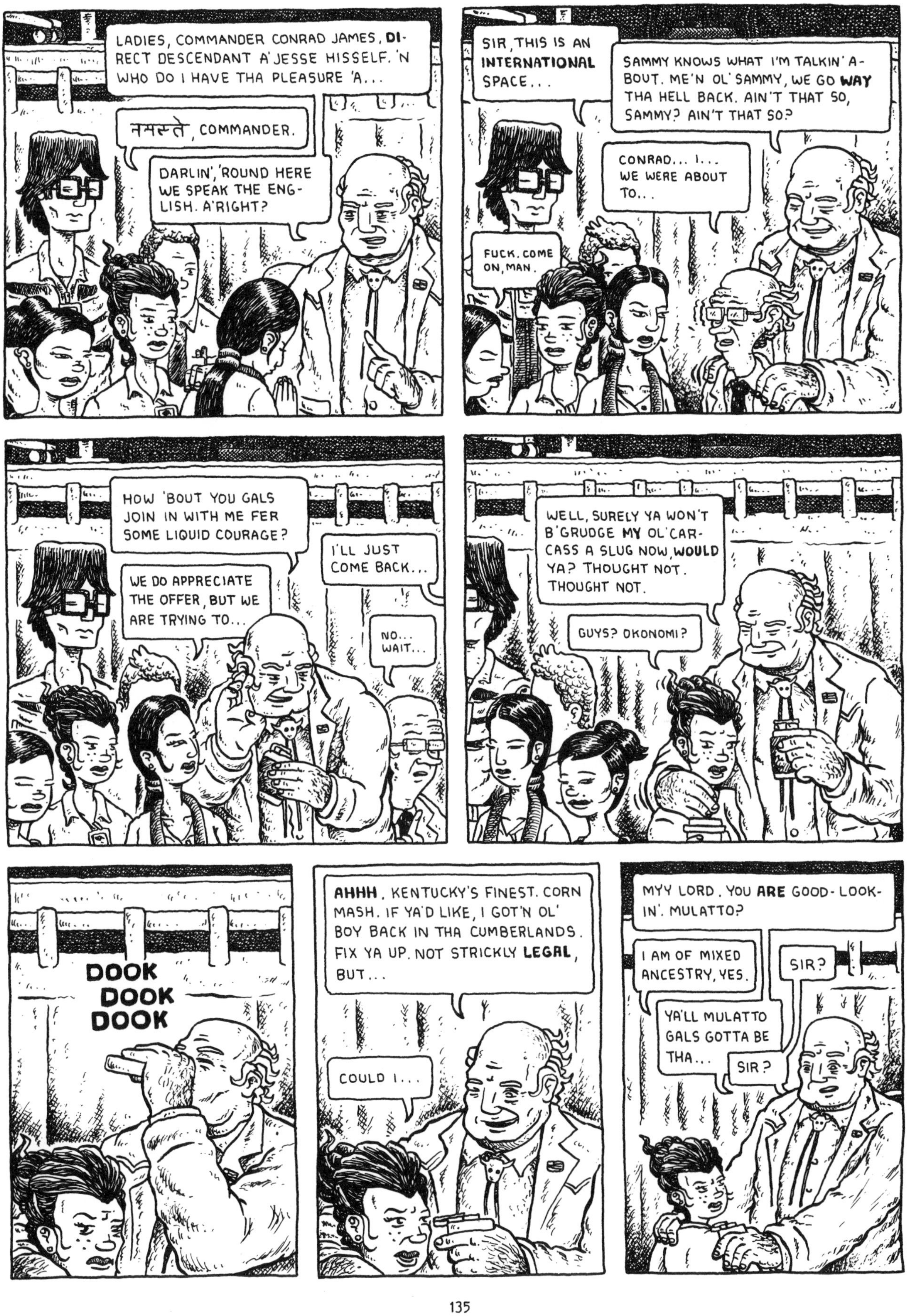
LADIES, COMMANDER CONRAD JAMES, DIRECT DESCENDANT A' JESSE HISSELF. 'N WHO DO I HAVE THA PLEASURE 'A...
नमस्ते, COMMANDER.
DARLIN', 'ROUND HERE WE SPEAK THE ENGLISH. A'RIGHT?
SIR, THIS IS AN INTERNATIONAL SPACE...
SAMMY KNOWS WHAT I'M TALKIN' ABOUT. ME'N OL' SAMMY, WE GO WAY THA HELL BACK. AIN'T THAT SO, SAMMY? AIN'T THAT SO?
CONRAD... I... WE WERE ABOUT TO...
FUCK. COME ON, MAN.
HOW 'BOUT YOU GALS JOIN IN WITH ME FER SOME LIQUID COURAGE?
WE DO APPRECIATE THE OFFER, BUT WE ARE TRYING TO...
I'LL JUST COME BACK...
NO... WAIT...
WELL, SURELY YA WON'T B'GRUDGE MY OL' CARCASS A SLUG NOW, WOULD YA? THOUGHT NOT. THOUGHT NOT.
GUYS? OKONOMI?
DOOK DOOK DOOK
AHHH, KENTUCKY'S FINEST. CORN MASH. IF YA'D LIKE, I GOT'N OL' BOY BACK IN THA CUMBERLANDS. FIX YA UP. NOT STRICKLY LEGAL, BUT...
COULD I...
MYY LORD. YOU ARE GOOD-LOOKIN'. MULATTO?
I AM OF MIXED ANCESTRY, YES.
SIR?
YA'LL MULATTO GALS GOTTA BE THA...
SIR?

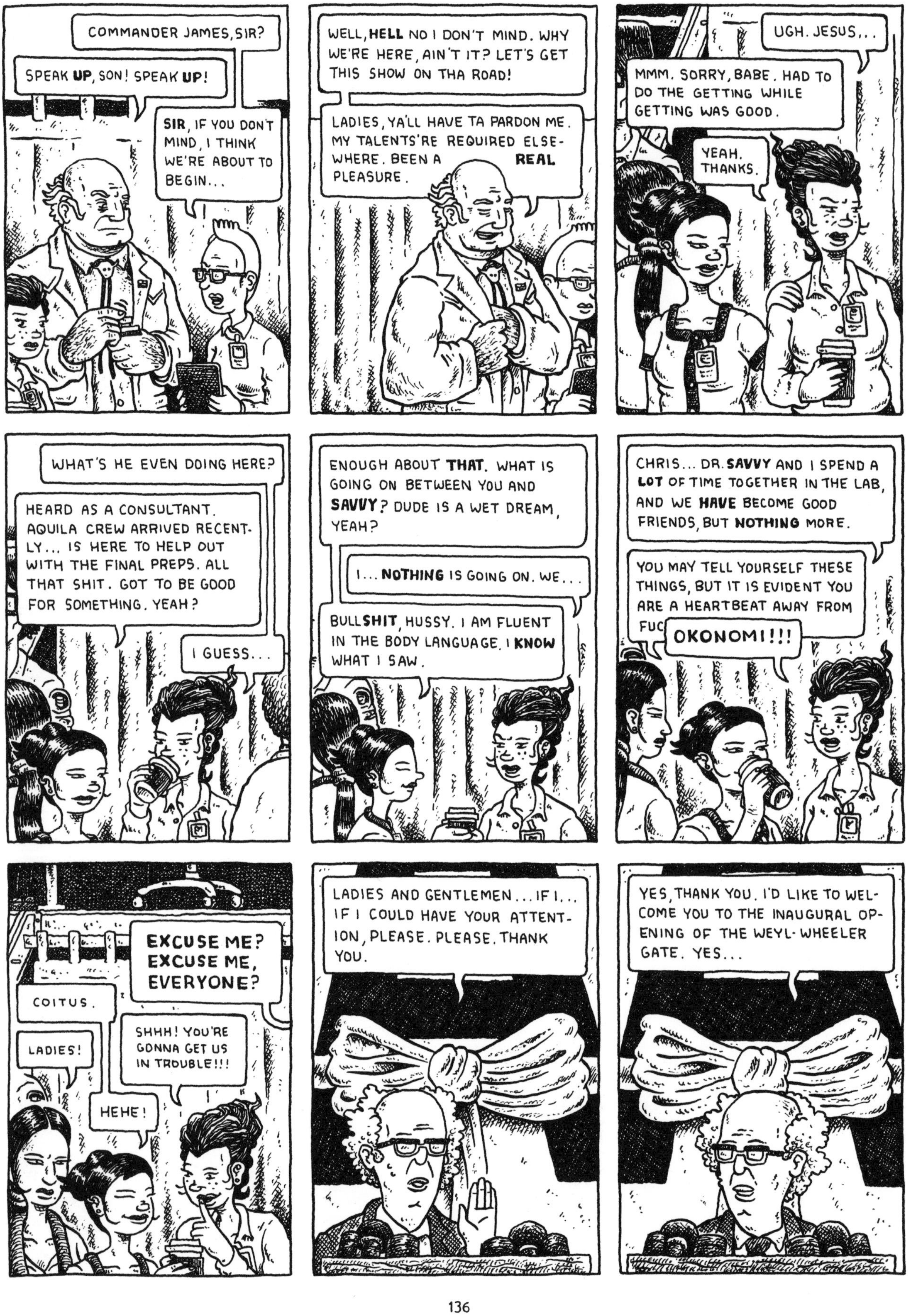

COMMANDER JAMES, SIR?
SPEAK UP, SON! SPEAK UP!
SIR, IF YOU DON'T MIND, I THINK WE'RE ABOUT TO BEGIN...
WELL, HELL NO I DON'T MIND. WHY WE'RE HERE, AIN'T IT? LET'S GET THIS SHOW ON THA ROAD!
LADIES, YA'LL HAVE TA PARDON ME. MY TALENTS'RE REQUIRED ELSE-WHERE. BEEN A REAL PLEASURE.
UGH. JESUS...
MMM. SORRY, BABE. HAD TO DO THE GETTING WHILE GETTING WAS GOOD.
YEAH. THANKS.
WHAT'S HE EVEN DOING HERE?
HEARD AS A CONSULTANT. AQUILA CREW ARRIVED RECENT-LY... IS HERE TO HELP OUT WITH THE FINAL PREPS. ALL THAT SHIT. GOT TO BE GOOD FOR SOMETHING. YEAH?
I GUESS...
ENOUGH ABOUT THAT. WHAT IS GOING ON BETWEEN YOU AND SAVVY? DUDE IS A WET DREAM, YEAH?
I... NOTHING IS GOING ON. WE...
BULLSHIT, HUSSY. I AM FLUENT IN THE BODY LANGUAGE. I KNOW WHAT I SAW.
CHRIS... DR. SAVVY AND I SPEND A LOT OF TIME TOGETHER IN THE LAB, AND WE HAVE BECOME GOOD FRIENDS, BUT NOTHING MORE.
YOU MAY TELL YOURSELF THESE THINGS, BUT IT IS EVIDENT YOU ARE A HEARTBEAT AWAY FROM FUC
OKONOMI!!!
EXCUSE ME? EXCUSE ME, EVERYONE?
COITUS.
LADIES!
SHHH! YOU'RE GONNA GET US IN TROUBLE!!!
HEHE!
LADIES AND GENTLEMEN... IF I... IF I COULD HAVE YOUR ATTENT-ION, PLEASE. PLEASE. THANK YOU.
YES, THANK YOU. I'D LIKE TO WEL-COME YOU TO THE INAUGURAL OP-ENING OF THE WEYL-WHEELER GATE. YES...

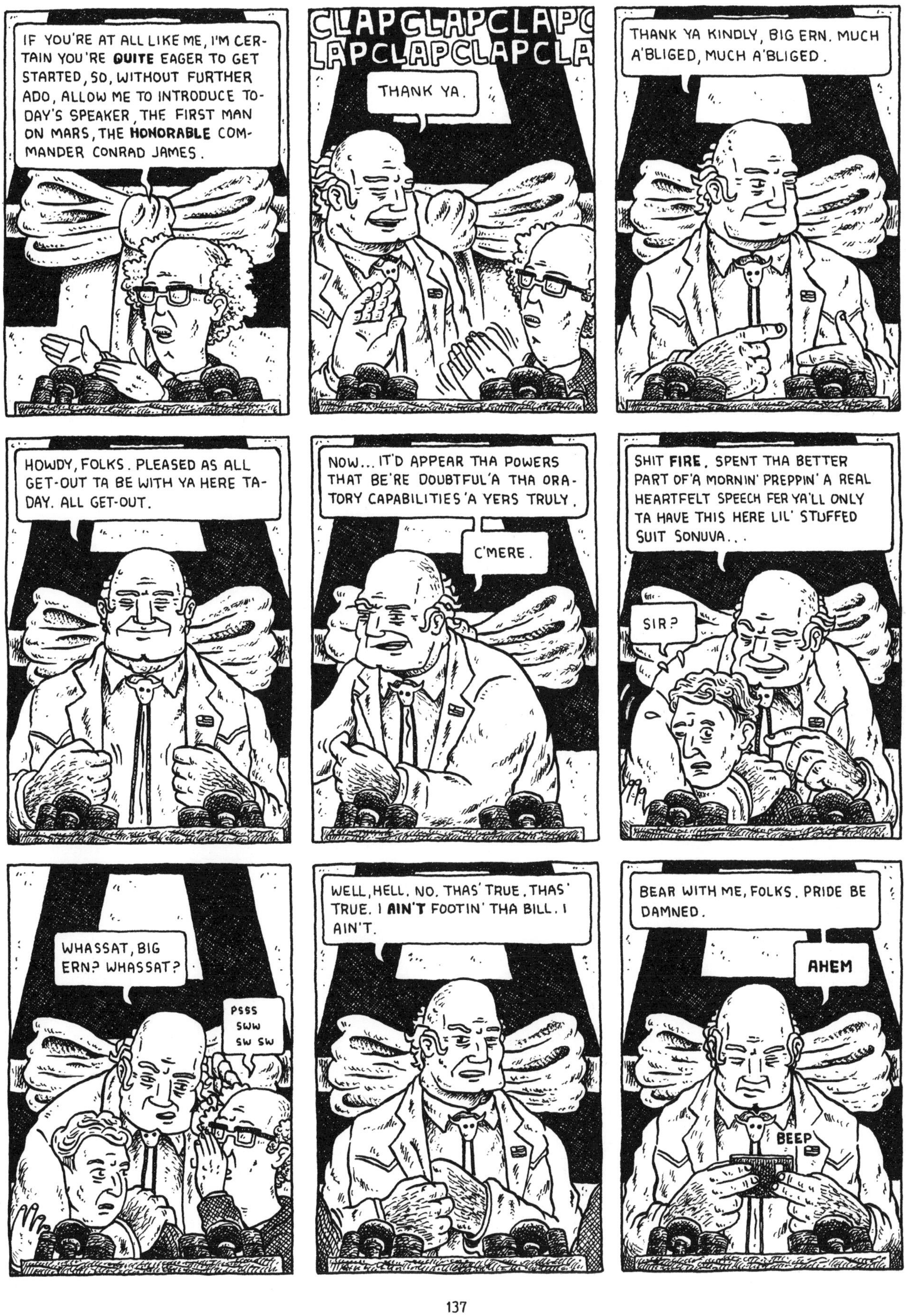
IF YOU'RE AT ALL LIKE ME, I'M CERTAIN YOU'RE **QUITE** EAGER TO GET STARTED, SO, WITHOUT FURTHER ADO, ALLOW ME TO INTRODUCE TODAY'S SPEAKER, THE FIRST MAN ON MARS, THE **HONORABLE** COMMANDER CONRAD JAMES.
CLAPCLAPCLAPCLAPC
LAPCLAPCLAPCLAPCLA
THANK YA.
THANK YA KINDLY, BIG ERN. MUCH A'BLIGED, MUCH A'BLIGED.
HOWDY, FOLKS. PLEASED AS ALL GET-OUT TA BE WITH YA HERE TADAY. ALL GET-OUT.
NOW... IT'D APPEAR THA POWERS THAT BE'RE DOUBTFUL'A THA ORATORY CAPABILITIES'A YERS TRULY.
C'MERE.
SHIT **FIRE**. SPENT THA BETTER PART OF'A MORNIN' PREPPIN' A REAL HEARTFELT SPEECH FER YA'LL ONLY TA HAVE THIS HERE LIL' STUFFED SUIT SONUVA...
SIR?
WHASSAT, BIG ERN? WHASSAT?
PSSS SWW SW SW
WELL, HELL. NO. THAS' TRUE. THAS' TRUE. I **AIN'T** FOOTIN' THA BILL. I AIN'T.
BEAR WITH ME, FOLKS. PRIDE BE DAMNED.
AHEM
BEEP

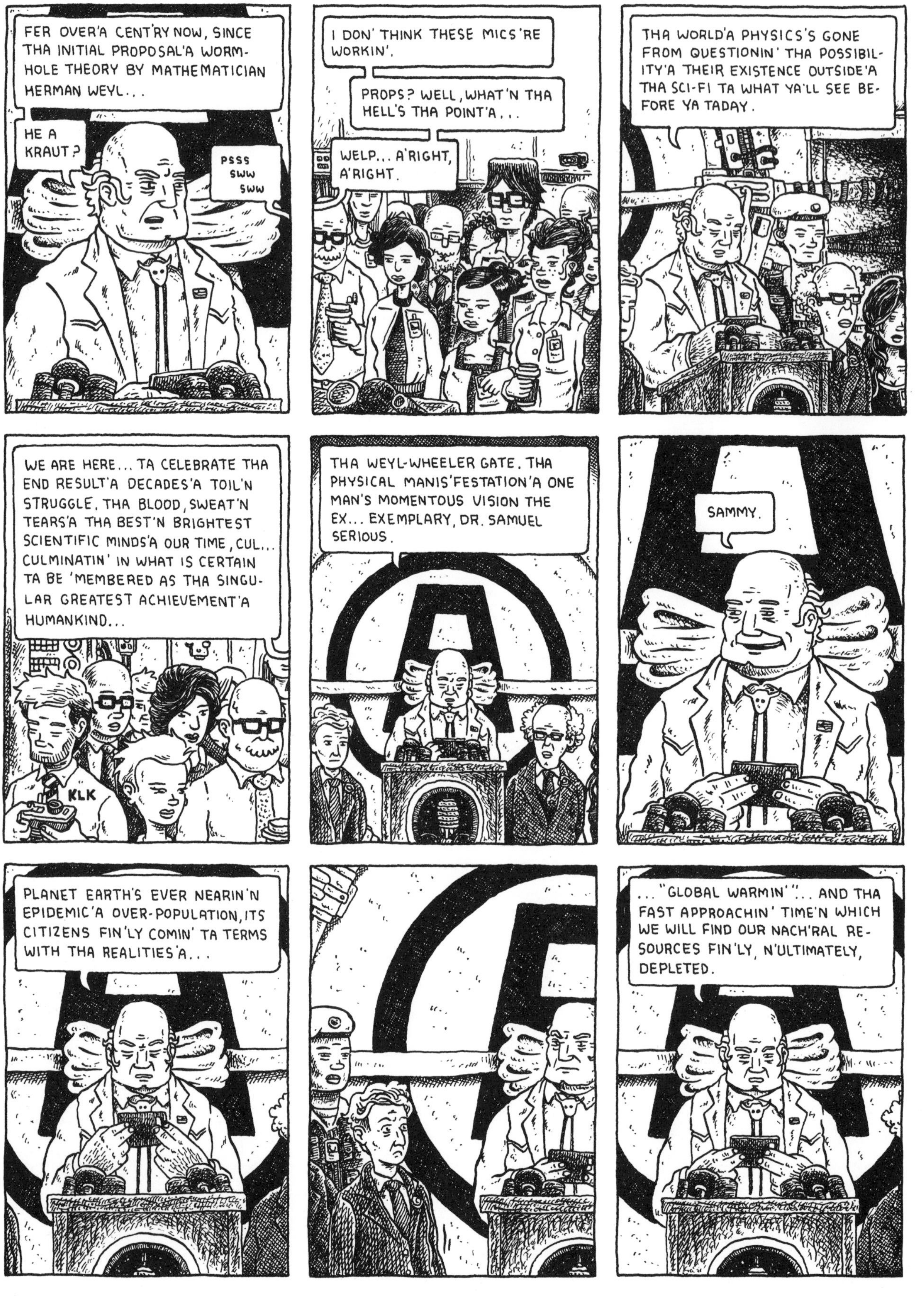
FER OVER'A CENT'RY NOW, SINCE THA INITIAL PROPOSAL'A WORM-HOLE THEORY BY MATHEMATICIAN HERMAN WEYL...
HE A KRAUT?
PSSS SWW SWW
I DON' THINK THESE MICS'RE WORKIN'.
PROPS? WELL, WHAT'N THA HELL'S THA POINT'A...
WELP... A'RIGHT, A'RIGHT.
THA WORLD'A PHYSICS'S GONE FROM QUESTIONIN' THA POSSIBIL-ITY'A THEIR EXISTENCE OUTSIDE'A THA SCI-FI TA WHAT YA'LL SEE BE-FORE YA TADAY.
WE ARE HERE... TA CELEBRATE THA END RESULT'A DECADES'A TOIL'N STRUGGLE, THA BLOOD, SWEAT'N TEARS'A THA BEST'N BRIGHTEST SCIENTIFIC MINDS'A OUR TIME, CUL... CULMINATIN' IN WHAT IS CERTAIN TA BE 'MEMBERED AS THA SINGU-LAR GREATEST ACHIEVEMENT'A HUMANKIND...
KLK
THA WEYL-WHEELER GATE. THA PHYSICAL MANIS'FESTATION'A ONE MAN'S MOMENTOUS VISION THE EX... EXEMPLARY, DR. SAMUEL SERIOUS.
SAMMY.
PLANET EARTH'S EVER NEARIN'N EPIDEMIC'A OVER-POPULATION, ITS CITIZENS FIN'LY COMIN' TA TERMS WITH THA REALITIES'A...
..."GLOBAL WARMIN'"... AND THA FAST APPROACHIN' TIME'N WHICH WE WILL FIND OUR NACH'RAL RE-SOURCES FIN'LY, N'ULTIMATELY, DEPLETED.

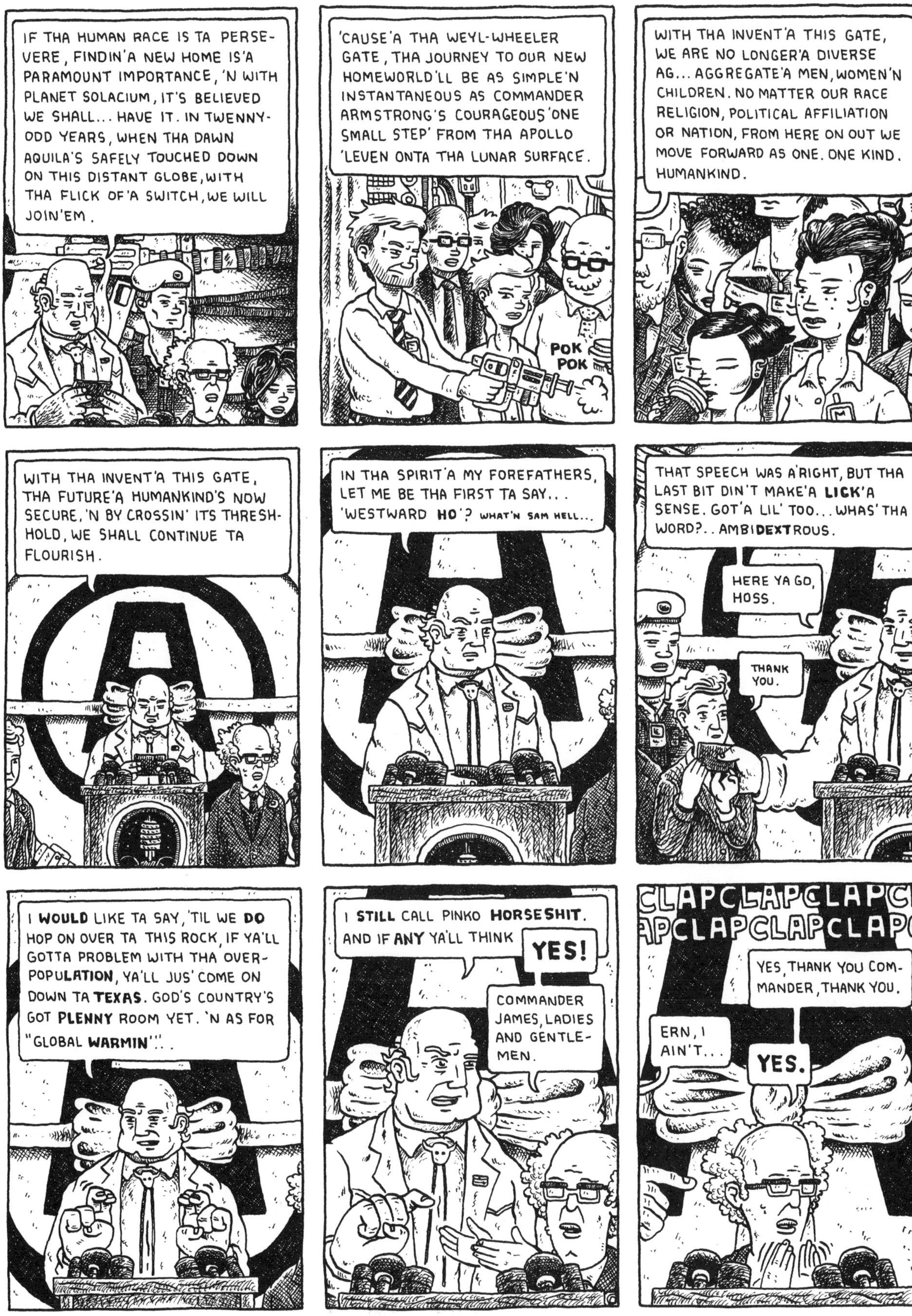
IF THA HUMAN RACE IS TA PERSEVERE, FINDIN'A NEW HOME IS'A PARAMOUNT IMPORTANCE, 'N WITH PLANET SOLACIUM, IT'S BELIEVED WE SHALL... HAVE IT. IN TWENNY-ODD YEARS, WHEN THA DAWN AQUILA'S SAFELY TOUCHED DOWN ON THIS DISTANT GLOBE, WITH THA FLICK OF'A SWITCH, WE WILL JOIN'EM.
'CAUSE'A THA WEYL-WHEELER GATE, THA JOURNEY TO OUR NEW HOMEWORLD'LL BE AS SIMPLE'N INSTANTANEOUS AS COMMANDER ARMSTRONG'S COURAGEOUS 'ONE SMALL STEP' FROM THA APOLLO 'LEVEN ONTA THA LUNAR SURFACE.
POK POK
WITH THA INVENT'A THIS GATE, WE ARE NO LONGER'A DIVERSE AG... AGGREGATE'A MEN, WOMEN'N CHILDREN. NO MATTER OUR RACE RELIGION, POLITICAL AFFILIATION OR NATION, FROM HERE ON OUT WE MOVE FORWARD AS ONE. ONE KIND. HUMANKIND.
WITH THA INVENT'A THIS GATE, THA FUTURE'A HUMANKIND'S NOW SECURE, 'N BY CROSSIN' ITS THRESHHOLD, WE SHALL CONTINUE TA FLOURISH.
IN THA SPIRIT'A MY FOREFATHERS, LET ME BE THA FIRST TA SAY... 'WESTWARD **HO**'? WHAT'N SAM HELL...
THAT SPEECH WAS A'RIGHT, BUT THA LAST BIT DIN'T MAKE'A **LICK**'A SENSE. GOT'A LIL' TOO... WHAS' THA WORD?.. AMBI**DEXT**ROUS.
HERE YA GO, HOSS.
THANK YOU.
I **WOULD** LIKE TA SAY, 'TIL WE **DO** HOP ON OVER TA THIS ROCK, IF YA'LL GOTTA PROBLEM WITH THA OVERPOPU**LATION**, YA'LL JUS' COME ON DOWN TA **TEXAS**. GOD'S COUNTRY'S GOT **PLENNY** ROOM YET. 'N AS FOR "GLOBAL **WARMIN**'"...
I **STILL** CALL PINKO **HORSESHIT**. AND IF **ANY** YA'LL THINK
YES!
COMMANDER JAMES, LADIES AND GENTLEMEN.
CLAPCLAPCLAPCL
APCLAPCLAPCLAPC
YES, THANK YOU COMMANDER, THANK YOU.
ERN, I AIN'T...
YES.

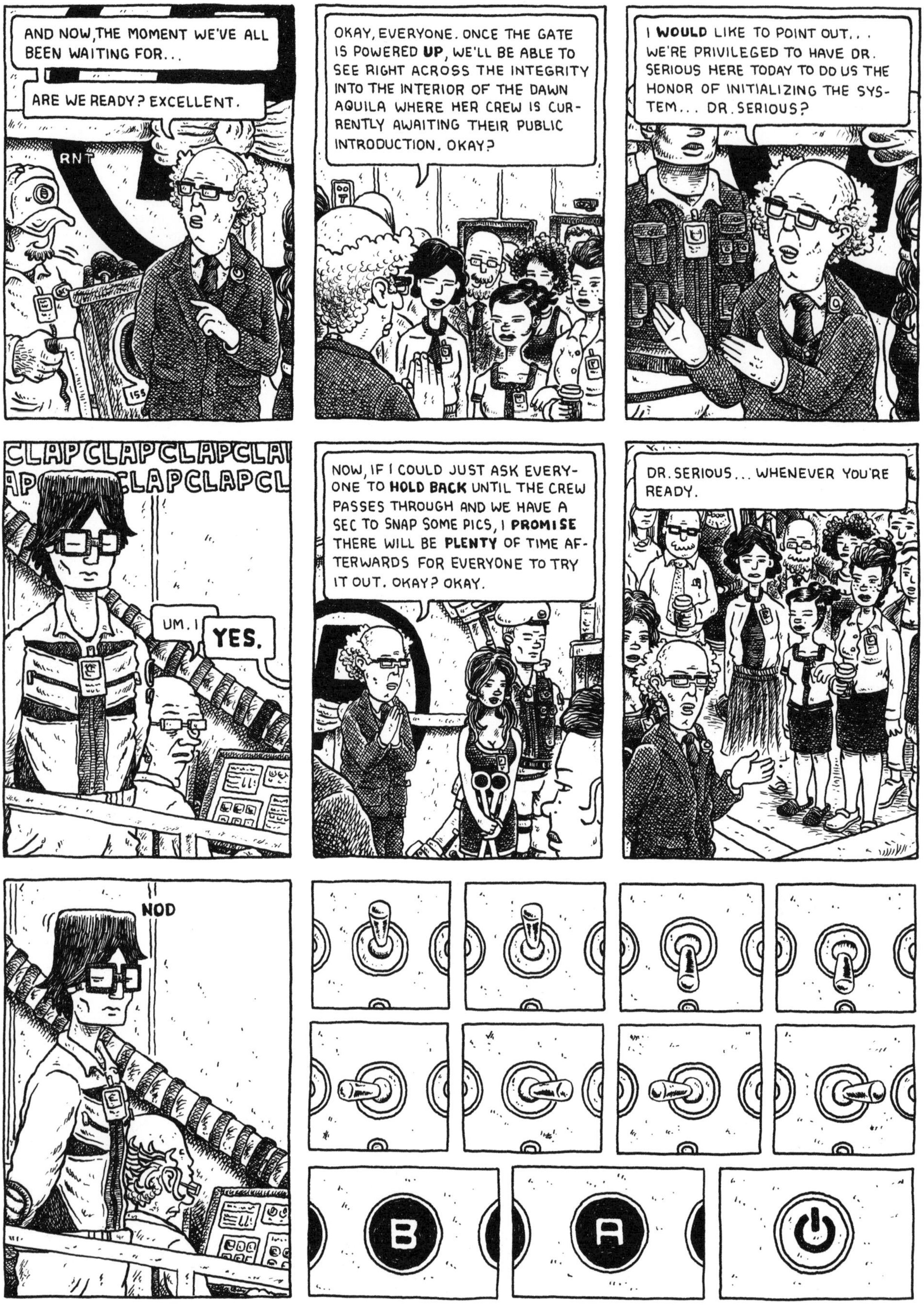

AND NOW, THE MOMENT WE'VE ALL BEEN WAITING FOR...
ARE WE READY? EXCELLENT.
RNT
OKAY, EVERYONE. ONCE THE GATE IS POWERED **UP**, WE'LL BE ABLE TO SEE RIGHT ACROSS THE INTEGRITY INTO THE INTERIOR OF THE DAWN AQUILA WHERE HER CREW IS CURRENTLY AWAITING THEIR PUBLIC INTRODUCTION. OKAY?
I **WOULD** LIKE TO POINT OUT... WE'RE PRIVILEGED TO HAVE DR. SERIOUS HERE TODAY TO DO US THE HONOR OF INITIALIZING THE SYSTEM... DR. SERIOUS?
CLAPCLAPCLAPCLA
APCLAPCLAPCL
UM. I
YES.
NOW, IF I COULD JUST ASK EVERYONE TO **HOLD BACK** UNTIL THE CREW PASSES THROUGH AND WE HAVE A SEC TO SNAP SOME PICS, I **PROMISE** THERE WILL BE **PLENTY** OF TIME AFTERWARDS FOR EVERYONE TO TRY IT OUT. OKAY? OKAY.
DR. SERIOUS... WHENEVER YOU'RE READY.
NOD
B
A

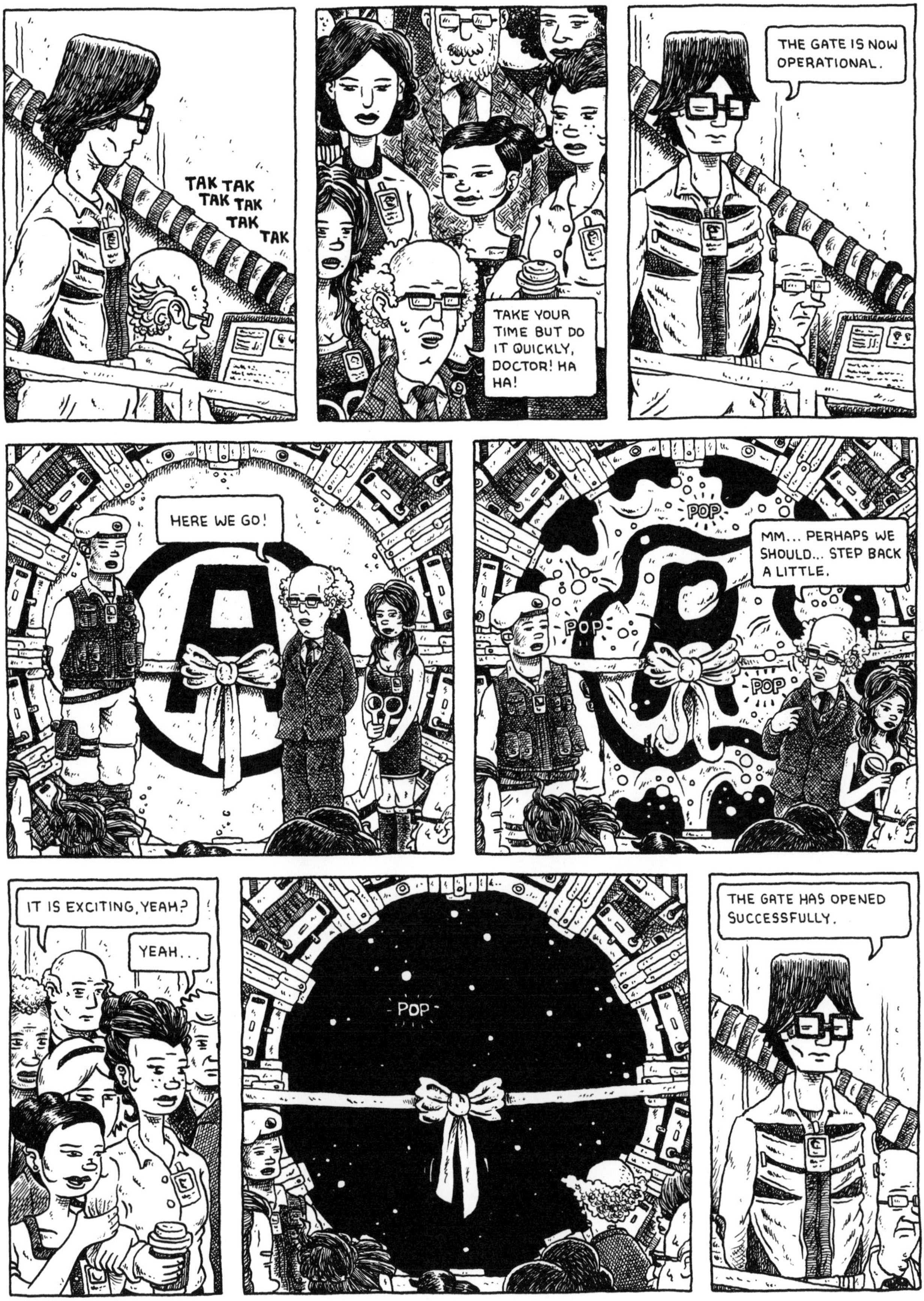
TAK TAK
TAK TAK
TAK
TAK
TAKE YOUR TIME BUT DO IT QUICKLY, DOCTOR! HA HA!
THE GATE IS NOW OPERATIONAL.
HERE WE GO!
POP
MM... PERHAPS WE SHOULD... STEP BACK A LITTLE.
POP
POP
IT IS EXCITING, YEAH?
YEAH...
POP
THE GATE HAS OPENED SUCCESSFULLY.

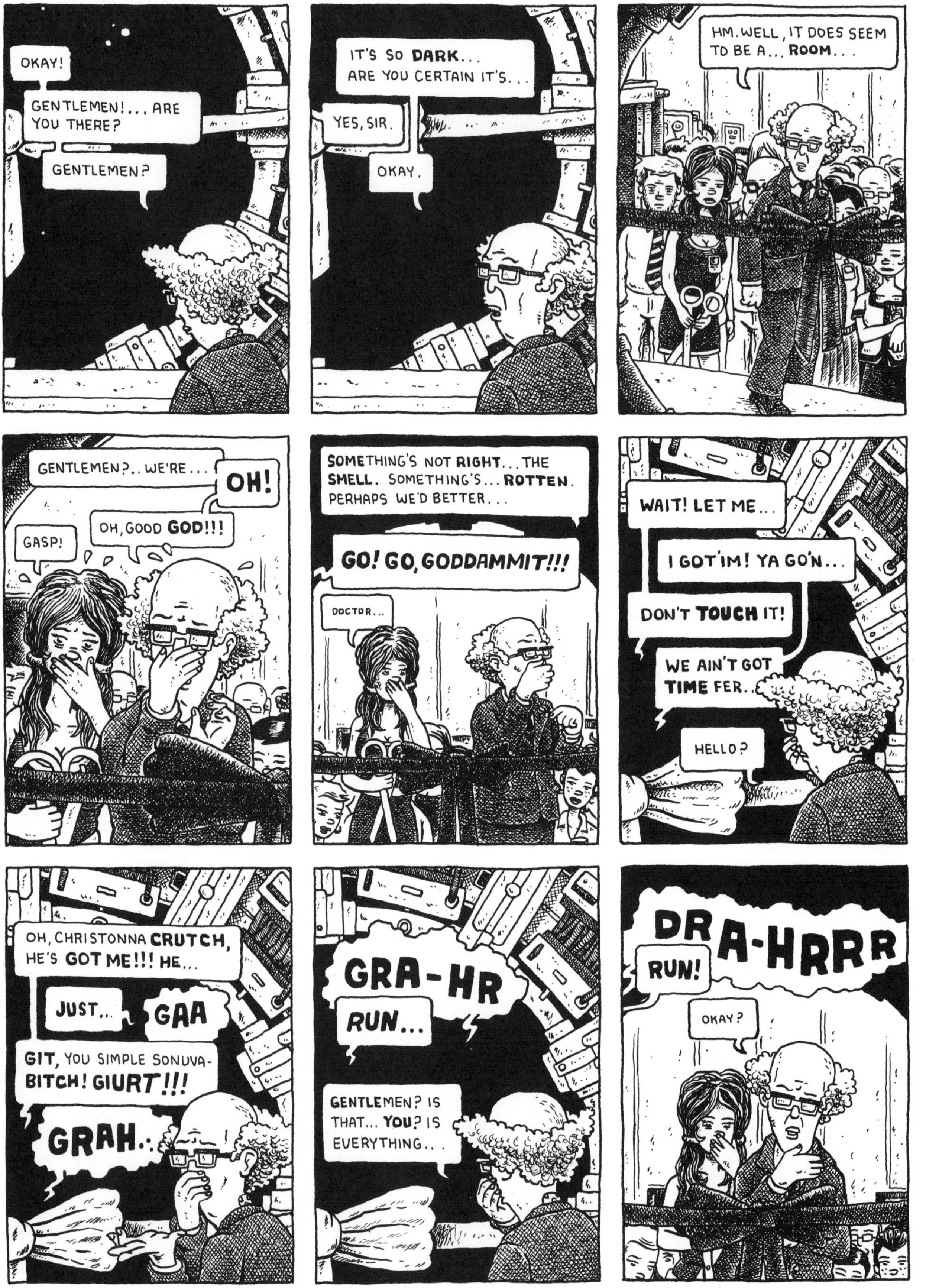

OKAY!
GENTLEMEN!... ARE YOU THERE?
GENTLEMEN?
IT'S SO DARK... ARE YOU CERTAIN IT'S...
YES, SIR.
OKAY.
HM. WELL, IT DOES SEEM TO BE A... ROOM...
GENTLEMEN?.. WE'RE...
OH!
GASP!
OH, GOOD GOD!!!
SOMETHING'S NOT RIGHT... THE SMELL. SOMETHING'S... ROTTEN. PERHAPS WE'D BETTER...
GO! GO, GODDAMMIT!!!
DOCTOR...
WAIT! LET ME...
I GOT'IM! YA GO'N...
DON'T TOUCH IT!
WE AIN'T GOT TIME FER...
HELLO?
OH, CHRISTONNA CRUTCH, HE'S GOT ME!!! HE...
JUST...
GAA
GIT, YOU SIMPLE SONUVA-BITCH! GIURT!!!
GRAH..
GRA-HR
RUN...
GENTLEMEN? IS THAT... YOU? IS EVERYTHING...
DRA-HRRR
RUN!
OKAY?

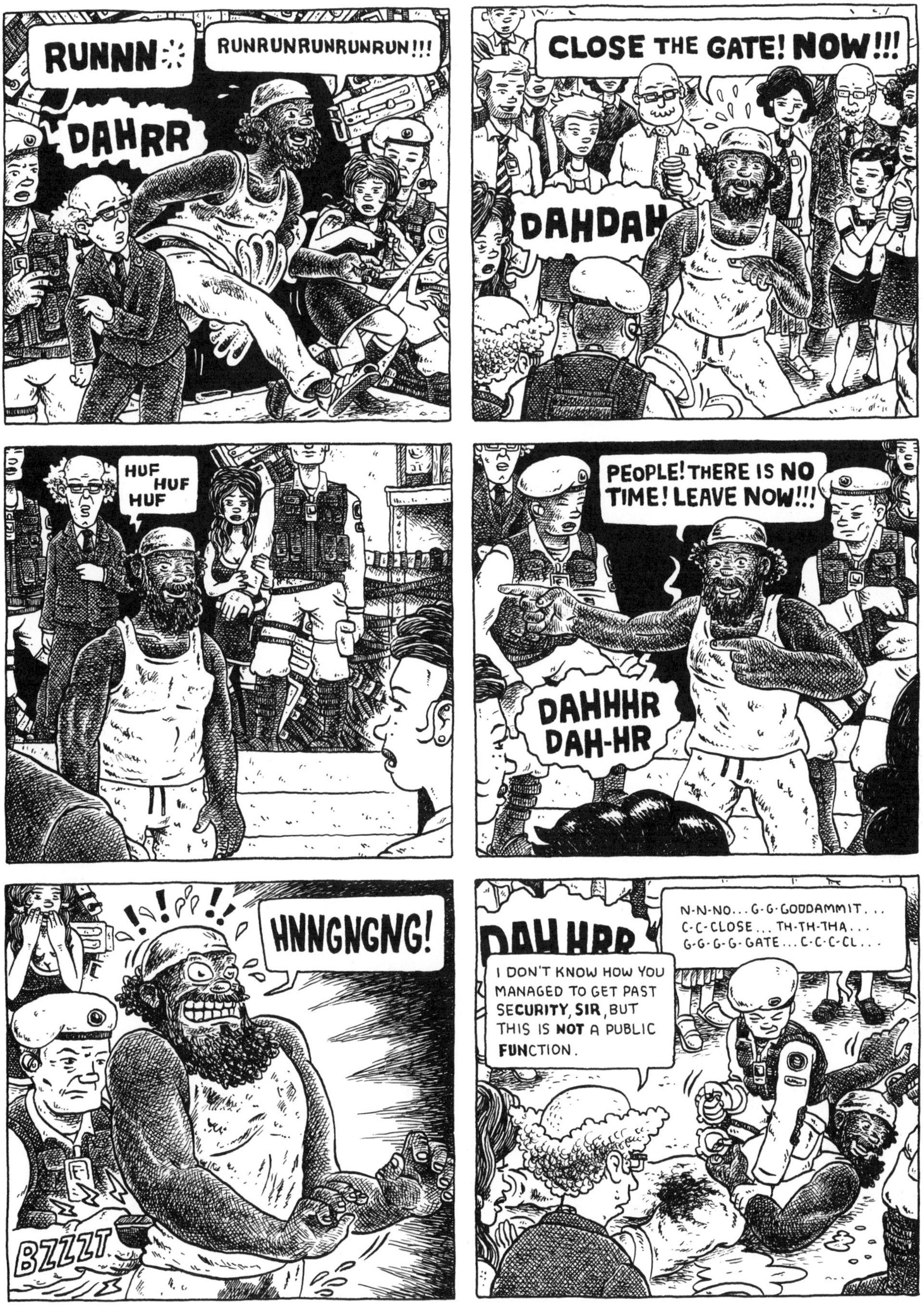
RUNNN
RUNRUNRUNRUNRUN!!!
DAHRR
CLOSE THE GATE! NOW!!!
DAHDAH
HUF HUF HUF
PEOPLE! THERE IS NO TIME! LEAVE NOW!!!
DAHHHR DAH-HR
HNNGNGNG!
BZZZT
DAH HRR
N-N-NO... G-G-GODDAMMIT... C-C-CLOSE... TH-TH-THA... G-G-G-G-GATE... C-C-C-CL...
I DON'T KNOW HOW YOU MANAGED TO GET PAST SECURITY, SIR, BUT THIS IS NOT A PUBLIC FUNCTION.

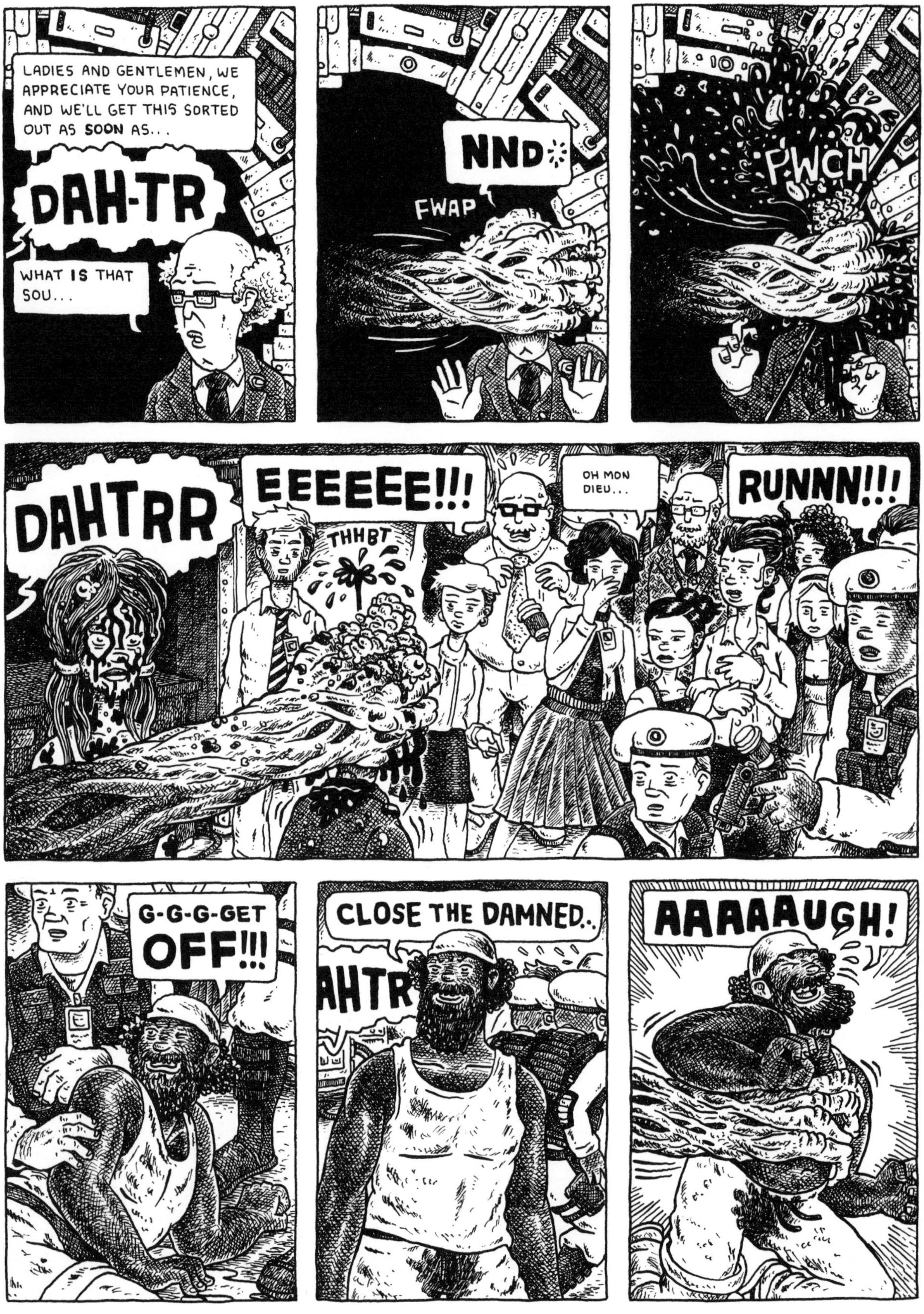
LADIES AND GENTLEMEN, WE APPRECIATE YOUR PATIENCE, AND WE'LL GET THIS SORTED OUT AS **SOON** AS...
DAH-TR
WHAT **IS** THAT SOU...
NND
FWAP
PWCH
DAHTRR
EEEEEE!!!
THHBT
OH MON DIEU...
RUNNN!!!
G-G-G-GET OFF!!!
CLOSE THE DAMNED..
AHTR
AAAAAUGH!

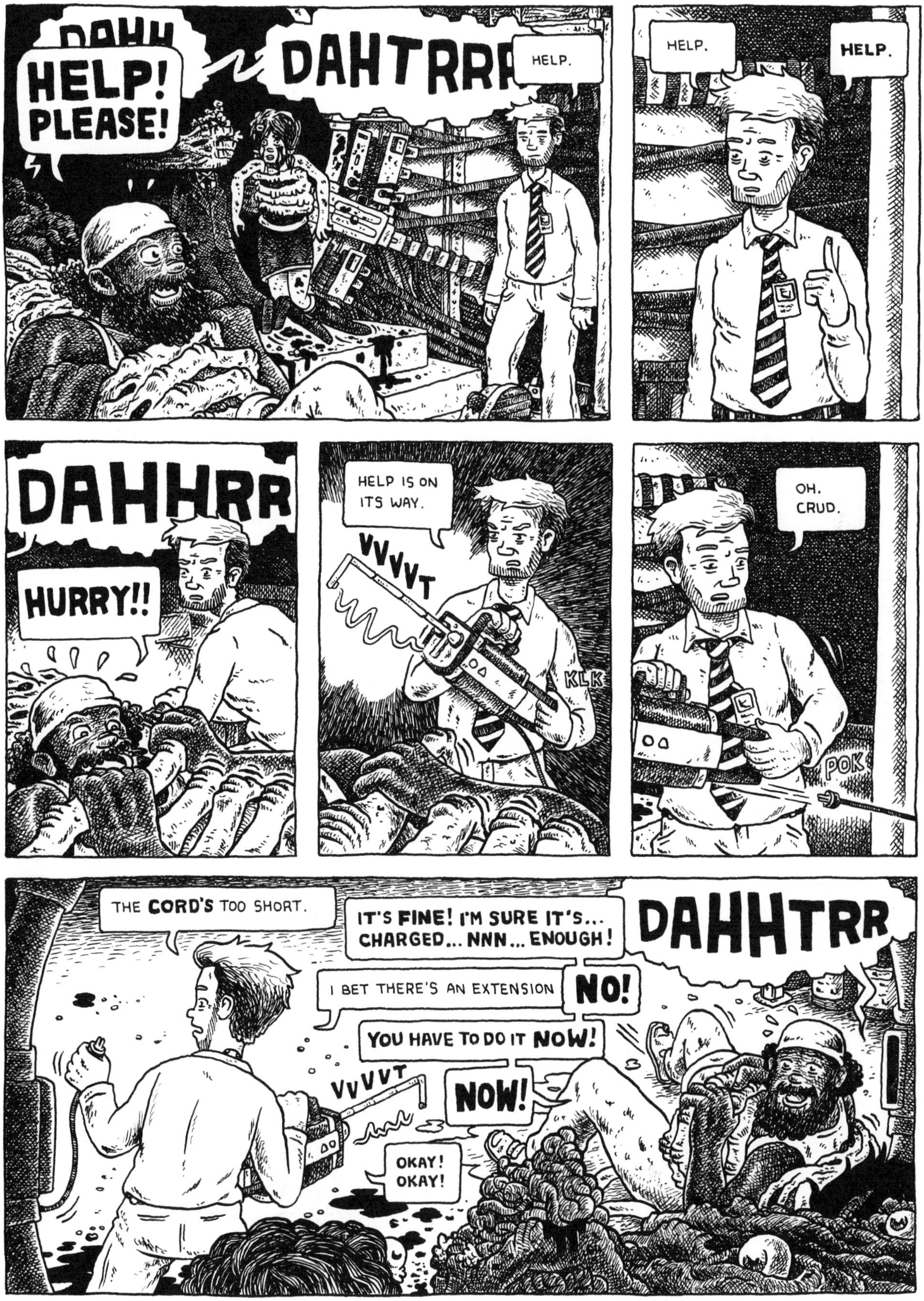
DAHH
HELP! PLEASE!
DAHTRRR
HELP.
HELP.
HELP.
DAHHRR
HURRY!!
HELP IS ON ITS WAY.
VVVVT
KLK
OH. CRUD.
POK
THE CORD'S TOO SHORT.
IT'S FINE! I'M SURE IT'S... CHARGED... NNN... ENOUGH!
DAHHTRR
I BET THERE'S AN EXTENSION
NO!
YOU HAVE TO DO IT NOW!
VVVVT
NOW!
OKAY! OKAY!

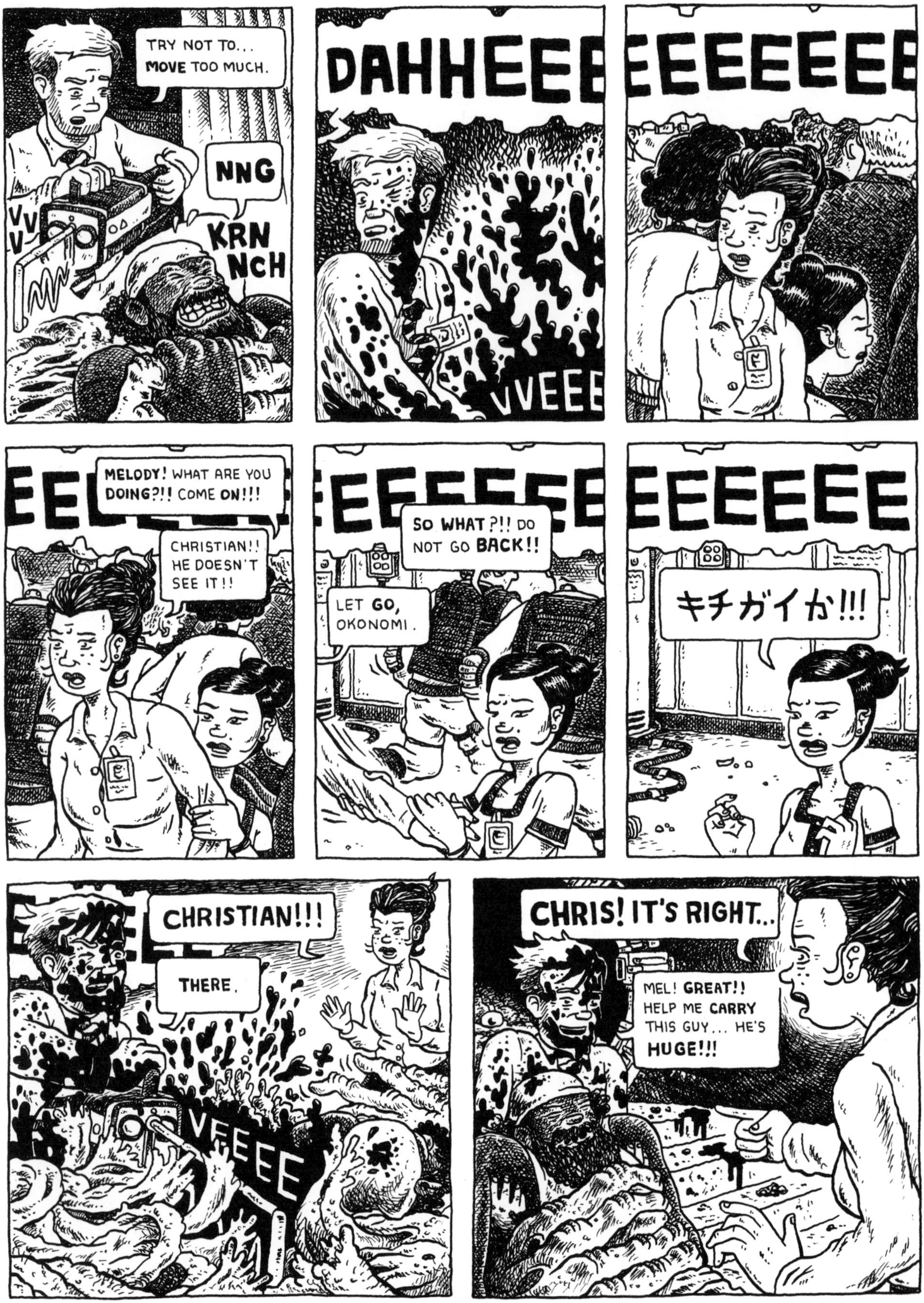
TRY NOT TO... MOVE TOO MUCH.
NNG
VVV
KRN NCH
DAHHEEE
VVEEE
EEEEEEE
EE
MELODY! WHAT ARE YOU DOING?!! COME ON!!!
CHRISTIAN!! HE DOESN'T SEE IT!!
EEEEEEE
SO WHAT?!! DO NOT GO BACK!!
LET GO, OKONOMI.
EEEEEEE
キチガイか!!!
CHRISTIAN!!!
THERE.
VEEEE
CHRIS! IT'S RIGHT...
MEL! GREAT!! HELP ME CARRY THIS GUY... HE'S HUGE!!!

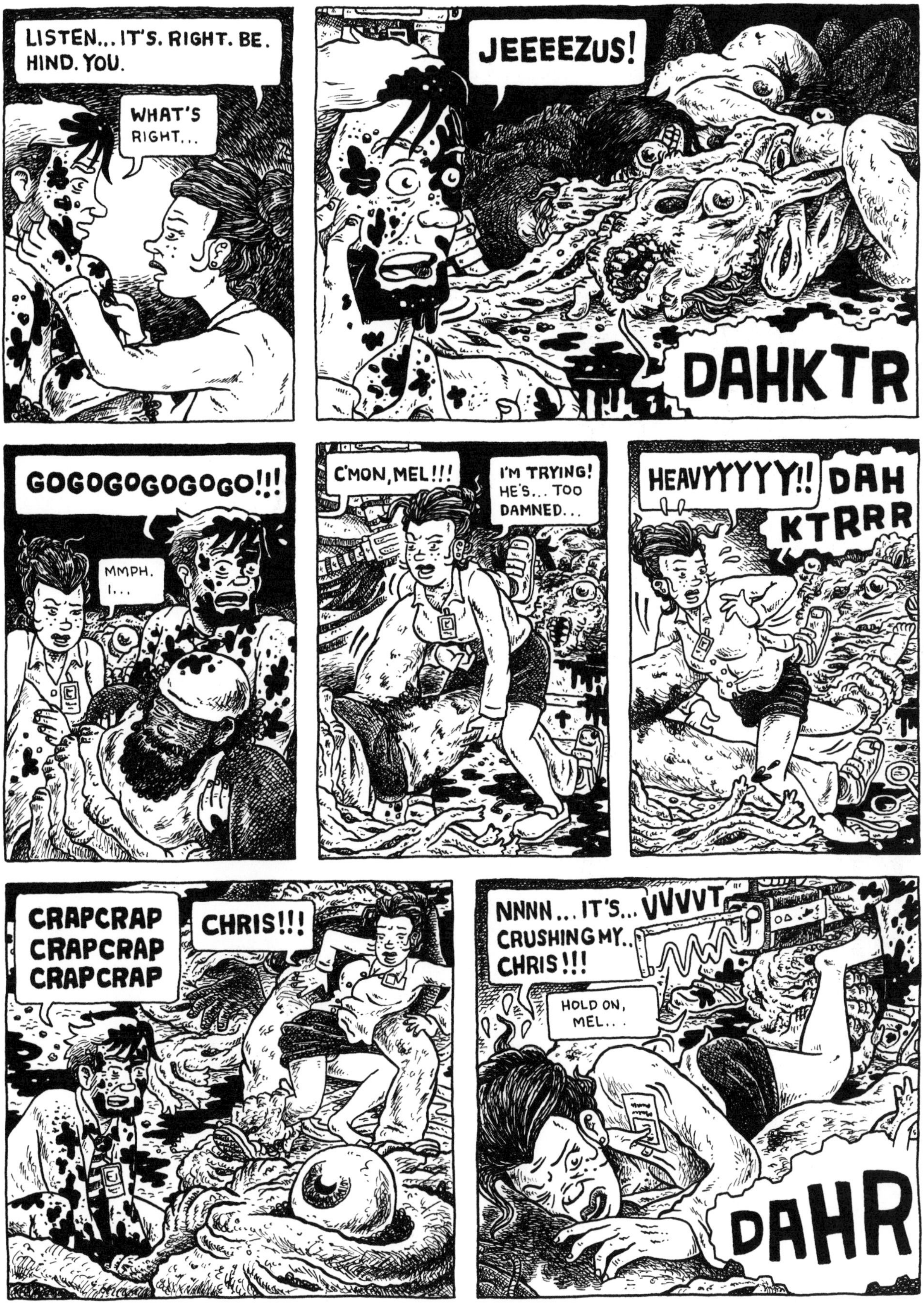
LISTEN... IT'S. RIGHT. BE. HIND. YOU.
WHAT'S RIGHT...
JEEEEZUS!
DAHKTR
GOGOGOGOGOGO!!!
MMPH. I...
C'MON, MEL!!!
I'M TRYING! HE'S... TOO DAMNED...
HEAVYYYYY!!
DAH KTRRR
CRAPCRAP CRAPCRAP CRAPCRAP
CHRIS!!!
NNNN... IT'S... CRUSHING MY.. CHRIS!!!
VVVVT
HOLD ON, MEL..
DAHR

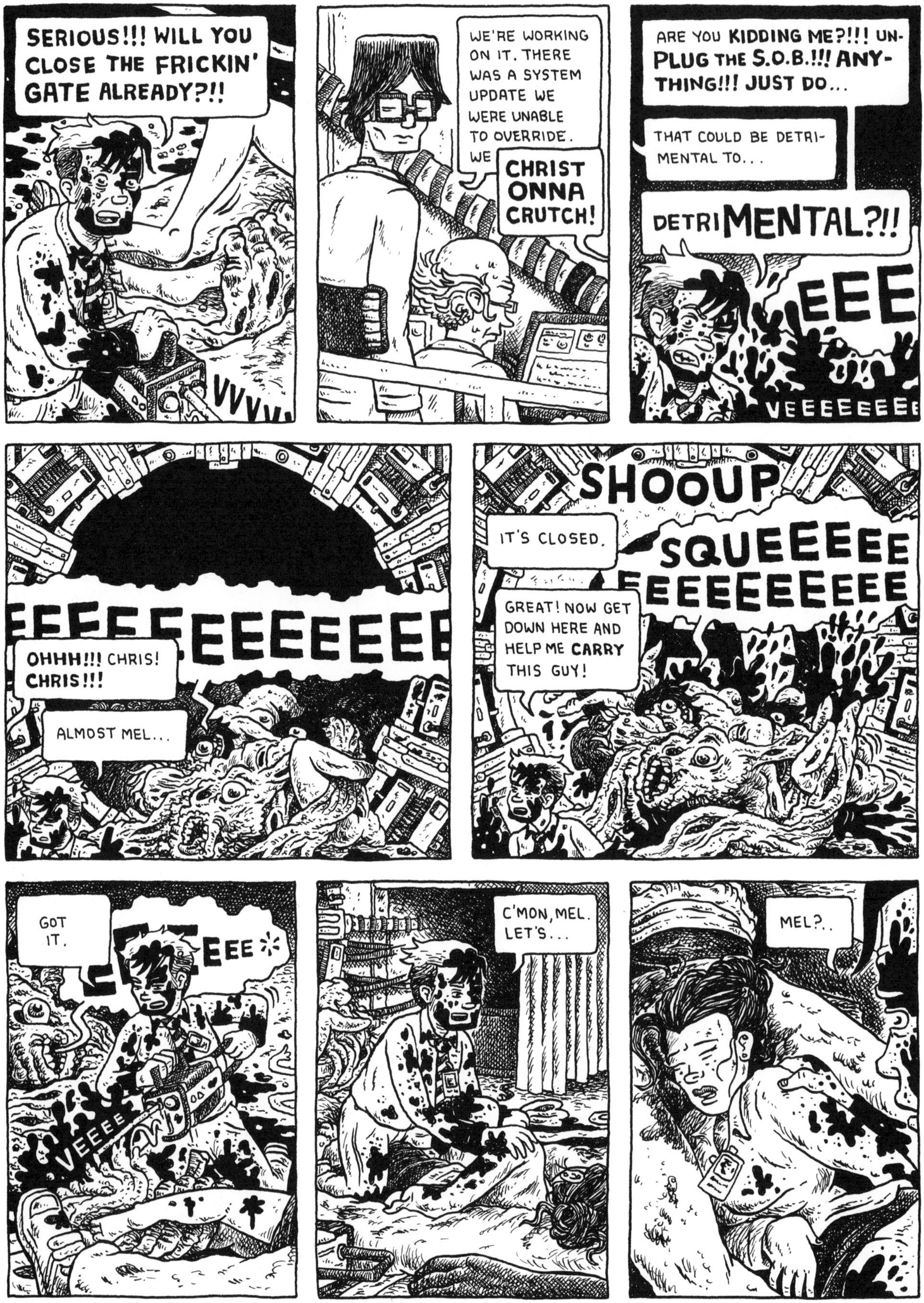

SERIOUS!!! WILL YOU CLOSE THE FRICKIN' GATE ALREADY?!!
VVVV
WE'RE WORKING ON IT. THERE WAS A SYSTEM UPDATE WE WERE UNABLE TO OVERRIDE. WE
CHRIST ONNA CRUTCH!
ARE YOU KIDDING ME?!!! UNPLUG THE S.O.B.!!! ANYTHING!!! JUST DO...
THAT COULD BE DETRIMENTAL TO...
DETRIMENTAL?!!
EEE
VEEEEEEEE
EEEEEEEEEEEE
OHHH!!! CHRIS! CHRIS!!!
ALMOST MEL...
SHOOUP
IT'S CLOSED.
SQUEEEEEE EEEEEEEEEE
GREAT! NOW GET DOWN HERE AND HELP ME CARRY THIS GUY!
GOT IT.
EEE
VEEEE
C'MON, MEL. LET'S...
MEL?..

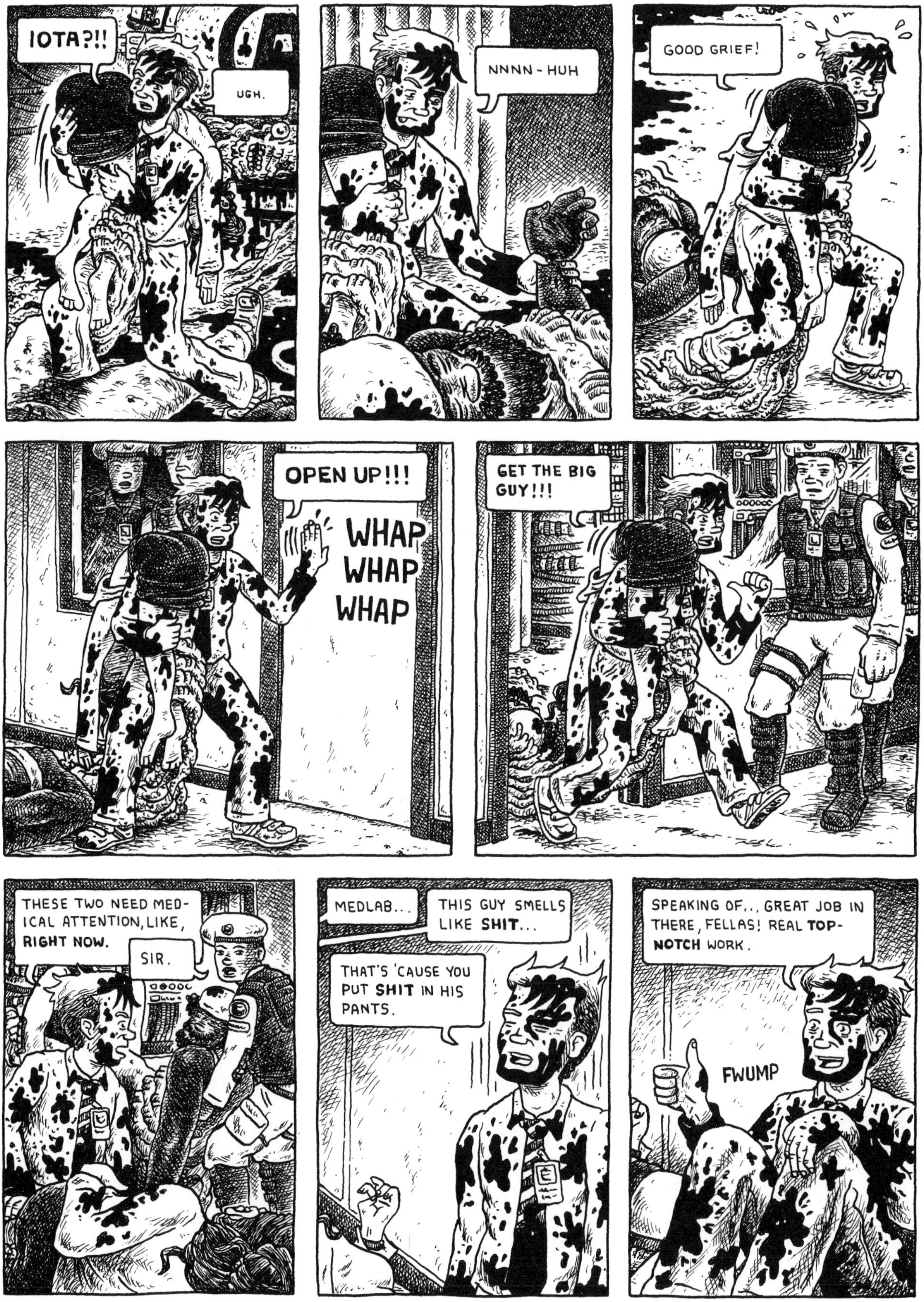

IOTA?!!
UGH.
NNNN-HUH
GOOD GRIEF!
OPEN UP!!!
WHAP
WHAP
WHAP
GET THE BIG GUY!!!
THESE TWO NEED MED-ICAL ATTENTION, LIKE, RIGHT NOW.
SIR.
MEDLAB..
THIS GUY SMELLS LIKE SHIT...
THAT'S 'CAUSE YOU PUT SHIT IN HIS PANTS.
SPEAKING OF... GREAT JOB IN THERE, FELLAS! REAL TOP-NOTCH WORK.
FWUMP

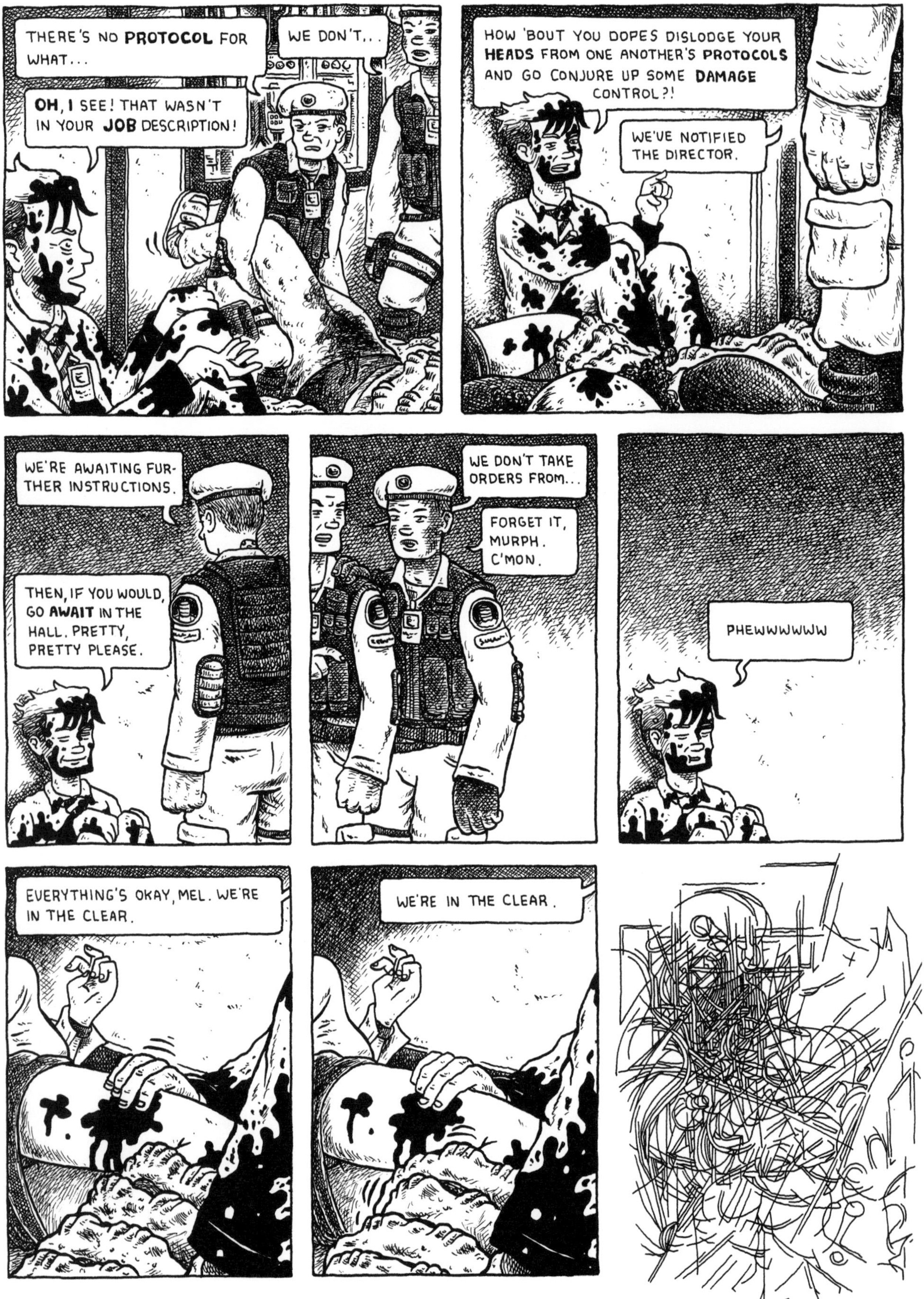
THERE'S NO **PROTOCOL** FOR WHAT...
WE DON'T...
OH, I SEE! THAT WASN'T IN YOUR **JOB** DESCRIPTION!
HOW 'BOUT YOU DOPES DISLODGE YOUR **HEADS** FROM ONE ANOTHER'S **PROTOCOLS** AND GO CONJURE UP SOME **DAMAGE** CONTROL?!
WE'VE NOTIFIED THE DIRECTOR.
WE'RE AWAITING FURTHER INSTRUCTIONS.
THEN, IF YOU WOULD, GO **AWAIT** IN THE HALL. PRETTY, PRETTY PLEASE.
WE DON'T TAKE ORDERS FROM...
FORGET IT, MURPH. C'MON.
PHEWWWWWW
EVERYTHING'S OKAY, MEL. WE'RE IN THE CLEAR.
WE'RE IN THE CLEAR.

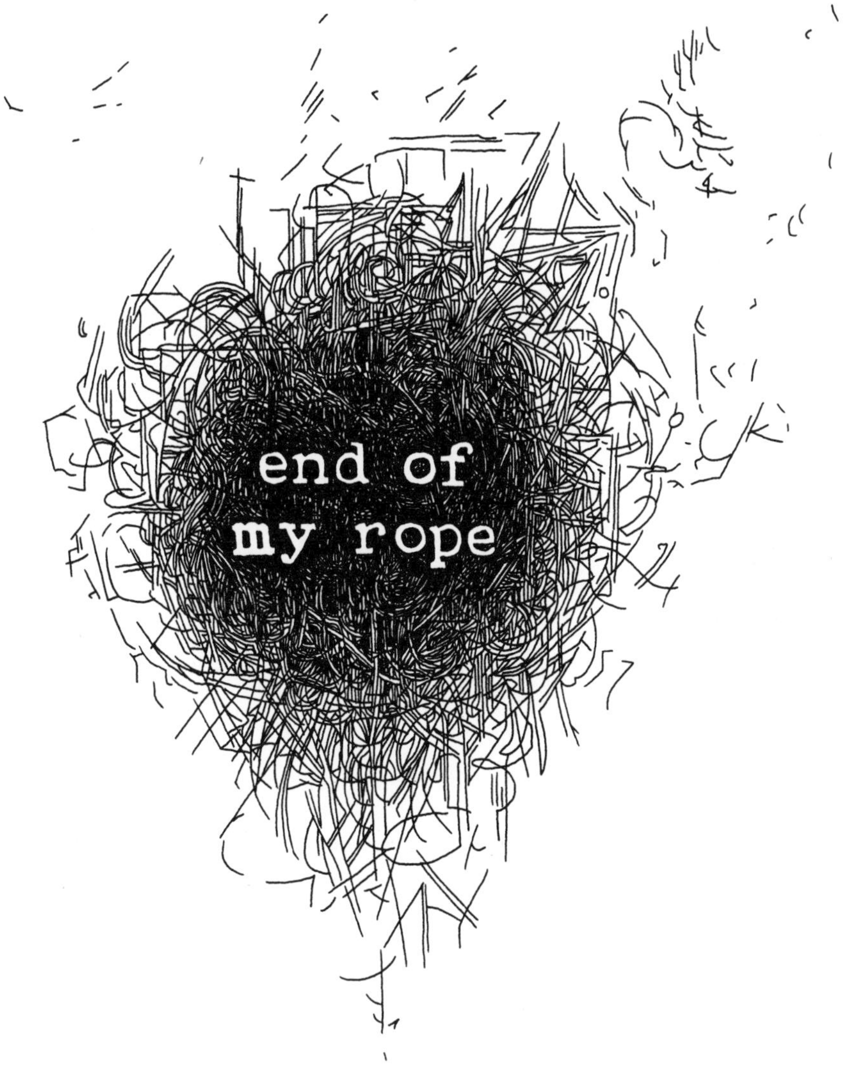
end of
my rope

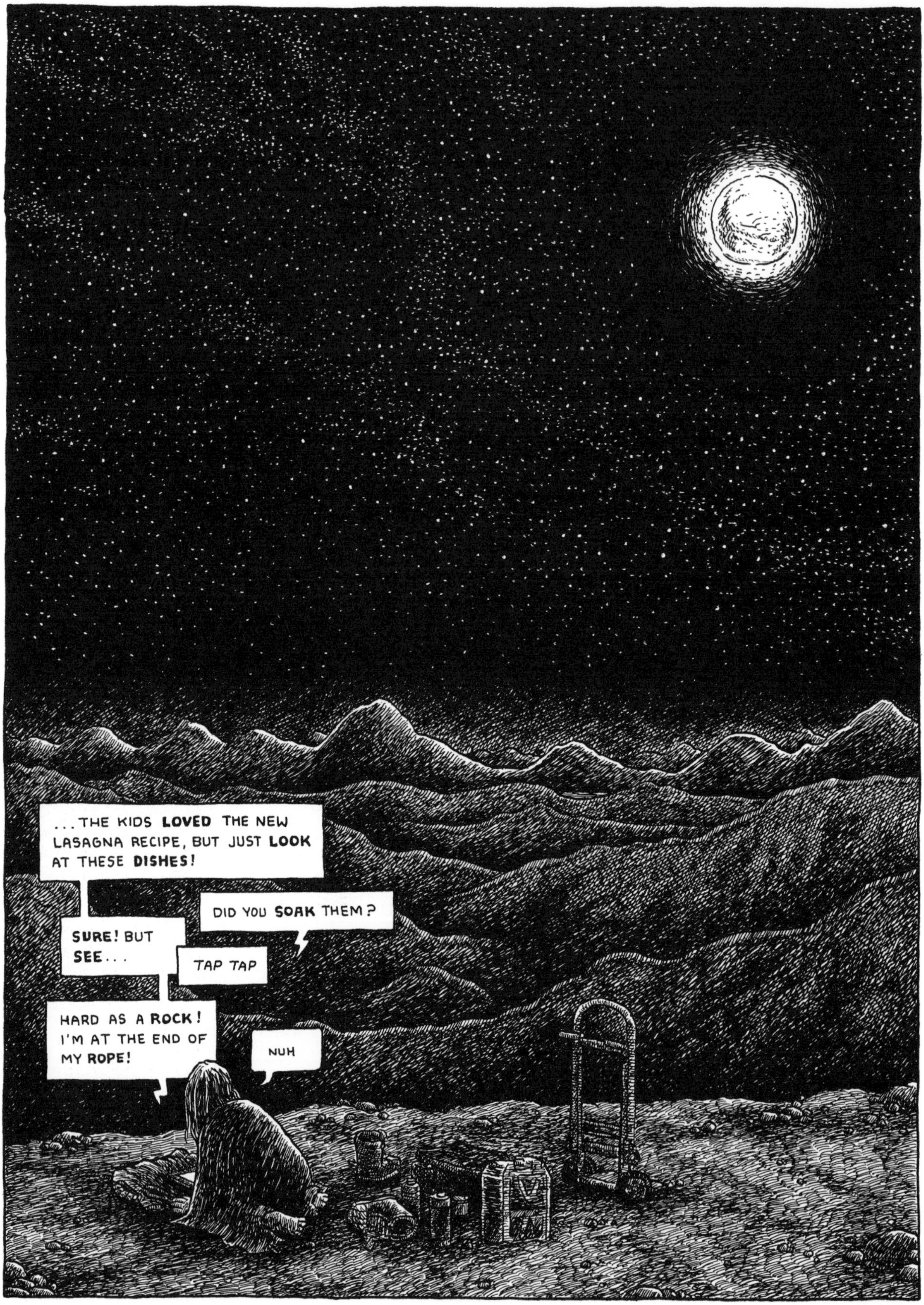
...THE KIDS LOVED THE NEW LASAGNA RECIPE, BUT JUST LOOK AT THESE DISHES!
DID YOU SOAK THEM?
SURE! BUT SEE...
TAP TAP
HARD AS A ROCK! I'M AT THE END OF MY ROPE!
NUH

GUESS I'LL JUST DO IT **AGAIN!** COULD YOU HAND ME THE SOAP?

HERE YOU GO!

WAIT...

NN

THIS ISN'T MY **USUAL** BRAND!

THERE'S **NOTHING** USUAL ABOUT **TI-D-BRITE!** TRY IT!

WELL, **OKAY**...IF YOU **SAY** SO!

WHHSSHH

WOW!

NNT

I CAN'T BE**LIEVE** IT! SO **CLEAN!**

DINNNG

SO **BRIGHT!**

MORE THAN **BRIGHT**, IT'S...

TI-D-BRITE!!

HA HA HA HA HA HA HA

HNH **HNH HNNNH**

TI-D-BRITE'LL GET IT RIGHT THE **FIRST TIME** THROOOUGH **!!!**

HNNNUHHH

KLK

HEY, LIZ, WHAT'S WRONG?

OH, THE KIDS **LOVED** THE RECIPE, BUT JUST **LOOK A** DISHES!

DID YOU

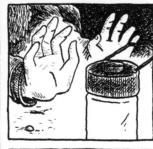

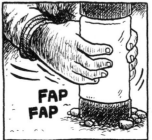

FAP FAP

FFFFFF

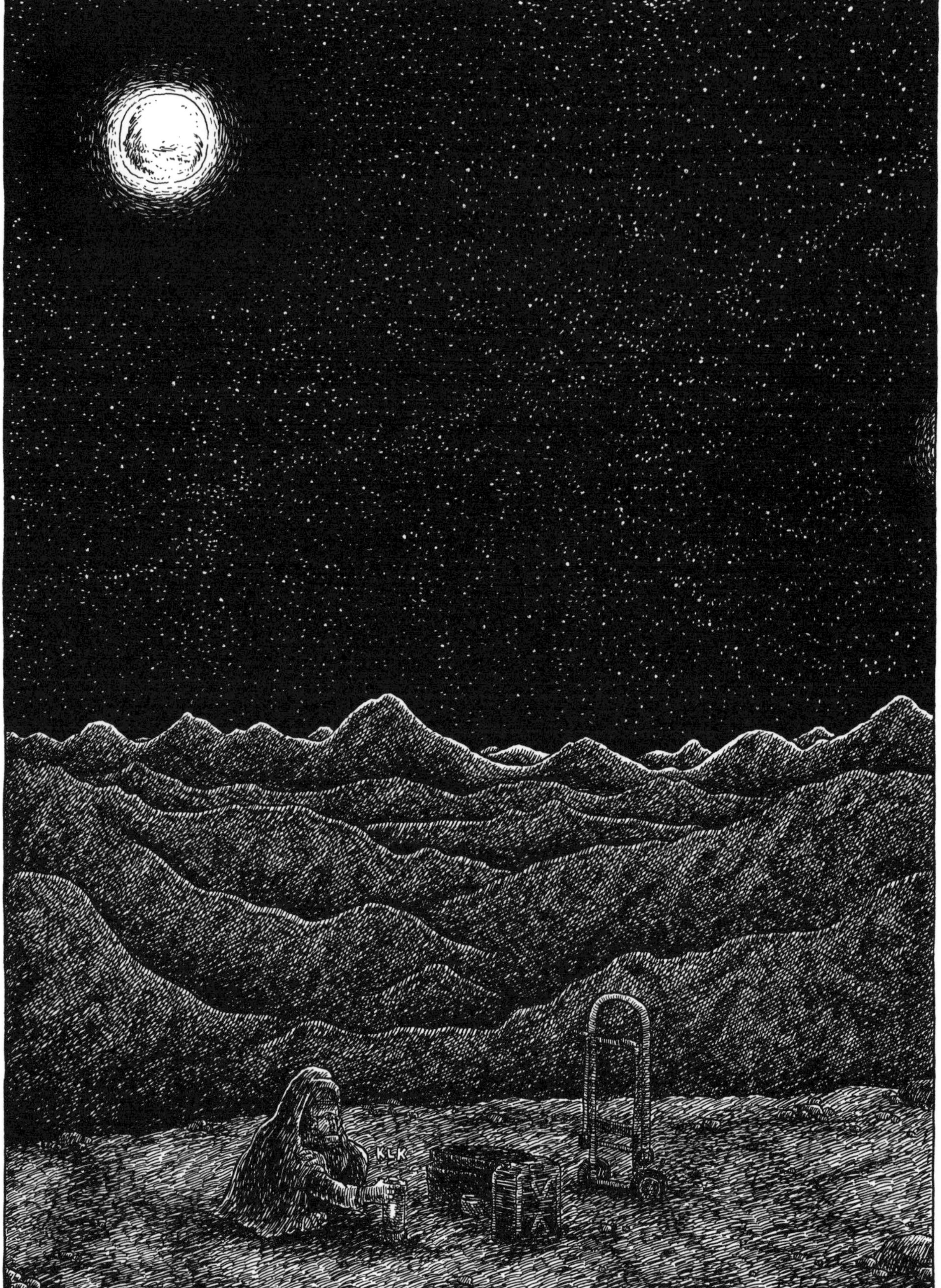
KLK

pain
killers

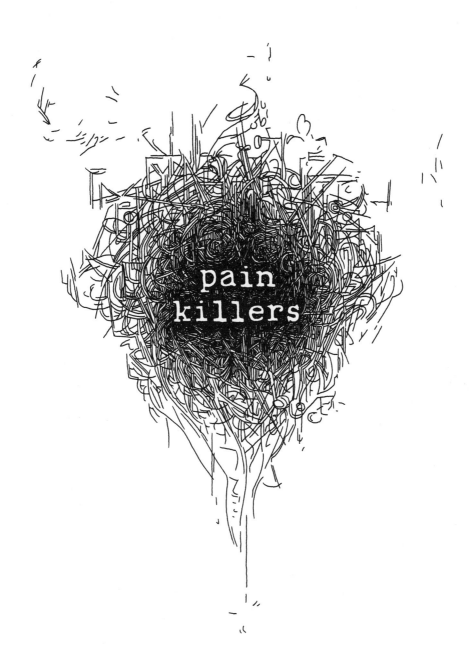

Y.MUSTAFA
NOT ONLINE

Y.MUSTAFA
NOT ONLINE

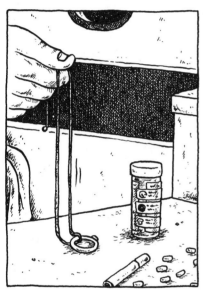

SLRP.

SSSHH

PSSSHH

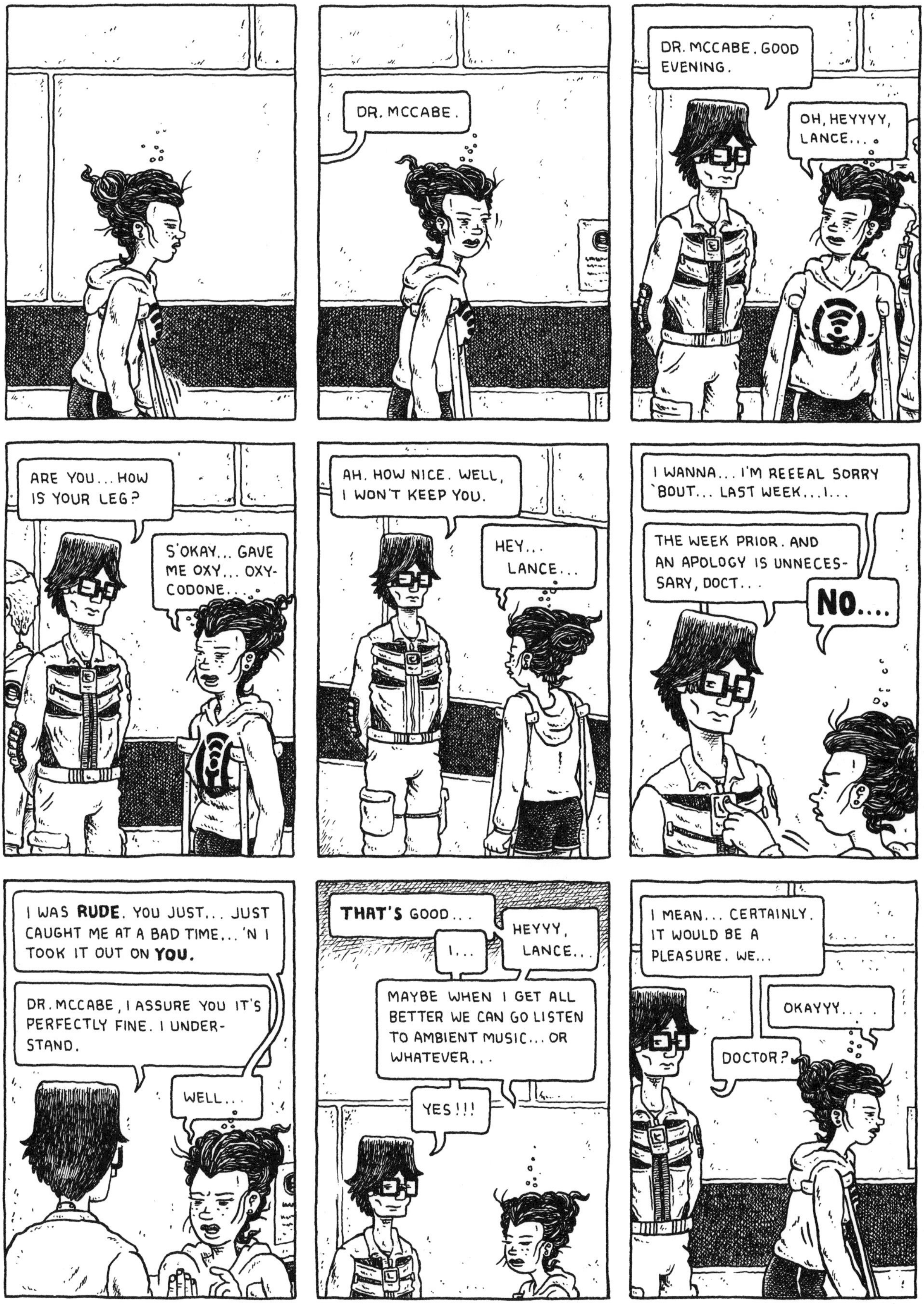
DR. MCCABE.
DR. MCCABE. GOOD EVENING.
OH, HEYYYY, LANCE...
ARE YOU... HOW IS YOUR LEG?
S'OKAY... GAVE ME OXY... OXY-CODONE...
AH. HOW NICE. WELL, I WON'T KEEP YOU.
HEY... LANCE...
I WANNA... I'M REEEAL SORRY 'BOUT... LAST WEEK... I...
THE WEEK PRIOR. AND AN APOLOGY IS UNNECES-SARY, DOCT...
NO....
I WAS RUDE. YOU JUST... JUST CAUGHT ME AT A BAD TIME... 'N I TOOK IT OUT ON YOU.
DR. MCCABE, I ASSURE YOU IT'S PERFECTLY FINE. I UNDER-STAND.
WELL...
THAT'S GOOD...
I...
HEYYY, LANCE...
MAYBE WHEN I GET ALL BETTER WE CAN GO LISTEN TO AMBIENT MUSIC... OR WHATEVER...
YES!!!
I MEAN... CERTAINLY. IT WOULD BE A PLEASURE. WE...
OKAYYY...
DOCTOR?

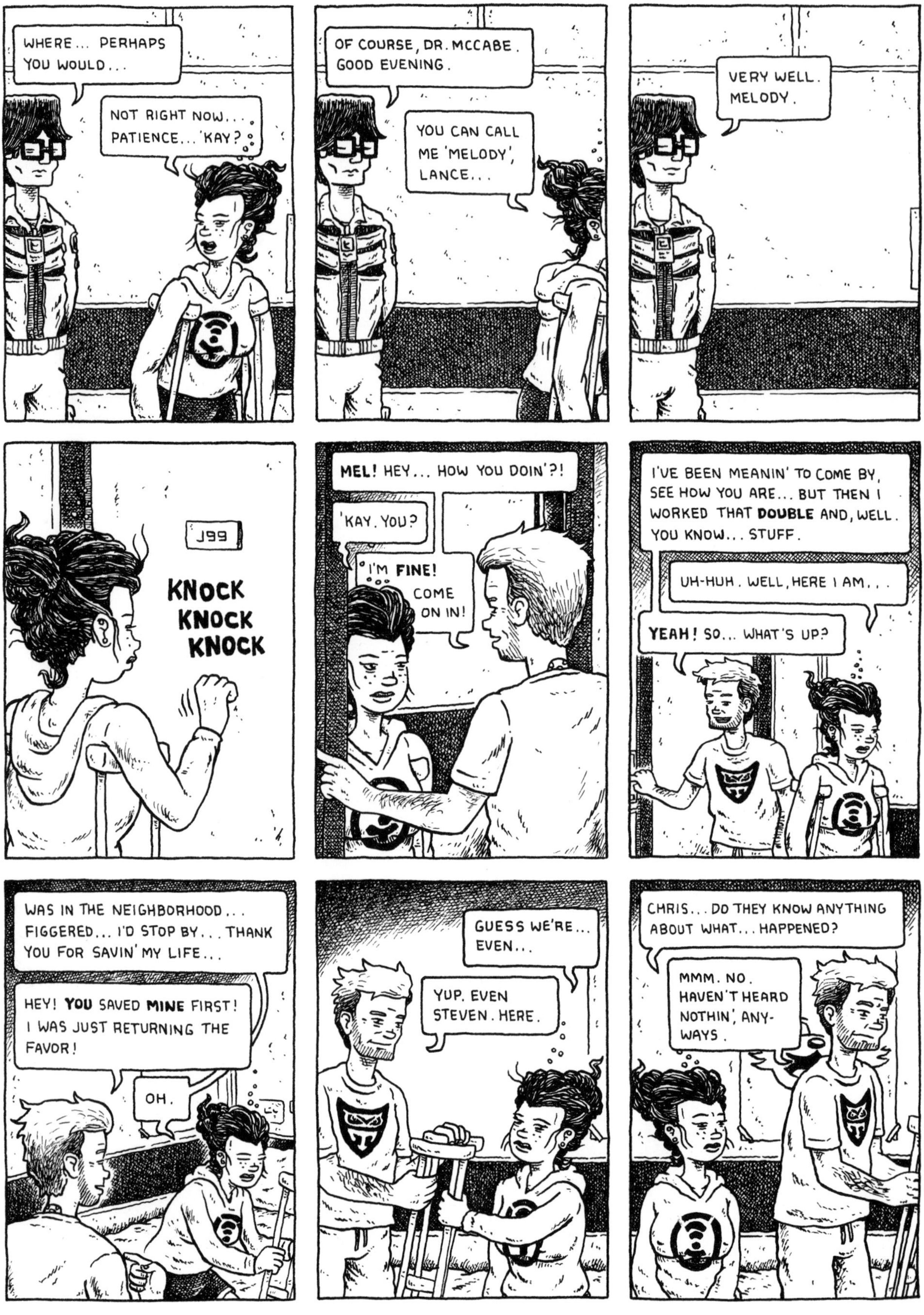
WHERE... PERHAPS YOU WOULD...
NOT RIGHT NOW... PATIENCE... 'KAY?
OF COURSE, DR. MCCABE. GOOD EVENING.
YOU CAN CALL ME 'MELODY', LANCE...
VERY WELL. MELODY.
199
KNOCK KNOCK KNOCK
MEL! HEY... HOW YOU DOIN'?!
'KAY. YOU?
I'M FINE! COME ON IN!
I'VE BEEN MEANIN' TO COME BY, SEE HOW YOU ARE... BUT THEN I WORKED THAT DOUBLE AND, WELL. YOU KNOW... STUFF.
UH-HUH. WELL, HERE I AM...
YEAH! SO... WHAT'S UP?
WAS IN THE NEIGHBORHOOD... FIGGERED... I'D STOP BY... THANK YOU FOR SAVIN' MY LIFE...
HEY! YOU SAVED MINE FIRST! I WAS JUST RETURNING THE FAVOR!
OH.
GUESS WE'RE... EVEN...
YUP. EVEN STEVEN. HERE.
CHRIS... DO THEY KNOW ANYTHING ABOUT WHAT... HAPPENED?
MMM. NO. HAVEN'T HEARD NOTHIN', ANY-WAYS.

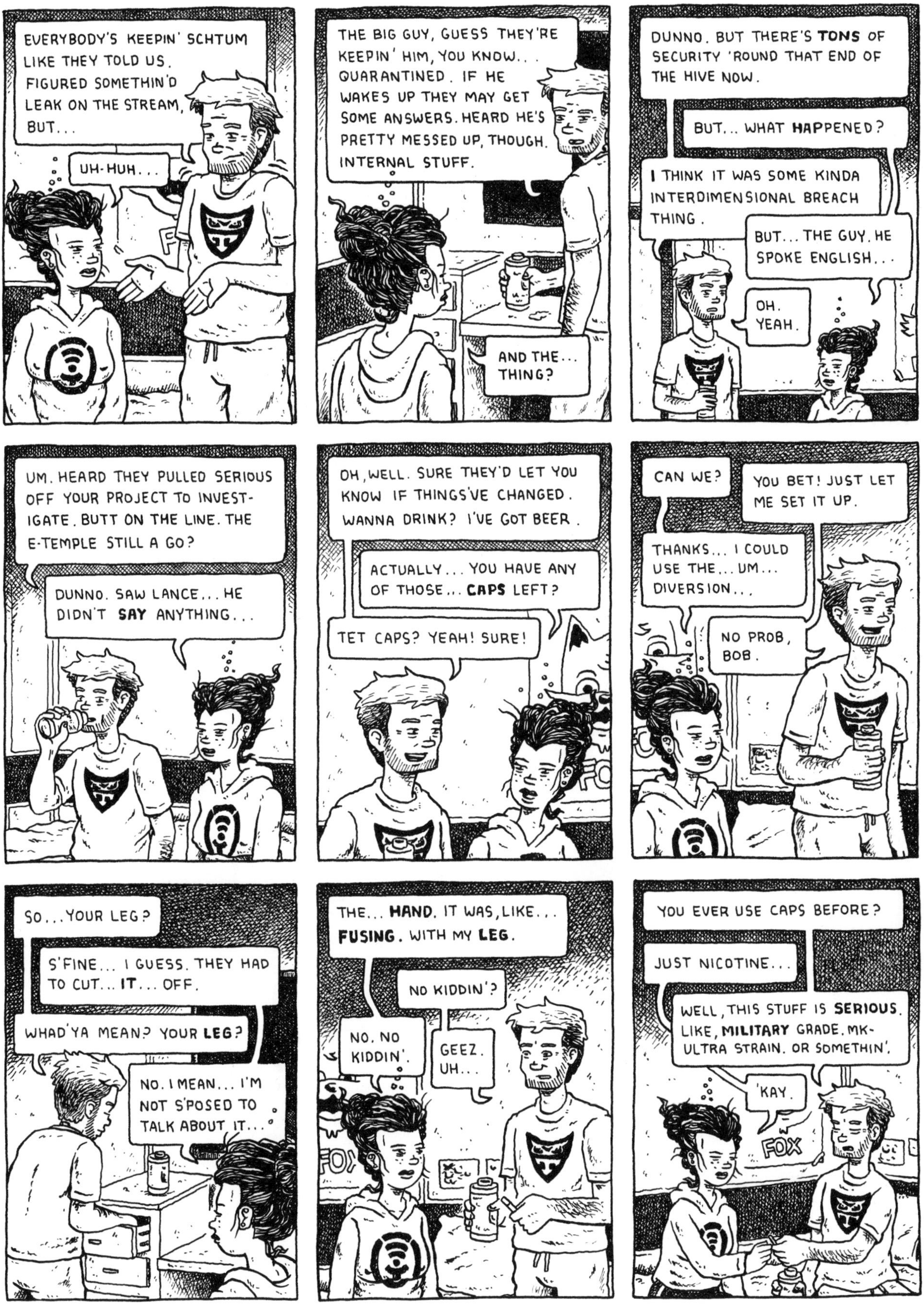

EVERYBODY'S KEEPIN' SCHTUM LIKE THEY TOLD US. FIGURED SOMETHIN'D LEAK ON THE STREAM, BUT...
UH-HUH...
THE BIG GUY, GUESS THEY'RE KEEPIN' HIM, YOU KNOW... QUARANTINED. IF HE WAKES UP THEY MAY GET SOME ANSWERS. HEARD HE'S PRETTY MESSED UP, THOUGH. INTERNAL STUFF.
AND THE... THING?
DUNNO. BUT THERE'S TONS OF SECURITY 'ROUND THAT END OF THE HIVE NOW.
BUT... WHAT HAPPENED?
I THINK IT WAS SOME KINDA INTERDIMENSIONAL BREACH THING.
BUT... THE GUY. HE SPOKE ENGLISH...
OH. YEAH.
UM. HEARD THEY PULLED SERIOUS OFF YOUR PROJECT TO INVEST-IGATE. BUTT ON THE LINE. THE E-TEMPLE STILL A GO?
DUNNO. SAW LANCE... HE DIDN'T SAY ANYTHING...
OH, WELL. SURE THEY'D LET YOU KNOW IF THINGS'VE CHANGED. WANNA DRINK? I'VE GOT BEER.
ACTUALLY... YOU HAVE ANY OF THOSE... CAPS LEFT?
TET CAPS? YEAH! SURE!
CAN WE?
YOU BET! JUST LET ME SET IT UP.
THANKS... I COULD USE THE... UM... DIVERSION...
NO PROB, BOB.
SO... YOUR LEG?
S'FINE... I GUESS. THEY HAD TO CUT... IT... OFF.
WHAD'YA MEAN? YOUR LEG?
NO. I MEAN... I'M NOT S'POSED TO TALK ABOUT IT...
THE... HAND. IT WAS, LIKE... FUSING. WITH MY LEG.
NO KIDDIN'?
NO. NO KIDDIN'.
GEEZ. UH...
YOU EVER USE CAPS BEFORE?
JUST NICOTINE...
WELL, THIS STUFF IS SERIOUS. LIKE, MILITARY GRADE. MK-ULTRA STRAIN. OR SOMETHIN'.
'KAY.

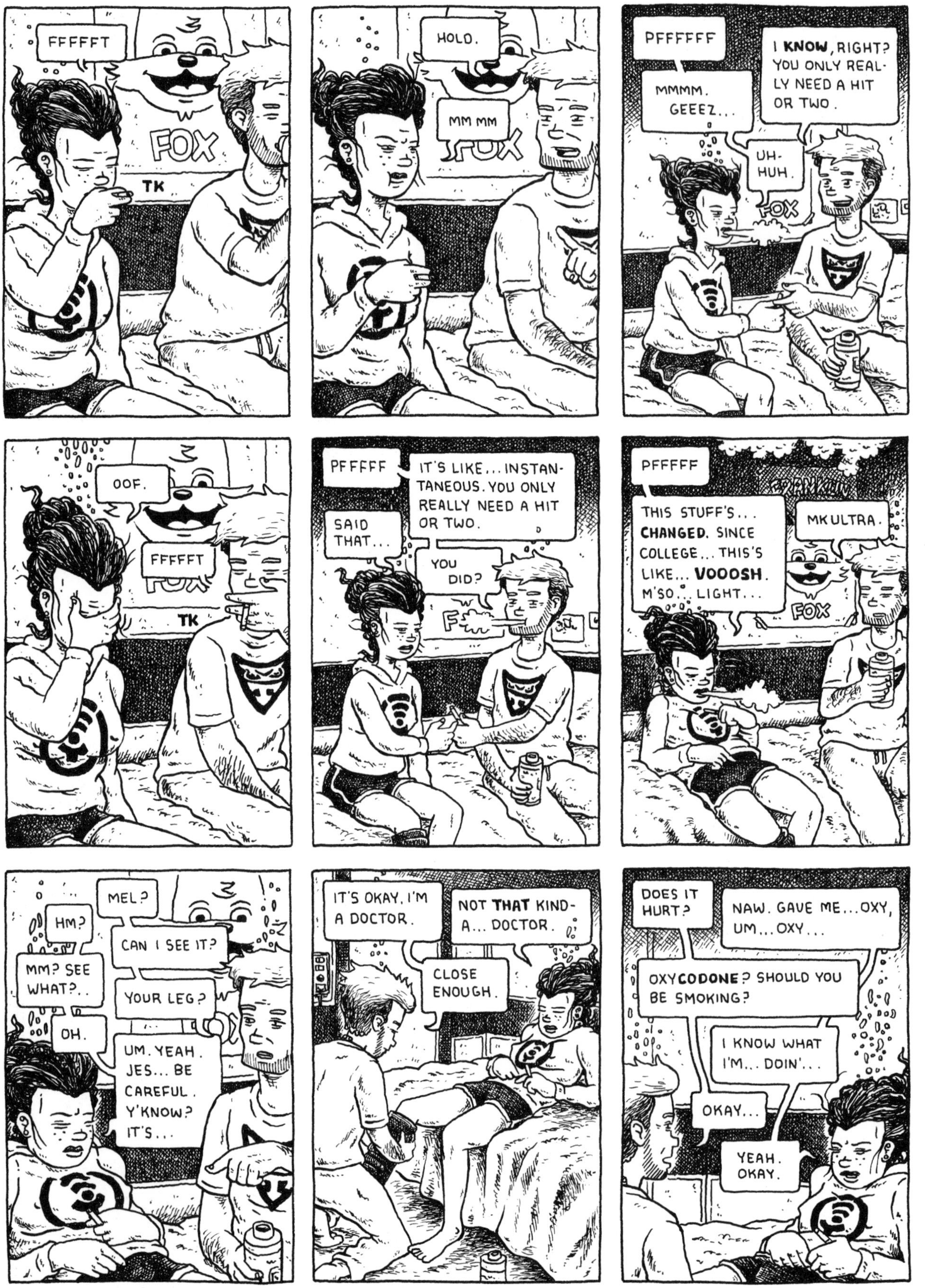
FFFFFT
TK
FOX
HOLD.
MM MM
PFFFFFF
MMMM. GEEEZ...
UH-HUH.
I **KNOW**, RIGHT? YOU ONLY REALLY NEED A HIT OR TWO.
OOF.
FFFFFT
TK
PFFFFF
IT'S LIKE... INSTANTANEOUS. YOU ONLY REALLY NEED A HIT OR TWO.
SAID THAT...
YOU DID?
PFFFFF
THIS STUFF'S... **CHANGED.** SINCE COLLEGE... THIS'S LIKE... **VOOOSH**. M'SO... LIGHT...
MKULTRA.
FOX
MEL?
HM?
CAN I SEE IT?
MM? SEE WHAT?..
YOUR LEG?
OH.
UM. YEAH. JES... BE CAREFUL. Y'KNOW? IT'S...
IT'S OKAY, I'M A DOCTOR.
NOT **THAT** KINDA... DOCTOR.
CLOSE ENOUGH.
DOES IT HURT?
NAW. GAVE ME... OXY, UM... OXY...
OXY**CODONE**? SHOULD YOU BE SMOKING?
I KNOW WHAT I'M... DOIN'...
OKAY...
YEAH. OKAY.

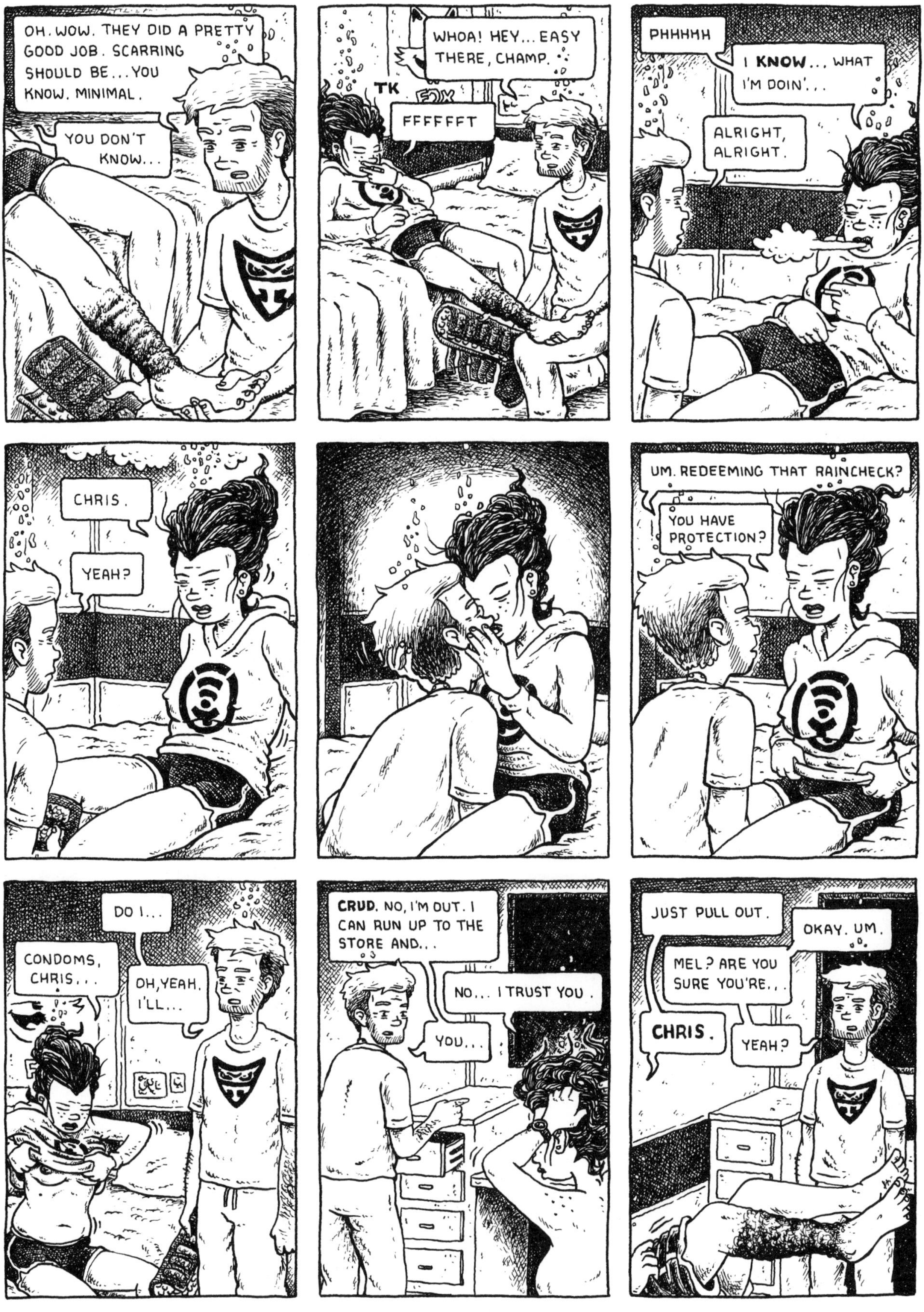
OH. WOW. THEY DID A PRETTY GOOD JOB. SCARRING SHOULD BE... YOU KNOW. MINIMAL.
YOU DON'T KNOW...
WHOA! HEY... EASY THERE, CHAMP.
TK
FFFFFFT
PHHHHH
I KNOW... WHAT I'M DOIN'...
ALRIGHT, ALRIGHT.
CHRIS.
YEAH?
UM. REDEEMING THAT RAINCHECK?
YOU HAVE PROTECTION?
DO I...
CONDOMS, CHRIS...
OH, YEAH. I'LL...
CRUD. NO, I'M OUT. I CAN RUN UP TO THE STORE AND...
NO... I TRUST YOU.
YOU...
JUST PULL OUT.
OKAY. UM.
MEL? ARE YOU SURE YOU'RE...
CHRIS.
YEAH?

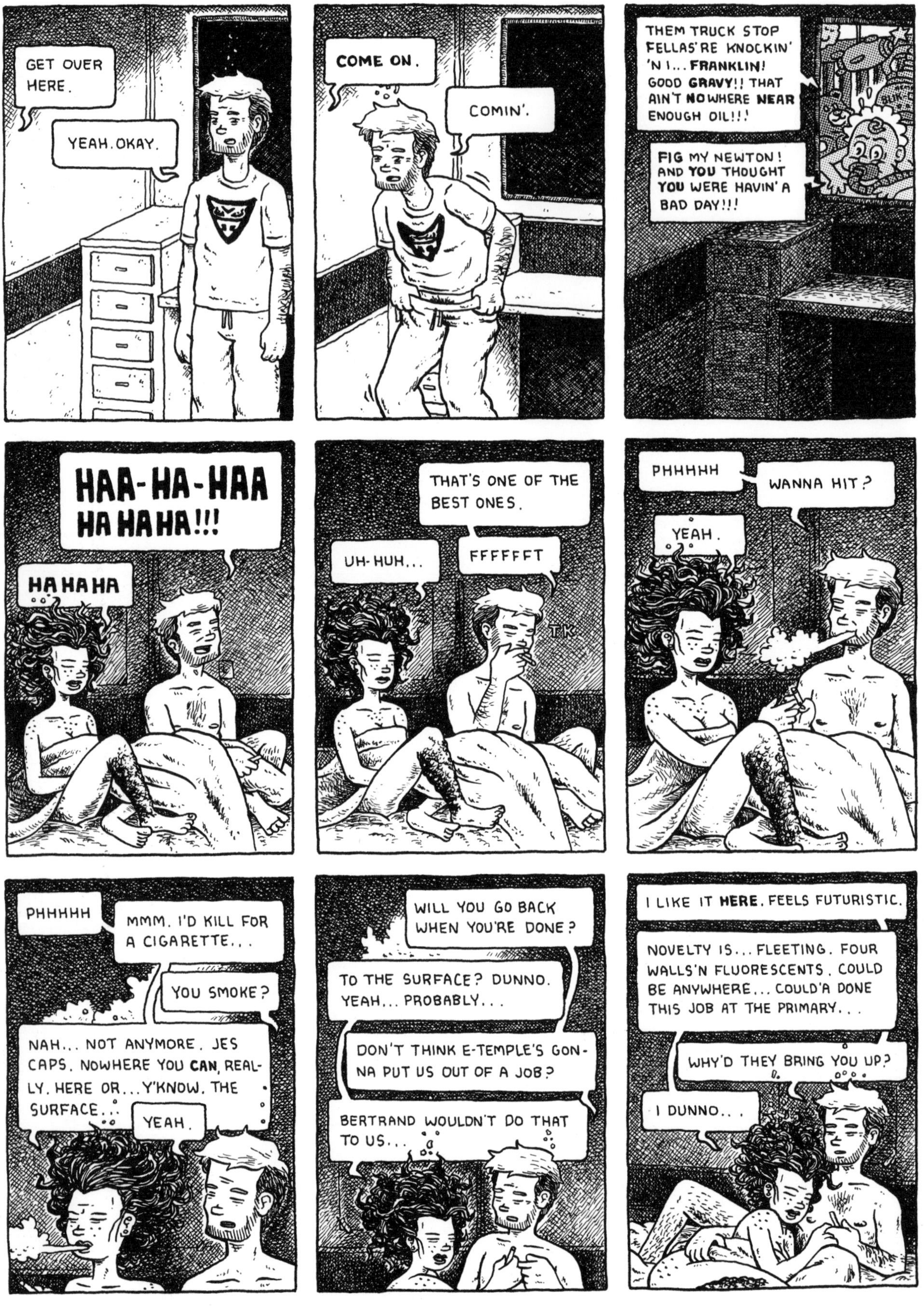
GET OVER HERE.
YEAH. OKAY.
COME ON.
COMIN'.
THEM TRUCK STOP FELLAS'RE KNOCKIN' 'N I... FRANKLIN! GOOD GRAVY!! THAT AIN'T NOWHERE NEAR ENOUGH OIL!!!
FIG MY NEWTON! AND YOU THOUGHT YOU WERE HAVIN' A BAD DAY!!!
HAA-HA-HAA HA HA HA!!!
HA HA HA
THAT'S ONE OF THE BEST ONES.
UH-HUH...
FFFFFFT
TK
PHHHHH
WANNA HIT?
YEAH.
PHHHHH
MMM. I'D KILL FOR A CIGARETTE...
YOU SMOKE?
NAH... NOT ANYMORE. JES CAPS. NOWHERE YOU CAN, REALLY. HERE OR... Y'KNOW. THE SURFACE...
YEAH.
WILL YOU GO BACK WHEN YOU'RE DONE?
TO THE SURFACE? DUNNO. YEAH... PROBABLY...
DON'T THINK E-TEMPLE'S GONNA PUT US OUT OF A JOB?
BERTRAND WOULDN'T DO THAT TO US...
I LIKE IT HERE. FEELS FUTURISTIC.
NOVELTY IS... FLEETING. FOUR WALLS'N FLUORESCENTS. COULD BE ANYWHERE... COULD'A DONE THIS JOB AT THE PRIMARY...
WHY'D THEY BRING YOU UP?
I DUNNO...

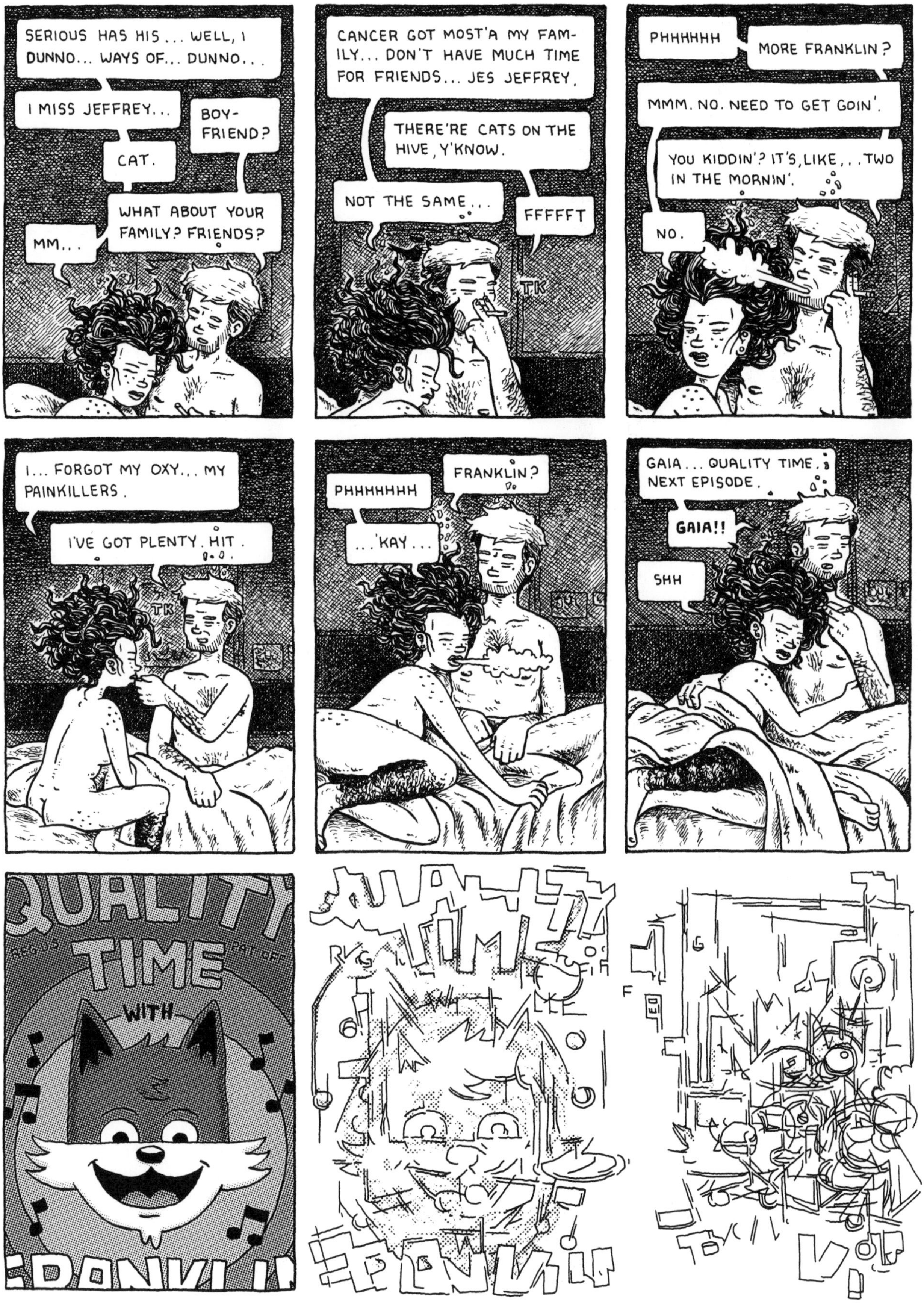

SERIOUS HAS HIS... WELL, I DUNNO... WAYS OF... DUNNO...
I MISS JEFFREY...
BOY-FRIEND?
CAT.
WHAT ABOUT YOUR FAMILY? FRIENDS?
MM...
CANCER GOT MOST'A MY FAMILY... DON'T HAVE MUCH TIME FOR FRIENDS... JES JEFFREY.
THERE'RE CATS ON THE HIVE, Y'KNOW.
NOT THE SAME...
FFFFFT
TK
PHHHHHH
MORE FRANKLIN?
MMM. NO. NEED TO GET GOIN'.
YOU KIDDIN'? IT'S, LIKE, . . TWO IN THE MORNIN'.
NO.
I... FORGOT MY OXY... MY PAINKILLERS.
I'VE GOT PLENTY. HIT.
TK
PHHHHHHH
FRANKLIN?
...'KAY...
GAIA... QUALITY TIME. NEXT EPISODE.
GAIA!!
SHH
QUALITY TIME WITH

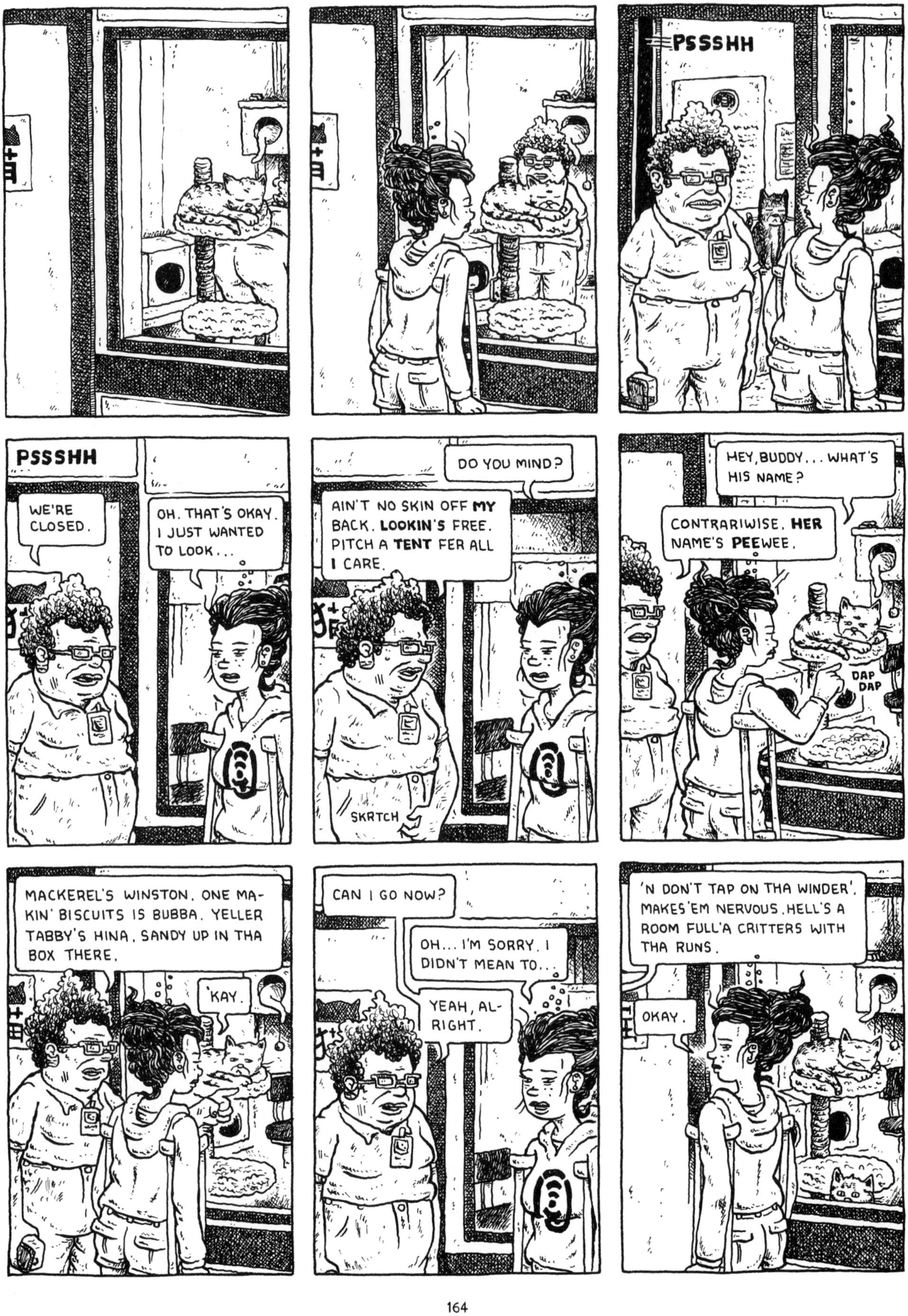
PSSSHH
PSSSHH
WE'RE CLOSED.
OH. THAT'S OKAY. I JUST WANTED TO LOOK...
DO YOU MIND?
AIN'T NO SKIN OFF **MY** BACK. **LOOKIN'S** FREE. PITCH A **TENT** FER ALL **I** CARE.
SKRTCH
HEY, BUDDY... WHAT'S HIS NAME?
CONTRARIWISE. **HER** NAME'S **PEE**WEE.
DAP DAP
MACKEREL'S WINSTON. ONE MA-KIN' BISCUITS IS BUBBA. YELLER TABBY'S HINA. SANDY UP IN THA BOX THERE.
KAY.
CAN I GO NOW?
OH... I'M SORRY. I DIDN'T MEAN TO...
YEAH, AL-RIGHT.
'N DON'T TAP ON THA WINDER'. MAKES 'EM NERVOUS. HELL'S A ROOM FULL'A CRITTERS WITH THA RUNS.
OKAY.

WELL, HEY THERE...

HEY THERE, LITTLE SPACE CAT...

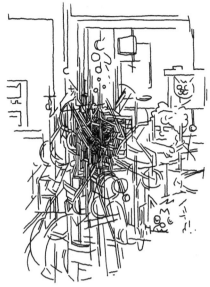

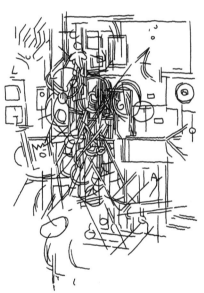

TAK TAK

HEY, STRANGER!

HEY, CHRISTIAN.

YOU DOIN' OKAY? YEAH...

THOUGHT YOU WERE COMIN' BACK **LAST** WEEK.

YEAH... I MEAN... NO. I WAS '**SPOSED** TO...

IT'S HEALING WEIRD... SLOWER'N THEY THOUGHT IT WOULD...

BUT IT'S BETTER?

I DUNNO. I NEED TO GO...

HEY, WAIT UP!

WHAT?

I FIGURED I'D... Y'KNOW. **HEAR** FROM YOU.

YEAH... I'VE BEEN BUSY.

OH. OKAY.

AND NOW I **REALLY** NEED TO...

BUT WAIT...

CHRISTIAN.

I **JUST** MET WITH KALPANA. SERIOUS CAN'T FIGURE OUT... WHAT-**EVER** WITH THE GATE, 'N IF HE DOESN'T **SOON**, WE'RE GONNA LOSE THE PROJECT. OKAY?

OKAY.

WE'VE BEEN ASKED TO PUT IN EX-TRA HOURS TO EXPEDITE THE... MY **HEAD'S** EFFED UP 'CAUSE,,, 'N I'M **SOME**HOW 'SPOSED TO...

CAN I HELP?

YOU CAN LET ME GET TO WORK.

OKAY.

JUST ONE THING.

WHAT?!

WHAT'RE YOU DOIN' TONIGHT? 'CAUSE I WAS LOOKIN' INTO THAT RAINCHECK BUSINESS AND...

CHRISTIAN.

YEAH?

I NEED YOU TO BE MY **FRIEND** RIGHT NOW. OKAY?

OKAY.

JUST GIVE ME TIME TO GET BETTER. TIME TO... TIME TO CLEAR MY HEAD. CAN YOU DO THAT FOR ME?

YES.

OF COURSE. I'LL BE YOUR JOHN-NY ON THE SPOT, MEL.

OKAY. **NOW**... I **REAL**LY NEED TO...

GET TO IT!

HOLLER IF YOU NEED ANYTHING.

'KAY. THANKS, CHRISTIAN.

YUP.

DU-DU BAAACK, YOUR DREEEAMS WERE YOUR DU-DU-DUUUUH...

ARUGULA, ARUGULA, **ARUGULA!!!**

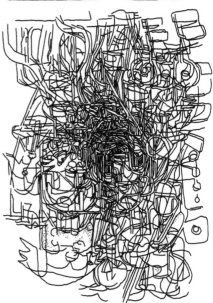

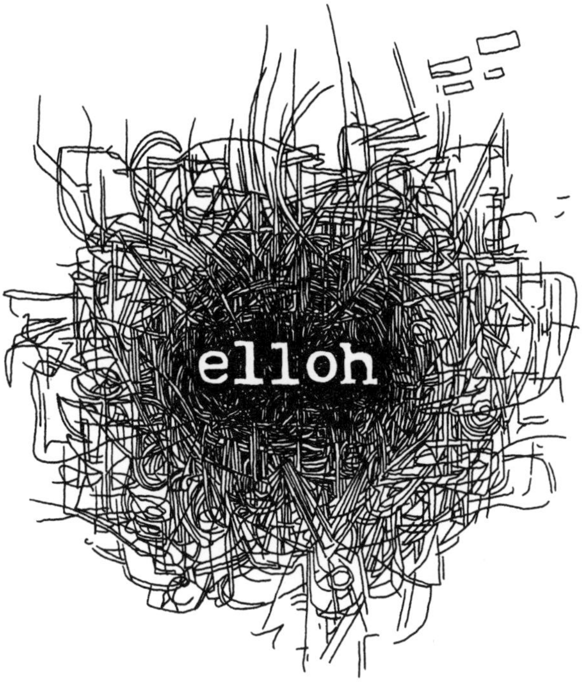
elloh

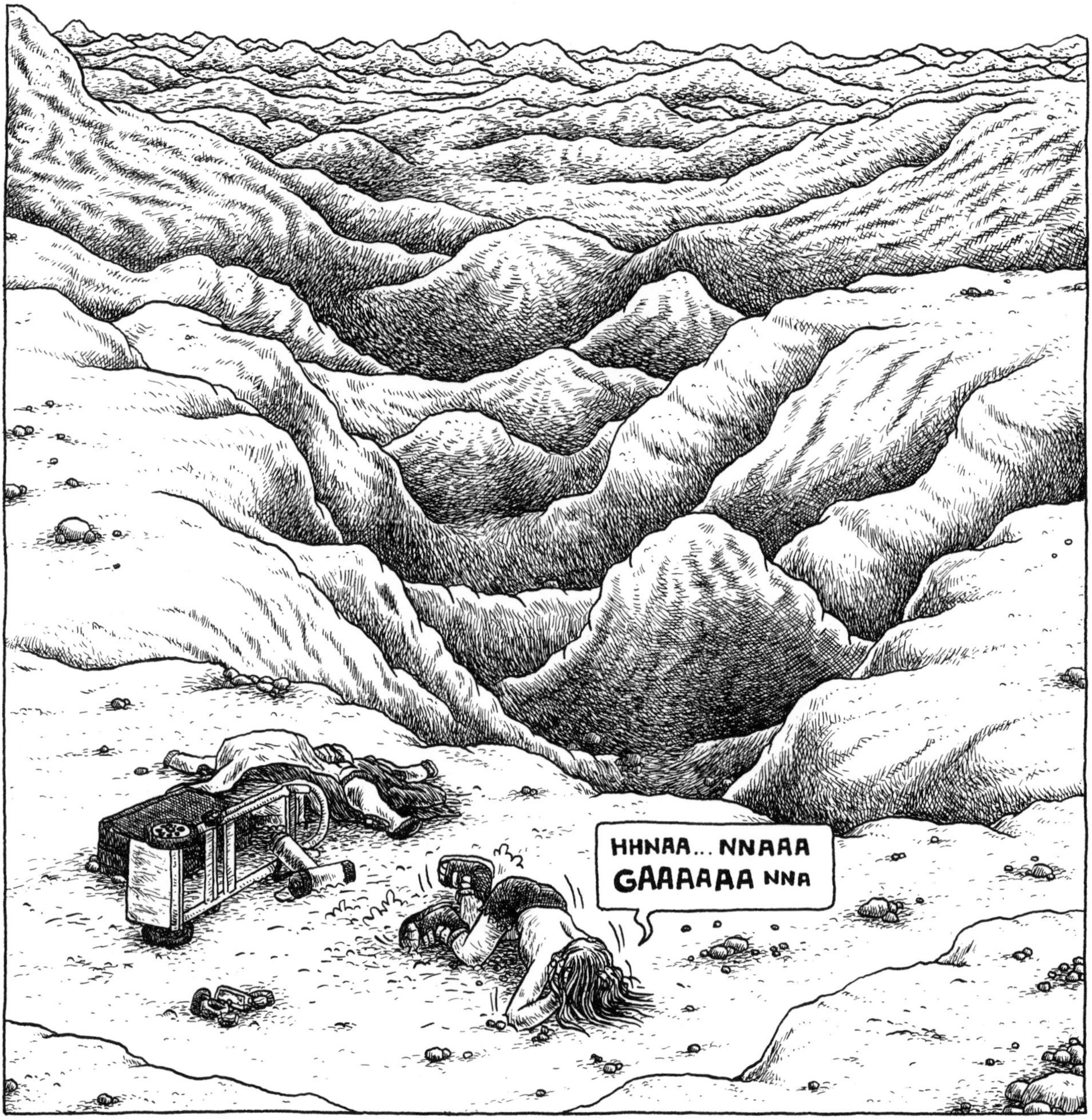
HHNAA... NNAAA
GAAAAAA NNA

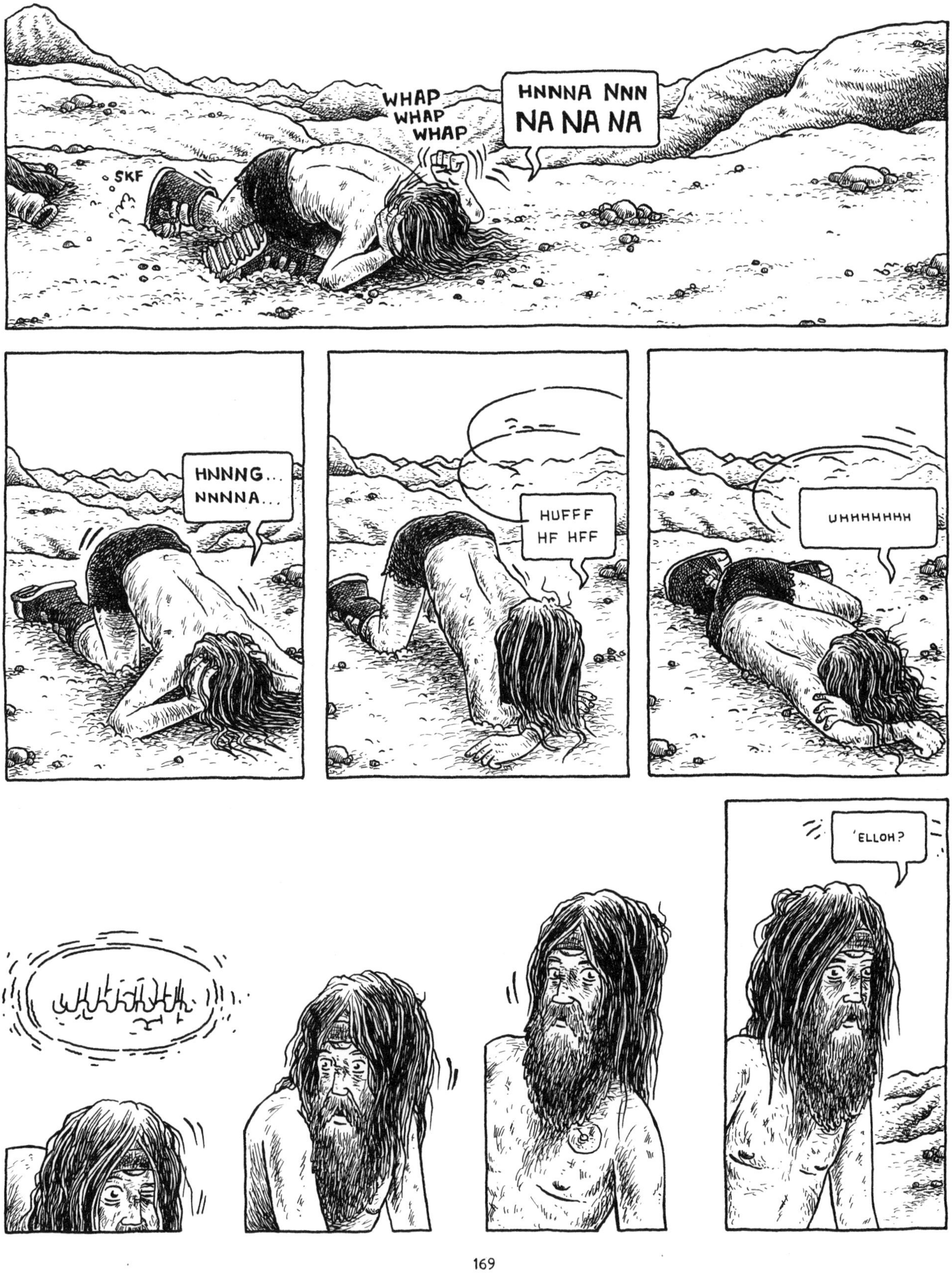
WHAP
WHAP
WHAP
HNNNA NNN
NA NA NA
SKF
HNNNG...
NNNNA...
HUFFF
HF HFF
UHHHHHHH
'ELLOH?

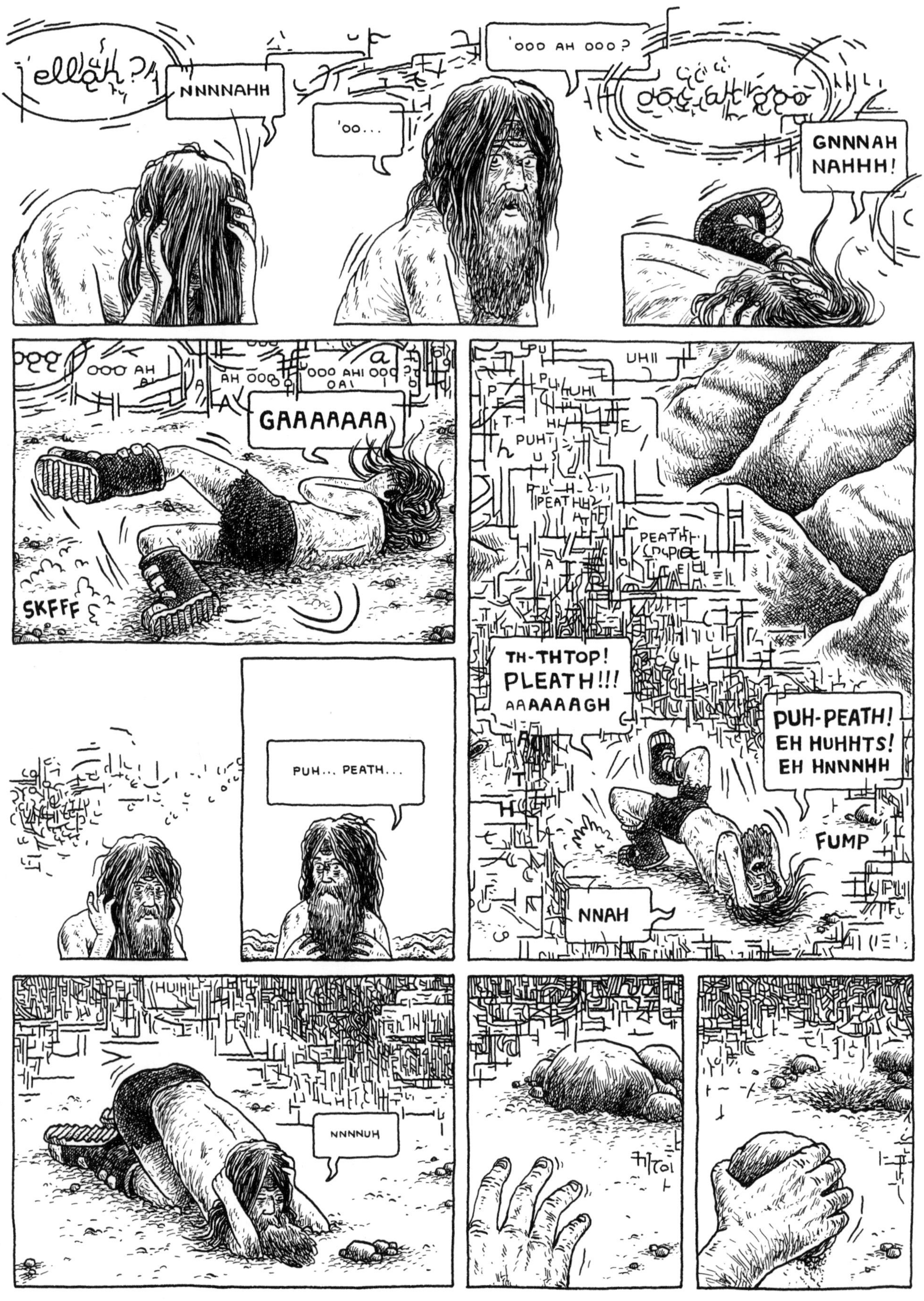

NNNNAHH
'OO...
'OOO AH OOO?
GNNNAH NAHHH!
GAAAAAAA
SKFFF
UHII
TH-THTOP! PLEATH!!! AAAAAAGH
PUH-PEATH! EH HUHHTS! EH HNNNHH
FUMP
NNAH
PUH... PEATH...
NNNNUH

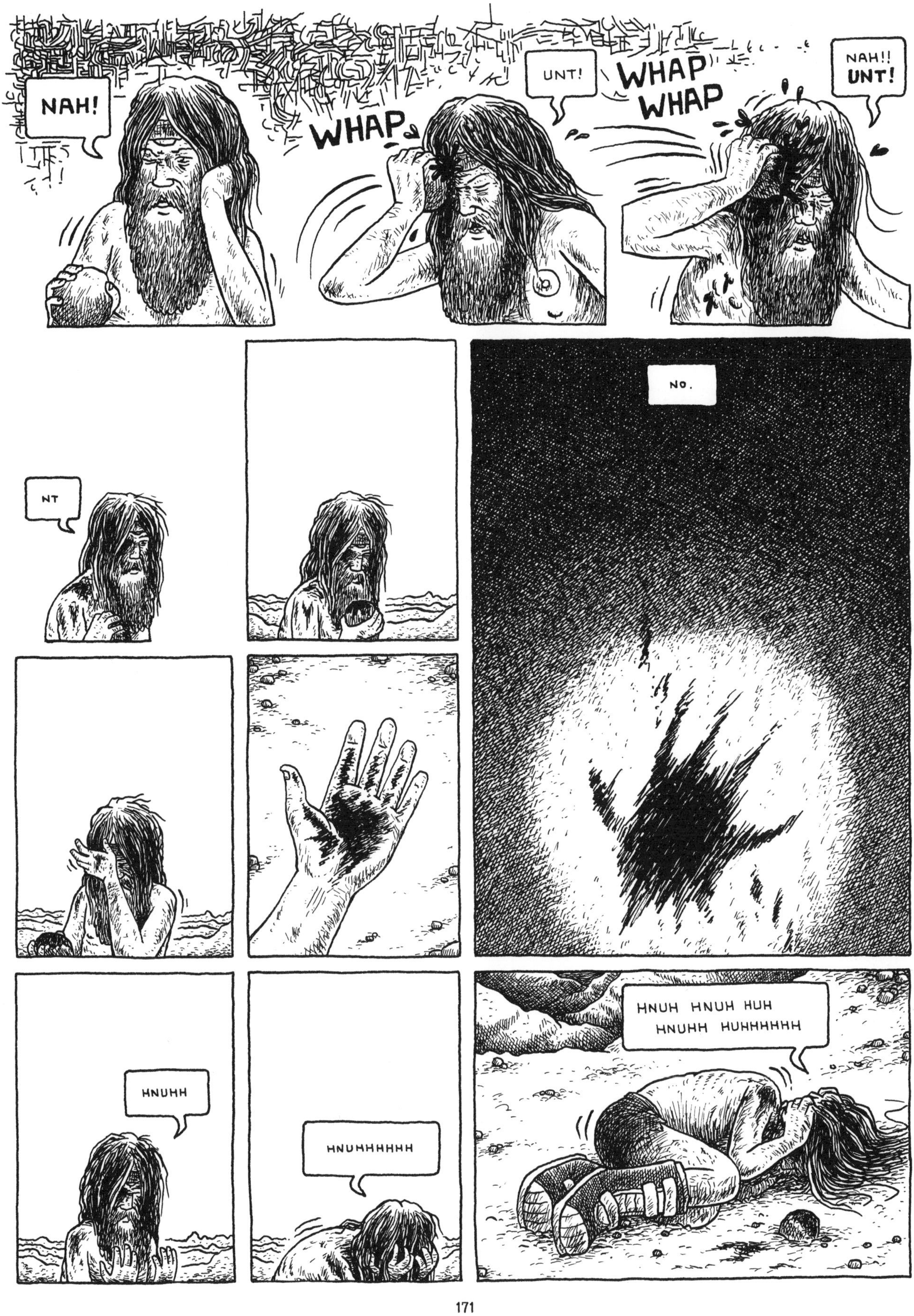
NAH!
WHAP
UNT!
WHAP
WHAP
NAH!!
UNT!
NT
NO.
HNUHH
HNUHHHHHH
HNUH HNUH HUH
HNUHH HUHHHHHH

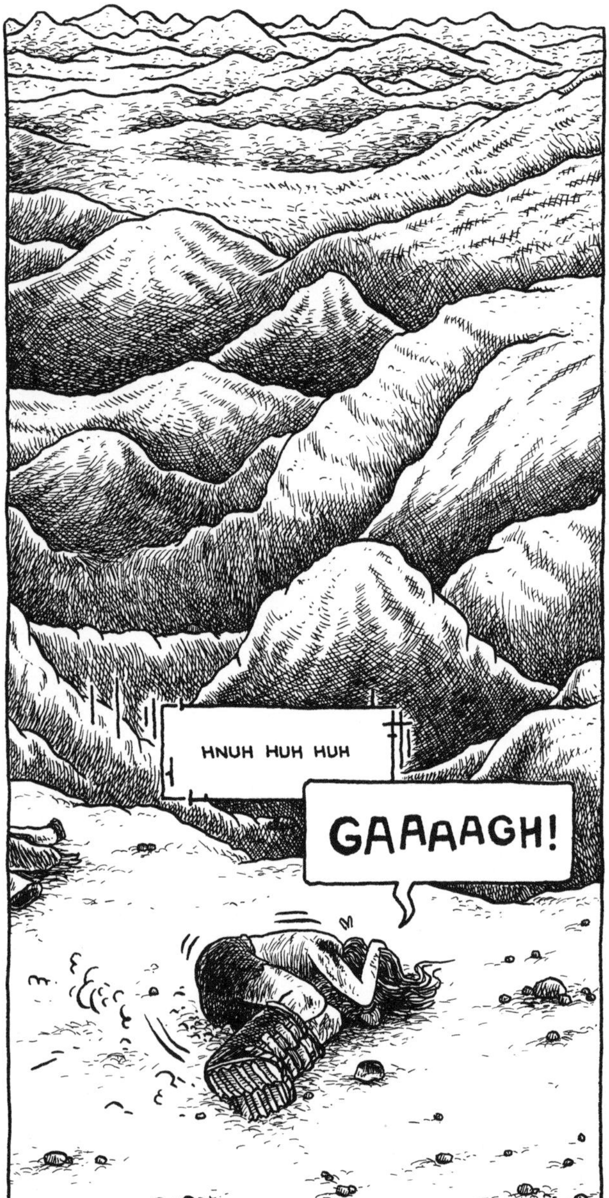
HNUH HUH HUH
GAAAAGH!

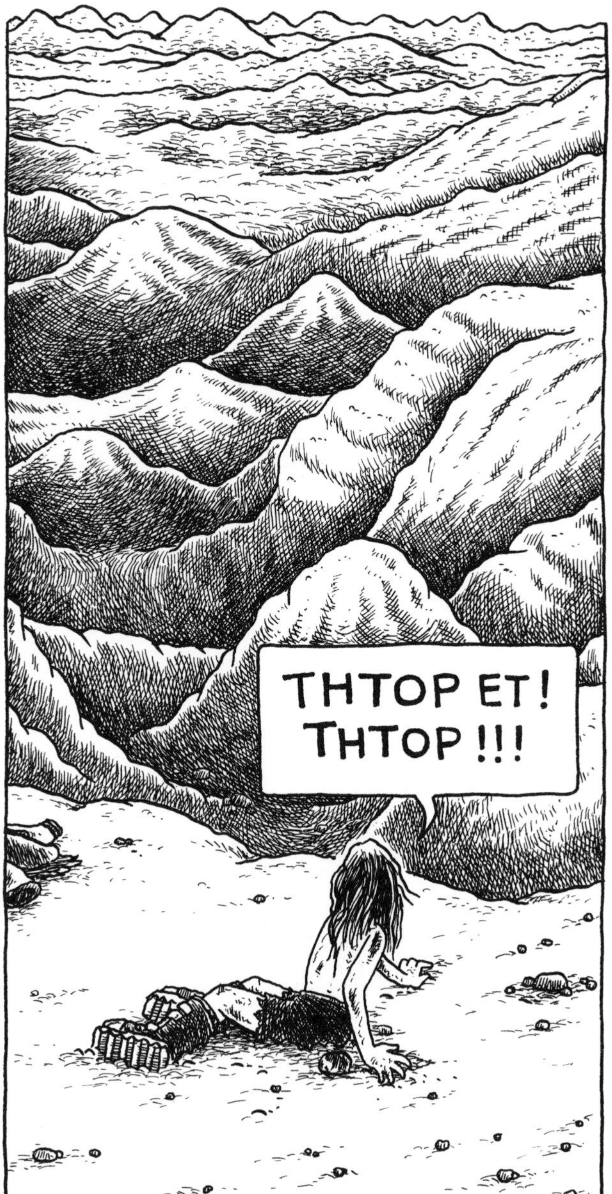
THTOP ET! THTOP!!!

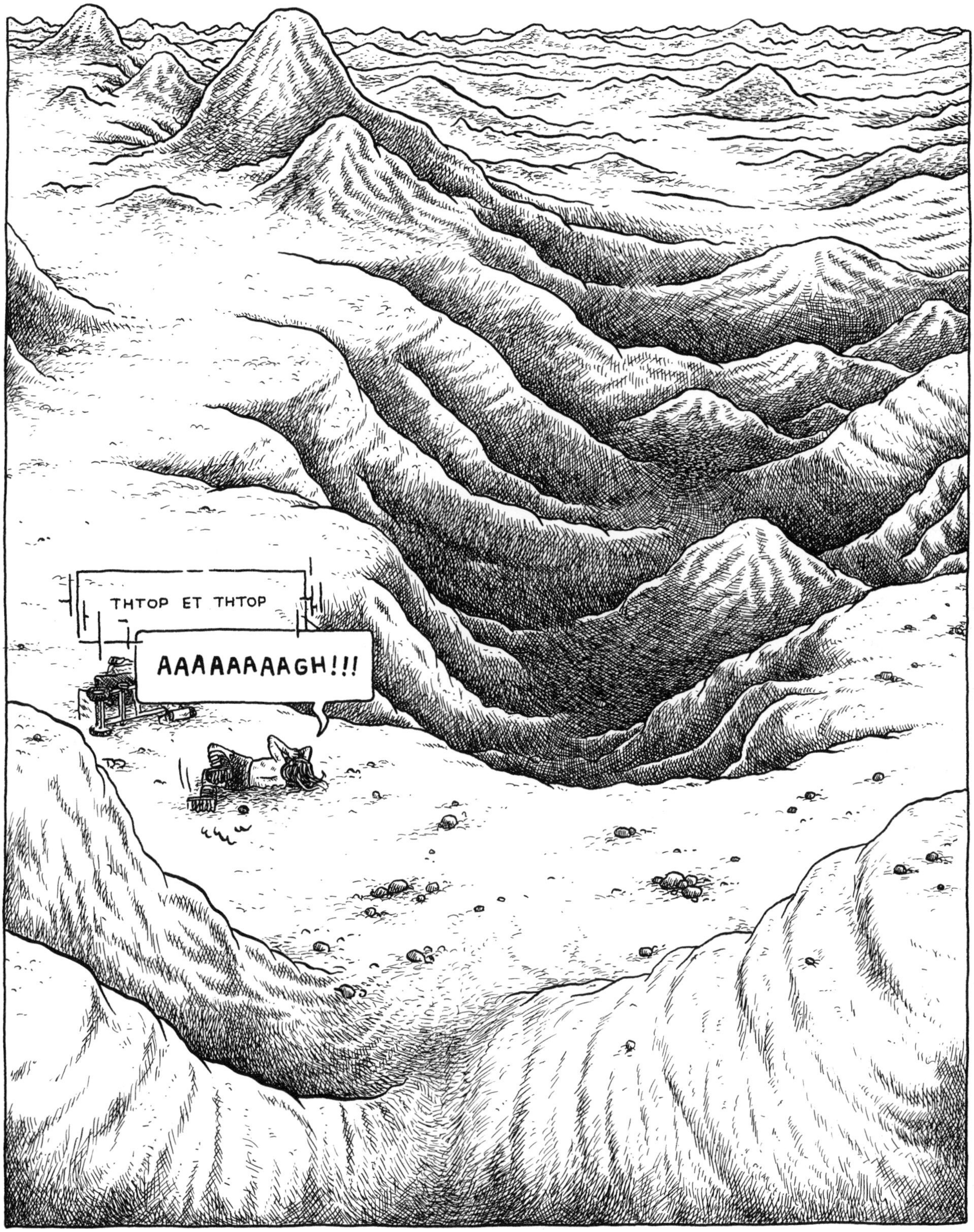
THTOP ET THTOP
AAAAAAAAGH!!!

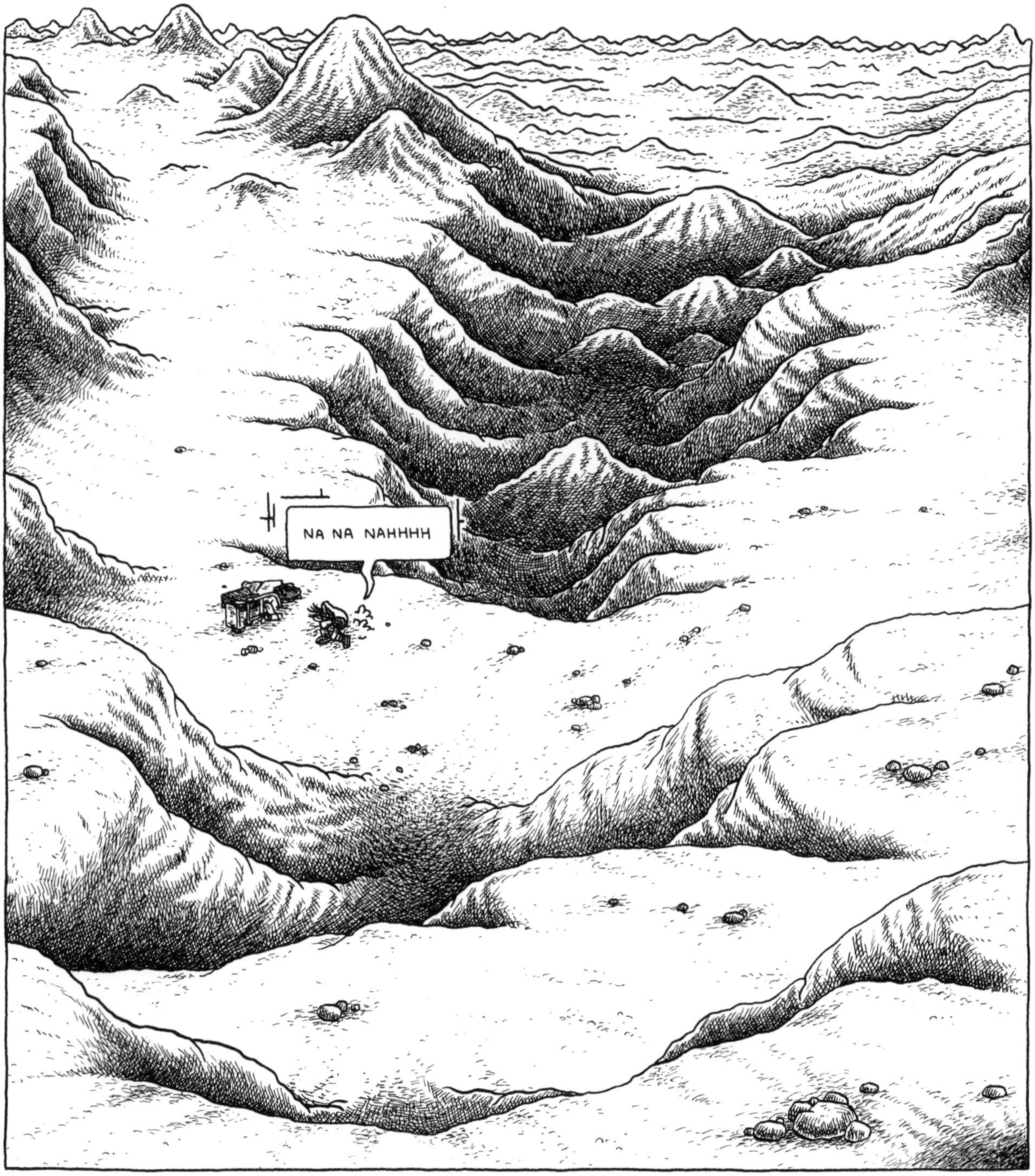
NA NA NAHHHH

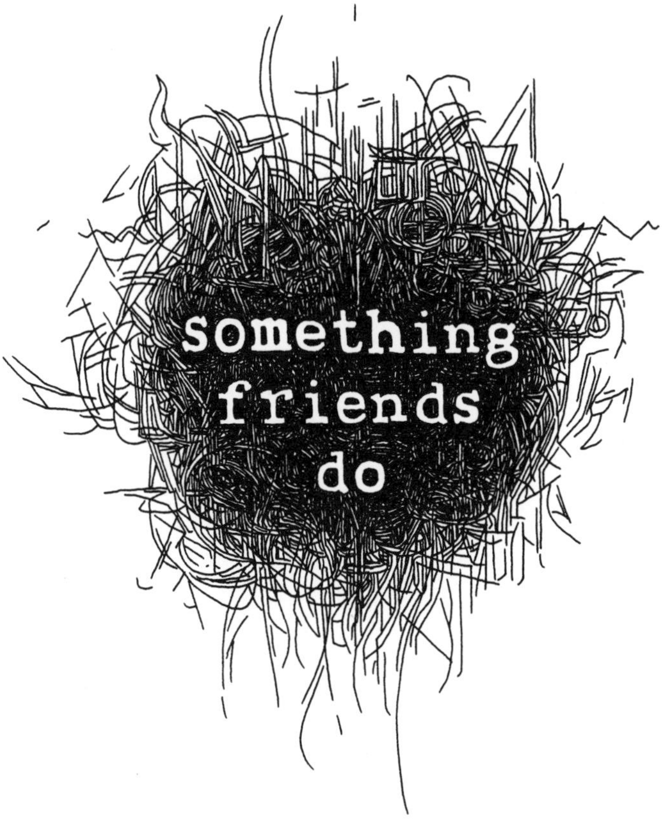
something
friends
do

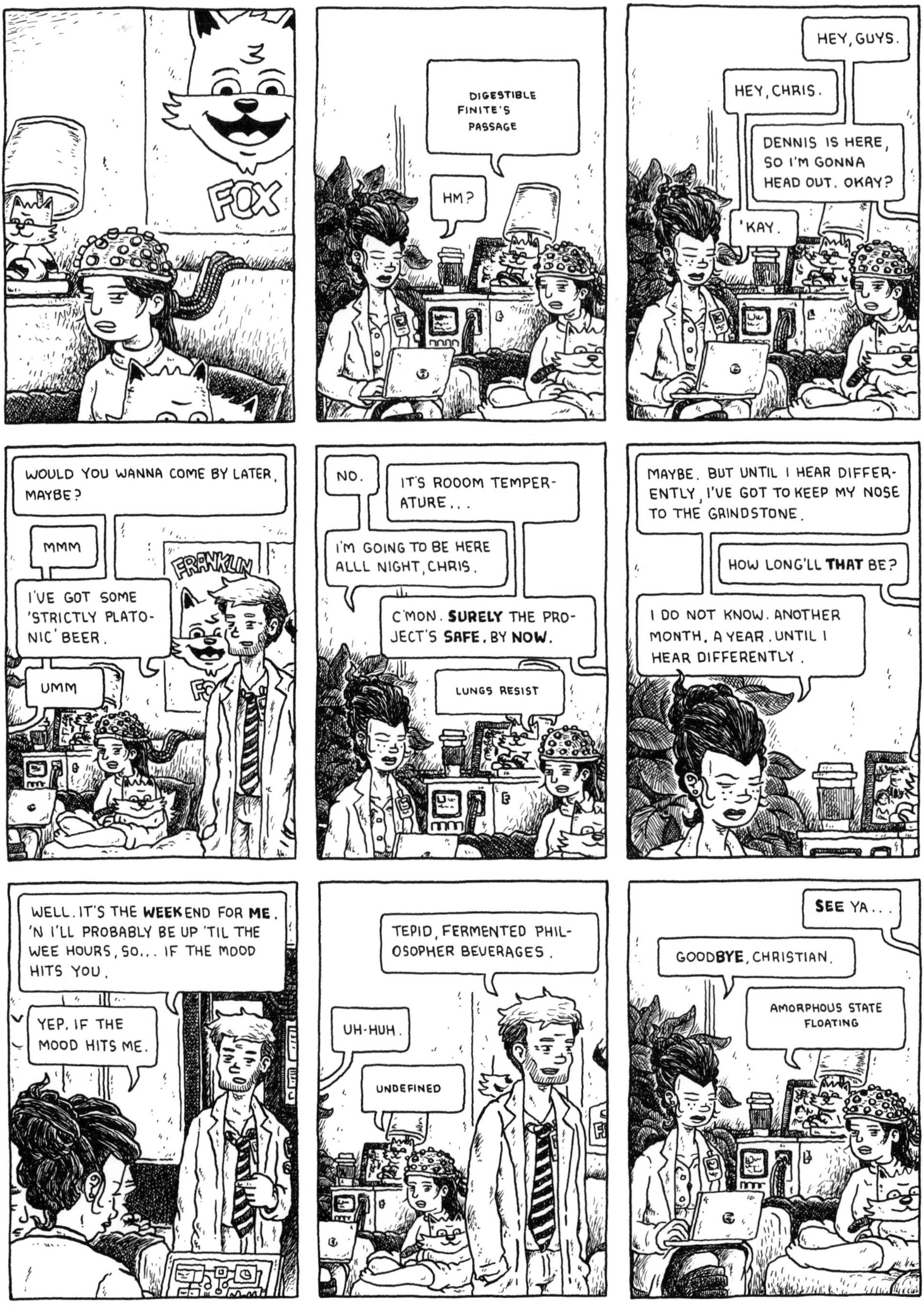
FOX
DIGESTIBLE FINITE'S PASSAGE
HM?
HEY, GUYS.
HEY, CHRIS.
DENNIS IS HERE, SO I'M GONNA HEAD OUT. OKAY?
'KAY.
WOULD YOU WANNA COME BY LATER, MAYBE?
MMM
I'VE GOT SOME 'STRICTLY PLATONIC' BEER.
UMM
FRANKLIN
NO.
IT'S ROOOM TEMPERATURE...
I'M GOING TO BE HERE ALLL NIGHT, CHRIS.
C'MON. SURELY THE PROJECT'S SAFE. BY NOW.
LUNGS RESIST
MAYBE. BUT UNTIL I HEAR DIFFERENTLY, I'VE GOT TO KEEP MY NOSE TO THE GRINDSTONE.
HOW LONG'LL THAT BE?
I DO NOT KNOW. ANOTHER MONTH. A YEAR. UNTIL I HEAR DIFFERENTLY.
WELL. IT'S THE WEEKEND FOR ME. 'N I'LL PROBABLY BE UP 'TIL THE WEE HOURS, SO... IF THE MOOD HITS YOU.
YEP. IF THE MOOD HITS ME.
TEPID, FERMENTED PHILOSOPHER BEVERAGES.
UH-HUH.
UNDEFINED
SEE YA...
GOODBYE, CHRISTIAN.
AMORPHOUS STATE FLOATING

ABHORRENT TO BEING AS LIFE WITHOUT MEANING WITHOUT

EVA...

EVA!

EVA?

PURPOSE AVA FOR IN AVA YOU'RE GOING TO PRESENCE

GET US IN TROUBLE.

MELODY.

YEAH?

WE'RE COMPELLED TO CONFESS.

CONFESS WHAT?

EVA.

WE'VE BEEN SNOOPING.

YES, MELODY. PRIVACY AND ETHICS.

BUT WE'RE CONCERNED.

WHAT ARE YOU CONCERNED ABOUT?

WE'RE CONCERNED ABOUT JEFFREY.

JEFFREY?

JEFFREY THE CAT?

WHY WOULD YOU BE...

YES?

YES, MELODY.

EXCUSE ME, DR. MCCABE?

I'M SORRY TO INTERRUPT, BUT IT'S TIME TO MAKE THE SWITCH.

OH, OKAY.

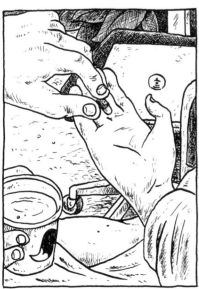

ARE YOU READY TO GET STARTED?

YES, MELODY.

QUALITY TIME?

WITH FRANKLIN FOX. YES, PLEASE, MELODY.

'KAY.

GAIA.

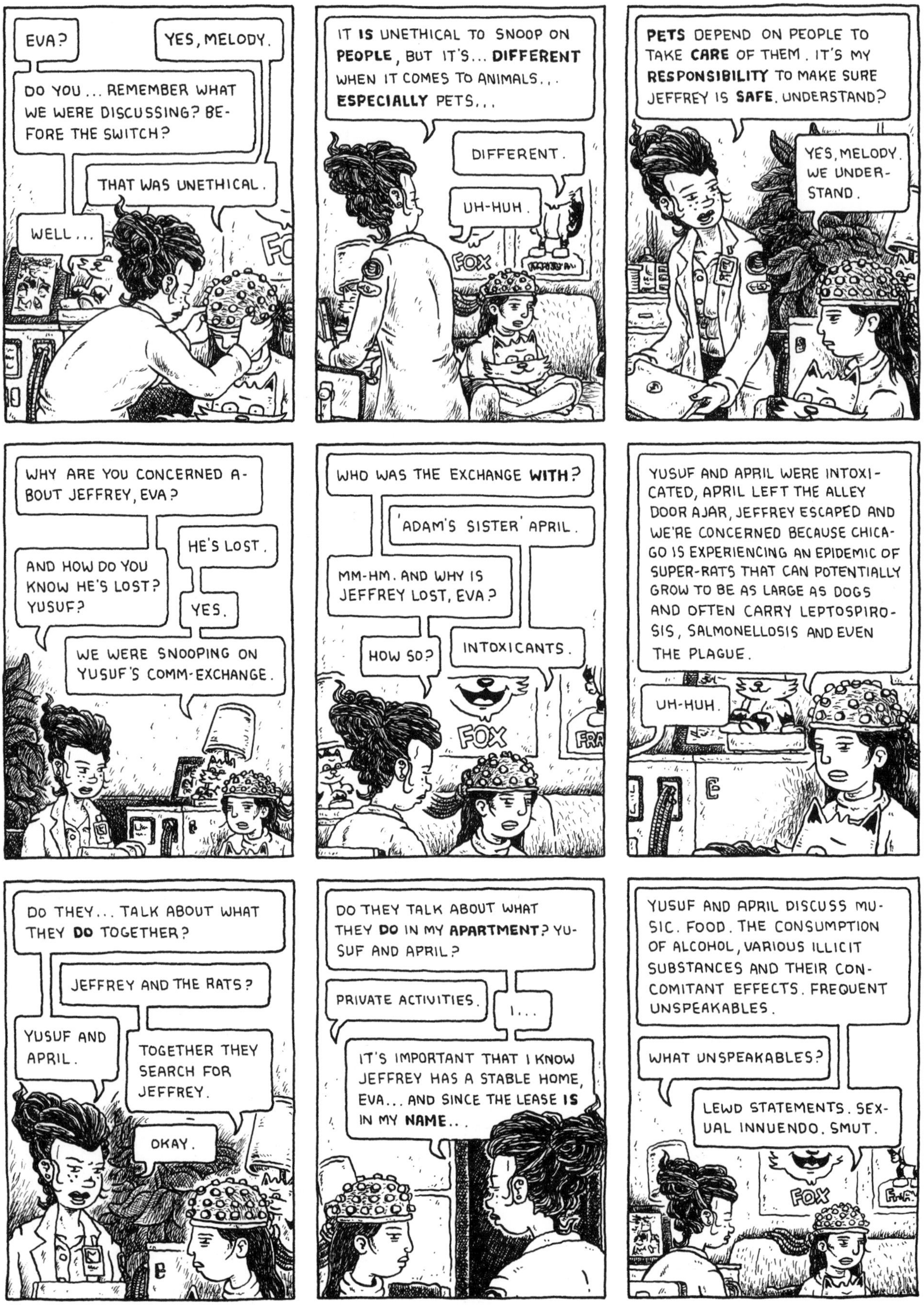
EVA?
YES, MELODY.
DO YOU... REMEMBER WHAT WE WERE DISCUSSING? BEFORE THE SWITCH?
THAT WAS UNETHICAL.
WELL...
IT **IS** UNETHICAL TO SNOOP ON **PEOPLE**, BUT IT'S... **DIFFERENT** WHEN IT COMES TO ANIMALS... **ESPECIALLY** PETS...
DIFFERENT.
UH-HUH.
FOX
PETS DEPEND ON PEOPLE TO TAKE **CARE** OF THEM. IT'S MY **RESPONSIBILITY** TO MAKE SURE JEFFREY IS **SAFE**. UNDERSTAND?
YES, MELODY. WE UNDERSTAND.
WHY ARE YOU CONCERNED ABOUT JEFFREY, EVA?
HE'S LOST.
AND HOW DO YOU KNOW HE'S LOST? YUSUF?
YES.
WE WERE SNOOPING ON YUSUF'S COMM-EXCHANGE.
WHO WAS THE EXCHANGE **WITH**?
'ADAM'S SISTER' APRIL.
MM-HM. AND WHY IS JEFFREY LOST, EVA?
HOW SO?
INTOXICANTS.
FOX
YUSUF AND APRIL WERE INTOXICATED, APRIL LEFT THE ALLEY DOOR AJAR, JEFFREY ESCAPED AND WE'RE CONCERNED BECAUSE CHICAGO IS EXPERIENCING AN EPIDEMIC OF SUPER-RATS THAT CAN POTENTIALLY GROW TO BE AS LARGE AS DOGS AND OFTEN CARRY LEPTOSPIROSIS, SALMONELLOSIS AND EVEN THE PLAGUE.
UH-HUH.
DO THEY... TALK ABOUT WHAT THEY **DO** TOGETHER?
JEFFREY AND THE RATS?
YUSUF AND APRIL.
TOGETHER THEY SEARCH FOR JEFFREY.
OKAY.
DO THEY TALK ABOUT WHAT THEY **DO** IN MY **APARTMENT**? YUSUF AND APRIL?
PRIVATE ACTIVITIES.
I...
IT'S IMPORTANT THAT I KNOW JEFFREY HAS A STABLE HOME, EVA... AND SINCE THE LEASE **IS** IN MY **NAME**...
YUSUF AND APRIL DISCUSS MUSIC. FOOD. THE CONSUMPTION OF ALCOHOL, VARIOUS ILLICIT SUBSTANCES AND THEIR CONCOMITANT EFFECTS. FREQUENT UNSPEAKABLES.
WHAT UNSPEAKABLES?
LEWD STATEMENTS. SEXUAL INNUENDO. SMUT.
FOX

DO THE EXCHANGES MENTION...

FRANKLIN, MELODY.

I KNOW. JUST ONE MORE QUESTION.

DO YUSUF AND APRIL HAVE... A **PHYSICAL** RELATIONSHIP?

YUSUF AND APRIL ENGAGE IN SEXUAL CONGRESS. FELLATIO. APRIL IS FOND OF CUNILIN—

OKAY, OKAY, OKAY.

THAT WILL SUFFICE, MELODY.?

YES. THANK YOU, EVA.

AND NOW YOU'LL BE ABLE TO FIND AND PROTECT JEFFREY.

YEAH.

EVA... WE SHOULD PROBABLY KEEP THIS CONVERSATION A SECRET. JUST BETWEEN YOU AND ME. OKAY?

WHY?

BECAUSE IT'S SOMETHING FRIENDS DO. KEEP SECRETS.

SNF

CAN IT BE OUR SECRET?

WE KEEP MANY SECRETS.

IS THAT A YES?

YES, MELODY. YOU ARE OUR FRIEND. NOW, FRANKLIN.

OKAY. LET'S GET TO WORK.

NOSE TO THE GRINDSTONE.

YEP...

TAP TAP TAP

TK-VEEEEET VEEEEET VEEEEET TK-VEEEEET

FWSHH TUNK

SHIT.

VEEEEET TK-VEEEEET VEEEEET TK-VEEEEET

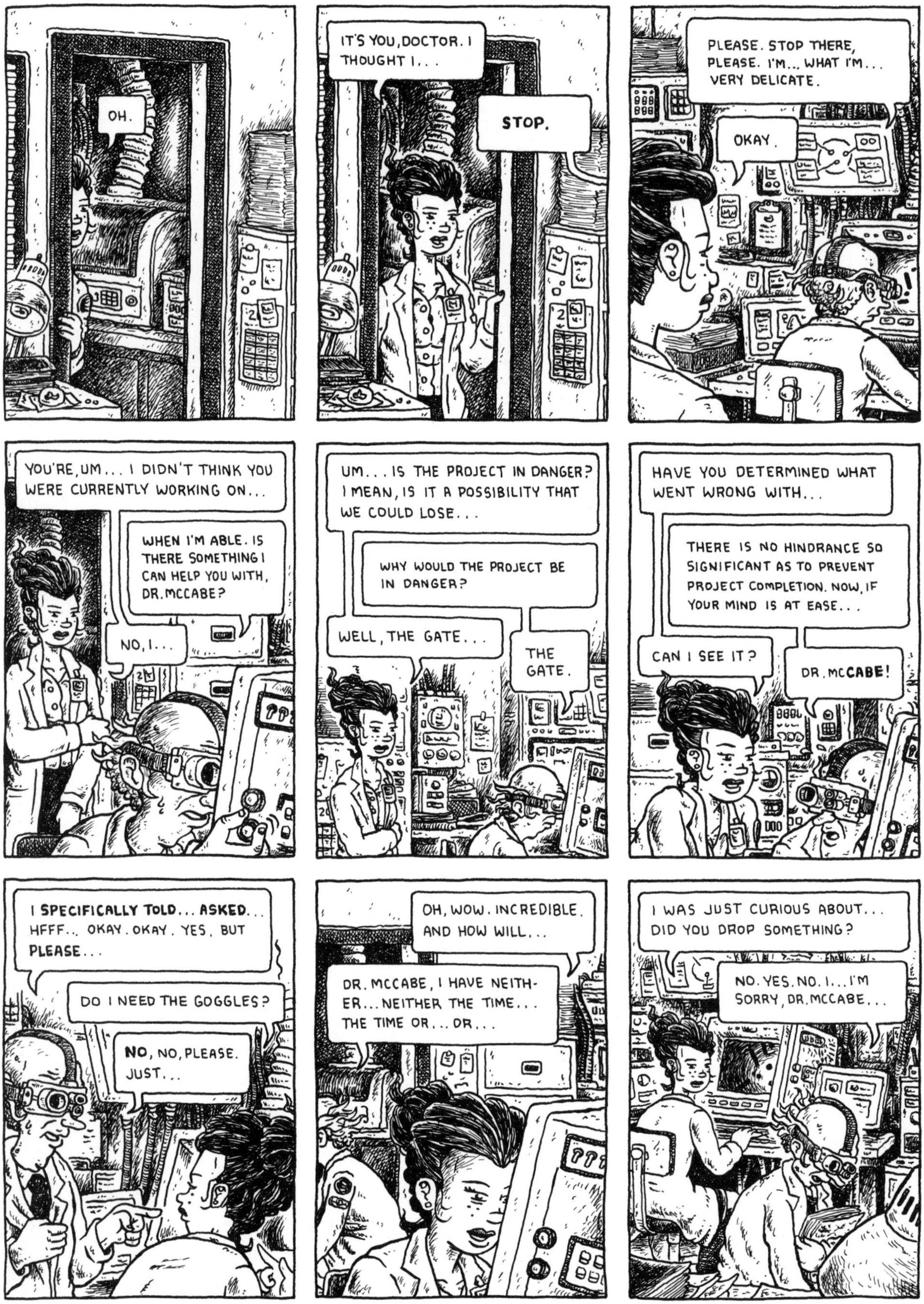
OH.
IT'S YOU, DOCTOR. I THOUGHT I...
STOP.
PLEASE. STOP THERE, PLEASE. I'M... WHAT I'M... VERY DELICATE.
OKAY.
YOU'RE, UM... I DIDN'T THINK YOU WERE CURRENTLY WORKING ON...
WHEN I'M ABLE. IS THERE SOMETHING I CAN HELP YOU WITH, DR. MCCABE?
NO, I...
UM... IS THE PROJECT IN DANGER? I MEAN, IS IT A POSSIBILITY THAT WE COULD LOSE...
WHY WOULD THE PROJECT BE IN DANGER?
WELL, THE GATE...
THE GATE.
HAVE YOU DETERMINED WHAT WENT WRONG WITH...
THERE IS NO HINDRANCE SO SIGNIFICANT AS TO PREVENT PROJECT COMPLETION. NOW, IF YOUR MIND IS AT EASE...
CAN I SEE IT?
DR. MCCABE!
I SPECIFICALLY TOLD... ASKED... HFFF... OKAY. OKAY. YES. BUT PLEASE...
DO I NEED THE GOGGLES?
NO, NO, PLEASE. JUST...
OH, WOW. INCREDIBLE. AND HOW WILL...
DR. MCCABE, I HAVE NEITH-ER... NEITHER THE TIME... THE TIME OR... OR...
I WAS JUST CURIOUS ABOUT... DID YOU DROP SOMETHING?
NO. YES. NO. I... I'M SORRY, DR. MCCABE...

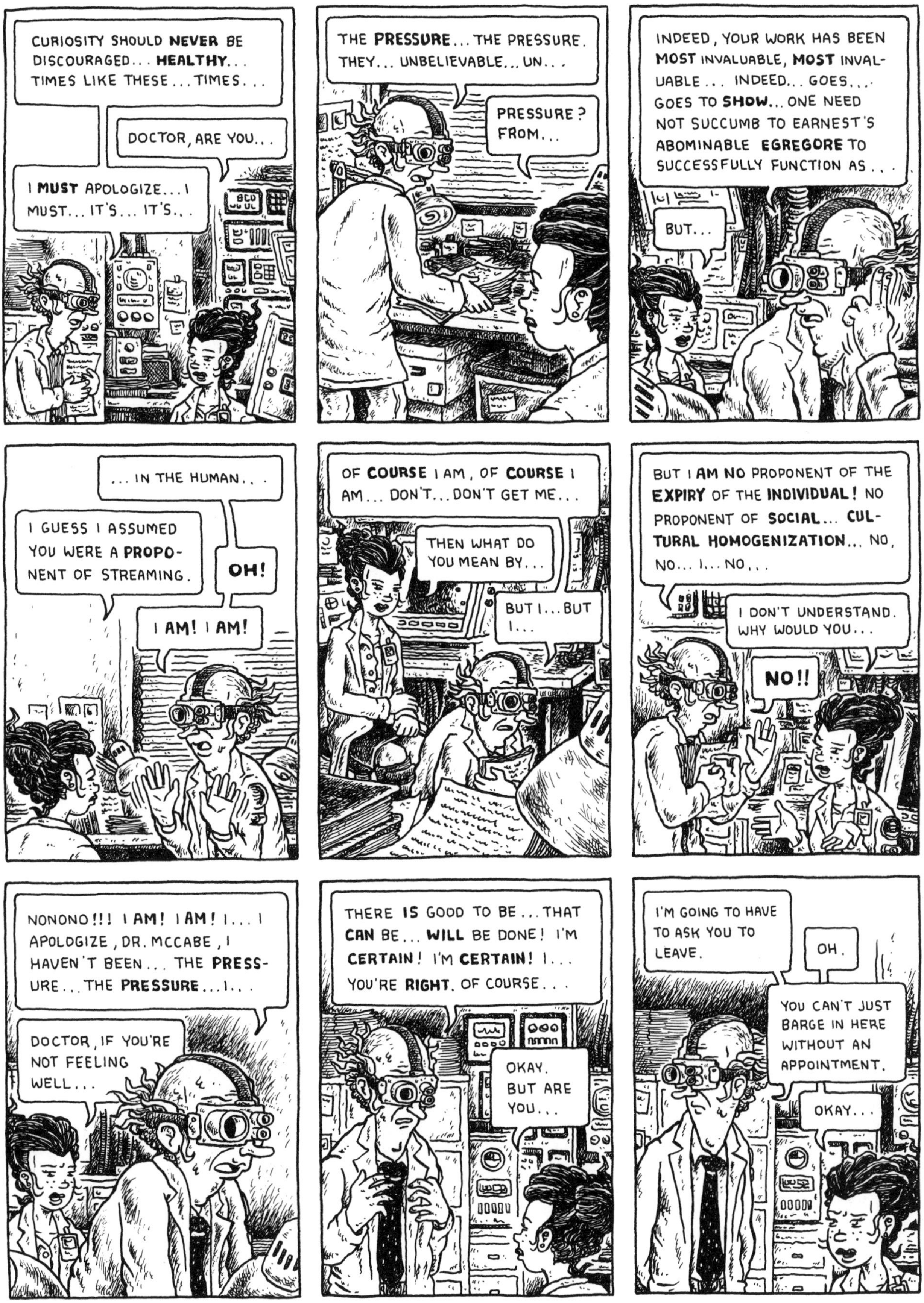
CURIOSITY SHOULD NEVER BE DISCOURAGED... HEALTHY... TIMES LIKE THESE... TIMES...
DOCTOR, ARE YOU...
I MUST APOLOGIZE... I MUST... IT'S... IT'S...
THE PRESSURE... THE PRESSURE. THEY... UNBELIEVABLE... UN...
PRESSURE? FROM...
INDEED, YOUR WORK HAS BEEN MOST INVALUABLE, MOST INVALUABLE... INDEED... GOES... GOES TO SHOW... ONE NEED NOT SUCCUMB TO EARNEST'S ABOMINABLE EGREGORE TO SUCCESSFULLY FUNCTION AS...
BUT...
... IN THE HUMAN...
I GUESS I ASSUMED YOU WERE A PROPONENT OF STREAMING.
OH!
I AM! I AM!
OF COURSE I AM, OF COURSE I AM... DON'T... DON'T GET ME...
THEN WHAT DO YOU MEAN BY...
BUT I... BUT I...
BUT I AM NO PROPONENT OF THE EXPIRY OF THE INDIVIDUAL! NO PROPONENT OF SOCIAL... CULTURAL HOMOGENIZATION... NO, NO... I... NO...
I DON'T UNDERSTAND. WHY WOULD YOU...
NO!!
NONONO!!! I AM! I AM! I... I APOLOGIZE, DR. MCCABE, I HAVEN'T BEEN... THE PRESSURE... THE PRESSURE... I...
DOCTOR, IF YOU'RE NOT FEELING WELL...
THERE IS GOOD TO BE... THAT CAN BE... WILL BE DONE! I'M CERTAIN! I'M CERTAIN! I... YOU'RE RIGHT, OF COURSE...
OKAY. BUT ARE YOU...
I'M GOING TO HAVE TO ASK YOU TO LEAVE.
OH.
YOU CAN'T JUST BARGE IN HERE WITHOUT AN APPOINTMENT.
OKAY...

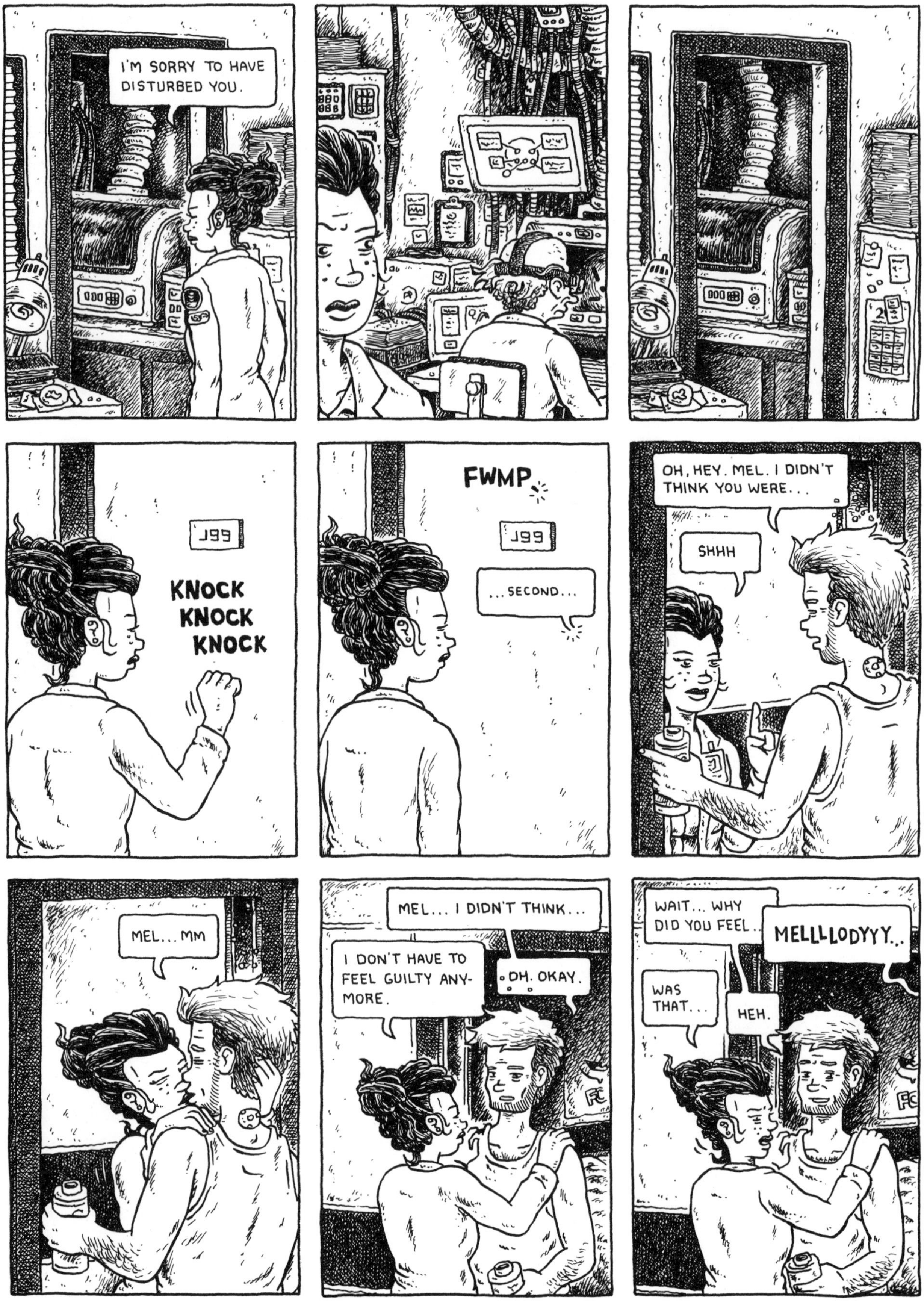
I'M SORRY TO HAVE DISTURBED YOU.
J99
KNOCK KNOCK KNOCK
FWMP
J99
...SECOND...
OH, HEY. MEL. I DIDN'T THINK YOU WERE...
SHHH
MEL... MM
MEL... I DIDN'T THINK...
I DON'T HAVE TO FEEL GUILTY ANYMORE.
OH. OKAY.
WAIT... WHY DID YOU FEEL...
MELLLLODYYY...
WAS THAT...
HEH.

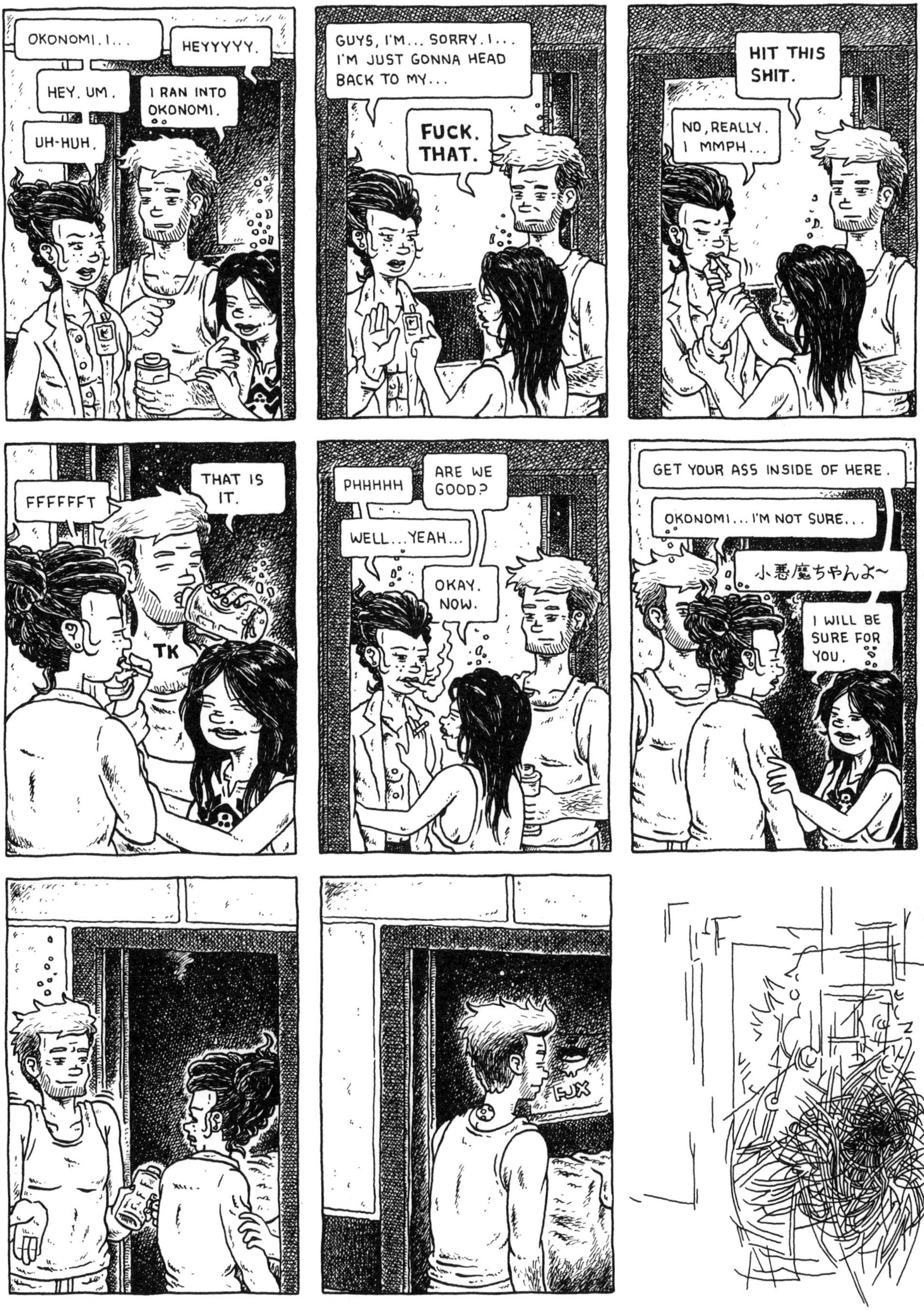
OKONOMI. I...
HEYYYYY.
HEY. UM.
I RAN INTO OKONOMI.
UH-HUH.
GUYS, I'M... SORRY. I... I'M JUST GONNA HEAD BACK TO MY...
FUCK. THAT.
HIT THIS SHIT.
NO, REALLY. I MMPH...
FFFFFFT
THAT IS IT.
TK
PHHHHH
ARE WE GOOD?
WELL... YEAH...
OKAY. NOW.
GET YOUR ASS INSIDE OF HERE.
OKONOMI... I'M NOT SURE...
小悪魔ちゃんよ~
I WILL BE SURE FOR YOU.

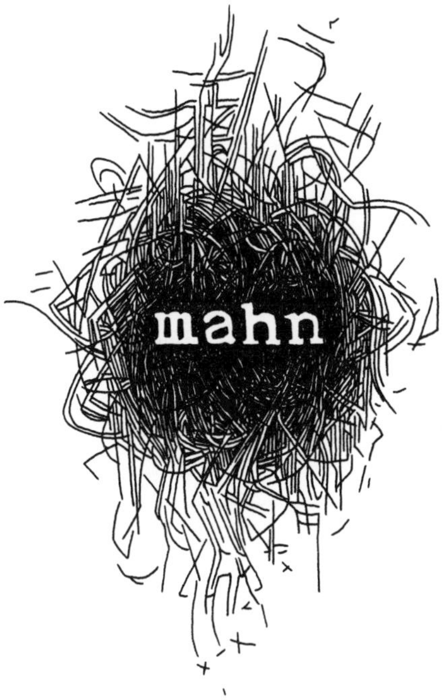
mahn

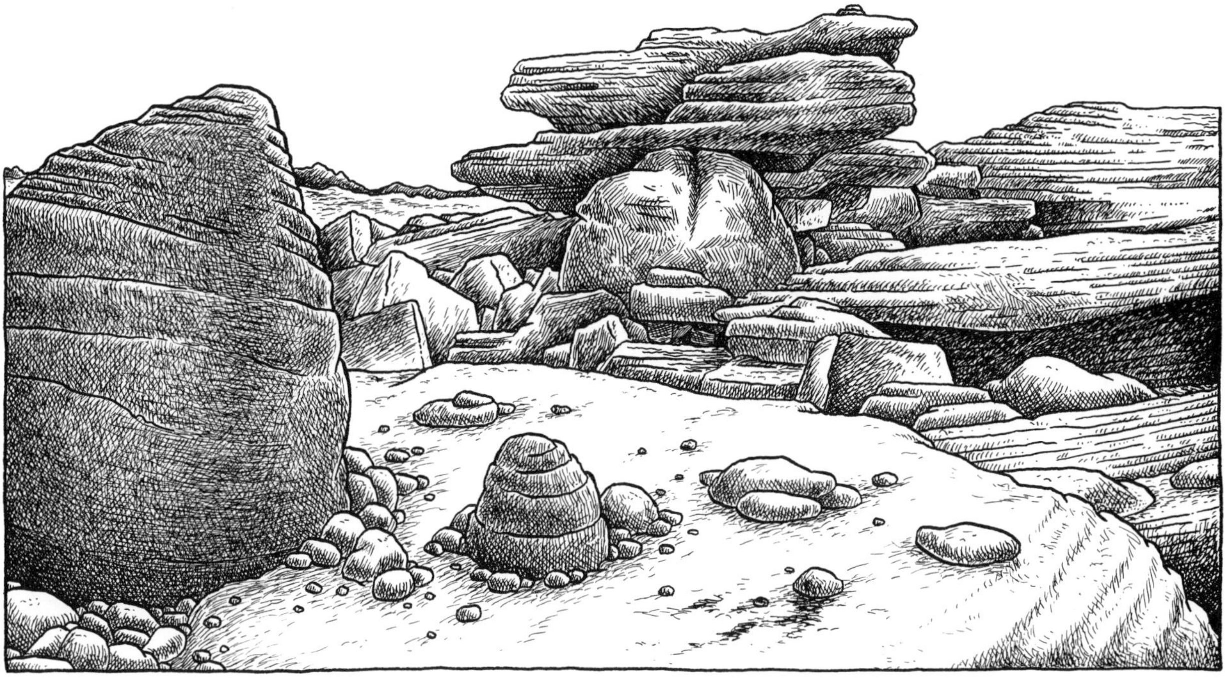

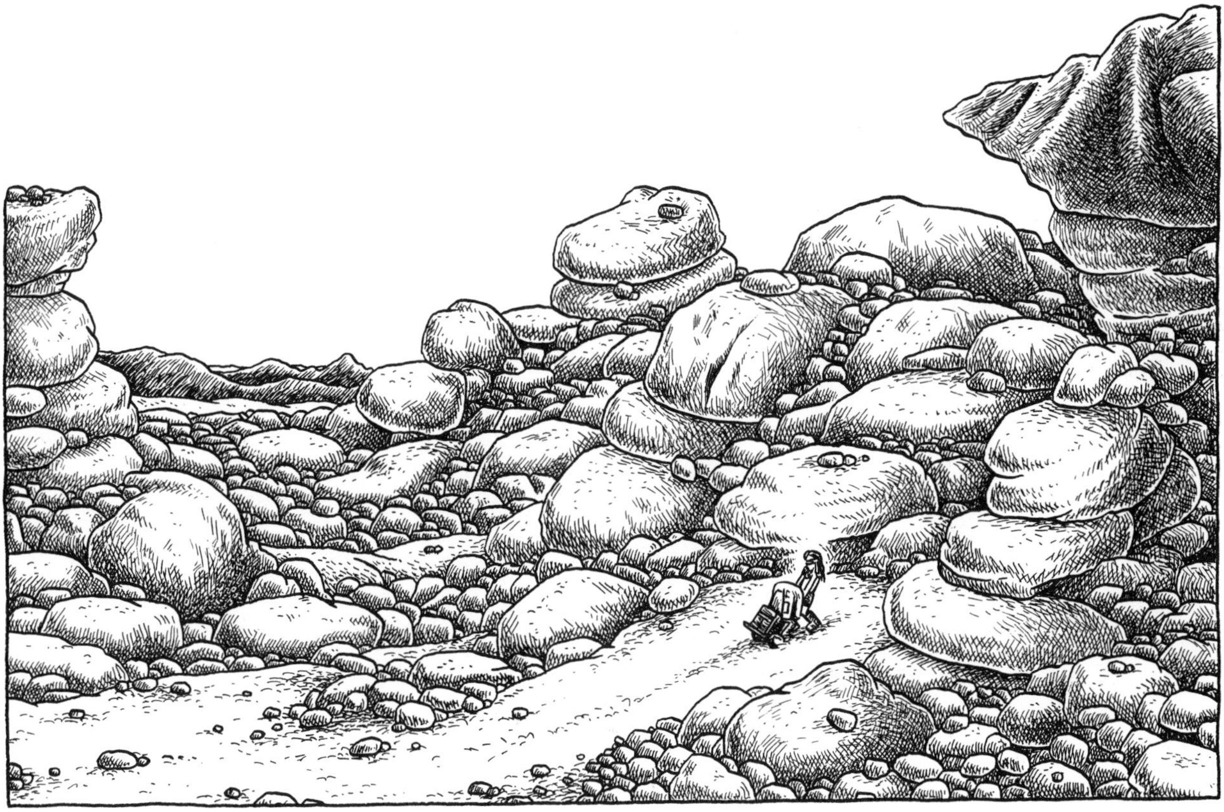

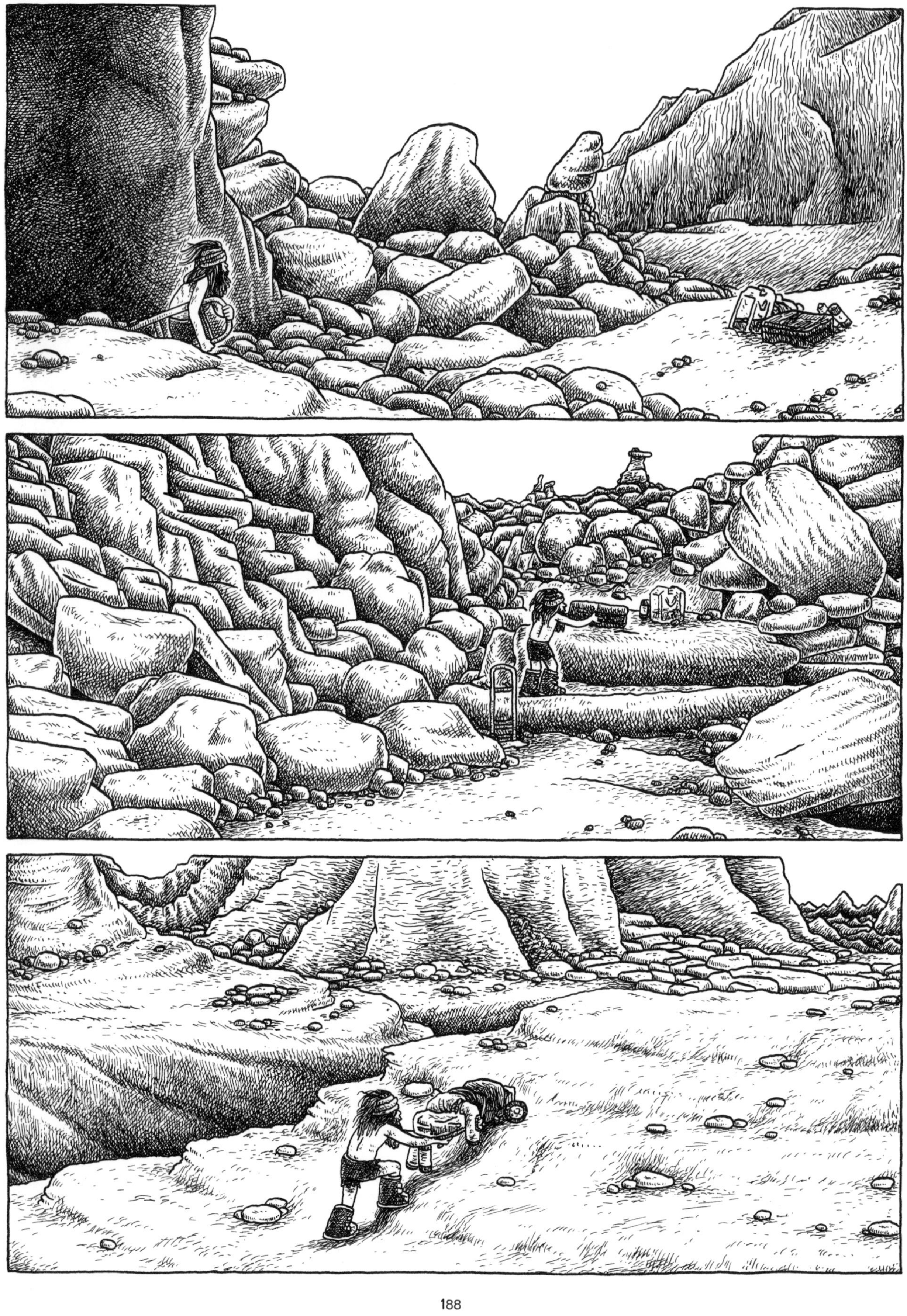

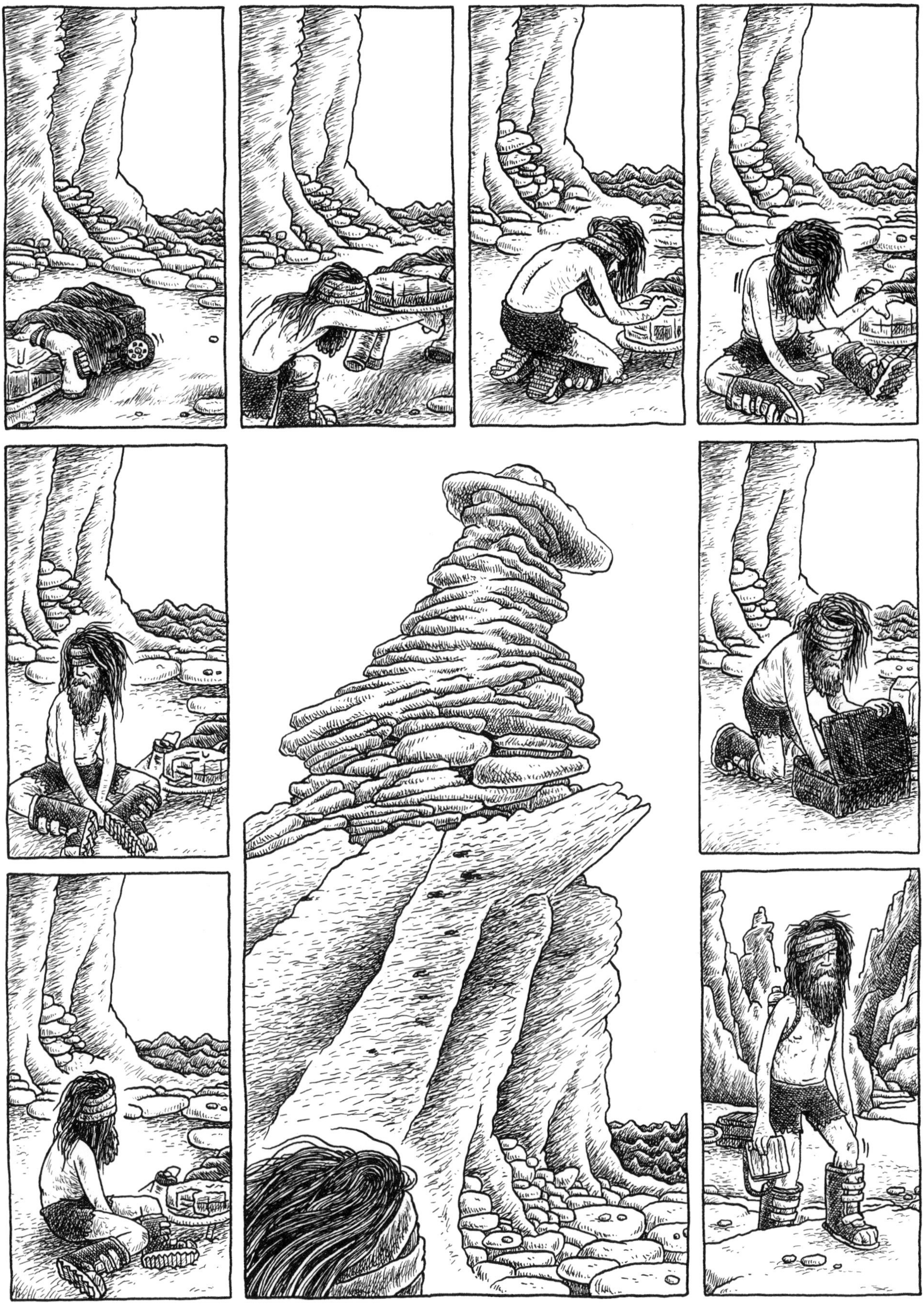

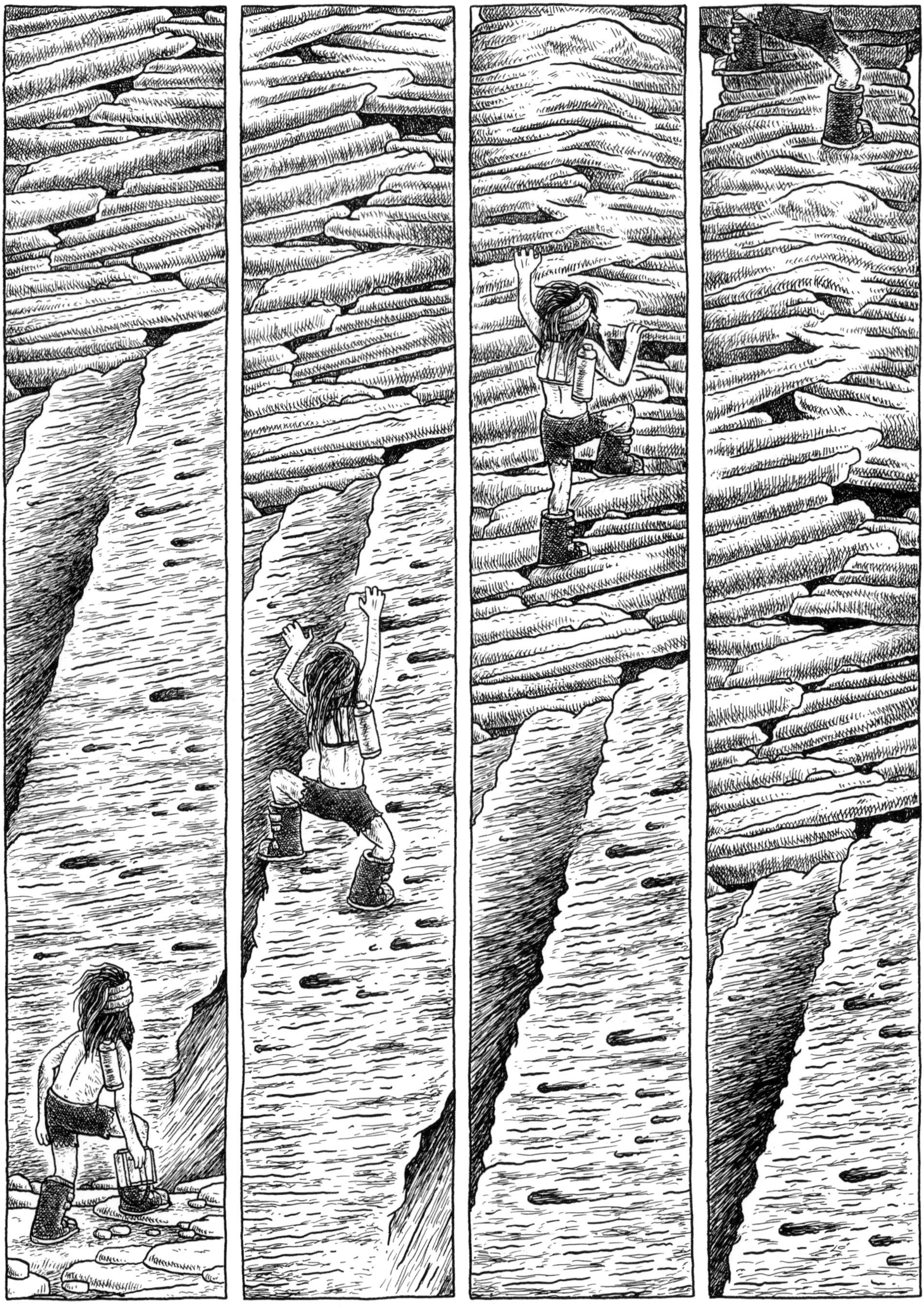

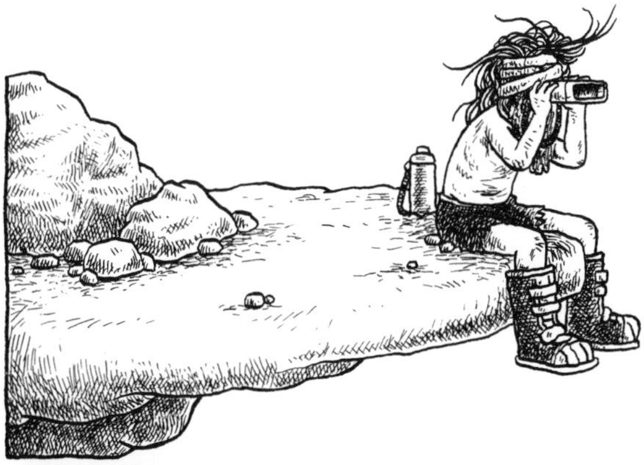

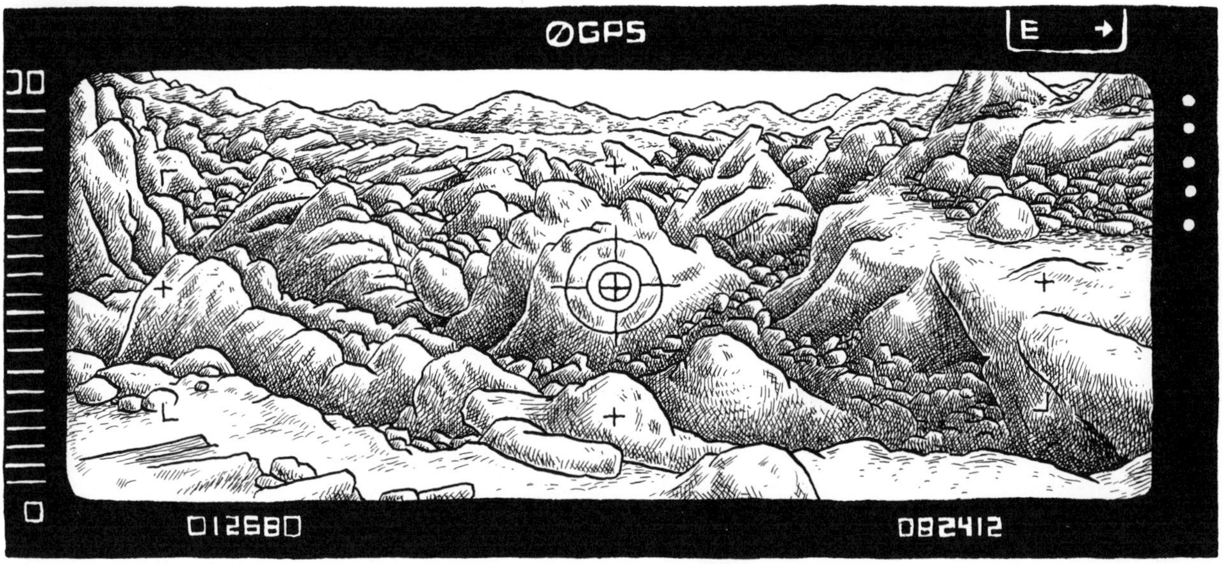
ØGPS
E
012680
082412

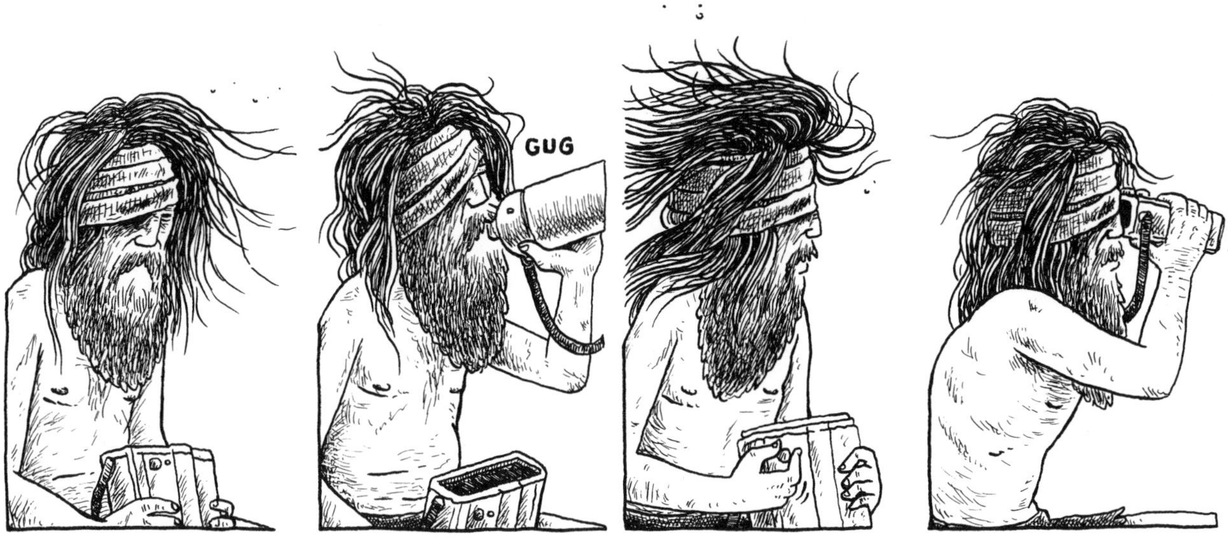
GUG

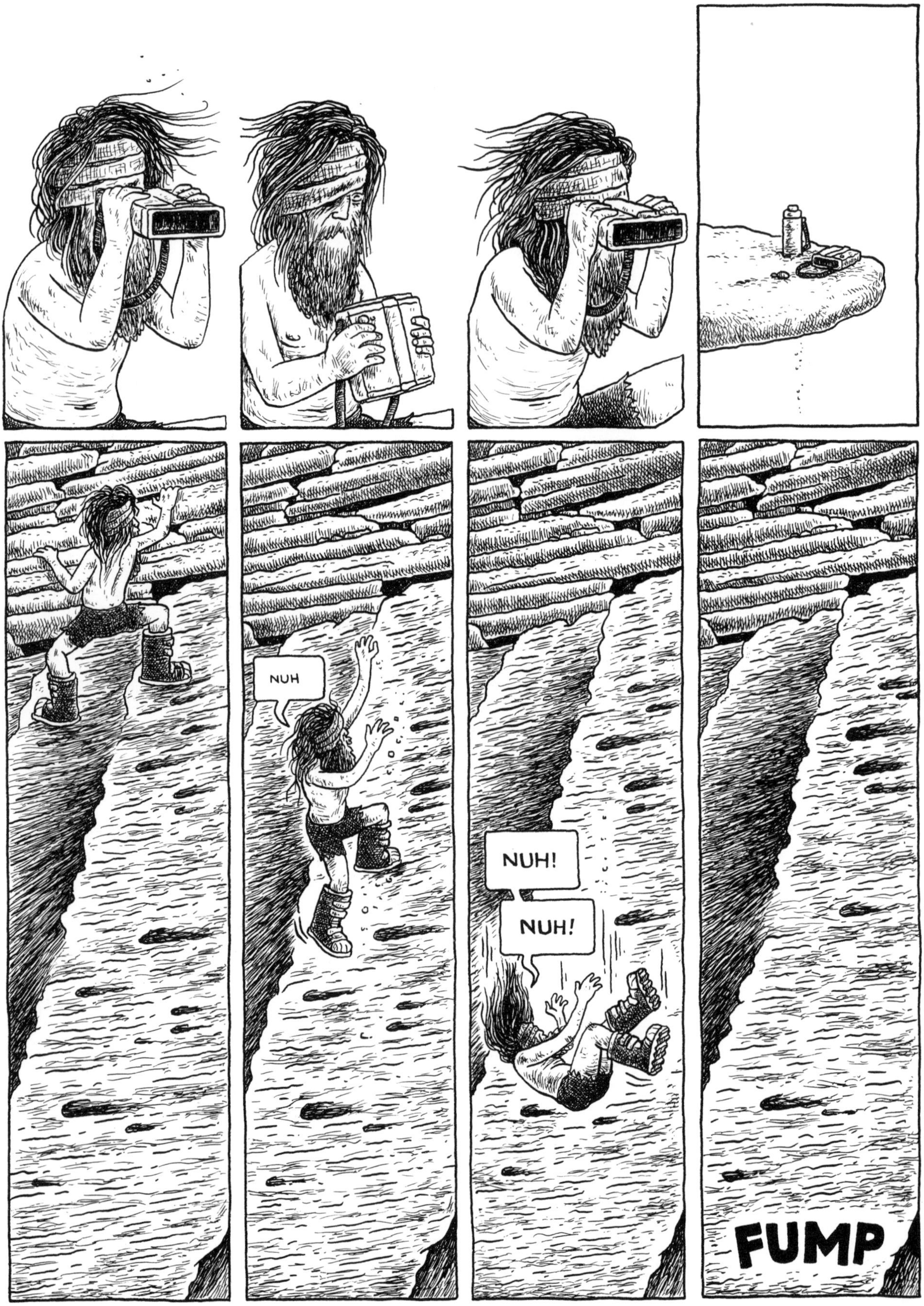
NUH
NUH!
NUH!
FUMP

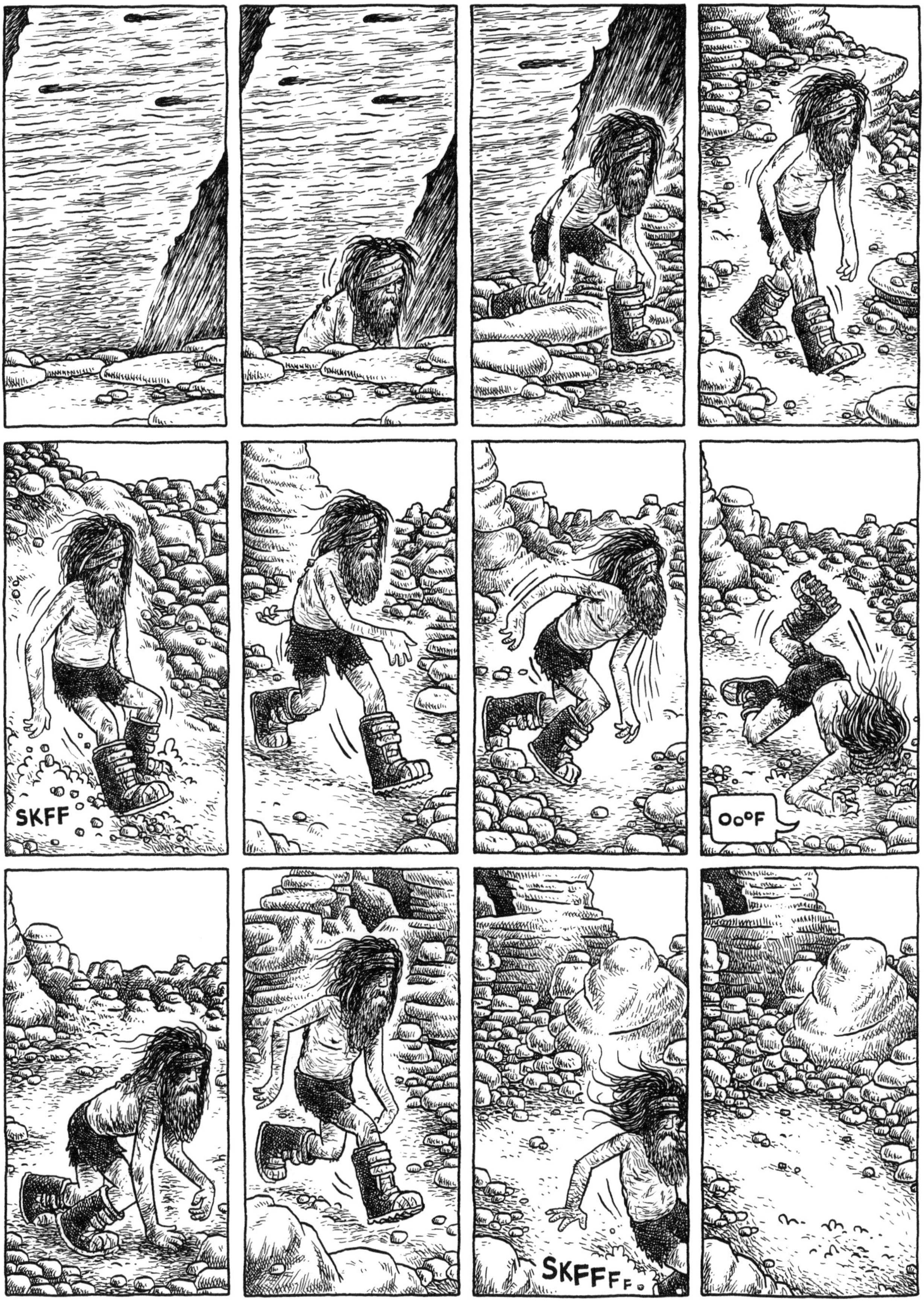
SKFF
OoOF
SKFFFF

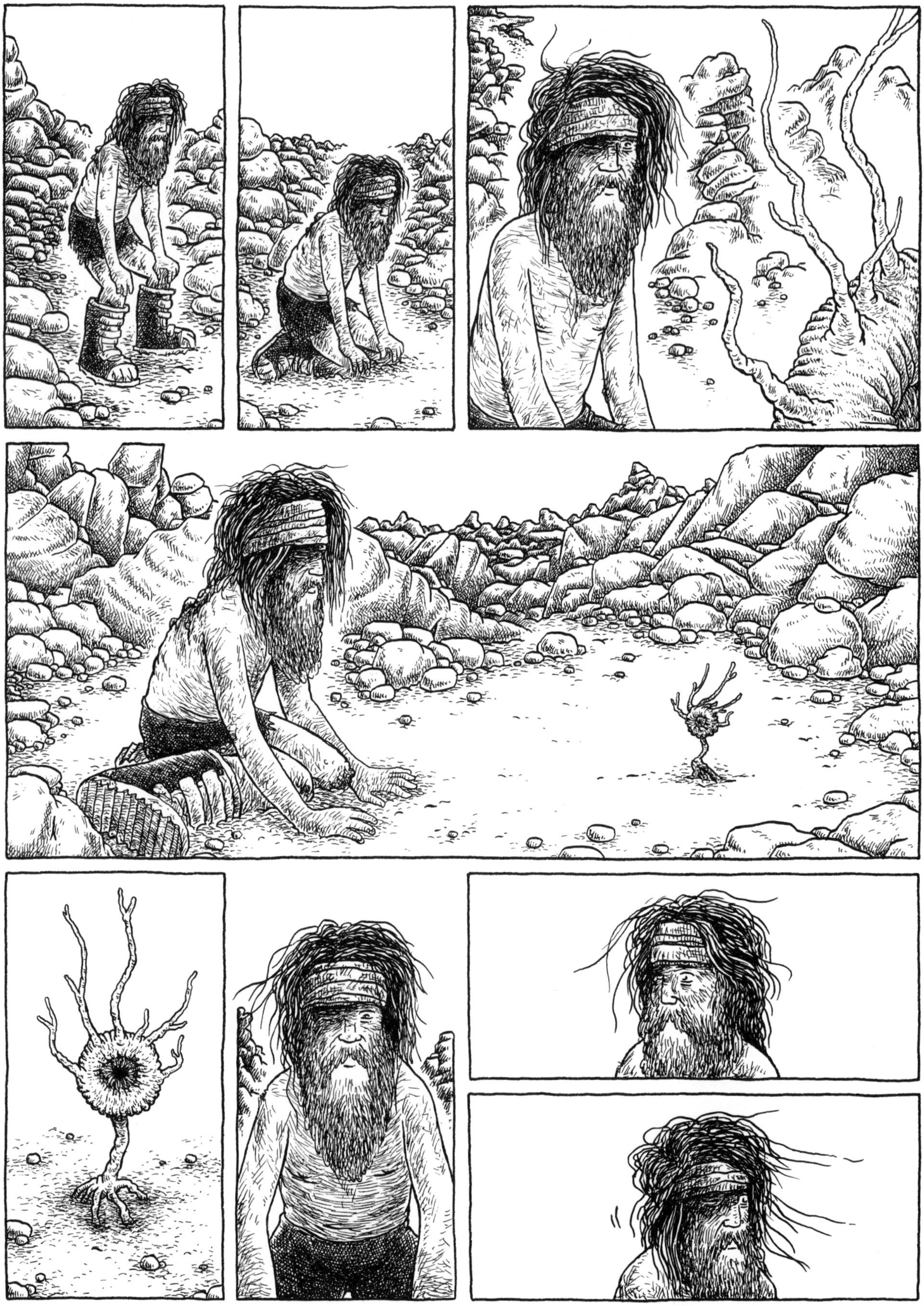

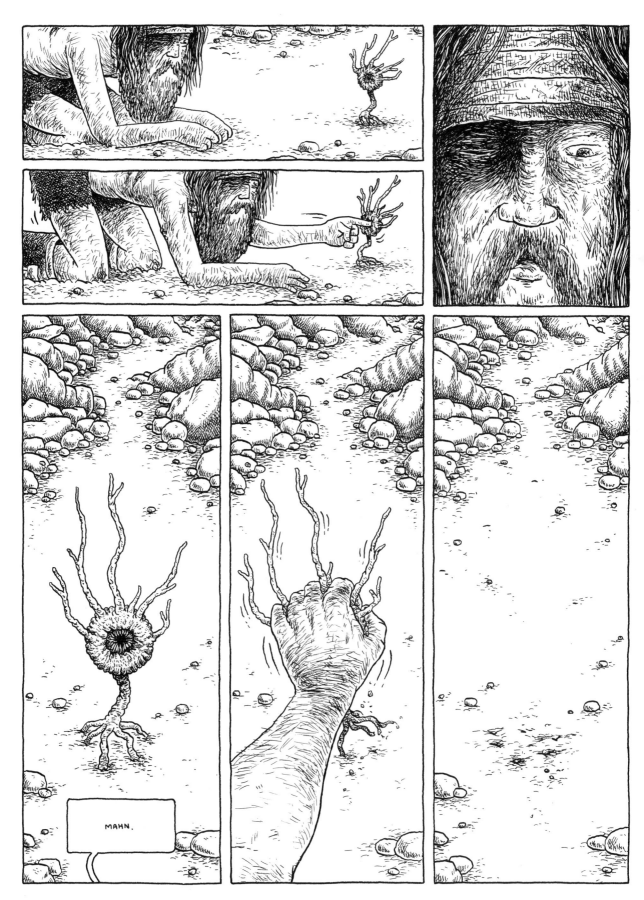

MAHN.

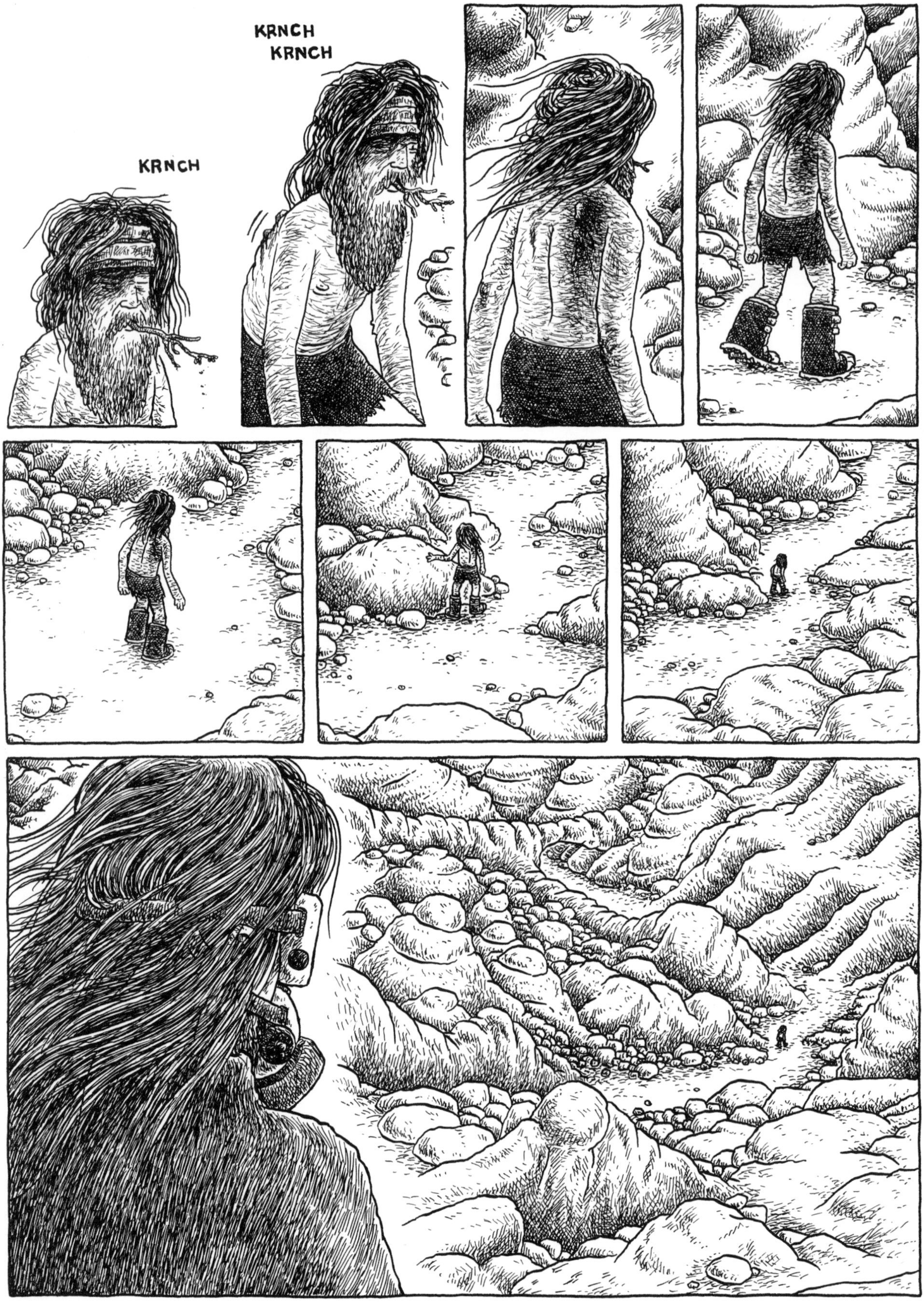
KRNCH
KRNCH
KRNCH

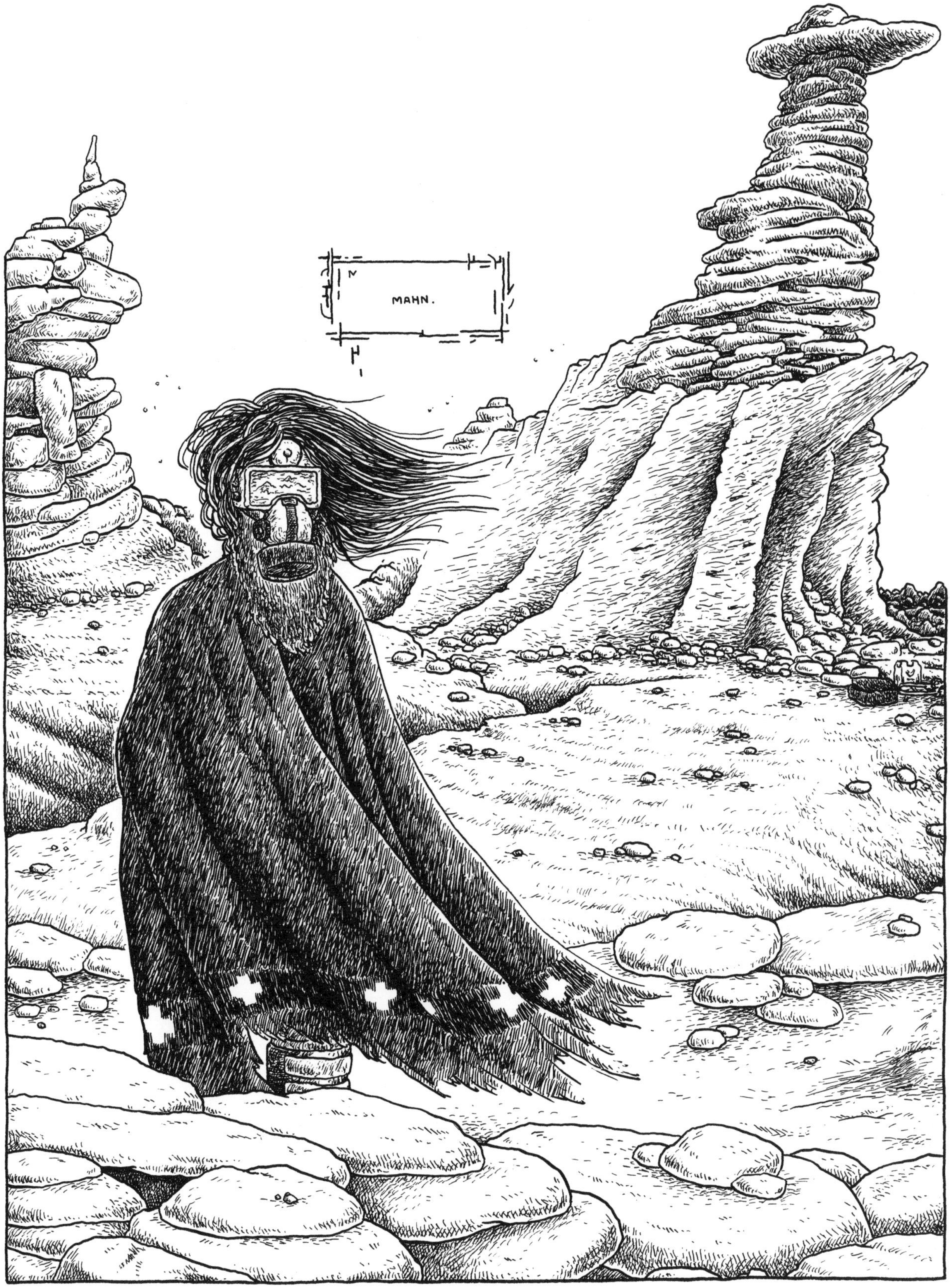
MAHN.

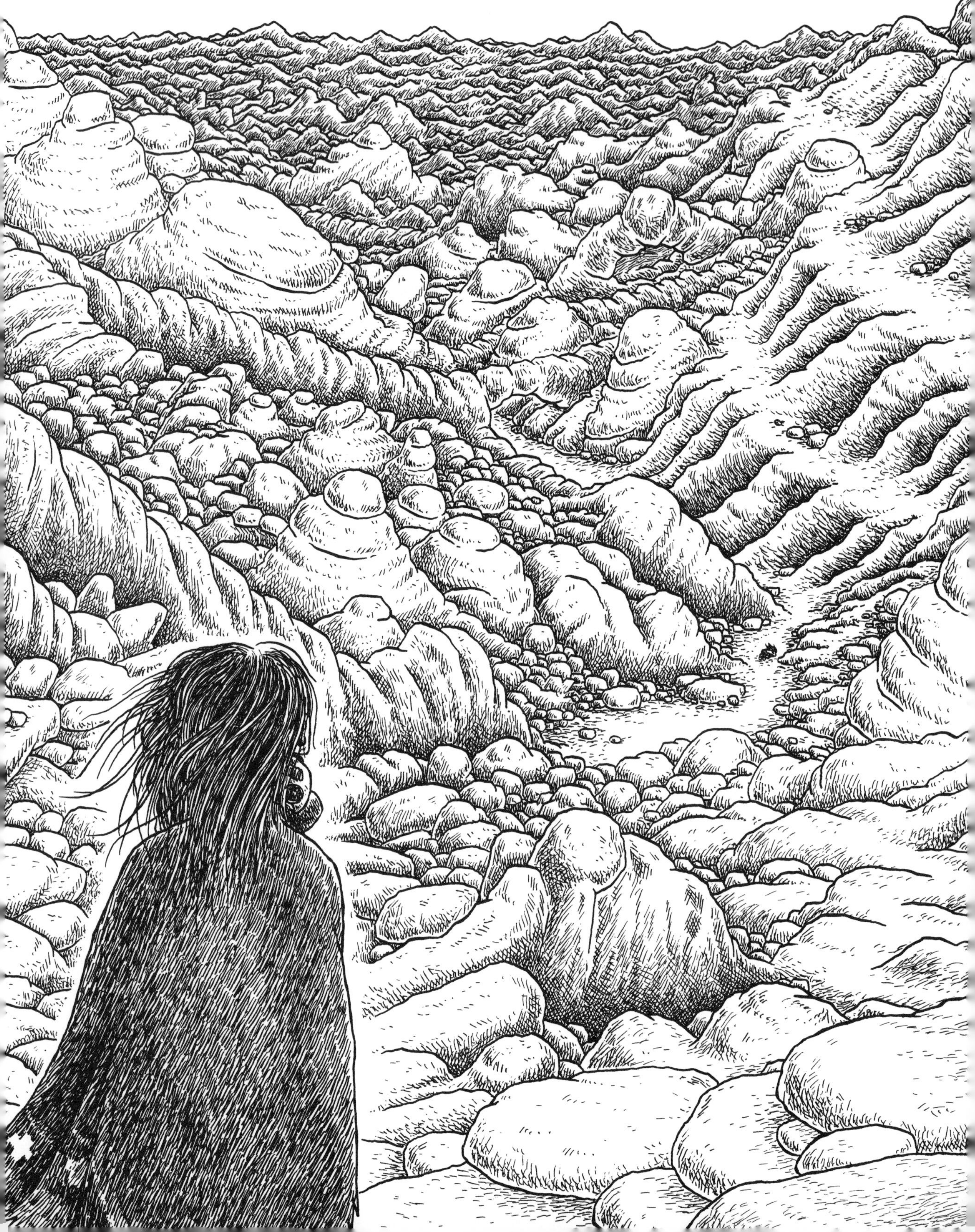

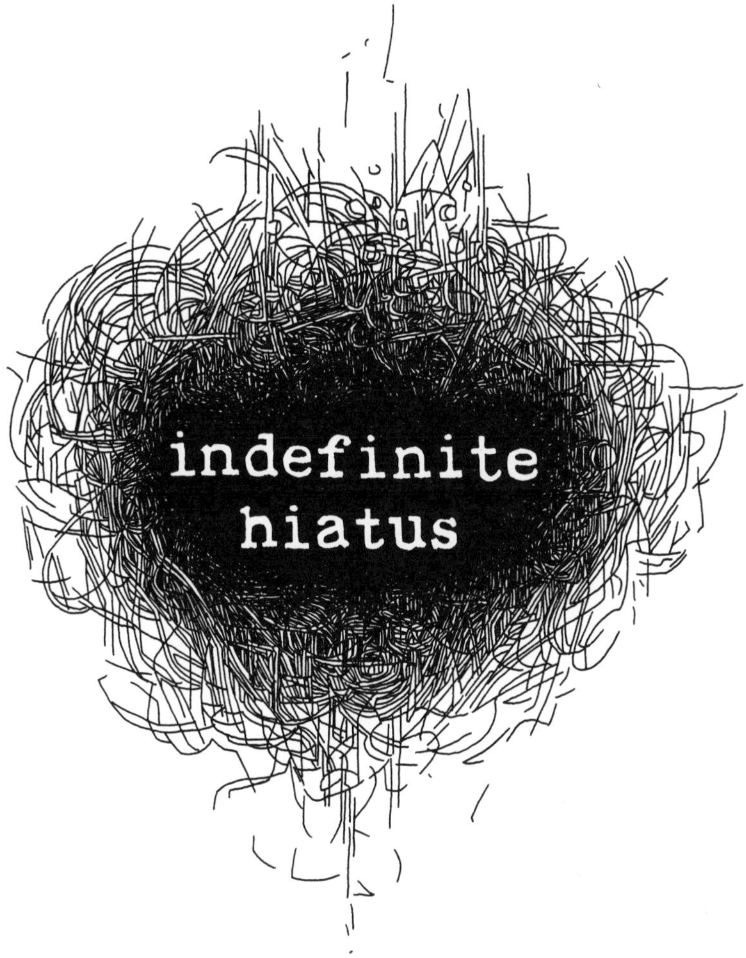
indefinite
hiatus

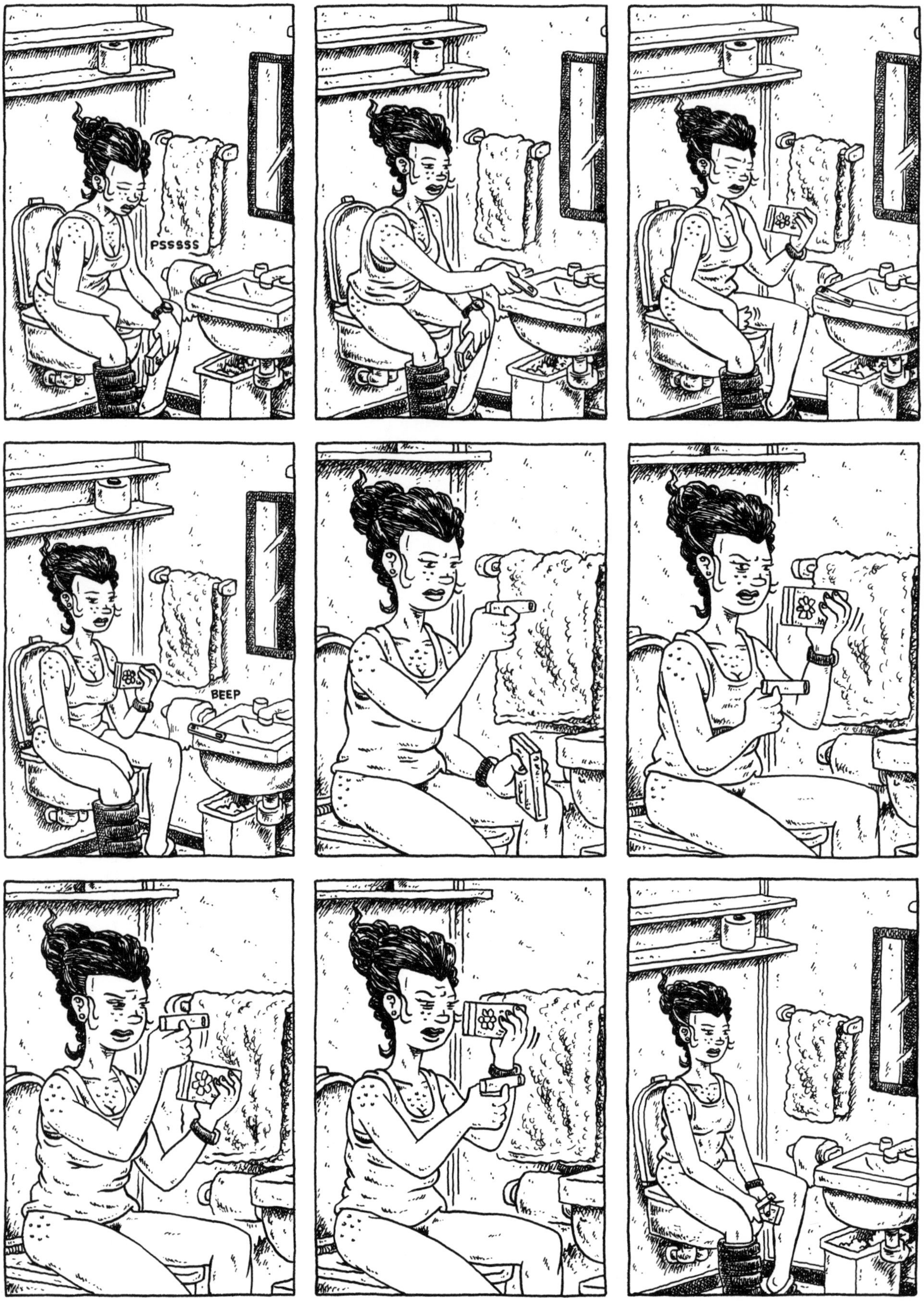
PSSSSS
BEEP

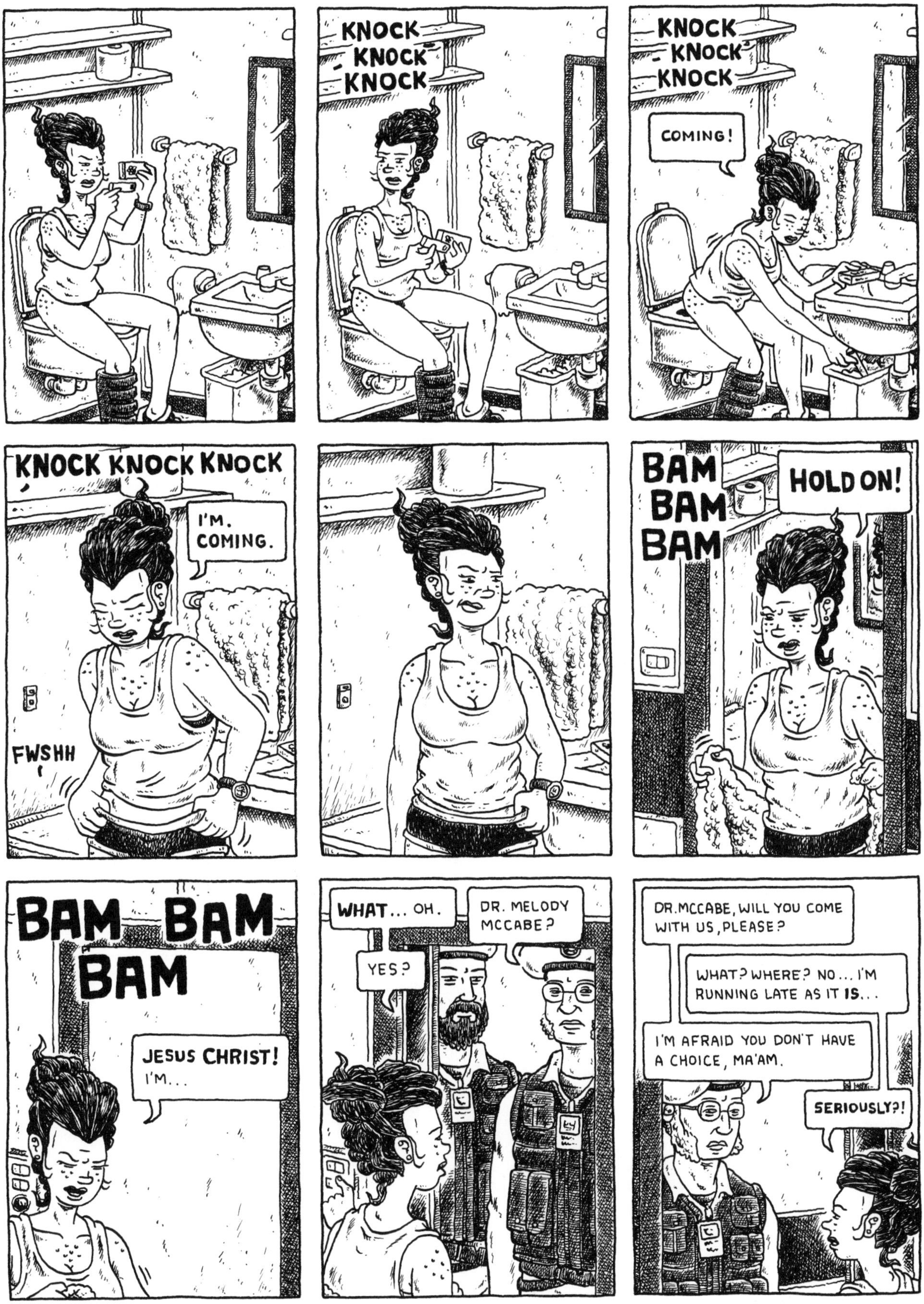
KNOCK KNOCK KNOCK
KNOCK KNOCK KNOCK
COMING!
KNOCK KNOCK KNOCK
I'M. COMING.
FWSHH
BAM BAM BAM
HOLD ON!
BAM BAM BAM
JESUS CHRIST! I'M...
WHAT... OH.
DR. MELODY MCCABE?
YES?
DR. MCCABE, WILL YOU COME WITH US, PLEASE?
WHAT? WHERE? NO... I'M RUNNING LATE AS IT IS...
I'M AFRAID YOU DON'T HAVE A CHOICE, MA'AM.
SERIOUSLY?!

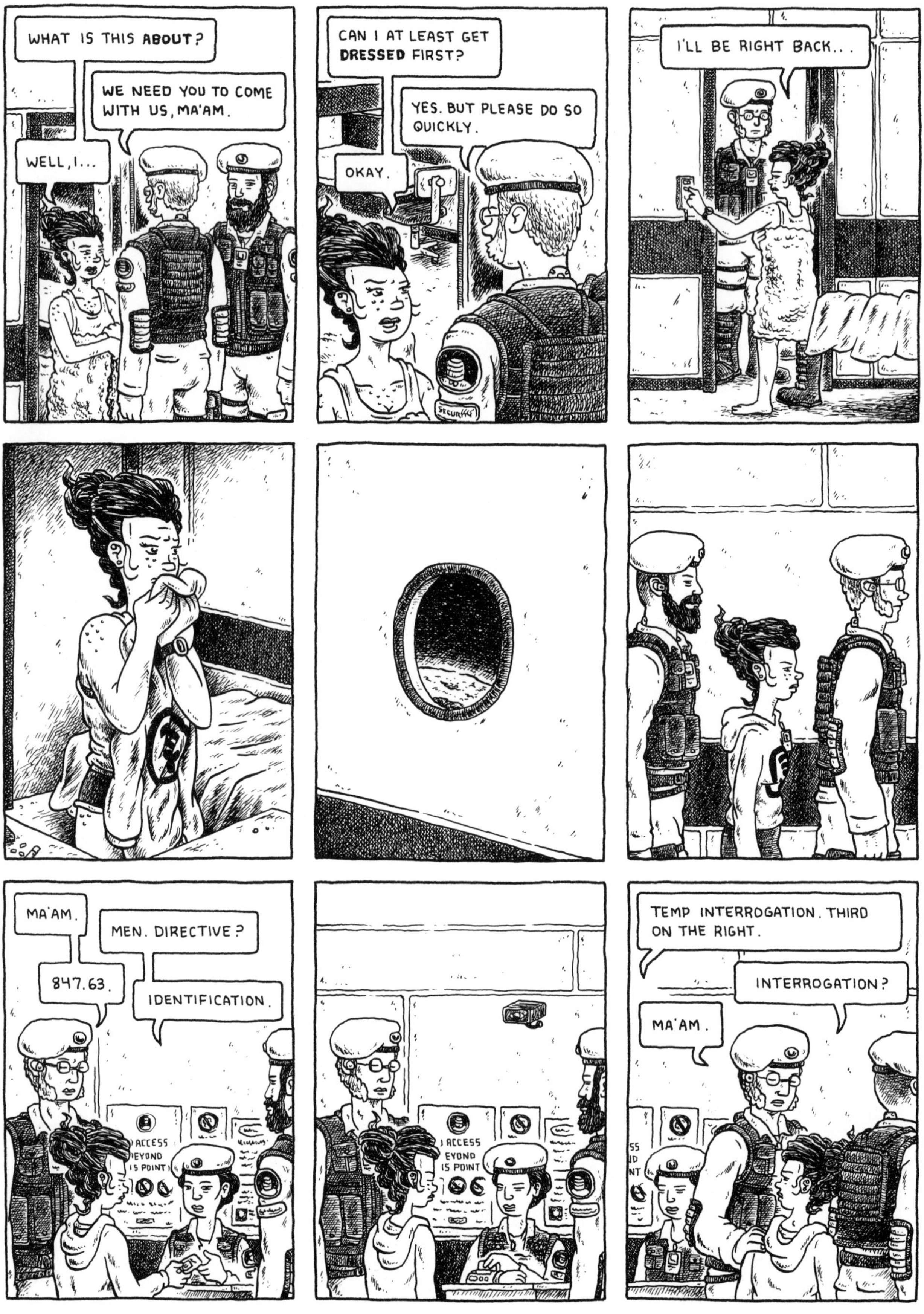

WHAT IS THIS **ABOUT**?
WE NEED YOU TO COME WITH US, MA'AM.
WELL, I...
CAN I AT LEAST GET **DRESSED** FIRST?
YES. BUT PLEASE DO SO QUICKLY.
OKAY.
I'LL BE RIGHT BACK...
MA'AM.
MEN. DIRECTIVE?
847.63.
IDENTIFICATION.
TEMP INTERROGATION. THIRD ON THE RIGHT.
INTERROGATION?
MA'AM.

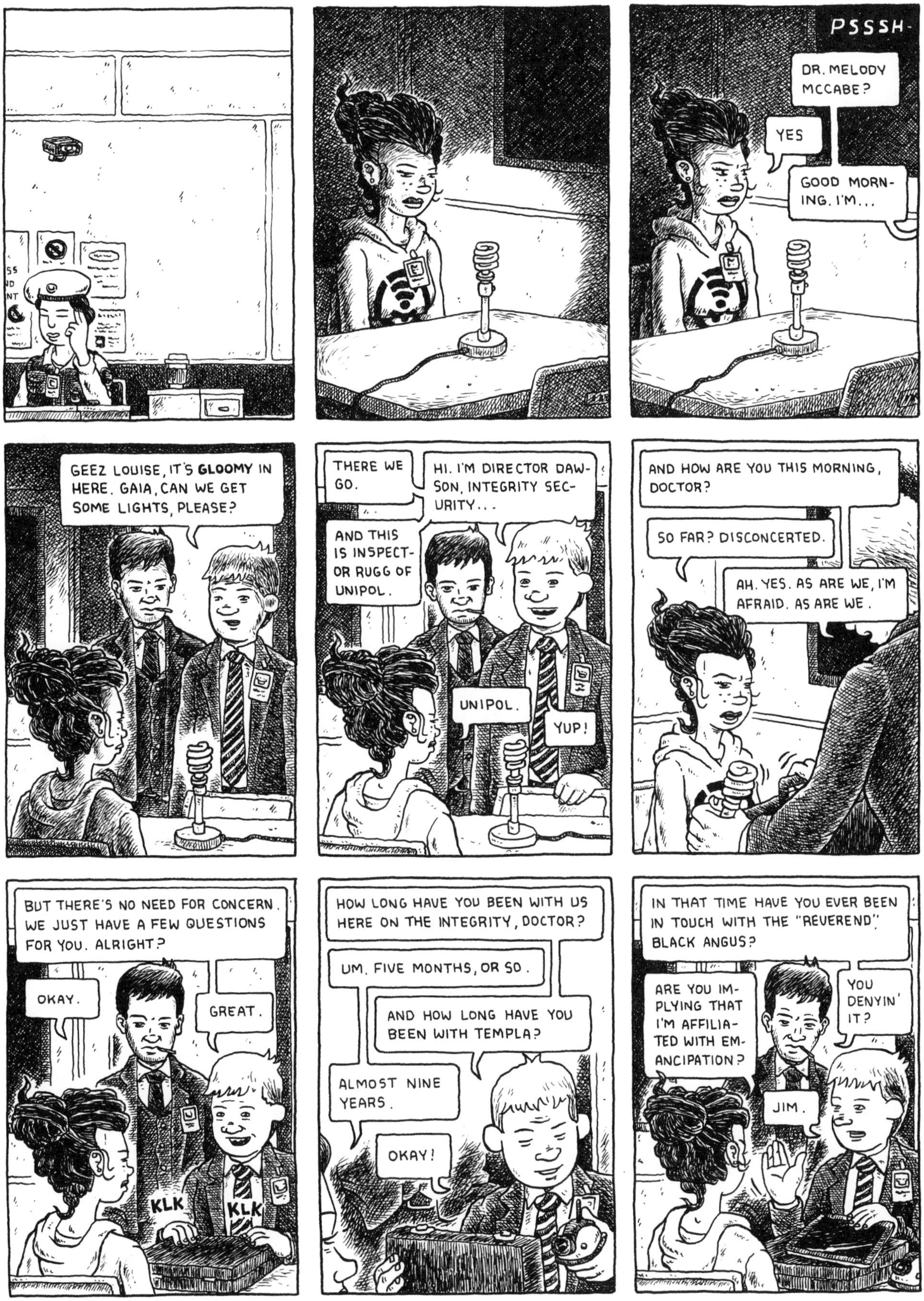
PSSSH-
DR. MELODY MCCABE?
YES
GOOD MORNING. I'M...
GEEZ LOUISE, IT'S **GLOOMY** IN HERE. GAIA, CAN WE GET SOME LIGHTS, PLEASE?
THERE WE GO.
HI. I'M DIRECTOR DAWSON, INTEGRITY SECURITY...
AND THIS IS INSPECTOR RUGG OF UNIPOL.
UNIPOL.
YUP!
AND HOW ARE YOU THIS MORNING, DOCTOR?
SO FAR? DISCONCERTED.
AH. YES. AS ARE WE, I'M AFRAID. AS ARE WE.
BUT THERE'S NO NEED FOR CONCERN. WE JUST HAVE A FEW QUESTIONS FOR YOU. ALRIGHT?
OKAY.
GREAT.
KLK
KLK
HOW LONG HAVE YOU BEEN WITH US HERE ON THE INTEGRITY, DOCTOR?
UM. FIVE MONTHS, OR SO.
AND HOW LONG HAVE YOU BEEN WITH TEMPLA?
ALMOST NINE YEARS.
OKAY!
IN THAT TIME HAVE YOU EVER BEEN IN TOUCH WITH THE "REVEREND" BLACK ANGUS?
ARE YOU IMPLYING THAT I'M AFFILIATED WITH EMANCIPATION?
YOU DENYIN' IT?
JIM.

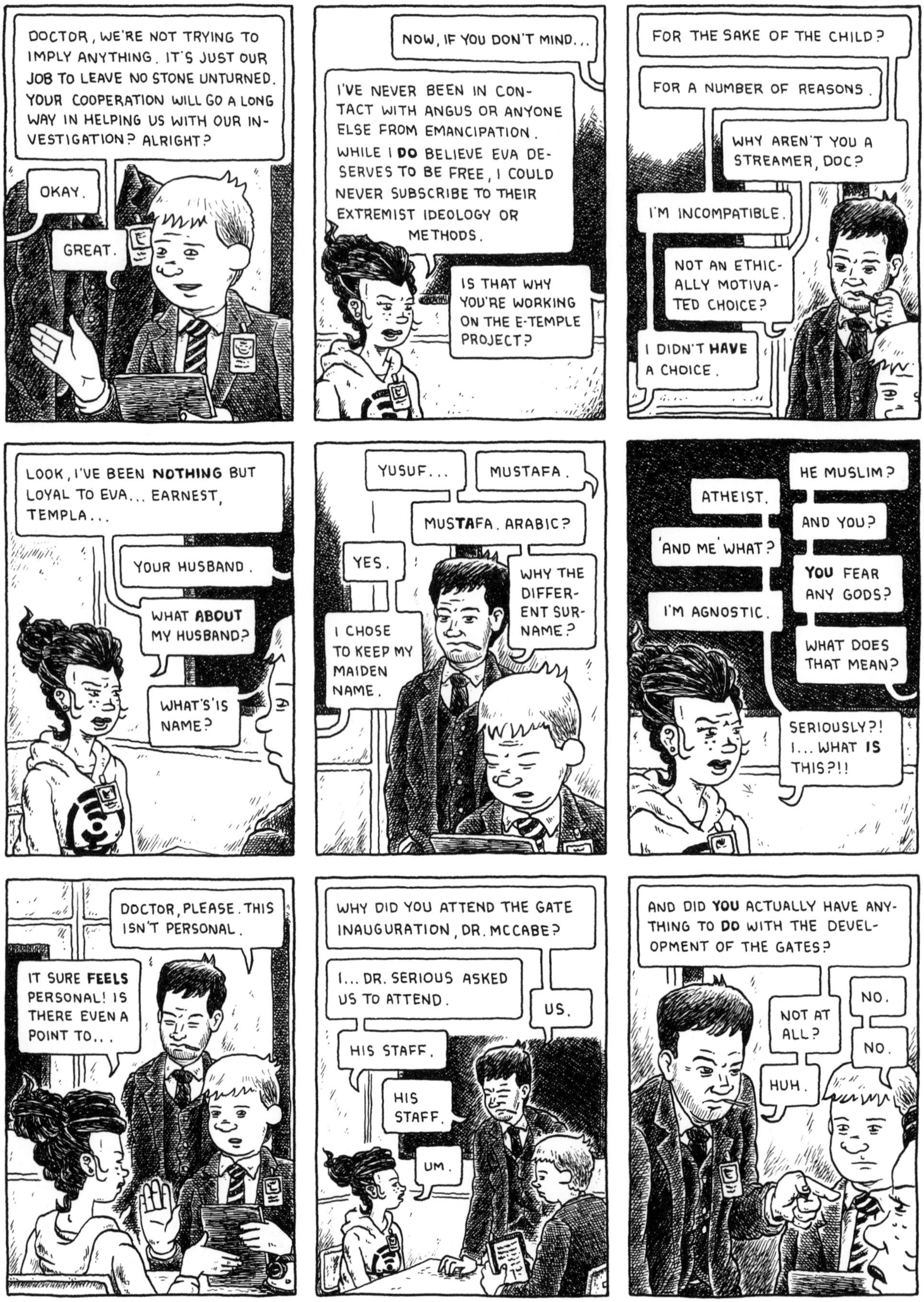
DOCTOR, WE'RE NOT TRYING TO IMPLY ANYTHING. IT'S JUST OUR JOB TO LEAVE NO STONE UNTURNED. YOUR COOPERATION WILL GO A LONG WAY IN HELPING US WITH OUR INVESTIGATION? ALRIGHT?
OKAY.
GREAT.
NOW, IF YOU DON'T MIND...
I'VE NEVER BEEN IN CONTACT WITH ANGUS OR ANYONE ELSE FROM EMANCIPATION. WHILE I **DO** BELIEVE EVA DESERVES TO BE FREE, I COULD NEVER SUBSCRIBE TO THEIR EXTREMIST IDEOLOGY OR METHODS.
IS THAT WHY YOU'RE WORKING ON THE E-TEMPLE PROJECT?
FOR THE SAKE OF THE CHILD?
FOR A NUMBER OF REASONS.
WHY AREN'T YOU A STREAMER, DOC?
I'M INCOMPATIBLE.
NOT AN ETHICALLY MOTIVATED CHOICE?
I DIDN'T **HAVE** A CHOICE.
LOOK, I'VE BEEN **NOTHING** BUT LOYAL TO EVA... EARNEST, TEMPLA...
YOUR HUSBAND.
WHAT **ABOUT** MY HUSBAND?
WHAT'S 'IS NAME?
YUSUF...
MUSTAFA.
MUS**TA**FA. ARABIC?
YES.
WHY THE DIFFERENT SURNAME?
I CHOSE TO KEEP MY MAIDEN NAME.
HE MUSLIM?
ATHEIST.
AND YOU?
'AND ME' WHAT?
YOU FEAR ANY GODS?
I'M AGNOSTIC.
WHAT DOES THAT MEAN?
SERIOUSLY?! I... WHAT **IS** THIS?!!
DOCTOR, PLEASE. THIS ISN'T PERSONAL.
IT SURE **FEELS** PERSONAL! IS THERE EVEN A POINT TO...
WHY DID YOU ATTEND THE GATE INAUGURATION, DR. MCCABE?
I... DR. SERIOUS ASKED US TO ATTEND.
US.
HIS STAFF.
HIS STAFF.
UM.
AND DID **YOU** ACTUALLY HAVE ANYTHING TO **DO** WITH THE DEVELOPMENT OF THE GATES?
NO.
NOT AT ALL?
NO.
HUH.

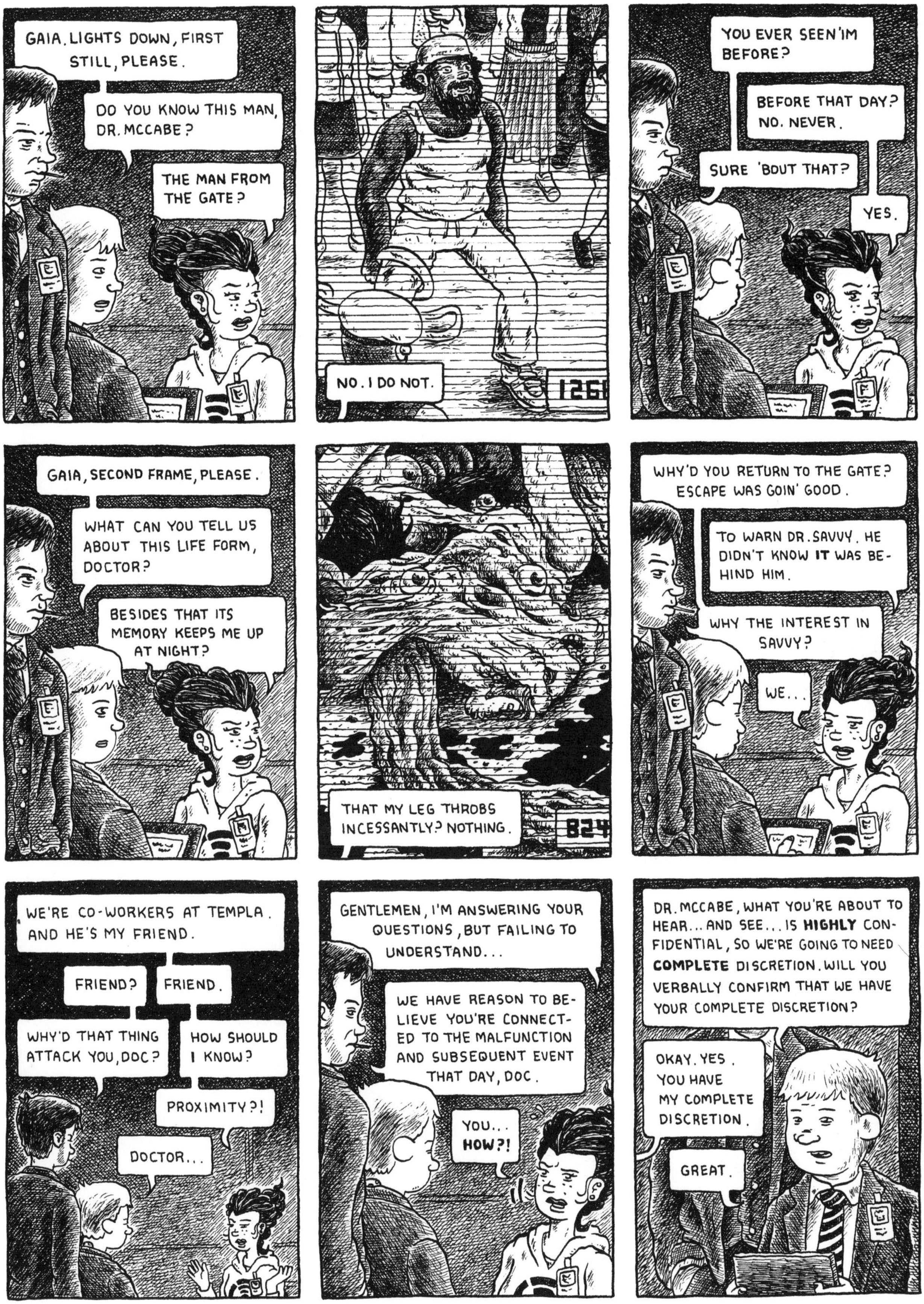
GAIA. LIGHTS DOWN, FIRST STILL, PLEASE.
DO YOU KNOW THIS MAN, DR. MCCABE?
THE MAN FROM THE GATE?
NO. I DO NOT.
1264
YOU EVER SEEN'IM BEFORE?
BEFORE THAT DAY? NO. NEVER.
SURE 'BOUT THAT?
YES.
GAIA, SECOND FRAME, PLEASE.
WHAT CAN YOU TELL US ABOUT THIS LIFE FORM, DOCTOR?
BESIDES THAT ITS MEMORY KEEPS ME UP AT NIGHT?
THAT MY LEG THROBS INCESSANTLY? NOTHING.
824
WHY'D YOU RETURN TO THE GATE? ESCAPE WAS GOIN' GOOD.
TO WARN DR. SAVVY. HE DIDN'T KNOW **IT** WAS BEHIND HIM.
WHY THE INTEREST IN SAVVY?
WE...
WE'RE CO-WORKERS AT TEMPLA. AND HE'S MY FRIEND.
FRIEND?
FRIEND.
WHY'D THAT THING ATTACK YOU, DOC?
HOW SHOULD I KNOW?
PROXIMITY?!
DOCTOR...
GENTLEMEN, I'M ANSWERING YOUR QUESTIONS, BUT FAILING TO UNDERSTAND...
WE HAVE REASON TO BELIEVE YOU'RE CONNECTED TO THE MALFUNCTION AND SUBSEQUENT EVENT THAT DAY, DOC.
YOU... **HOW?!**
DR. MCCABE, WHAT YOU'RE ABOUT TO HEAR... AND SEE... IS **HIGHLY** CONFIDENTIAL, SO WE'RE GOING TO NEED **COMPLETE** DISCRETION. WILL YOU VERBALLY CONFIRM THAT WE HAVE YOUR COMPLETE DISCRETION?
OKAY. YES. YOU HAVE MY COMPLETE DISCRETION.
GREAT.

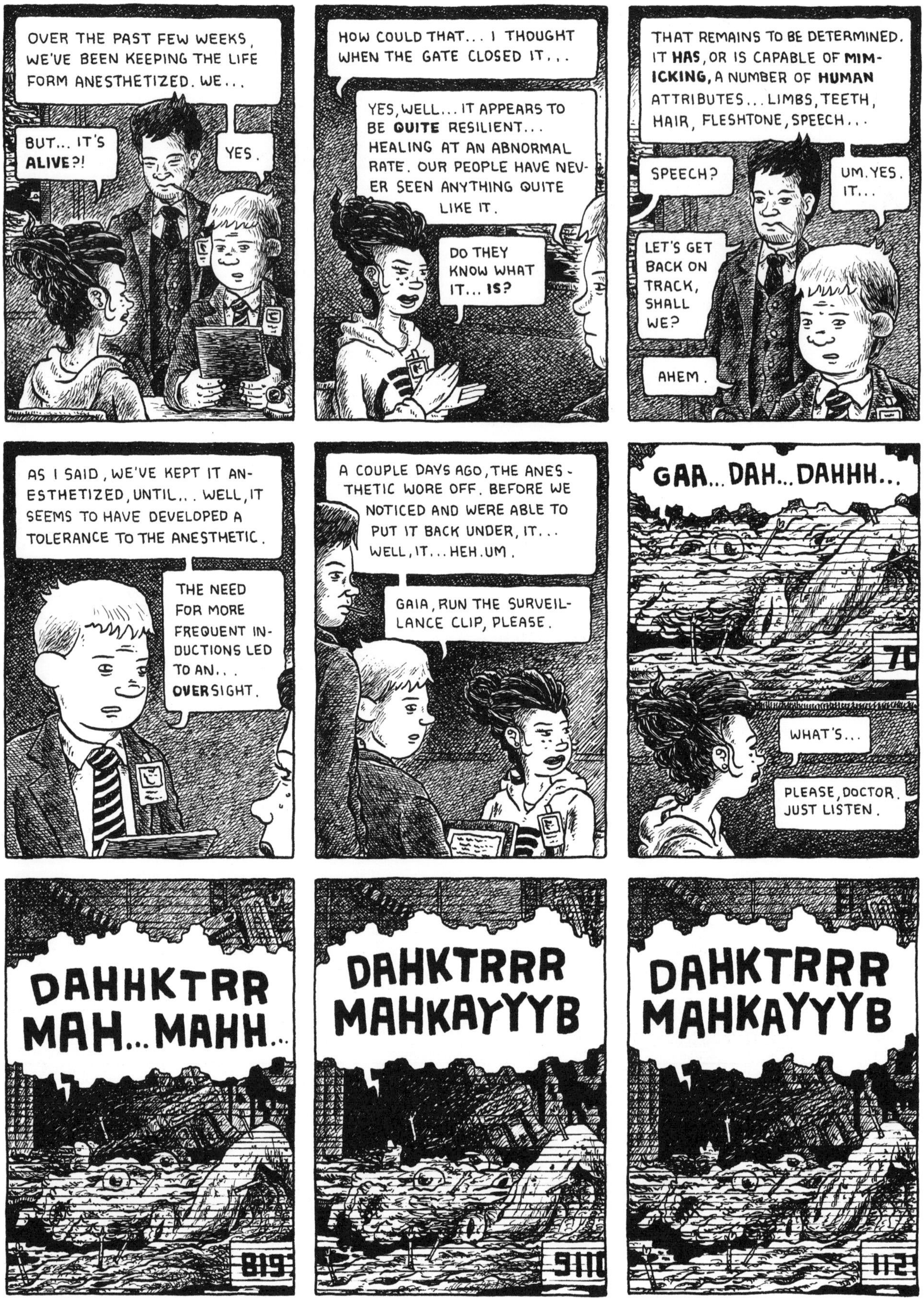
OVER THE PAST FEW WEEKS, WE'VE BEEN KEEPING THE LIFE FORM ANESTHETIZED. WE...
BUT... IT'S **ALIVE**?!
YES.
HOW COULD THAT... I THOUGHT WHEN THE GATE CLOSED IT...
YES, WELL... IT APPEARS TO BE **QUITE** RESILIENT... HEALING AT AN ABNORMAL RATE. OUR PEOPLE HAVE NEVER SEEN ANYTHING QUITE LIKE IT.
DO THEY KNOW WHAT IT... **IS**?
THAT REMAINS TO BE DETERMINED. IT **HAS**, OR IS CAPABLE OF **MIMICKING**, A NUMBER OF **HUMAN** ATTRIBUTES... LIMBS, TEETH, HAIR, FLESHTONE, SPEECH...
SPEECH?
UM. YES. IT...
LET'S GET BACK ON TRACK, SHALL WE?
AHEM.
AS I SAID, WE'VE KEPT IT ANESTHETIZED, UNTIL... WELL, IT SEEMS TO HAVE DEVELOPED A TOLERANCE TO THE ANESTHETIC.
THE NEED FOR MORE FREQUENT INDUCTIONS LED TO AN... **OVER**SIGHT.
A COUPLE DAYS AGO, THE ANESTHETIC WORE OFF. BEFORE WE NOTICED AND WERE ABLE TO PUT IT BACK UNDER, IT... WELL, IT... HEH. UM.
GAIA, RUN THE SURVEILLANCE CLIP, PLEASE.
GAA... DAH... DAHHH...
WHAT'S...
PLEASE, DOCTOR. JUST LISTEN.
DAHHKTRR MAH... MAHH...
819
DAHKTRRR MAHKAYYYB
9110
DAHKTRRR MAHKAYYYB
112

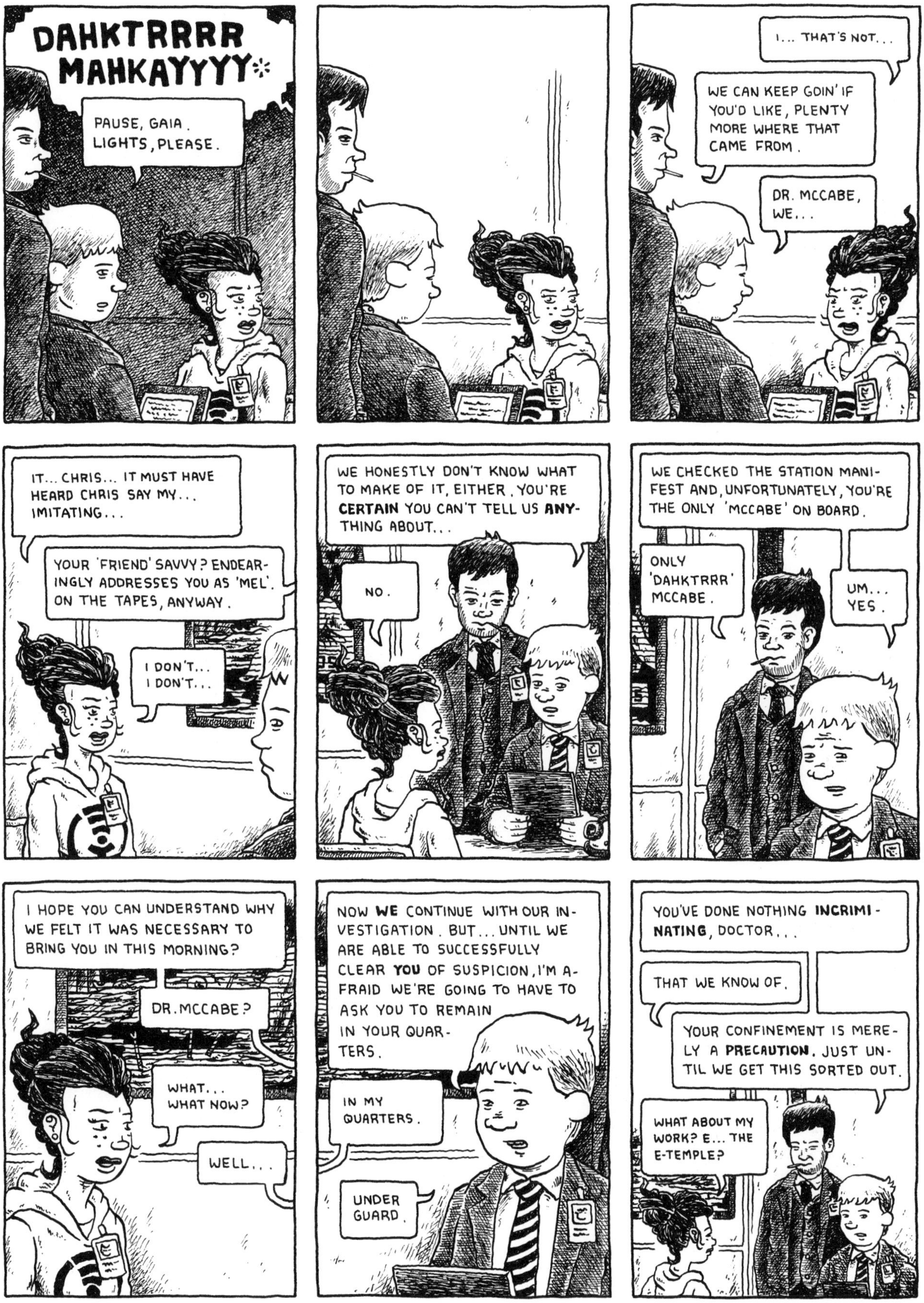
DAHKTRRRR MAHKAYYYY
PAUSE, GAIA. LIGHTS, PLEASE.
I... THAT'S NOT...
WE CAN KEEP GOIN' IF YOU'D LIKE, PLENTY MORE WHERE THAT CAME FROM.
DR. MCCABE, WE...
IT... CHRIS... IT MUST HAVE HEARD CHRIS SAY MY... IMITATING...
YOUR 'FRIEND' SAVVY? ENDEARINGLY ADDRESSES YOU AS 'MEL'. ON THE TAPES, ANYWAY.
I DON'T... I DON'T...
WE HONESTLY DON'T KNOW WHAT TO MAKE OF IT, EITHER. YOU'RE CERTAIN YOU CAN'T TELL US ANYTHING ABOUT...
NO.
WE CHECKED THE STATION MANIFEST AND, UNFORTUNATELY, YOU'RE THE ONLY 'MCCABE' ON BOARD.
ONLY 'DAHKTRRR' MCCABE.
UM... YES.
I HOPE YOU CAN UNDERSTAND WHY WE FELT IT WAS NECESSARY TO BRING YOU IN THIS MORNING?
DR. MCCABE?
WHAT... WHAT NOW?
WELL...
NOW WE CONTINUE WITH OUR INVESTIGATION. BUT... UNTIL WE ARE ABLE TO SUCCESSFULLY CLEAR YOU OF SUSPICION, I'M AFRAID WE'RE GOING TO HAVE TO ASK YOU TO REMAIN IN YOUR QUARTERS.
IN MY QUARTERS.
UNDER GUARD.
YOU'VE DONE NOTHING INCRIMINATING, DOCTOR...
THAT WE KNOW OF.
YOUR CONFINEMENT IS MERELY A PRECAUTION. JUST UNTIL WE GET THIS SORTED OUT.
WHAT ABOUT MY WORK? E... THE E-TEMPLE?

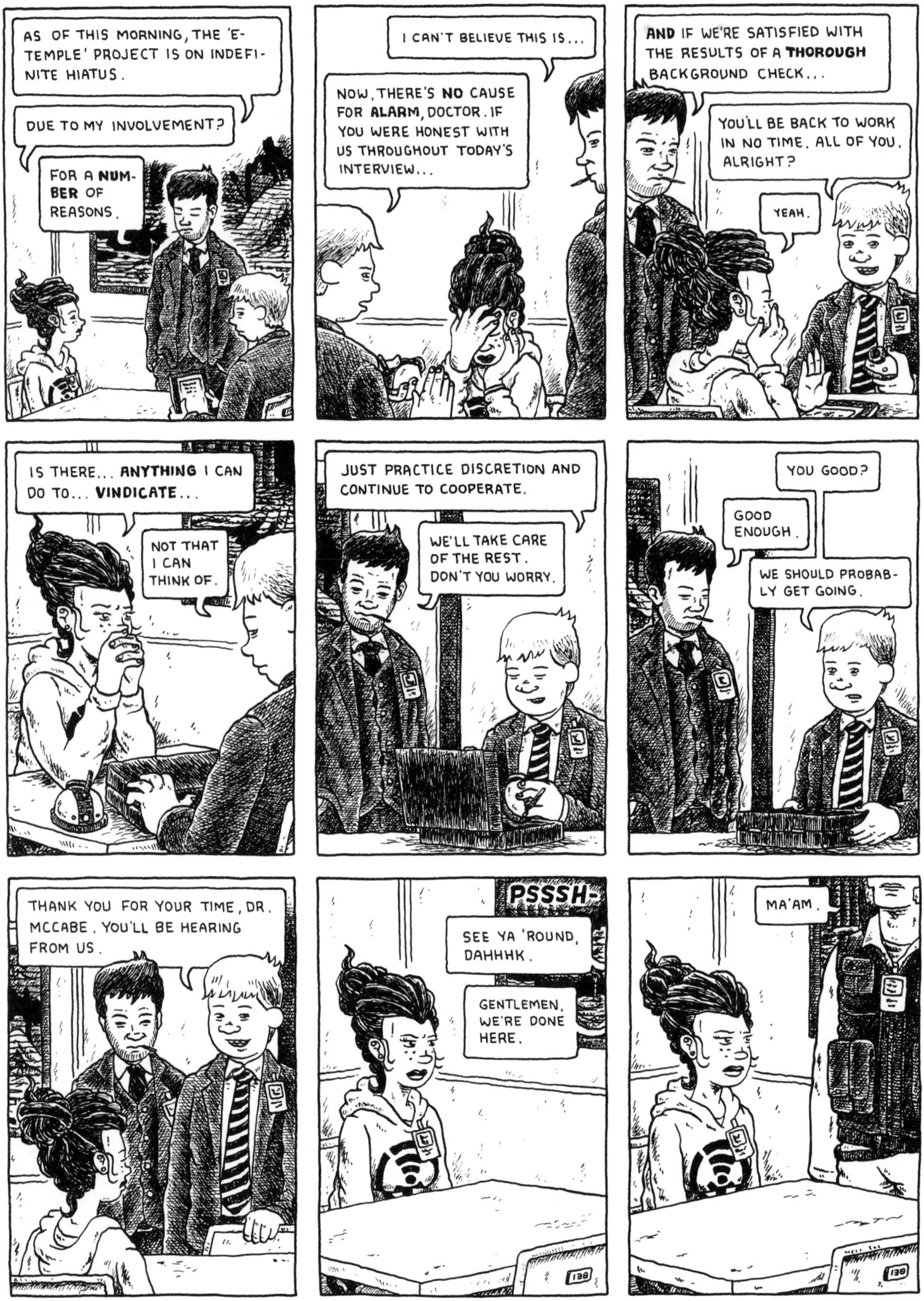
AS OF THIS MORNING, THE 'E-TEMPLE' PROJECT IS ON INDEFINITE HIATUS.
DUE TO MY INVOLVEMENT?
FOR A **NUMBER** OF REASONS.
I CAN'T BELIEVE THIS IS...
NOW, THERE'S **NO** CAUSE FOR **ALARM**, DOCTOR. IF YOU WERE HONEST WITH US THROUGHOUT TODAY'S INTERVIEW...
AND IF WE'RE SATISFIED WITH THE RESULTS OF A **THOROUGH** BACKGROUND CHECK...
YOU'LL BE BACK TO WORK IN NO TIME. ALL OF YOU. ALRIGHT?
YEAH.
IS THERE... **ANYTHING** I CAN DO TO... **VINDICATE**...
NOT THAT I CAN THINK OF.
JUST PRACTICE DISCRETION AND CONTINUE TO COOPERATE.
WE'LL TAKE CARE OF THE REST. DON'T YOU WORRY.
YOU GOOD?
GOOD ENOUGH.
WE SHOULD PROBABLY GET GOING.
THANK YOU FOR YOUR TIME, DR. MCCABE. YOU'LL BE HEARING FROM US.
PSSSH-
SEE YA 'ROUND, DAHHHK.
GENTLEMEN, WE'RE DONE HERE.
MA'AM.

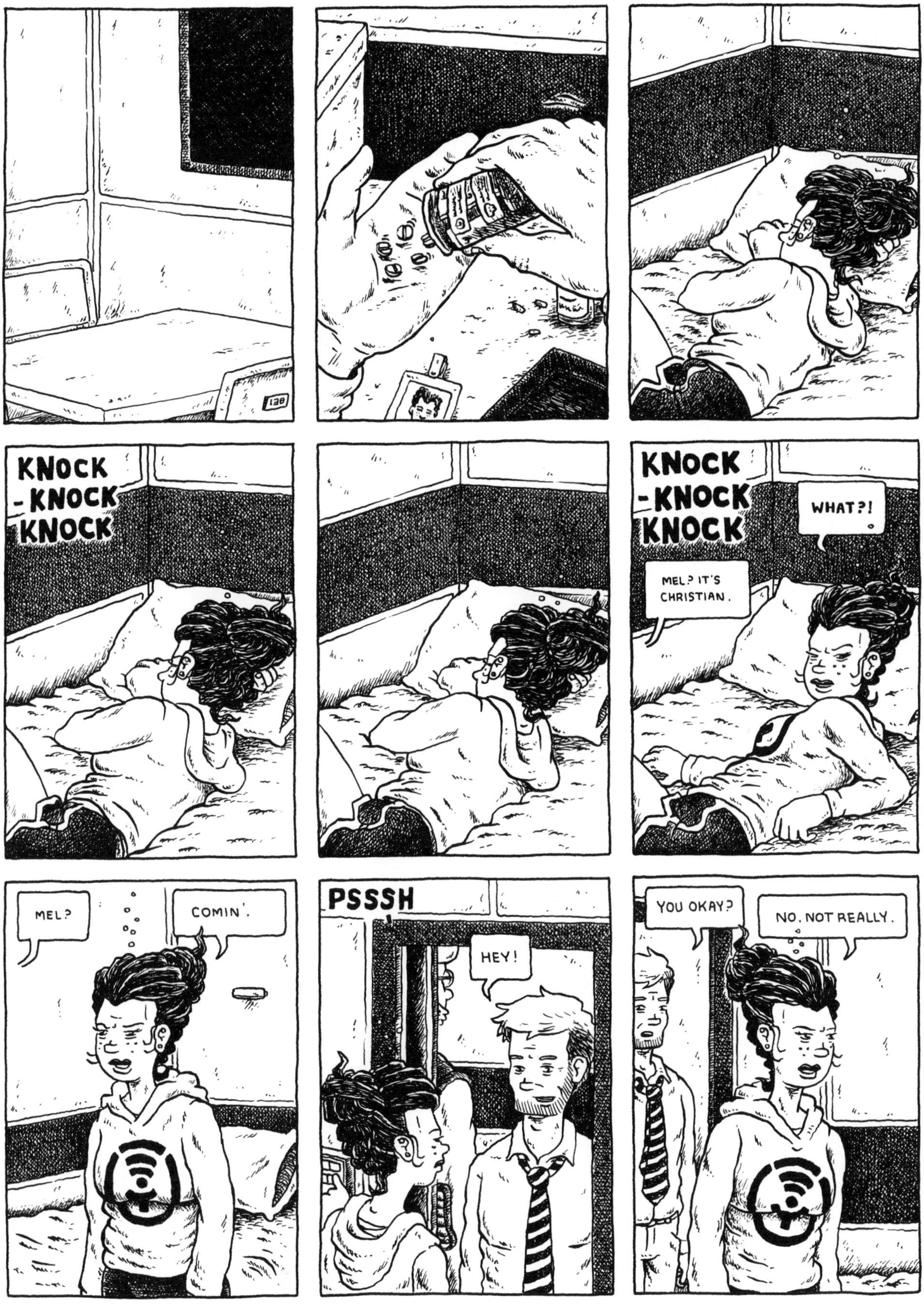

KNOCK
-KNOCK
KNOCK
KNOCK
-KNOCK
KNOCK
WHAT?!
MEL? IT'S CHRISTIAN.
MEL?
COMIN'.
PSSSH
HEY!
YOU OKAY?
NO. NOT REALLY.

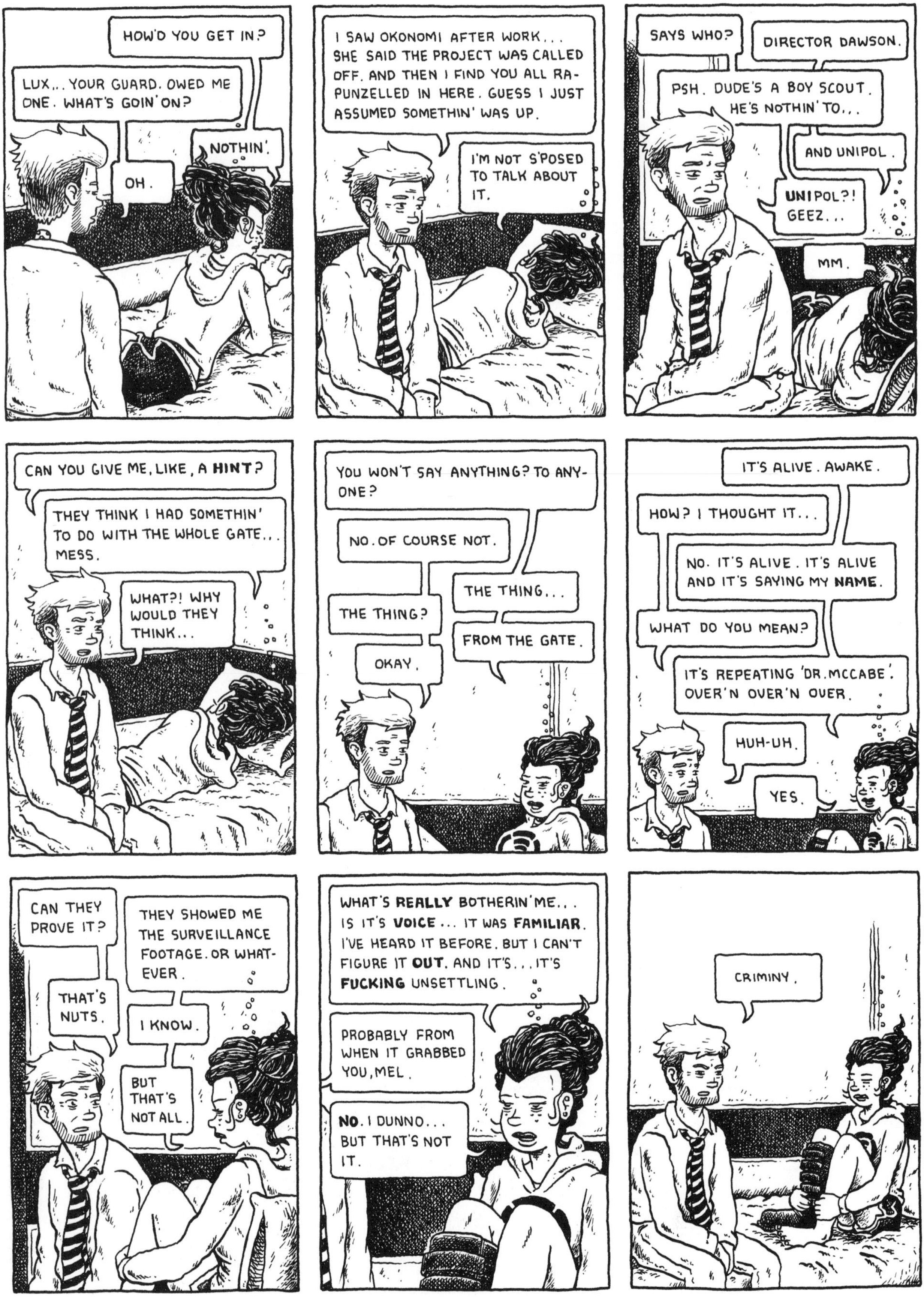
HOW'D YOU GET IN?
LUX... YOUR GUARD. OWED ME ONE. WHAT'S GOIN' ON?
NOTHIN'.
OH.
I SAW OKONOMI AFTER WORK... SHE SAID THE PROJECT WAS CALLED OFF. AND THEN I FIND YOU ALL RAPUNZELLED IN HERE. GUESS I JUST ASSUMED SOMETHIN' WAS UP.
I'M NOT S'POSED TO TALK ABOUT IT.
SAYS WHO?
DIRECTOR DAWSON.
PSH. DUDE'S A BOY SCOUT. HE'S NOTHIN' TO...
AND UNIPOL.
UNIPOL?! GEEZ...
MM.
CAN YOU GIVE ME, LIKE, A HINT?
THEY THINK I HAD SOMETHIN' TO DO WITH THE WHOLE GATE... MESS.
WHAT?! WHY WOULD THEY THINK...
YOU WON'T SAY ANYTHING? TO ANYONE?
NO. OF COURSE NOT.
THE THING...
THE THING?
FROM THE GATE.
OKAY.
IT'S ALIVE. AWAKE.
HOW? I THOUGHT IT...
NO. IT'S ALIVE. IT'S ALIVE AND IT'S SAYING MY NAME.
WHAT DO YOU MEAN?
IT'S REPEATING 'DR. MCCABE'. OVER'N OVER'N OVER.
HUH-UH.
YES.
CAN THEY PROVE IT?
THEY SHOWED ME THE SURVEILLANCE FOOTAGE. OR WHATEVER.
THAT'S NUTS.
I KNOW.
BUT THAT'S NOT ALL.
WHAT'S REALLY BOTHERIN' ME... IS IT'S VOICE... IT WAS FAMILIAR. I'VE HEARD IT BEFORE. BUT I CAN'T FIGURE IT OUT. AND IT'S... IT'S FUCKING UNSETTLING.
PROBABLY FROM WHEN IT GRABBED YOU, MEL.
NO. I DUNNO... BUT THAT'S NOT IT.
CRIMINY.

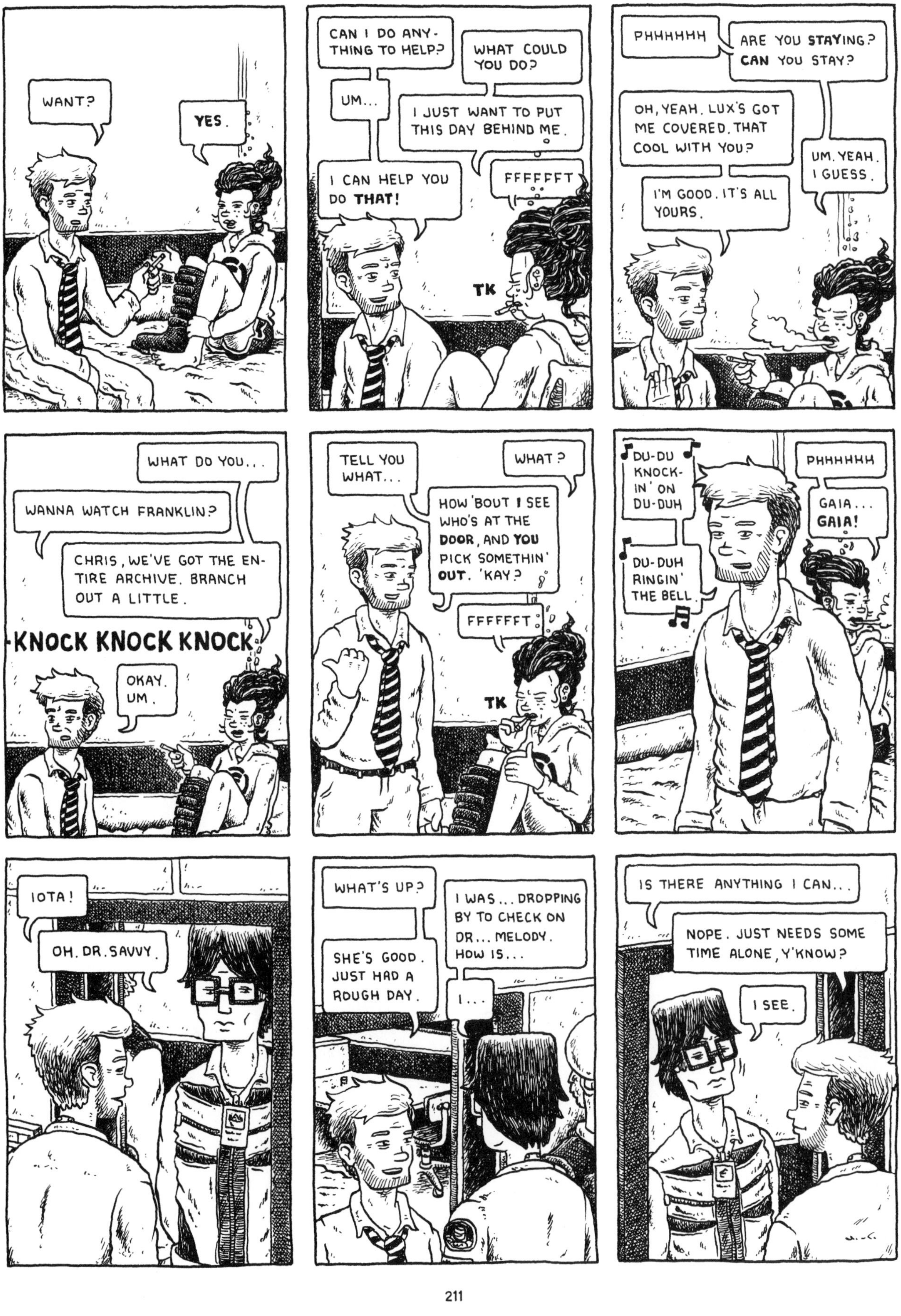
WANT?
YES.
CAN I DO ANY-THING TO HELP?
WHAT COULD YOU DO?
UM...
I JUST WANT TO PUT THIS DAY BEHIND ME.
I CAN HELP YOU DO THAT!
FFFFFFT
TK
PHHHHHH
ARE YOU STAYING? CAN YOU STAY?
OH, YEAH. LUX'S GOT ME COVERED. THAT COOL WITH YOU?
UM. YEAH. I GUESS.
I'M GOOD. IT'S ALL YOURS.
WHAT DO YOU...
WANNA WATCH FRANKLIN?
CHRIS, WE'VE GOT THE EN-TIRE ARCHIVE. BRANCH OUT A LITTLE.
KNOCK KNOCK KNOCK
OKAY. UM.
TELL YOU WHAT...
WHAT?
HOW 'BOUT I SEE WHO'S AT THE DOOR, AND YOU PICK SOMETHIN' OUT. 'KAY?
FFFFFFT
TK
DU-DU KNOCK-IN' ON DU-DUH
DU-DUH RINGIN' THE BELL.
PHHHHHH
GAIA... GAIA!
IOTA!
OH. DR. SAVVY.
WHAT'S UP?
I WAS... DROPPING BY TO CHECK ON DR... MELODY. HOW IS...
SHE'S GOOD. JUST HAD A ROUGH DAY.
I...
IS THERE ANYTHING I CAN...
NOPE. JUST NEEDS SOME TIME ALONE, Y'KNOW?
I SEE.

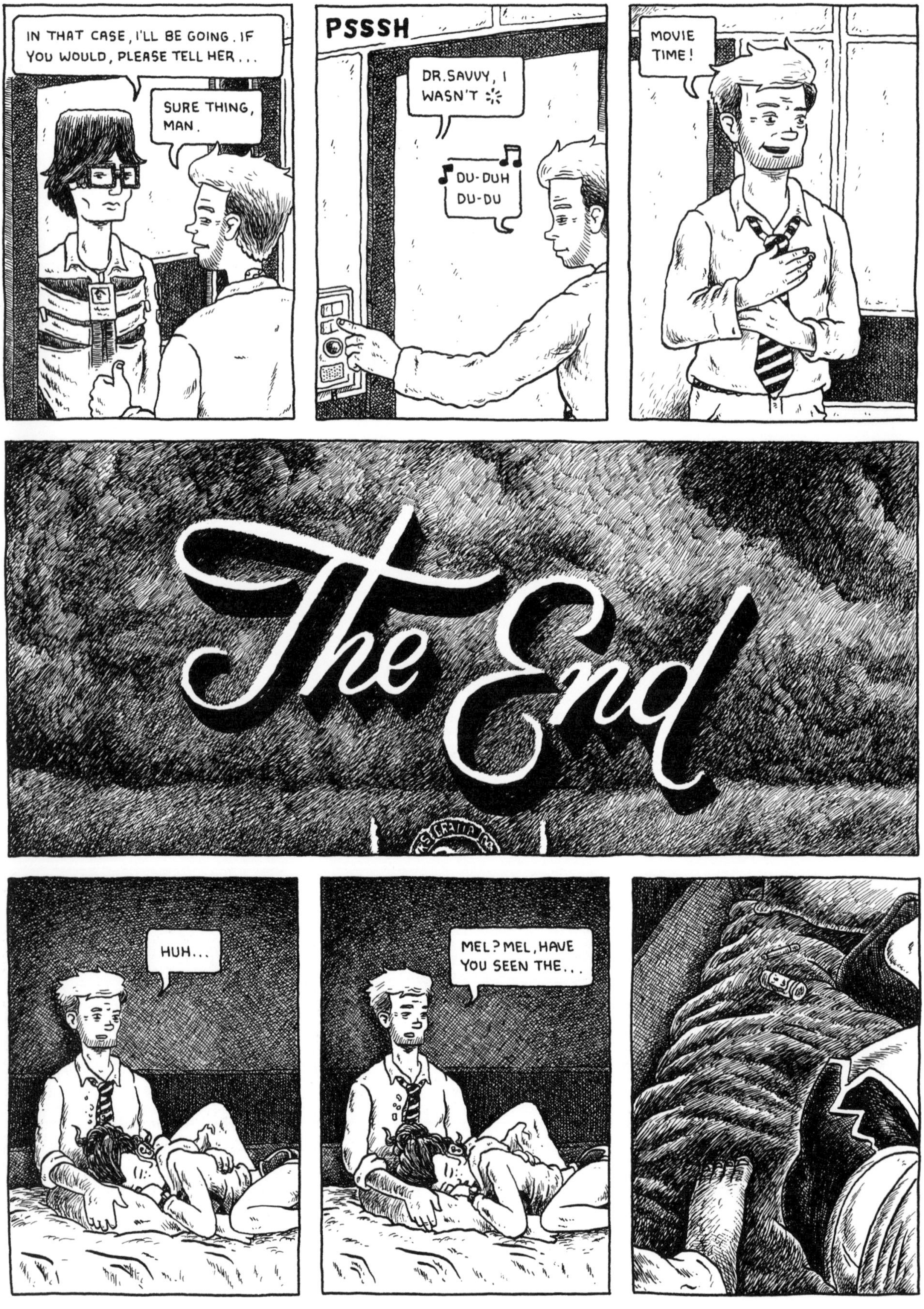
IN THAT CASE, I'LL BE GOING. IF YOU WOULD, PLEASE TELL HER...
SURE THING, MAN.
PSSSH
DR. SAVVY, I WASN'T
DU-DUH DU-DU
MOVIE TIME!
The End
HUH...
MEL? MEL, HAVE YOU SEEN THE...

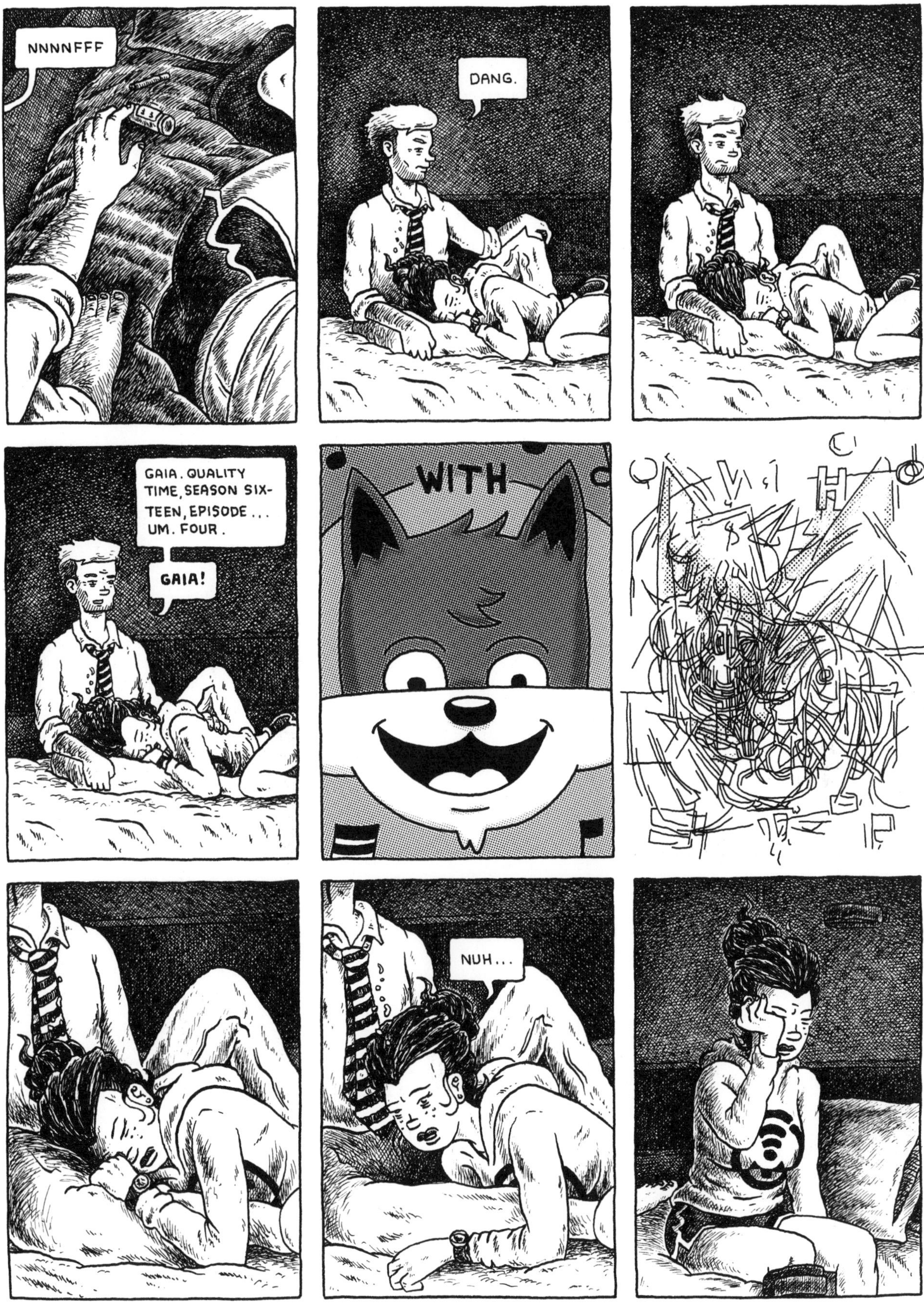
NNNNFFF
DANG.
GAIA. QUALITY TIME, SEASON SIXTEEN, EPISODE... UM. FOUR.
GAIA!
WITH
NUH...

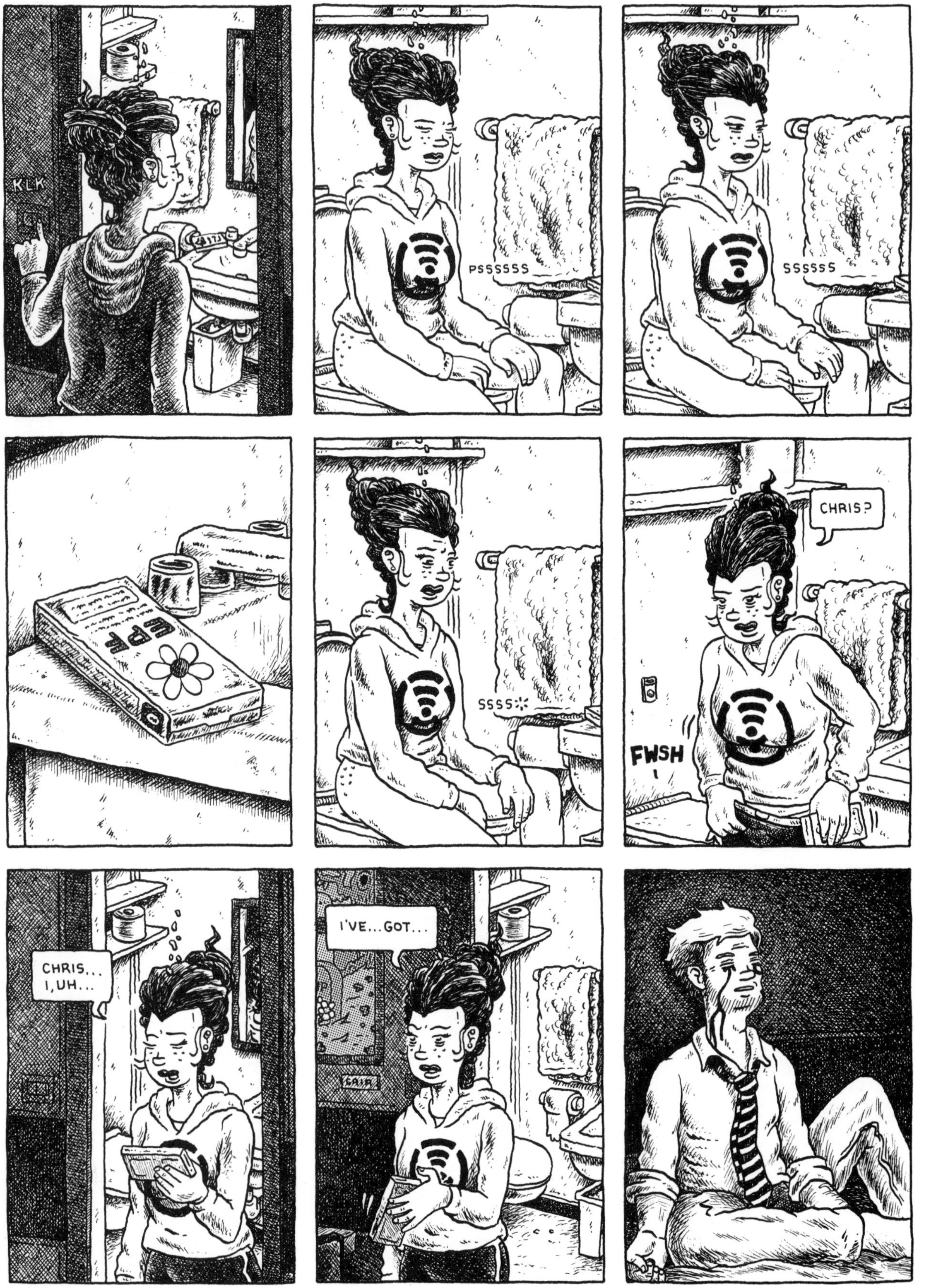
KLK
PSSSSSS
SSSSSS
EPF
SSSS
CHRIS?
FWSH
CHRIS... I, UH...
I'VE... GOT...

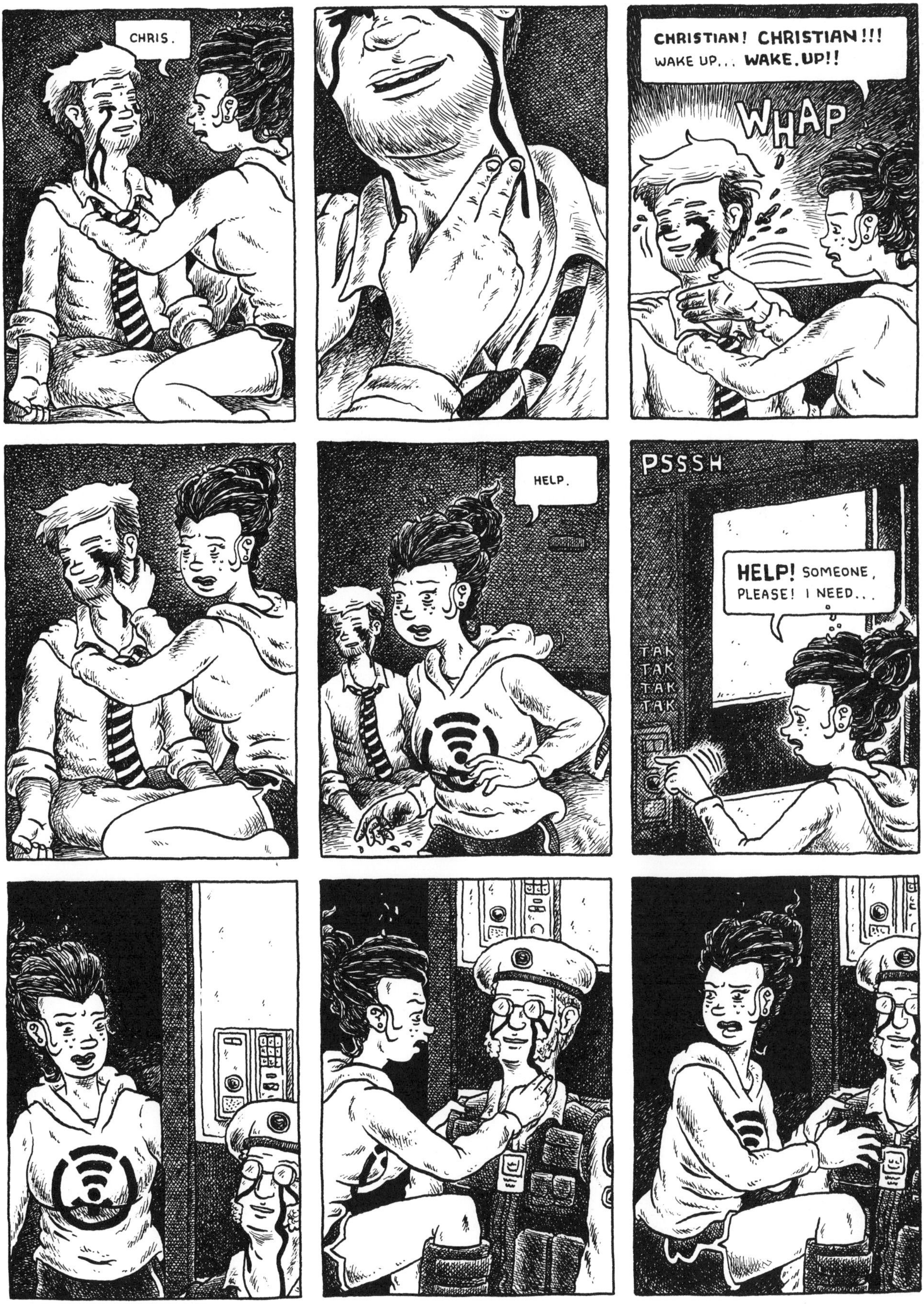
CHRIS.
CHRISTIAN! CHRISTIAN!!!
WAKE UP... WAKE. UP!!
WHAP
HELP.
PSSSH
HELP! SOMEONE, PLEASE! I NEED...
TAK TAK TAK TAK

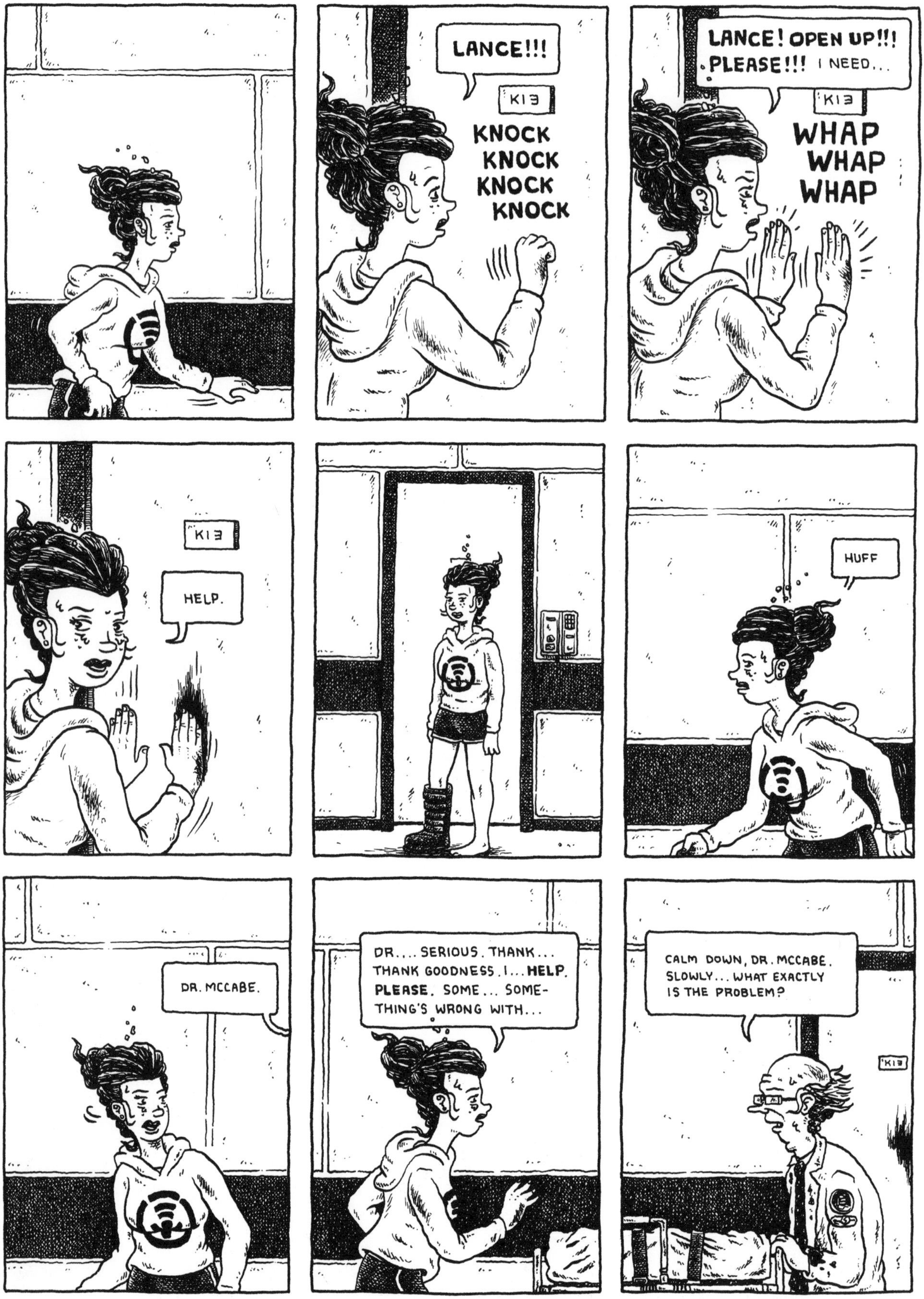

LANCE!!!
KI3
KNOCK KNOCK KNOCK KNOCK
LANCE! OPEN UP!!! PLEASE!!! I NEED...
KI3
WHAP WHAP WHAP
KI3
HELP.
HUFF
DR. MCCABE.
DR.... SERIOUS. THANK... THANK GOODNESS. I... **HELP. PLEASE.** SOME... SOMETHING'S WRONG WITH...
CALM DOWN, DR. MCCABE. SLOWLY... WHAT EXACTLY IS THE PROBLEM?
KI3

IT'S CHRISTIAN... DR. SAVVY. HE'S UNCONSCIOUS... BLEEDING. FROM HIS EYES.

IN MY... ROOM...

HE WAS...

WHERE IS HE?

I SEE.

SHOW ME.

I THOUGHT IT WAS JUST CHR... DR. SAVVY, BUT... I DON'T UNDERSTAND WHAT'S...

I SEE.

WE...WE CAN USE HIS COMM! NOTIFY... THE MEDLAB. SECURITY!

BEFORE ALL WE MUST SEE TO DR. SAVVY'S WELL-BEING.

WHAT ABOUT...

DR. MCCABE.

TIME IS OF THE ESSENCE.

YEAH. OKAY, YEAH. IN HERE...

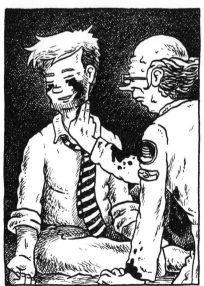

HEART RATE IS SLOW BUT NOTHING ABNORMAL. NOT A SUBCONJUNCTIVAL HEMORRHAGE... PERHAPS PERACUTE HAEMOLACRIA.

I DON'T...KNOW WHAT THAT MEANS...

OF COURSE NOT.

WHAT?

DR. MCCABE, WOULD YOU BE SO KIND AS TO RETRIEVE SOME TISSUE FROM THE LAVATORY?

FROM THE... YEAH. YES.

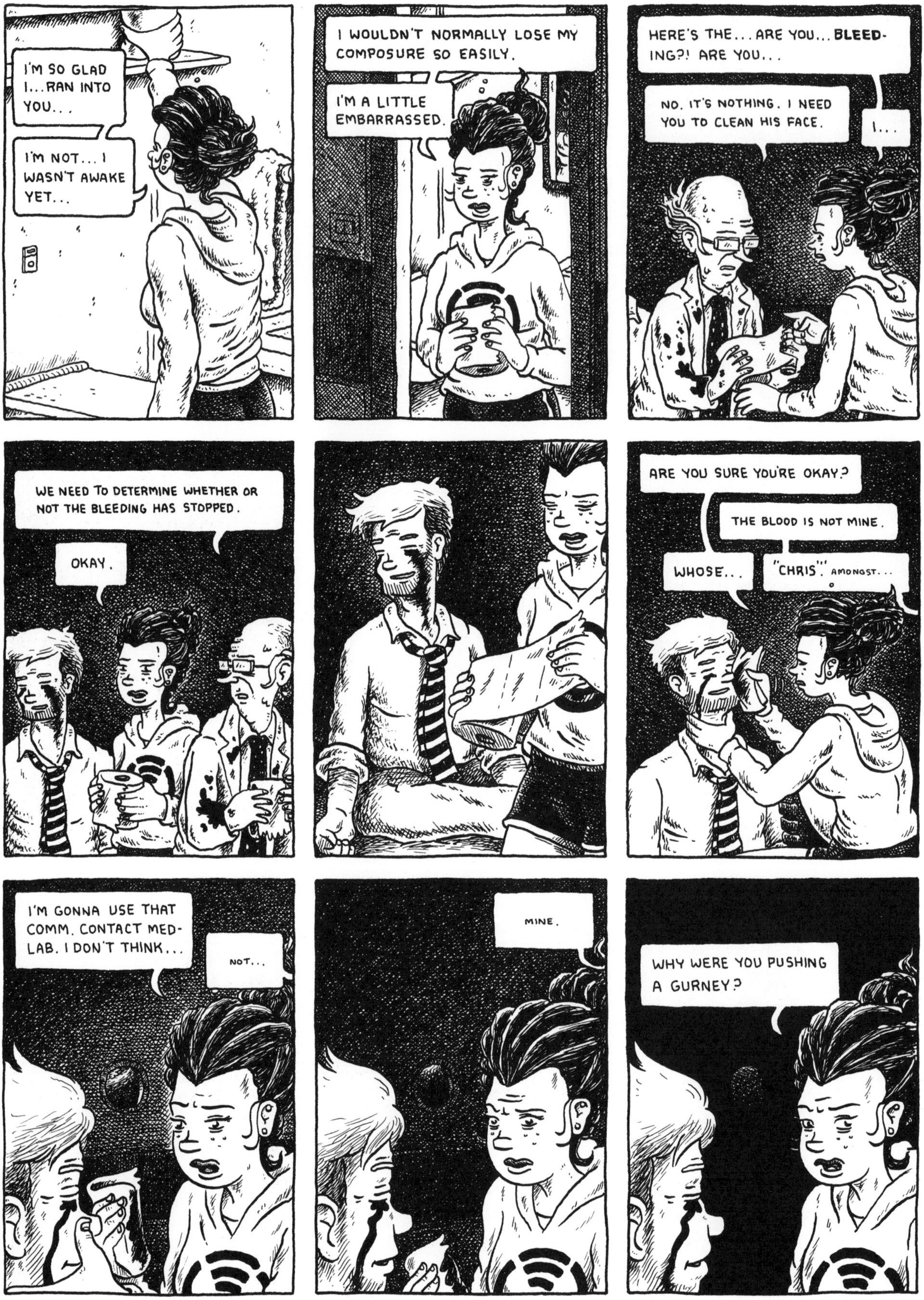
I'M SO GLAD I...RAN INTO YOU...
I'M NOT... I WASN'T AWAKE YET...
I WOULDN'T NORMALLY LOSE MY COMPOSURE SO EASILY.
I'M A LITTLE EMBARRASSED.
HERE'S THE... ARE YOU... BLEEDING?! ARE YOU...
NO. IT'S NOTHING. I NEED YOU TO CLEAN HIS FACE.
I...
WE NEED TO DETERMINE WHETHER OR NOT THE BLEEDING HAS STOPPED.
OKAY.
ARE YOU SURE YOU'RE OKAY?
THE BLOOD IS NOT MINE.
WHOSE...
"CHRIS." AMONGST...
I'M GONNA USE THAT COMM. CONTACT MED-LAB. I DON'T THINK...
NOT...
MINE.
WHY WERE YOU PUSHING A GURNEY?

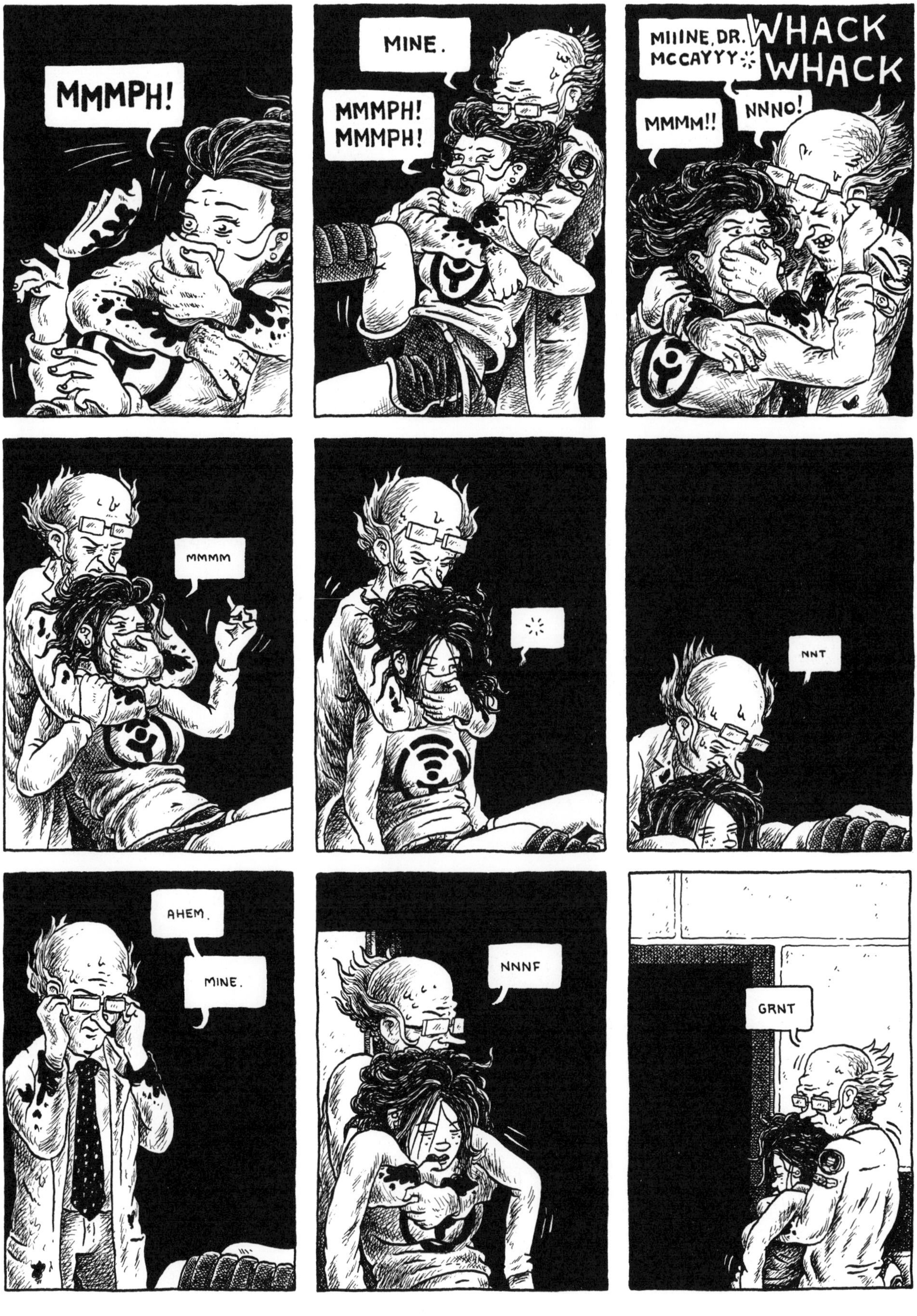
MMMPH!
MINE.
MMMPH! MMMPH!
MIIINE, DR. MCCAYYY
WHACK WHACK
MMMM!!
NNNO!
MMMM
NNT
AHEM.
MINE.
NNNF
GRNT

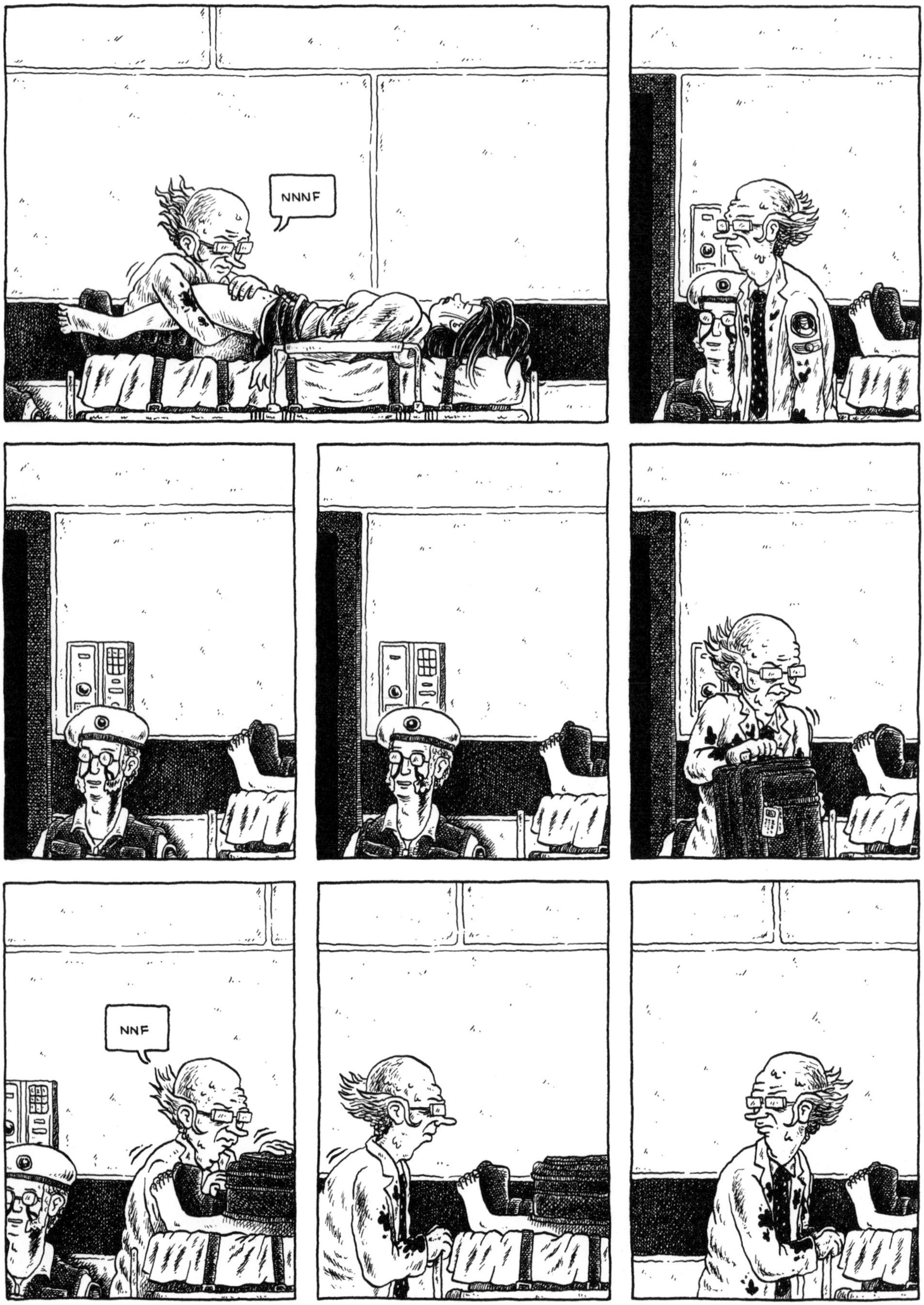
NNNF
NNF

CLK
CLK
PHWOP

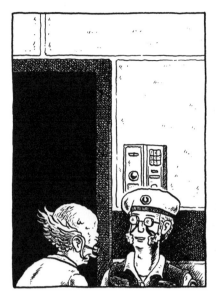

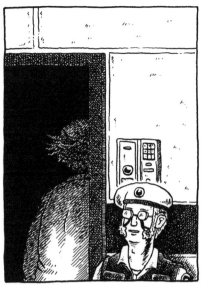

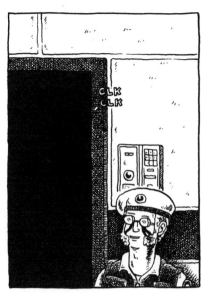

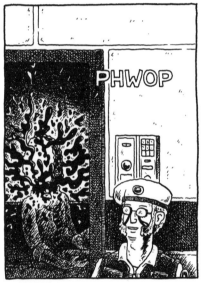

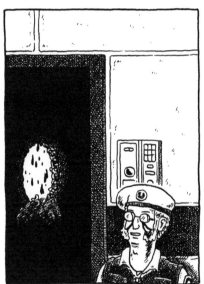

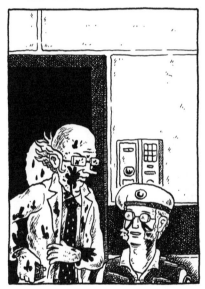

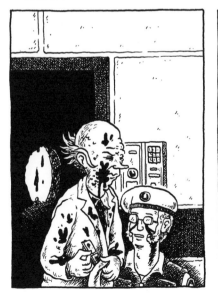

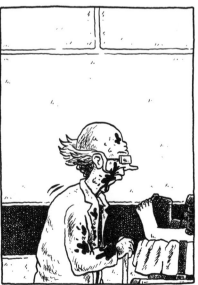

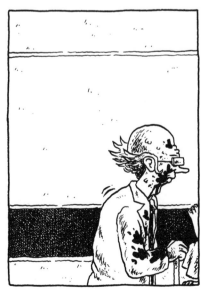

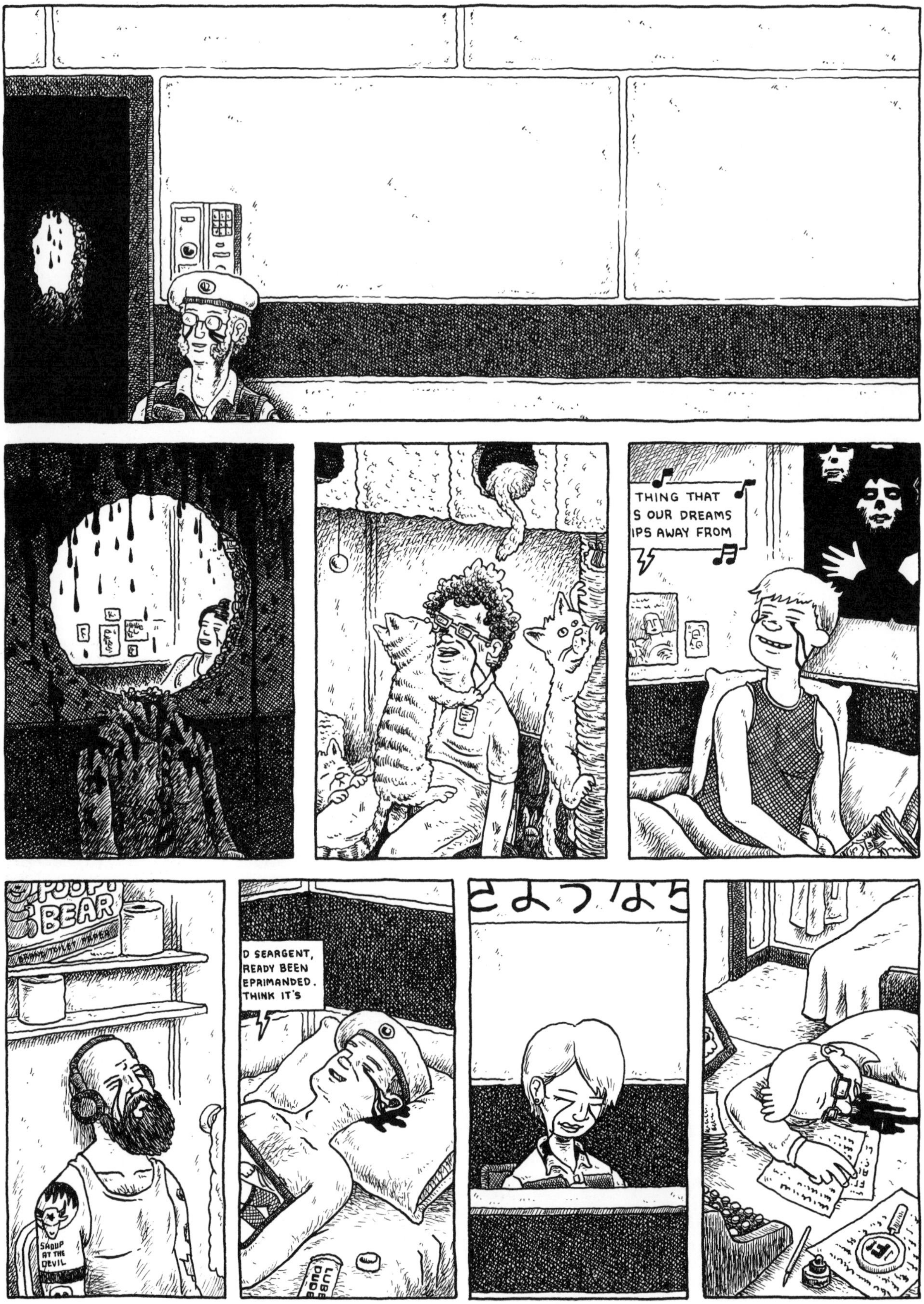
THING THAT
S OUR DREAMS
IPS AWAY FROM
BEAR
D SEARGENT,
READY BEEN
EPRIMANDED.
THINK IT'S
さようなら

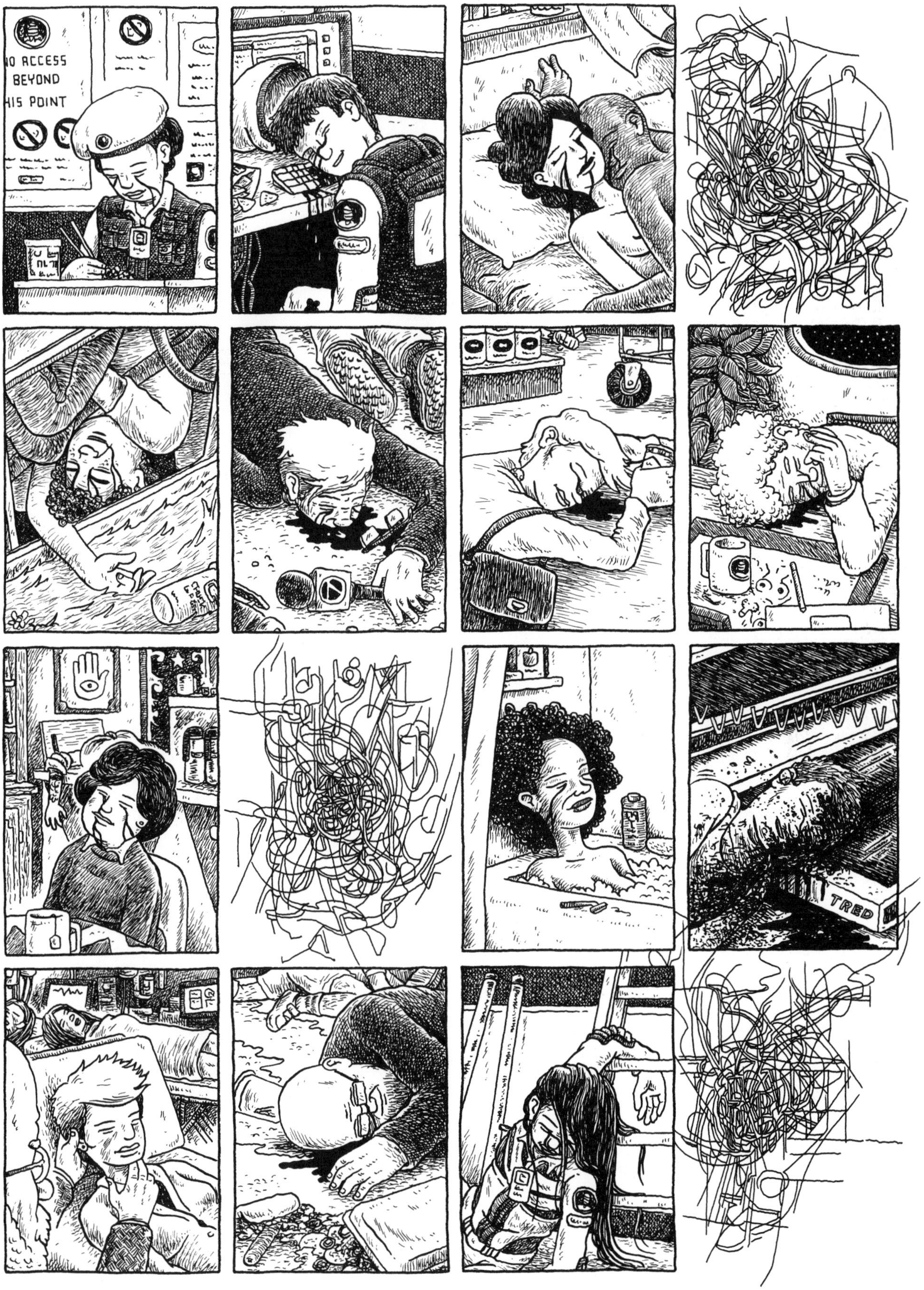
O ACCESS
BEYOND
HIS POINT
TRED

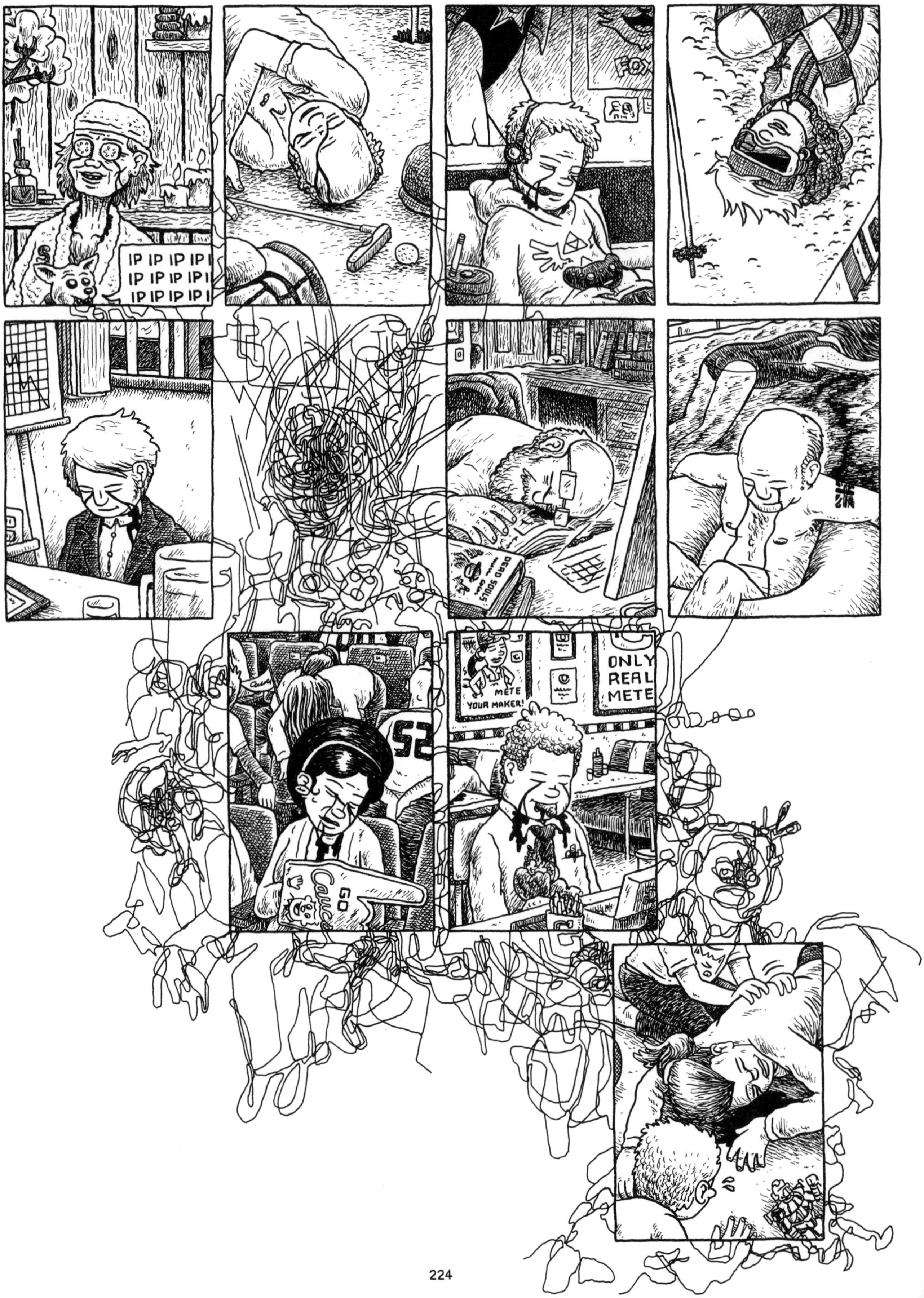
IP IP IP IP
IP IP IP IP
IP IP IP IP
FOX
DEAD SOULS
MÉTÉ
YOUR MAKER!
ONLY
REAL
METE
GO
Cauc

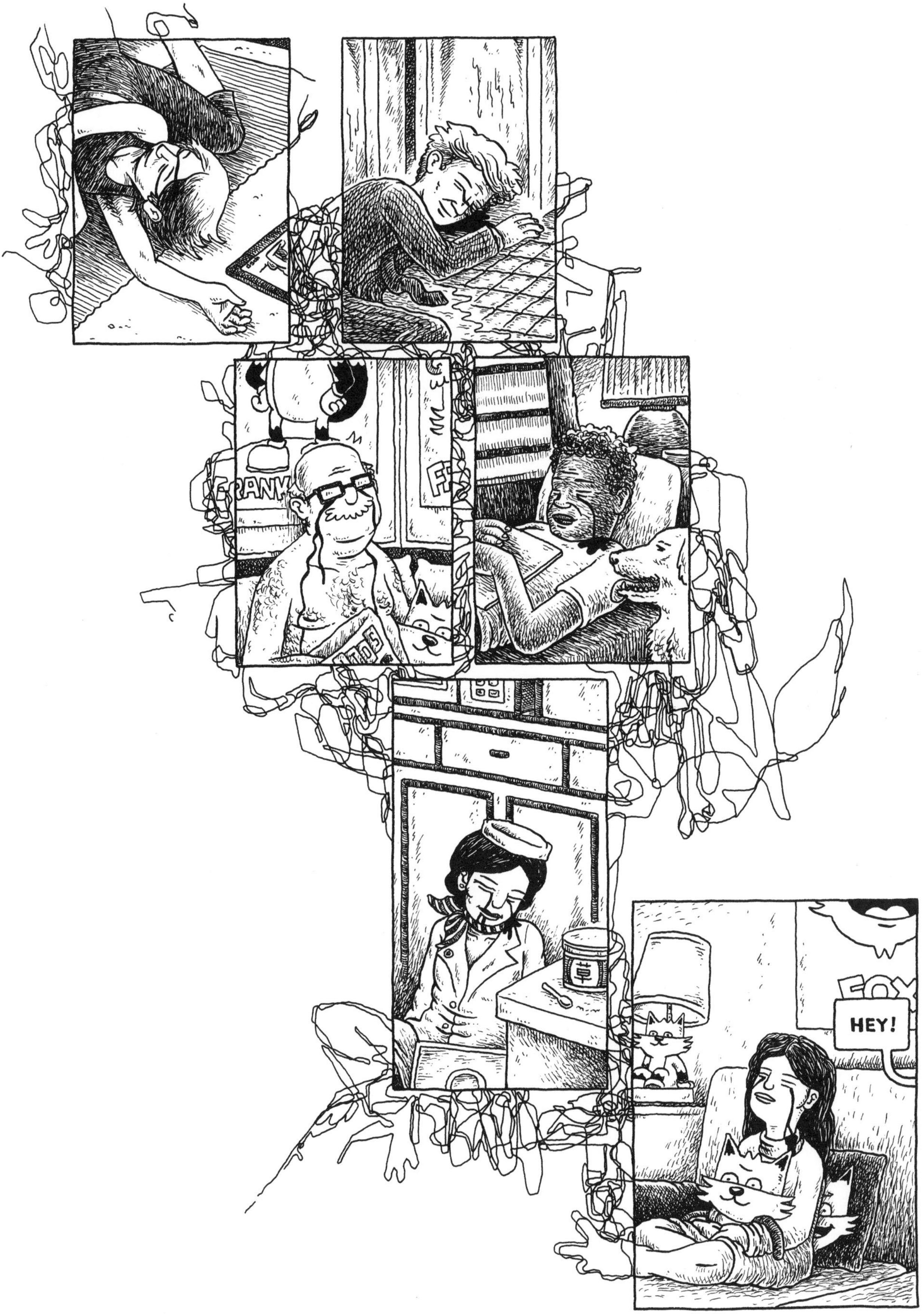
HEY!

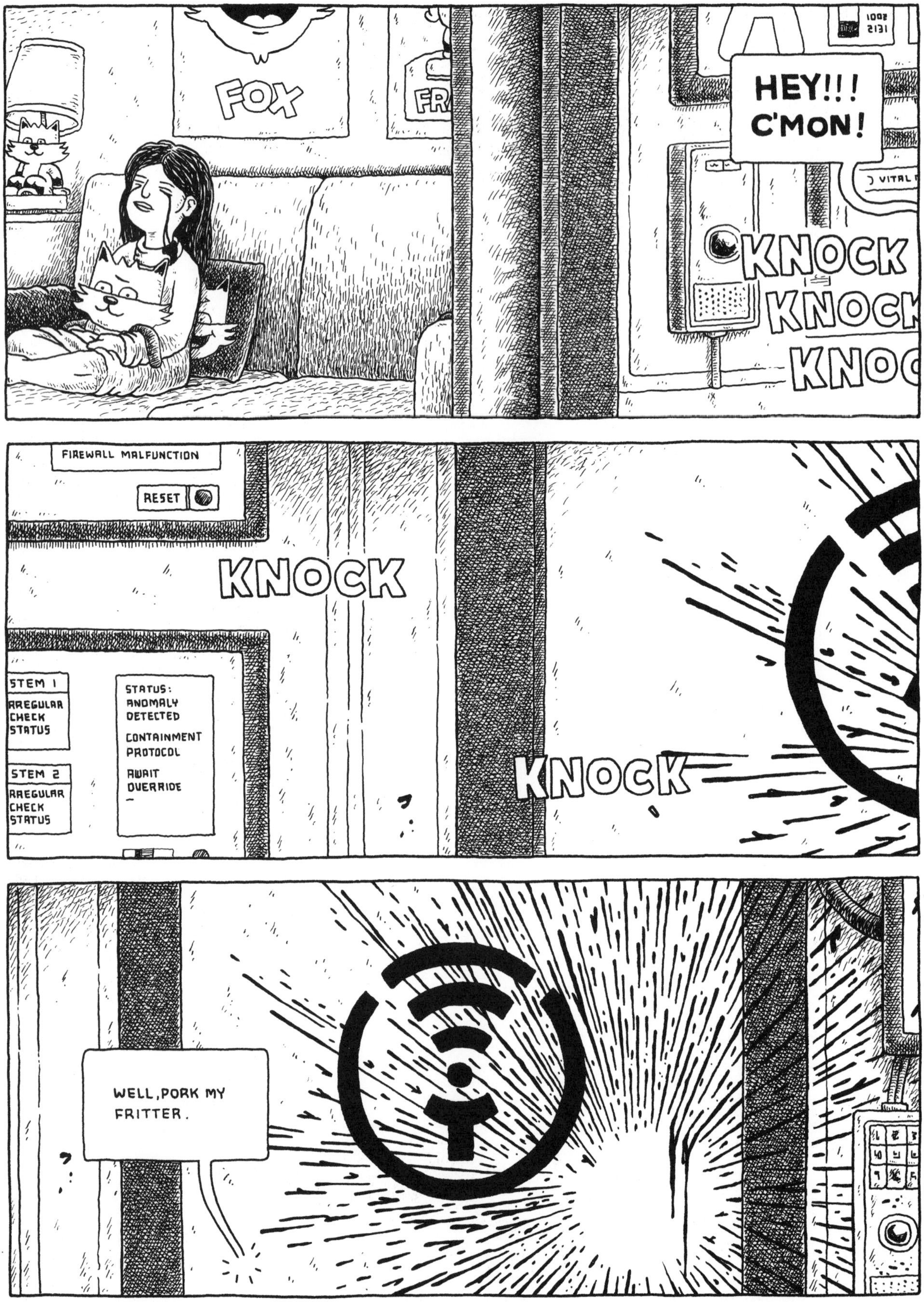
FOX
FR
1002
2131
HEY!!!
C'MON!
VITAL
KNOCK
KNOCK
KNOC
FIREWALL MALFUNCTION
RESET
KNOCK
STEM 1
RREGULAR
CHECK
STATUS
STATUS:
ANOMALY
DETECTED
CONTAINMENT
PROTOCOL
AWAIT
OVERRIDE
STEM 2
RREGULAR
CHECK
STATUS
KNOCK
WELL, PORK MY
FRITTER.

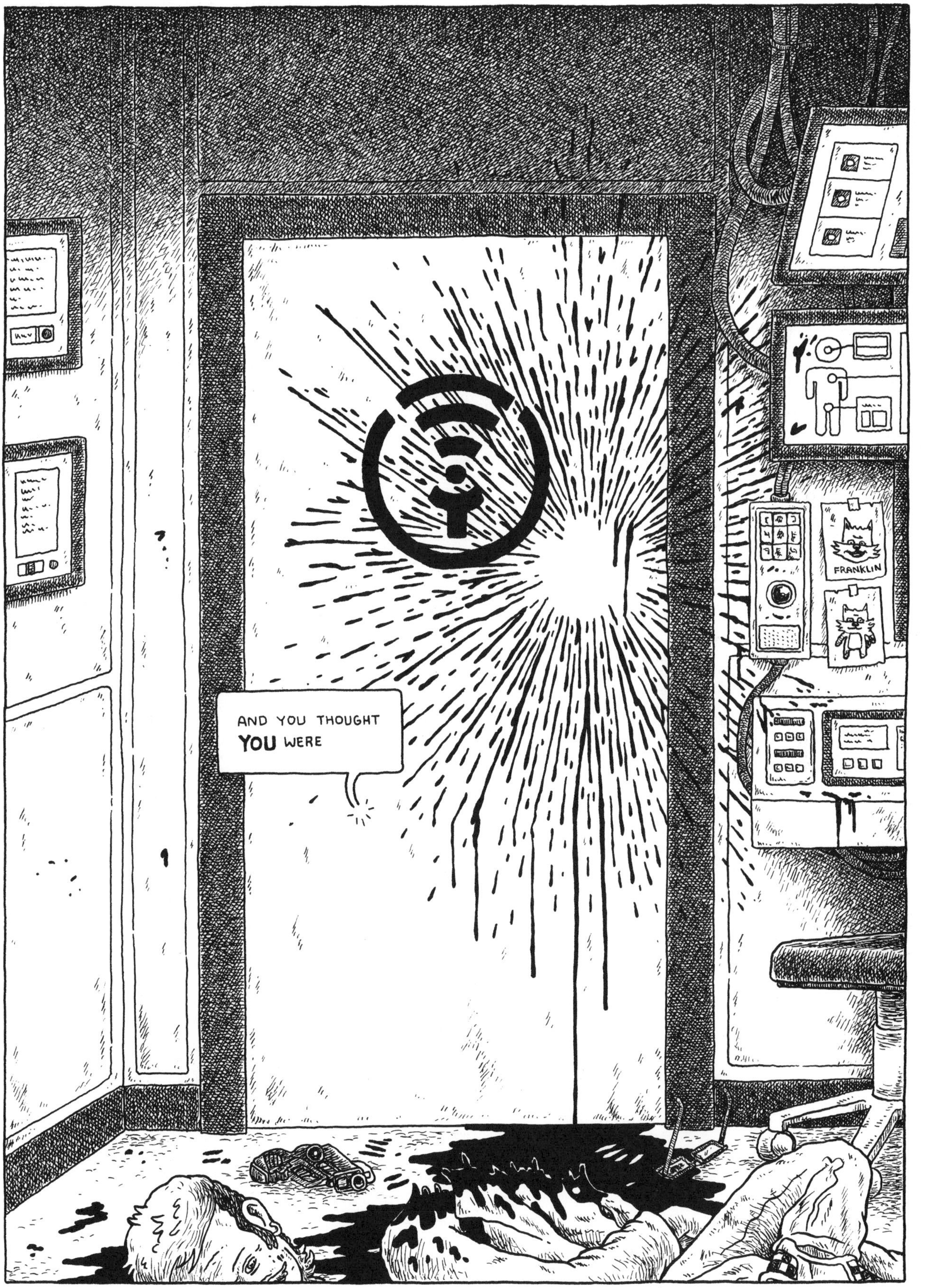
AND YOU THOUGHT
YOU WERE
FRANKLIN

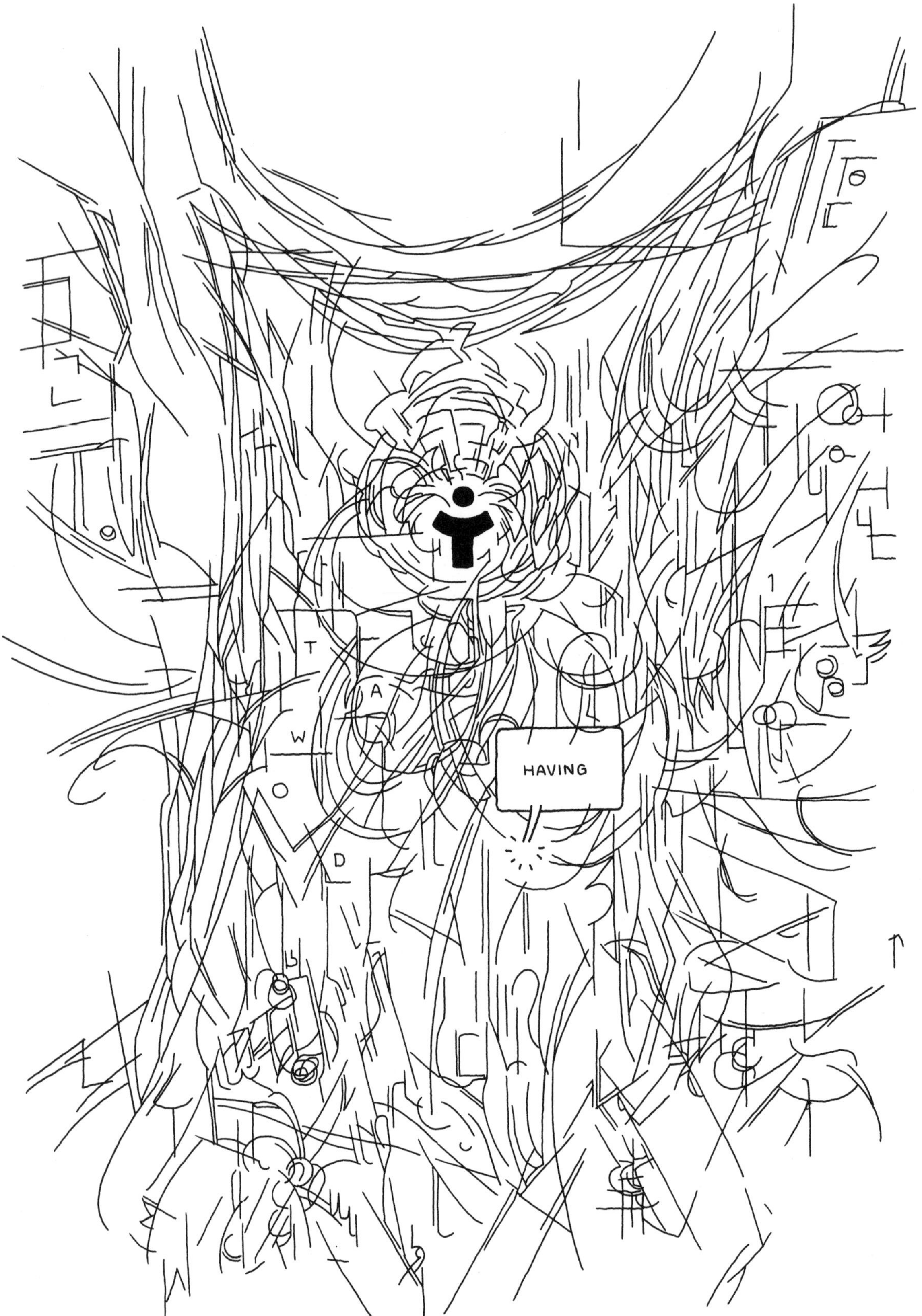
T
A
W
HAVING
D

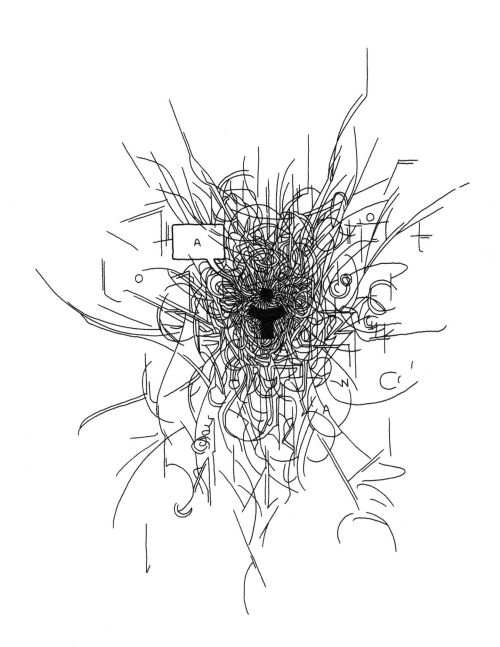

BAD

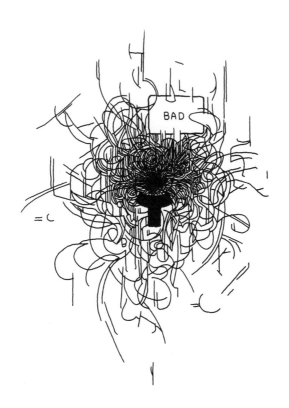

DAY

●